Architecture of Modern China

Architecture of Modern China provides a theoretical and historical perspective of the architecture of modern China, covering the period from 1729 to 2008.

Analysing a large number of subjects, from relationships between architects and political authority, to the changes brought about by liberalization in the post-Mao era, to the present-day interactions between China and the West, the chapter topics integrate to form a picture of Chinese architecture as a whole.

The distinctive features of the book include a blending of 'critical' and 'historical' research and a long-range perspective encompassing the current scene and the Maoist period. The book provides both an empirical historical narrative and an in-depth analysis of social and formal issues in modern Chinese architecture. This elegant book cuts a large subject into key topics and as such is a book any student, architect or academic interested in modern and contemporary architecture of China would do well to read.

Jianfei Zhu is Associate Professor in the Faculty of Architecture Building & Planning at the University of Melbourne. His research explores analytical and international perspectives on the Chinese experience in architecture, urbanity and social practice.

Architecture of Modern China

A historical critique

Jianfei Zhu

Routledge
Taylor & Francis Group

LONDON AND NEW YORK

First published 2009
by Routledge
2 Park Square, Milton Park, Abingdon, Oxon OX14 4RN

Simultaneously published in the USA and Canada
by Routledge
270 Madison Avenue, New York, NY 10016, USA

*Routledge is an imprint of the Taylor & Francis Group, an
informa business*

© 2009 Jianfei Zhu

Typeset in Frutiger by Prepress Projects Ltd, Perth, UK
Printed and bound in Great Britain by The Cromwell Press,
Trowbridge, Wiltshire

British Library Cataloguing in Publication Data
A catalogue record for this book is available from the British
Library

Library of Congress Cataloging in Publication Data
Zhu, Jianfei, 1962–
Architecture of Modern China / Jianfei Zhu.
p. cm.
Includes bibliographical references and index.
1. Architecture—China. I. Title.
NA1540.Z57 2008
720.951'0903—dc22
2008014925

ISBN10: 0-415-45780-7 (hbk)
ISBN10: 0-415-45781-5 (pbk)

ISBN13: 978-0-415-45780-4 (hbk)
ISBN13: 978-0-415-45781-1 (pbk)

Front Cover The Great Hall of the People and the National
Grand Theatre, Beijing.

献给我的父母朱国学和黄娇英

For my parents, Zhu Guoxue and Huang Jiaoying

Contents

Credits for texts

Chapter 6: Jianfei Zhu, 'Criticality in between China and the West', *Journal of Architecture*, 10, no. 5 (November 2005), 479–98. © 2005 The Journal of Architecture.

Comments from G. Baird, Y. H. Chang, P. Eisenman, J. Liu, M. Speaks and other Architects/Critics: George Baird, 'The Criticality Debate: some further thoughts'; Yung Ho Chang, 'Criticalities or What the West Meant for Me'; Peter Eisenman, 'Contro lo Spettacolo'; Liu Jiakun, 'An Open Letter to Jianfei Zhu'; Michael Speaks, 'Ideals, Ideology, Intelligence in China and the West', *Shidai Jianzhu: Time + Architecture*, 91, no. 5 (September 2006), 61–8. © 2006 Time + Architecture.

Chapter 10: Jianfei Zhu, 'Guanyu "20 pian gaodi": zhongguo dalu xiandai jianzhu de xipu miaoshu (1910s–2010s)', *Shidai Jianzhu: Time + Architecture*, 97, no. 5 (September 2007), 16–21. © 2007 Time + Architecture.

Illustration credits

10.1: © Jianfei Zhu

(1, 2, 4, 6, 7, 10, 13, 16): © Jianfei Zhu

(3): Liang Sicheng, *Liang Sicheng Quanji*, Beijing: Zhongguo Jianzhu Gongye Chubanshe, 2001, vol. 8, p. 63.

(5): Fu Chao-ching, *Zhongguo Gudian Shiyang Xinjianzhu*, Taipei: Nantian Press, 1993, Figures 13–44, p. 288.

(8): Zhao Chen.

(9, 11, 12): Gong Deshun, Zou Denong, Dou Yide, *Zhongguo Xiandai Jianzhu Shigang*, Tianjin: Tianjin Kexue Jishu Chubanshe, 1989, Figures 6-22, 2-7, 6-4, on pp. 119, 32, 108 respectively.

(14): CAG (China Architecture Design and Research Group). Photographer: Zhang Guangyuan.

(15): OMA (Office for Metropolitan Architecture).

(17): Atelier FCJZ.

(18): MADA s.p.a.m.

(19): Cui Kai. Photographer: Zhang Guangyuan.

(20): Chen Mun Wai.

Acknowledgements

This book is a result of writings and lectures I have delivered since the late 1990s at the request of editors and scholars in Europe and China, a time during which interest in modern and contemporary architecture of China has emerged and developed swiftly. The book, now as a collection of essays, is a formalized response to this demand to know and to explain the phenomenon that is modern Chinese architecture. It is also a result of focused investigations on specific topics such as Western linear perspective adopted in China, the Nanjing Decade of the 1930s, Liang Sicheng in the 1950s, the new generation and its criticality in the late 1990s, and forms of Beijing today, among others. For this journey of development, I would first like to thank Mark Cousins and Mary Wall who invited me to write a piece on modern Chinese architecture in 1994–5 (which resulted in 'Beyond Revolution', *AA Files*, 35, 1998), and Zou Denong who shared his knowledge with me and invited me to contribute a piece in 1998 for *Zhongguo Jianzhu Wushinian* (Fifty years of Chinese architecture, 1999).

I would like to thank those who have invited me to lecture at the following institutions on my research through which my ideas were tested and developed: Yung Ho Chang at Peking University (2002) and for the Shenzhen Biennale (2005); Cui Kai at China Architecture Design & Research Group Beijing (2001); Wu Jiang and Chang Qing (2002) and Lu Yongyi, Zhi Wenjun and Peng Nu (2006) at Tongji University Shanghai; Ding Wowo and Zhao Chen at Nanjing University Nanjing (2002); Mark Cousins at the Architectural Association London (2004); Wang Jianguo, Zhu Guangya and Ge Ming at Southeast University Nanjing (2005); Kate Goodwin at the Royal Academy of Arts London (2006); Iain Borden and Jonathan Hill at the Bartlett School of Architecture (2006); Verdran Mimica and Linda Vlassenrood at the Berlage Institute in Rotterdam (2006); George Baird and Adrian Blackwell at the University of Toronto (2006); Wang Shu at China Academy of Art in Hongzhou (2006); Jia Beisi at Hong Kong University (2006); Zhou Rong and *Domus China* (Qin Lei) for a debate with Zhu Tao at Peking University Beijing (2006); Junichiro Okata and Darko Radovic at Tokyo University (2007); Alan Penn for a research group at London University (2007); and recently Dietmar Steiner, Johannes Porsch, Ylva Haberlandt and Mladen Jadric for a symposium on 'China production' at Architecture Centre Vienna on 24 November 2007.

I have benefited a lot from conversations with many. Besides those already mentioned, they include Bu Zhengwei, Zhang Fuhe, Ai Weiwei,

Wang Mingxian, Shi Jian, Zhang Jie, Li Xinggang, Wang Lu, Wang Yun, Li Xiaodong, Wang Hui, Zhu Pei, Qi Xin, Wang Jun and Ou Ning in Beijing; Yang Bingde, Zhou Kai and Zeng Jian in Tianjin; Qi Kang, Zhen Xin, Chen Wei, Wang Qun and Zhang Lei in Nanjing; Liu Jiakun in Chengdu; Luo Xiaowei, Zheng Shiling, Lu Jiwei, Sun Jiwei, Qingyun Ma, Bu Bing, Li Xiangning, Ma Weidong, Tong Ming, Zhang Bin and Li Ding in Shanghai; William Lim and Heng Chye Kiang in Singapore; Li Shiqiao, Charlie Q. L. Xue, Wang Weijen, Gu Daqing, Gary Chang, Du Juan and Zhu Tao in Hong Kong; Stephan Feuchtwang, Li Hua and Zhang Hongxing in London; Winy Maas, Kayoko Ota, Shi Wenqian, Shiuan-Wen Chu and Yang Yang in Rotterdam; Bart Reuser in Amsterdam; Wei Wei Shannon from New York; Michael Speaks from Los Angeles; Eduard Kögel, Felix Zwoch and Barbara Münch from Berlin; Arata Isozaki, Kengo Kuma and Jinnai Hidenobu from Tokyo; and Tom Kvan, Kim Dovey, Philip Goad, Paul Walker, John Denton, Andrew Olszewski, Steve Whitford and Anoma Pieris in Melbourne.

I would also like to thank Xu Jia, who has shown great patience in preparing the English and Chinese version of the chart 'Twenty Plateaus'. Thanks must also be extended to Lu Fuxun in Beijing and Ji Guohua in Nanjing, who have helped me on Russian names; Tong Ming and Du Ming, who have collected information in Shanghai; Ding Qing, who has forwarded archive materials from Nanjing; and Mairo Gutjahr in Melbourne on German names and article titles (as they appeared in Chinese in the 1950s). Acknowledgement must also be extended to my research students Wu Ming, Chia Shi Chee, Zhang Yanjing and Karey Huang Fengyi, who have provided various assistance in the preparation of this manuscript. For constant and enduring support, my gratitude goes to Hong Zhang. For the publication of this book, I would like to thank Caroline Mallinder for her initial support for the project, and Grant Womack, Andrew R. Davidson, Georgina Johnson, Fran Ford and Victoria Johnson for the editing and production at Taylor & Francis.

CHAPTER 1

MODERN CHINESE ARCHITECTURE

A social, historical and formal analysis

International scholarship on the architecture of modern China has emerged dramatically in recent years. Publications in 1998, 1999 and 2002 have marked the beginning of a torrent of publications and media features on the topic.[1] The increasing visibility of China, the preparation for the Beijing Olympics of 2008, and the opening of the Chinese design market to the world, have all contributed to this rising interest. Yet China had developed a modern architecture long before. This history can stretch to the 1910s if not the 1840s or earlier. The research on the subject matter, within China, also started well before, in the mid-1980s and further back in the early 1960s. By now, if we put all this research within and without China together, we can recognize a few characteristics of the work as a whole. First, most of the research is carried out *within* one of several historical periods. There are works on *jindai* or 'early modern' Chinese architecture from 1840 to 1949, those on 'modern' Chinese architecture that are predominantly on the post-1949 periods, and those that focus on 'new architecture' of recent years, after the late 1990s. It is rare to find research that crosses these periods. Long historical analysis in search of latent social and formal currents is even harder to find. Second, these studies are primarily empirical and descriptive, rather than analytical in method and socio-political in focus. Intending to capture basic historical material, these works are rarely concerned with focused historical moments and political and formal problems, let alone long relations across these periods and social-ideological systems.

Against such a background, this book aims to develop an analytical study of modern Chinese architecture across historical periods. This book focuses on problems emerging in historical environments. It is a collection of studies on analytical problems (social, historical, formal) of historical moments. It is also a study of interrelations across these times in which long-range currents may be identified. The subject matter is 'modern Chinese architecture', which includes designs and practices in architecture that have been internalized into the modern Chinese context as it evolved since 1600. The primary historical range stretches from 1729 to 2008, that is, from a time when European perspective and formal geometry were introduced into China, to the present time when China assumes a new position in nation building and international relations. In this historical range, a predominant focus in coverage is on the century from the 1910s to the present, when modern architecture in a functional and structural sense has arrived and evolved in China. This book aims to be critical *and* historical. It focuses on both analytical problems and the condition of the problems of specific moments. Focusing on specific themes at specific moments, the work also explores underlying currents across these times and social environments.

Studies on architecture of modern China

Existing scholarship on the subject is of course rich and complex. There is first of all a large group of scholars working on the *jindai* or 'early modern' period from 1840 to 1949, that is, after China was partially colonized and before it was reunified under the People's Republic. From an initial collaboration between Wang Tan and Terunobu Fujimori in the mid-1980s, it has grown into a large-scale project of surveys and local empirical investigations assembled in regular conferences under Zhang Fuhe.[2] A large quantity of empirical work has been collected, which awaits focused analysis and interpretation. Parallel to this are some individual scholars' influential work. This includes Jeffrey W. Cody's research on Henry K. Murphy, the American architect practising in China from the 1910s to the 1930s, which offers rigorous historical information.[3] Lai Delin's various case studies on Liang Sicheng and the Chinese Style of the 1930s offer detailed information and rigorous analysis.[4] Hou Youbin, on the other hand, in his various writings, has offered a systematic interpretation of the entire 'early modern' century with a comprehensive set of analytical categories (cities, typologies, technology, institution, the profession, styles and thoughts).[5] Yang Bingde's overall take on the century charts another path that focuses upon 'cities' and 'cultures', that is, on the subject matter conceived as urban-historical settings and as clashes of 'architectural cultures' between China and the West.[6] These individual scholars' works have reintegrated in specific ways a vast body of empirical work by Zhang and Fujimori (or by their teams). Yet they are restricted to the time before 1949. More importantly, there are tendencies to morally idealize certain 'heroic' architects and styles, to avoid dark political complicities with oppressive regimes, and to employ vague and neutral categories of 'architectural culture' in some cases among these studies. Analytical studies on social and political productions of design, at specific local moments and across different periods, are needed for further analysis and understanding.

Among those that have crossed the 1949 mark, Fu Chao-ching's research is one of the earliest. His research focuses on 'new architecture based on the Chinese palace styles', those modern buildings that have employed the Chinese roofs as best exemplified in Nanjing, Beijing and Taipei in the 1930s, 1950s and 1970s respectively.[7] The work has covered an impressive amount of empirical examples in many cities over a long historical duration. It has also provided interpretations that situate the buildings in the political periods with ideological prescriptions.

Another two ambitious works that have crossed the 1949 mark, covering a history from the late nineteenth century to 2000, are by Zou Denong and by Peter G. Rowe with Seng Kuan. Zou's *Zhongguo Xiandai Jianzhu Shi* (A history of modern Chinese architecture) is a descriptive account of a large number of buildings and projects across this historical span, with a focus on the post-1949 period and its complex and shifting political movements from the 1950s to the 1980s.[8] Rowe and Kuan's book, *Architectural Encounters with Essence and Form in Modern China*, provides an interpretative reading of this long history.[9] Whereas the first is a large compendium of projects situated mostly within the political periods after 1949, the second is a concise sketch of different design approaches across these times with a thematic concern with methods of relating Chinese and Western traditions in design. Yet the two share a comparable basis. Both have privileged developments after 1949; both have implicitly adopted an official perspective in the account of design ideas and practice. Both, because of this perspective, have ignored a crucial breakthrough from the post-Maoist generation that have characteristically practised outside official circles with their experimental designs. Despite these features, Zou's book is empirically the most substantial published so far, whereas Rowe and Kuan's has offered one of the first readings of the history of modern Chinese architecture in the West.

There are also studies that have focused specifically on recent decades and a 'new architecture' from China in recent years. Among those illustrated collections of projects, Caroline Klein and Eduard Kögel's *Made in China: neue Chinesische Architektur* is arguably the most observant and rigorously prepared.[10] Academic or research publication on this topic is represented by Charlie Q. L. Xue's *Building a Revolution: Chinese Architecture since 1980*.[11] This book is consistent with Zou's history in research method in that comprehensive coverage is secured at the expanse of analytical focus. The book nevertheless is rich and informative. There are also recent interpretative attempts dealing with the same period, such as Hao Shuguang's work on 'architectural thoughts in contemporary China'.[12] This is new in that systematic efforts are devoted exclusively to studying ideas in design practice in contemporary China. Yet, once again, the work is broad and comprehensive, with an implicit reproduction of official perspectives and popular vocabulary. Critical distancing from conventional vocabulary and a careful and analytical use of key terms and perspectives are needed if contemporary design practice in China is to be analysed and theorized in this direction. It must be added that young critics such as Li Xiangning and Peng Nu are emerging in China who are exploring architectural criticism and historical research on this path (they are also related to an emerging group of public voices such as Wang Jun, Zhou Rong and Zhu Tao, and senior critics Shi Jian and Wang Mingxian).

The more analytical work can be found from a group of new scholars. Employing methods of related social sciences and humanities, their work is emerging as a substantial challenge to the existing body of work. This can be found in Li Shiqiao's writings (on various cases before 1949) in relation to cultural studies, history of ideas and theory, in Lai Delin's writings (on the 1910s to the 1930s) in relation to art and social history, in Duanfang Lu's publications (on socialist modernism of the 1960s and 1970s) in relation to urban sociology, and in Wang Chun-Hsiung's researches (on the 1930s) in relation to sociology of knowledge.[13]

Lu and Wang's researches, furthermore, overlap with another body of research that shares some common concerns with modern Chinese architecture. This is a large area with scholars of different disciplinary backgrounds working on modern and contemporary 'Chinese cities', 'urban spaces' and processes of 'urbanization'. Economists, social theorists, planners and geographers converge here. Whereas social theorists' observation can be tangible, analytical, or critical, with theoretical insights, as in Michael Dutton's *Streetlife China*, economists' work often covers macro spatial developments such as Laurence J. C. Ma and Fulong Wu's *Restructuring the Chinese City*, and scholars in planning history offer both macro and micro observations as in John Friedmann's *China's Urban Transition*. Urban geographers and urban historians, on the other hand, can offer descriptions of urban space that are detailed and grounded, while still retaining relations with the political process at local or national-historical level, as in the case of *Remaking the Chinese City: Modernity and National Identity, 1900–1950*, edited by Joseph W. Esherick.[14] These works, however, owing to disciplinary perspectives, cannot deal with constructed space and form in a detailed and analytical way, let alone issues of design, creativity, the profession of the architect, and relations between buildings and urban spaces and forms. Integration of sociological methods with detailed reading or analysis of built spaces and forms and of the design practice is needed and must be carried out by scholars concerned most immediately with architecture.

In summary, a large body of empirical research has been produced, and a few focused attempts have been made. However, analytical studies on modern Chinese architecture, with a focus on social production of design, and on political and formal problems of specific moments, with a long historical view across different periods and a critical distance from official and conventional perspectives, are rare and much needed for a deepening of our understanding of design and architectural practice in modern China.

About this book

This book is a collection of essays I have developed in the past few years, in an attempt to coordinate focused and long views, analysis and history, and issues of political production and formal logic. In this collection, each essay deals with a 'critical moment'. A critical moment is conceived as a historical moment in which one problem or one set of problems has emerged which deserves close investigation and theoretical reflection. These essays are then arranged in the book to form a list that is chronological and critical.

The research carried out in the book has three analytical focuses: *social* practice, *historical* condition, and *formal* evolution across time and geography. (1) Regarding the first, focus is placed on the production of ideas, designs and buildings in a social and political context. Some of the key issues to be explored are the role of the profession, the relation between the profession and state authorities, and interactions between design knowledge and a certain ideological prescription and political demand. (2) Regarding historical condition, the research here emphasizes local and national-historical conditions of a specific time, as well as their relation to other localities (especially the advanced Western countries) and other times (especially formal and political developments in the following decades in China). The particularity of China (and Asia and the 'peripheral' or developing countries) in relation to world or international architecture, which is itself a specific historical product of the West, is emphasized. 'New' or 'breakthrough' developments in the Chinese history are identified and studied in a local and international context. (3) Regarding formal evolution, this research pays close attention to concepts of space and form, and evolutions of forms and design approaches across historical periods. It deals with European concepts in China, the interaction of Chinese and foreign traditions, the trajectory of localization of Western ideas in China, the shift of formal language in design in 'modern Chinese architecture', and theoretical legacies of the Chinese formal and spatial traditions.

Employing these focuses as guiding questions, these essays explore historical development as well as analytical problems. Together they cover a history and a range of social and formal issues. These essays, however, are not exhaustive for all important moments and problems in the architecture and urban design of modern China. They cover instead a basic set of primary problems and critical moments in the entire history of modern Chinese architecture conceived as a long historical development from the mid-eighteenth century to the present. The studies here provide a basis for a social, historical and formal critique of modern Chinese architecture.

The chapters

From Chapter 2 to 9, a historical reading of specific times and problems is provided. Chapter 2 deals with the arrival of European sciences and visual-formal technologies after 1607 and in the 1730s and the following decades. It covers the arrival of Euclidian geometry, linear perspective, realist painting and quasi-Baroque buildings in China. It explores the ways in which the visual breakthroughs of the 1730s to 1780s in China brought about the problem of style, form, the object, truthfulness and the presence of a scientific gaze, in design practice in architecture as well as in related practices such as painting and systems of graphic representation. Chapter 3 deals with the arrival of the Chinese architect in the 1920s, the institutionalization of the profession, the knowledge–power contract, the 'collaboration' between the profession and the first nation-state of China in the 1930s in Nanjing, then the national capital, and the joint production of ideas, buildings and planning schemes of a 'Chinese style'. Issues of criticality or progressive, ethical commitment in the profession are also raised, in which a Chinese and Asian case for a geo-political project is affirmed. Chapter 4 examines Beijing of the 1950s, the national capital of the People's Republic. Standing in the 1950s, with earlier and new currents joining up here, issues of Soviet and American influences, of the scientific gaze, and of the impact of historical research with this gaze upon design thinking can be studied. Examining Liang Sicheng's trajectory, situating the research in a nexus of knowledge–power relations, this chapter focuses on 1954 and 1959 as two peak moments in which 'National Style', 'socialist new styles' and a radical urban transformation at the centre of Beijing materialized.

Chapter 5 explores a larger picture of transition from the earlier and the Maoist time before 1976 to the decades of the 1980s and 1990s. It identifies three primary design languages established before 1976: the national style of the state, the political expressionism of the Cultural Revolution, and socialist modernism. It then explores formal languages after 1976 in two sections, on the 1980s and on a new era since the late 1990s. Whereas the 1980s witnessed a neo-national style, a new vernacular, a formalistic late modernism and a commercial modernism or the International Style, the new era witnessed two new streams emerging in current China: a hyper-modernism of the state and an experimental modernism of the individual. This chapter also offers a preliminary reading of this experimental modernism in the social and historical context of post-Maoist China.

Chapter 6 and 7 deal with interactions between China and the West around 2000, and the relationship between criticality and instrumentality as it emerged in a recent debate. Chapter 6 identifies a symmetrical tendency occurring between China and the West in which criticality was transferred from the West into China as a Chinese instrumentality was displayed in the West. This essay contributes to a 'post-critical' debate in North America in suggesting that there is a global, Asian and Chinese impetus that should not be ignored. This research examines both a 'Western' voice in China resulting from the new generation of Chinese architects developing experimental designs using purist and tectonic modernism, as well as a 'Chinese/Asian' voice arising from explorations by Rem Koolhaas in particular of what may be termed as a post-critical pragmatism. Chapter 6 is followed by a special section that features a debate in relation to this essay organized in *Time + Architecture* (Shanghai, 2006). Eleven critics and architects from China and North America aired their views. This section includes a reprint of five of these comments, and my review and response as part of an ongoing discussion. Chapter 7 examines the 'symmetrical tendency' in the larger picture of China as a global construction site, and explores the possibility of China as a site for developing a new criticality. In this second aspect, it examines a material scenario of a post-capitalist world-system in which China plays a crucial part, and the cultural and intellectual basis in the Chinese tradition in which a relational ethics defines how society coheres and functions. It argues that an instrumentalist architecture of quantity and a relational ethics for a new critical attitude in design are likely to be the influence of the Chinese approach in the world.

Chapter 8 deals with Beijing in 2008. It offers a description of the historical development of the city in the past and then especially in the three decades of the post-Maoist era, from 1978 to 2008. It then focuses on the form of Beijing as it emerged in 2008: (1) the symbolic expression of a new confidence using a formal language in a joint effort of the East and West, (2) a horizontal Beijing of the imperial past in contrast to a vertical capitalist metropolis, (3) difference and similarity between 1959 and 2008 in organizing a representation of the nation on the world stage. This essay ends with an observation on a synthetic approach to state–market and state–society relationships in contemporary China.

Chapter 9 returns to historical Beijing and makes an attempt to theorize the Chinese urban tradition revealed in this city. The purpose is to theorize historical Beijing for today's critical re-employment and for international debate in a China–Europe comparison. Modern European readings of Chinese traditions are discussed first as mirror reflections before direct observations are made on imperial or historic Beijing (1420–1911). Beijing is found to be a synthesis of conceived geometries and lived spaces. The incorporation of nature, the use of levels of scales in a geometry of similarity and quantity, and the emphasis of the local and the informal are identified as three crucial aspects. They make historical Beijing a city of ordered geometries but also a field of life and formlessness. An order of disorder, a form of the informal, may offer useful ideas for a reconstruction of liveability and public sphere in contemporary China.

Chapter 10 offers a general reading of modern Chinese architecture of the twentieth century (1910s–2010s). It includes a map of all primary design positions found in mainland China in these hundred years. The positions are organized into five 'mountain ranges' and twenty 'plateaus'. It is a first step towards a more comprehensive mapping of a larger territory and a longer time. Together with Chapter 5, it provides a hindsight or an aerial view of the 'critical moments' or 'plateaus' of this architecture in modern China, some of the most important of which have been analysed in the previous chapters. Apart from identifying these moments, the map also reveals macro patterns or lines of flights and energetic currents moving through these moments or plateaus. Again the previous chapters have covered some of the most important currents and trajectories, such as that of the national style, the representation of the state, Western influence and the tortured path of modernism.

Problems: form, power, autonomy, criticality and geo-cultural difference

A series of critical problems are discovered and dealt with in these chapters. These problems may be listed here briefly. The first problem concerns 'form' and 'formlessness' in analysing the Euclidian geometry and linear perspective that arrived in China and their impact, and a Chinese tradition in geometrical studies and urban forms. If the European tradition has provided a geometry of form, then the Chinese have provided a geometry of quantity, organic life and informality. This set of issues is dealt with in Chapter 2 where the arrival of European geometry and linear perspective are studied, and in Chapter 9 where a Chinese approach to the lived and the formless is studied in relation to historical Beijing.

The second problem deals with power–knowledge interactions in the case of the profession working with state authority when the first nation-states of China were constructed in the 1930s and 1950s. The arrival and the shape of the modern profession of the architect, the institutionalization of skills, knowledge and design practice for the profession, the production of scientific knowledge on the Chinese tradition, and the use of Western design methods (of the Beaux-Arts tradition) and historical knowledge for a new national style to represent the nation-state in a specific ideological framework of a certain moment are dealt with in Chapters 3 and 4 for the two critical decades. The representation of the nation on the world stage is also dealt with in Chapter 8, in which urban forms of Beijing from the past to the 1950s and to 2008 are studied. The interaction between overseas architects and state authority is also observed.

The third problem deals with the liberalization of the economy and the arrival of private practice and the individual in design positioning.

A commercial modernism and an experimental modernism come hand in hand. The presence of the market economy and the freedom available for the profession contribute significantly to the arrival of the individual in design thinking and the appearance of a critical and experimental architecture from the architect as a modern bourgeois individual. The use of purist and tectonic modernism, exploring an internal language of building construction and its poetics, always emerges as its main form of expression. This happened very briefly (or, strictly speaking, insignificantly) in the 1930s, 1940s and 1950s on account of economic and ideological restrictions, and has been happening substantially since the late 1990s (Chapters 5, 6 and 7).

The next important problem concerns 'criticality' or, to use broader phrasing, the issue of a self-conscious commitment to an ethical and progressive cause in design. Here it is found that in China a nationalist architecture, in so far as it is engaged in a progressive political cause against imperialism (in the 1920s to the 1950s), can be understood as critical even though criticality here is not 'autonomous' and opposing authority and convention as defined in the West. It entails a questioning of the European definition of the critical conceived as an autonomous position against authority and tradition within a social and national boundary (Chapter 3). The research also deals with the arrival of individualist criticality with Western influence in the new market economy since the late 1990s (Chapters 6 and 7). This research then moves on to observe more closely these 'critical individuals' in the emerging civil society of contemporary China in which new characteristics can be identified. This includes a synthetic 'compromise' between criticality and participation, and a re-employment of indigenous Chinese ideas and concepts. These signs indicate the possibilities of a new formulation of the critical which requires theoretical constructions (Chapter 7).

These are specific problems arising from historical conditions in modern China. They share to a varying degree with other Asian countries and 'peripheral' or developing countries, in a structural relation and in contrast to the West, the origin of this modern world and this modern architecture which has spread worldwide since the nineteenth century. These problems are therefore useful for a further understanding of modern architecture in the non-Western world. Among all the specific historical problems identified in this study, two appear most basic or important in characterizing this modern architecture of the non-West and of China: relations with the West and alternative formulations of the critical.

Modern Chinese architecture has not developed from within, but has been stimulated or generated at its earliest moments by Western forces. The result, however, is not a Western or European architecture transplanted, but a hybrid, with various ways of combining and synthesizing different traditions: some crude and literal, others more abstract and developed. This hybrid condition was primarily the result of historical imperative in the earlier times. Yet it now becomes a certain advantage in that it provides a broader perspective incorporating both Western and indigenous Chinese traditions, and a space of new possibilities. In this hybrid modern architecture, now already a century old at least, we can identify some Chinese characteristics re-emerging or re-articulated. These include an architecture of scale and quantity, a socially embedded design practice, a pervasive role of the state and a different approach to the ethical and critical.

Resulting from the position of a (partial) colony after 1840 and from cultural tradition, two forms of criticality can be identified in China, which are structurally different from Western formulations. In the first, because of the colonial past, a nationalist criticality in design has emerged in the 1920s to the 1950s, with a progressive agenda not defined as that of an autonomous position against authority and tradition but constructed in a joint effort of the architect and state authority against external colonial domination. In the second, with Western individualistic criticality having arrived recently, signs of a reformulation of Western criticality with Chinese reality and tradition have emerged, indicating a (re-)surfacing of relational ethics of compromise and synthesis, for which a progressive agenda can be facilitated not through confrontation but interaction with different agents and powers. In both cases, we discover specificities of Western criticality formulated in social theory and architectural discourse since early modern times. They reveal the Western formulation as autonomous, confrontational and negative, but also illuminating in defining a task clearly and helpful in asserting this agenda at an initial moment. If the Chinese cases are persuasive at all, then a reform of the idea of criticality is possible. Critical architecture can be progressive *and* affirmative, with distinctive agendas *and* with relational ethics. Abandoning a self-centred autonomy, a new critical practice can be relational, embedded and constructive.

CHAPTER 2

PERSPECTIVE AS SYMBOLIC FORM

Beijing, 1729–35

Since a primary source of modernity in China in the past few centuries lies in Europe, processes of 'Westernization' and 'modernization' have been intertwined in complex ways. Have the Chinese ever attempted to separate the two processes, to select what was needed for China, to reorganize foreign influence and to synthesize it with local traditions? How did these interventions play out in architecture, art and visual culture in early modern China? To answer these questions, we need to investigate the earliest moment in history when European modern science and culture entered China. In the early seventeenth century, through an encounter of European Jesuits with Chinese Confucian scholars at the imperial court of Beijing, 'Western Learning' in science was embraced, although Christianity did not receive a comparable reception. Western mathematics, astronomy and cartography were introduced early in the century, which generated organized applications of the knowledge and great compilations of Western and Chinese studies in these fields in the late seventeenth century. One major consequence of this was a visual 'revolution' taking place around the 1730s, a breakthrough marked by an introduction of Renaissance linear perspective into China. A Chinese court official, Nian Xiyao, published a study on the subject in 1729 and then a revised edition in 1735 titled *Shi Xue* (Principles of visual perspective). Giuseppe Castiglione, an Italian Jesuit painter serving at the Chinese court since 1715, developed in the following decades a new style in which Renaissance realism with the use of perspective and chiaroscuro was integrated into the Chinese painting tradition. With the help of Castiglione and other Jesuits, 'Western-Style Pavilions' or 'Xiyanglou', a group of pleasure villas, fountains and gardens in a quasi-Baroque style with Chinese elements, was constructed in the 1740s to the 1780s, which had an impact on 'modern' buildings emerging afterwards.

This sequence of events, with scientific learning followed by a visual breakthrough, includes important cases in which critical problems concerning Chinese selection and reorganization of Western influences can be studied. The issue here concerns not only a general process of internalizing foreign influence, but also the specific characteristics of Renaissance scientific knowledge, the assumptions of its visual culture, the interrelation between a Greek–European 'bias' in the use of geometry and a 'universal' positivist rationality, as well as a

Chinese reaction, response and subsequent path of development in science and in visual culture including architecture and urban design. This essay provides a brief history of the events with a focus on the visual revolution of the 1730s. The purpose is to establish preliminary observations so that these critical issues can be addressed.

'Western Learning', 1600–1723

Matteo Ricci (1552–1610), an Italian Jesuit who studied in Rome and Lisbon, arrived in Macau in 1582, and visited the imperial palace in Beijing in 1601. He became the first Christian missionary who successfully entered the palace, settled in Beijing and was freely allowed to preach Christianity in China.[1] Ricci's approach was conciliatory: he learned the local language, studied Chinese classics and assumed the position of a 'Confucian scholar' with due customs and rituals. What made him attractive to the Chinese elite was not only his interest in Confucianism but also his scientific knowledge and his willingness to share this with the Chinese. It is known that Ricci's transfer of scientific knowledge to the Chinese and his adoption of Confucian rites and terminology were the means to achieve his goal, which was to convert the Chinese to Christianity.[2] The Chinese scholars, on the other hand, were open to all that he was offering although their stronger interest in science is obvious. While spreading the religion and converting many, Ricci also made maps of the world and presented these to the Chinese, and translated with Chinese scholars European books on mathematics and science. The most notable of these was his translation with Xu Guangqi (1562–1633) of the first six volumes of Euclid's *Elements* into a Chinese book in 1607 titled *Jihe Yuanben* (which may be translated as 'Elements of Geometry').

Ricci's tolerance of local rites and customs among Chinese converts soon attracted criticism from other orders of the Catholic Church.[3] In 1645 Pope Innocent X in Rome denounced the 'Ricci practice' and banned indigenous offerings and worship for the Chinese Christians. After rounds of debate, in 1704 Pope Clement XI issued an articulated decree banning local rites and customs among Chinese converts, a policy which was reaffirmed in 1715 (and was not changed until 1939). The Kangxi Emperor in Beijing (r. 1662–1722), who was tolerant of the Christian mission for a long time and had a great interest in Western science, finally retaliated by banning Christian teaching in China in 1721, a position that was closely maintained in the following reigns for more than a century. Despite this, some Jesuits remained at the Chinese court, as the Chinese learning of Western sciences continued actively regardless of the controversy with Rome. This 'Western learning' may be briefly described in three areas: astronomy, mathematics and geography.

In astronomy, the Chinese had the longest continuous history of observing celestial phenomena including eclipses, comets and sunspots; proposed the idea of the Earth as a sphere and of the universe as open and boundless; adopted an equator-based coordinate; initiated a quantified astronomy; and built devices for studies in astronomy.[4] Chinese astronomy however suffered from a lack of geometry as developed in Greece and quantified physics as emerged after the Renaissance. What the Jesuits offered to the Chinese at this juncture was a precise geometric explanation of heavenly movements (and Greek geometry itself), advanced algebra and new devices of calculation, a verified knowledge of the Earth as a sphere, advanced devices, especially the telescope, and a mathematical method of describing and predicting heavenly movements including eclipses.[5] However, on account of the denunciation of Galileo in 1616 and 1632 and of Copernicus's theory of a heliocentric universe by the Catholic Church, the Jesuits in China continued to uphold an Aristotelian theory of the universe with the Earth at the centre, delaying the arrival of new knowledge for almost a century (until after 1800).[6] But, because this option doesn't interfere with an accurate description of heavenly bodies as observed on the Earth, the Jesuits were still able to offer a system of calculation for calendar making that was better than the Chinese practice. Proved superior, the European method was adopted at the Chinese court in the 1620s and 1630s. In 1635, a great compilation of Western methods in mathematics and astronomy was made by Johannes Terrentius (Deng Yuhan), Adam Schall von Bell (Tang Ruowang), James Rho (Luo Yagu) and Nicolas Longobardi (Long Huamin), with the assistance of Xu Guangqi, Li Zhizao and Li Tianjing. In 1645, at the opening of the Qing dynasty (1644–1911), the book was republished as *Xiyang Xinfa Lishu* (Calendrical Science according to New Western Methods) by Schall von Bell. In that year, Schall von Bell was appointed Director of the Imperial Bureau of Astronomy (*Qin Tian Jian*) in Beijing. From 1645 to 1805, for 160 years, eleven European Jesuit scientists continued to occupy this position.[7] Chinese scientists, on the other hand, learned from the Europeans with a rather rational attitude. A team of Chinese made this comment:

> At first we also had our doubts about the astronomy from Europe when it was used in the Jisi Year (1629), but after having read many clear explanations our doubts diminished by half, and finally by participating in precise observations of the stars, and of the positions of the Sun and Moon, our hesitations were altogether overcome. Recently we received the imperial order to study these sciences, and every day we have been discussing them with the Europeans. Truth must be sought not only in books, but in making actual experiments with instruments; it is not enough to listen

with one's ears, one must also carry out manipulations with one's hands. All the new astronomy is then found to be exact.[8]

In mathematics, the Chinese were the first to develop algebra and had passed this to India, Arabia and Europe.[9] As Chinese interest declined after 1200, developed algebra re-entered China from Arabia from 1300 onwards. The Chinese had also developed geometry, but in a manner different from that of the Greeks: whereas in Greece theories of geometry dealt with pure formal relations, in China geometry was not 'pure' but numerical, and defined in terms of empirical problems.[10] According to historians of mathematics, whereas the Chinese and Indians developed algebra, it is the Greeks who developed pure geometry. Despite all these earlier differences, from the Renaissance onwards it was the Europeans who made continuous breakthroughs culminating in calculus in the late seventeenth century. Geometry, algebra and calculus then provided a precise description of movements of objects and celestial bodies at the birth of modern science. For China, from the early seventeenth century, Greek and Renaissance mathematics were translated and absorbed gradually.

In this process, the translation of Euclid's *Elements* by Ricci and Xu Guangqi was the first and remained important in China. Ricci and Xu translated the first six volumes of the *Elements* which dealt with plane geometry in 1607 (whereas the following nine volumes dealing with numbers, three-dimensional geometry and five regular solids were translated into Chinese in 1857 by Alexander Wylie and Li Shanlan).[11] The impact of the 1607 text was twofold. On the one hand, it brought into China a Greek approach to geometry: deductive, axiomatic and purely geometrical or formal, complementing a Chinese tradition that was algorithmic, numerical, empirical and problem-based.[12] The effect of a purely geometric theory was immediately evident in the new physics that so successfully explained the movement of objects and celestial bodies. On the other hand, the translation also served as a Chinese reassertion of its own tradition. The new knowledge stimulated a revitalization of Chinese mathematics; it generated pragmatic learning in the Qing dynasty (1644–1911); and it confirmed a neo-Confucian emphasis on *gewu*, *li* and *shixue* ('analysis', 'reason' and 'pragmatic studies').[13] The Chinese terms adopted for Euclidian geometry such as *jihe* ('how-much', which was corrupted into a term for 'geometry'), and *qiu*, *fa*, *liangfa* ('problem', 'method' and 'a method of measuring'), also rendered Euclidian formal geometry with a Chinese numerical emphasis.[14]

Altogether, the introduction of Greek and Renaissance mathematics generated a rediscovery of China's ancient tradition neglected since the fourteenth century, and a new interest in the discipline with an international perspective. As a result, *Shuli Jingyun* (Essence of number and reason), a large compilation of Western and Chinese mathematics commissioned by Emperor Kangxi, was made in 1723. It concluded the first stage of Western learning in mathematics, and inaugurated a confluence of Chinese mathematics into a shared international discipline thereafter.[15]

In geography and cartography, the Chinese had a long and continuous history of mapping the land with regulated grids at a scale since the second and third centuries (introduced by Zhang Heng of 78–139 and Pei Xue of 224–271).[16] Large maps of China and Asia were made in 801, 1043, 1100 and 1315 (Figure 2.1). The map of Asia made in the Mongolian Yuan dynasty in 1315, and subsequent expansions in 1555 and after in the Ming dynasty, covered Europe, Asia and Africa, based on knowledge obtained through Mongolian contacts with Europe and Chinese maritime expeditions to Arabia and east Africa.[17] The Chinese had had a theory of the Earth as a globe since the Han dynasty yet the idea was not verified. The Chinese had also made real measurements of units of length of latitudes and altitudes in 725, the first such attempts in the world.[18] In Europe, after a period of scientific cartography with parallel latitudes and curved longitudes developed by Ptolemy (active in AD 120–70), a 'dark age' reigned for a long time when religious 'wheel-maps' dominated the scene, until between 1300 and 1400 maritime charts and scientific maps emerged again. The rest of the story, of European 'voyages of discovery' and overseas expansion, is well known. What the Jesuits were bringing

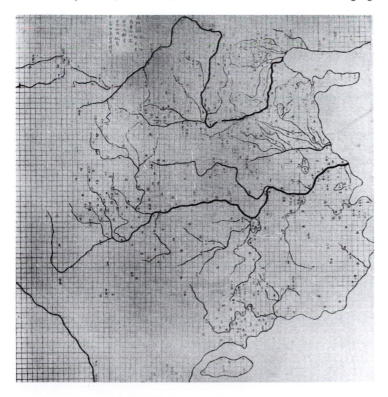

2.1 A map of central China entitled *Yuji Tu* (Map of the tracks of Yu the Great), made in 1100, stone cut in 1137, on grid scale of 100 li to the division.

into China at this moment, that is, what Ricci was presenting to the Chinese in 1584, 1600 and 1602, was a latest map of the world that covered the Americas, the Atlantic and the Pacific Oceans, a verified knowledge of the Earth as a sphere, many accurate locations and translated names now still in use in modern Chinese, and Renaissance cartography based on real surveys of positions in latitude and longitude using astronomical observations (Figure 2.2).[19]

With the support of King Louis XIV in Paris and competent Jesuit scientists sent from France, the Kangxi Emperor conducted a large project of land surveying across the empire from 1707 to 1717, using Renaissance methods to measure some 630 positions, in a net of triangles over the territory in twenty provinces including Taiwan and Mongolia.[20] The result was the *Huangyu Quanlantu*, or 'A Complete Map of the Empire' in 1718, which was 'not only the best map which had ever been made in Asia, but better and more accurate than any European map of its time'.[21]

What had happened to China at this moment in cartography, in terms of basic attitude, was a confluence of the two scientific traditions,

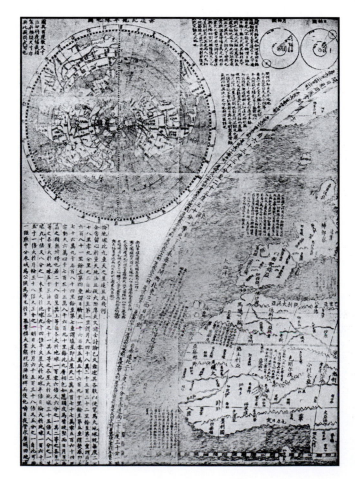

2.2 A corner (one-twelfth) of the Definitive World Map of Matteo Ricci made in 1602 entitled *Kunyu Wanguo Quantu*.

a long *continuous* one in China and a Greek–Renaissance one with a 'religious' break in its history. In this sense, China at this juncture underwent not a shift from a religious 'dark age' to an enlightened scientific era, but a step of transformation *from a first rationality to a second or new rationality*. In this process, a secular, materialist and disciplined attitude in Chinese antiquity remained unchanged. In fact, in so far as cartography reflects other disciplines in China such as geography, astronomy and mathematics, the same can be said of other technological disciplines and empirical studies in China. We will come to this issue of different forms of rationality at the end of this essay.

The years 1718 for cartography, 1723 for mathematics and 1645 for astronomy and calendar making can be regarded as moments of a Chinese internalization of Greek and Renaissance sciences. At these moments we can identify a Chinese screening of Western influence in that while rational scientific knowledge was embraced Christian teaching was left aside. There was a Chinese reading and reorganization when Greek geometry was absorbed in China and when scientific study was understood as a neo-Confucian enterprise. Nevertheless the European impact was real: a transformation of traditional rational studies into modern scientific pursuits, with a Greek geometric 'bias' and a Renaissance mathematical positivism. The issue of cultural 'bias' and special kinds of rationality will be explored in the following sections and at the end of the essay.

A visual breakthrough after 1700

One consequence of this transmission of Western science into China was the arrival of linear perspective and a change of visual culture after 1700. When Ricci presented his Christian paintings at the Chinese court in 1601, the realistic images with the use of chiaroscuro and elements of perspective greatly impressed the Chinese. Subsequent distribution of Christian books with illustrations using these techniques spread much further this new visual possibility to the Chinese in the following decades. In the 1680s, court paintings in Beijing began to use linear perspectives. In the 1730s, popular prints from the south, the New Year Painting produced in Suzhou, began to use linear perspectives and shades and shadows as distinctive features.

If we trace the development more closely, there were a few lines at the imperial court that were critical in establishing and popularizing this practice. One connection was between Jiao Bingzhen (active 1660s–80s) and Ferdinandus Verbiest (Nan Huairan, 1591–1688) at the Imperial Bureau of Astronomy.[22] Verbiest, Director of the Bureau from 1663 to 1688, refitted the Imperial Observatory with new devices, and produced a collection of 117 illustrations of these instruments in perspective views with shades and shadows in 1674 (Figure 2.3).

2.3 Beijing Observatory refitted by Ferdinandus Verbiest, engraving on paper, the first in a set of 117 leaves depicting the new instruments, drawings by artists under Verbiest in 1674.

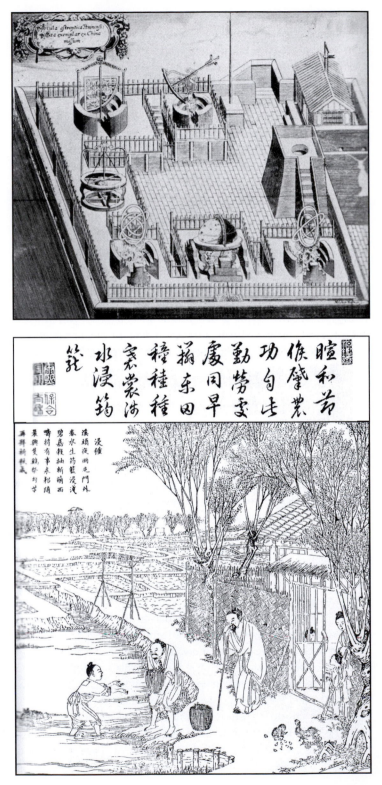

2.4 Illustration 1 in a set of forty-six leaves entitled *Gengzhi Tu* (Farming and weaving illustrated), wood engravings on paper, drawings by Jiao Bingzhen in 1696.

Jiao, a painter and also a court official working at the bureau, studied the drawing techniques with Verbiest. Jiao then applied this to his own work, producing a famous set of forty-six woodcut engravings in 1696, *Gengzhi Tu* (Farming and weaving illustrated), in which linear perspective was used (Figure 2.4). Jiao with his student Leng Mei, and other artists such as Chen Mei, Jiang Tingxi and Mang Guli, in the following years effectively developed a style of painting in which linear perspective was accommodated in a Chinese composition of aerial views.

Another critical connection was between Nian Xiyao (?–1739) and Giuseppe Castiglione (Lang Shining, 1688–1766). After Brunelleschi's experiments in 1417 and Alberti's book *On Painitng* of 1435, many mathematicians, architects and artists made contributions to improving either practical methods of perspective drawing or theoretical principles to unify different systems of projection used before. In this lineage, Andrea Pozzo (1642–1709), an Italian architect and painter, published his two-volume book *Perspectiva Pictorum et Architectorum* (Perspective in architecture and painting) in 1693 and 1698. Castiglione, a Jesuit from Milan, studied painting under Pozzo, and became a well-known painter in Lisbon, before arriving in Macau and

2.5 An illustration in Nian Xiyao's *Shi Xue* (Principles of visual perspective), 1735: instruments needed for a perspective drawing.

2.6 An illustration in Nian Xiyao's *Shi Xue*: basic concepts of a perspective projection.

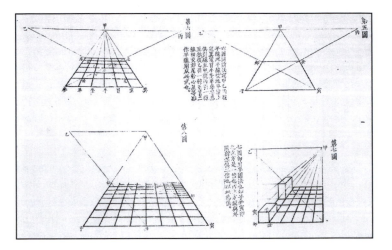

2.7 An illustration in Nian Xiyao's *Shi Xue*: European architectonic parts viewed in perspective.

2.8 An illustration in Nian Xiyao's *Shi Xue*: a scene of a Chinese lantern festival viewed in a one-point perspective.

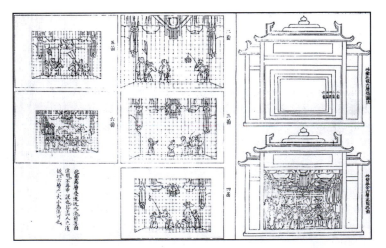

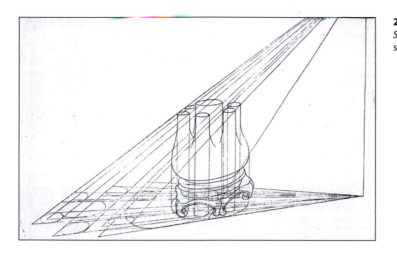

2.9 An illustration in Nian Xiyao's *Shi Xue*: a Chinese utensil with shadows in perspective.

Beijing in 1715.[23] While serving at the Chinese court and developing a synthesized style of painting using selectively European and Chinese methods, Castiglione also met Nian Xiyao and presented Pozzo's book to him.[24] Nian, a court official who had studied linear perspective for some ten years before, received enlightening explanations on the subject matter from Castiglione in these meetings, as Nian acknowledged.[25] With this, Nian published *Shixue Jingyun* in 1729, and republished the book with additions in 1735 with a simpler title *Shi Xue* (Principles of visual perspective). Nian thus produced the first treatise on geometrical principles of linear perspective in China. Judging by any standard, Nian's book and Castiglione's painting are the climax of this visual revolution. One special legacy of this connection was 'Western-Style Pavilions' or 'Xiyanglou', a group of buildings and gardens in a quasi-Baroque style built as part of an imperial villa outside Beijing in the 1740s to 1780s. These three incidents and their 'products', that is, Nian's book, Castiglione's painting and the Western-Style Pavilions, deserve a closer examination.

1 *Nian Xiyao and* Shi Xue, *1729–35*

Only the second edition of the book survives today (Figures 2.5, 2.6, 2.7, 2.8 and 2.9). The 1735 book contains the preface of the first edition (pp. 1–2), the preface of the second (pp. 3–5), an illustration of instruments needed for the drawings (p. 6) and the content of the book of 125 pages, which included sixty problems, seventy-five illustrations and explanatory notes of some 11,000 words.[26] Of these problems, the first part deals with perspective drawing of objects and the second objects with shadows. The objects depicted here include squares (placed on a horizontal surface), cubes, cylinders, other geometrical solids, Greek and Roman capitals and column bases, and Chinese utensils such as teapots and vases, as well as a scene of a

Chinese lantern festival viewed in a one-point central perspective.

It is important to note that, whereas the 1607 translation of Euclid's *Elements* in *Jihe Yuanben* introduced plane geometry, this book of 1729–35 for the first time introduced a geometric description of vision, and projected this scientific vision upon a Chinese world of things along with European architectonic objects. It introduced into China not only Greek geometry and its formal purity, but also the Renaissance science of a fixed monocular vision in which both the position of the eye and that of the viewer in relation to the 'world' are fixed. Since traditional Chinese methods taught artists to view a landscape in different and shifting angles with an interactive relation with the world, this book of 1729–36, and the paintings emerging then, imposed a European 'bias' and a fixation of the eye with a scientific realism in attitude. It defined a position of the human subject with an assumed split or dualist distance between humans and nature, mind and body, subject and object. In other words, in philosophical terms, this was a 'Cartesian' moment in China, in the positioning of a vision of the human subject, although its consequences may be felt decades and centuries later (we will come back to this issue in the last section of this essay).

There was however debate amongst the Chinese, as evidenced in Nian's prefaces in 1729 and 1735. In the preface of 1729, Nian says the ancient Chinese method teaches us to view from different angles yet it is difficult to learn and is not clear.[27] The Western method is clear as evidenced in the book. It requires fixed points and regulated lines drawn from these points; and once the viewing position is anchored all the rest can be generated without any doubt or uncertainty. Nian then says 'people are commenting that these drawings are *truthful* but not *lively* (*zhen er bu miao*). But how can you make them lively if they are not truthful first?' In the second preface, Nian was more accommodating to the Chinese method. Here he says the idea of a perspective where a distant thing is smaller is well understood to the Chinese. The Chinese tradition is able to handle mountains and valleys in careful compositions with great ease, with no need to consider literal dimensions and specific forms. However, when we are depicting buildings and utensils and when accuracy is needed, we have to use the Western method. (Nian then explained that he had consulted Castiglione again, reconsidered the content, researched diligently, and added some fifty more illustrations in the second edition). It is obvious that there was criticism of the Western method around that time in China. And the issue here in the debate concerned (1) a realist, 'truthful' approach versus a 'lively', dynamic approach in representation (*zhen* versus *miao*) and (2) the precise usefulness of the Western and Chinese methods respectively, given a close comparison of the two and a re-appreciation of the native tradition. Debate on these issues, especially on the *zhen–miao* dichotomy, continued with respect to Castiglione's painting.

2.10 *Jurui Tu* (An auspicious collection), by Giuseppe Castiglione, 1723, ink and colour on silk, 173 cm × 86.1 cm.

2.11 *Baijun Tu* (One hundred horses), Section Two, by Giuseppe Castiglione, 1728, ink and colour on silk, 94.5 cm × 776.2 cm.

2 Castiglione and a new style of painting, 1715–66

Before Castiglione arrived in Beijing in 1715, two Jesuit painters had briefly visited the palace: Giovanni Gherardini in 1700–4 and Matteo Ripa (Ma Guoxian) in 1710–23. Neither of them left behind a substantial body of work.[28]

When Castiglione died in 1766, none of the younger Jesuit artists or Chinese students was comparable to Castiglione in skills and creative synthesis.[29] Because of the intensification of the rites dispute between Rome and Beijing in the 1770s and after, there were no longer any Jesuit artists left at the Chinese court from the 1810s onwards. In the special eighteenth century, then, Castiglione stood out as the leading figure of a group of artists who were responsible for creating a new style of painting in which Renaissance and Chinese traditions were synthesized in specific ways.[30]

Castiglione's initial contribution was teaching Chinese students oil painting and the use of perspective, as well as producing oil paintings for the interiors of palaces in which Chinese themes (of mountains, rivers, flowers) presented from a predominantly European point of view and featuring the use of chiaroscuro were included.[31] From 1723 onwards, with the new Emperor Yongzheng (r. 1723–35) on the

throne, thanks to his rigorous institutional reform and his close interest in and even direct comments on Castiglione's painting that encouraged an adoption of Chinese methods (in conjunction with European), and certainly thanks to Castiglione's own innovative experiments, a new approach emerged. Chinese materials (silk, brush, colour), themes (auspicious flowers and animals) and formats (vertical or horizontal scrolls) were used while at the same time European techniques in the use of perspective, chiaroscuro and complex colours to express light, space, volume, texture and materiality were also employed. The use of directional light and the effect of shades and shadows were softened so that, as it were, the 'European' object may be slightly eroded and submerge better in a 'Chinese' surface where light was diffused and lines and decorative qualities (emphasizing surfaces) played a greater part. Castiglione's *Jurui Tu* (An auspicious collection, 1723), *Songxian Yingzhi Tu* (Auspicious flowers, 1724) and *Baijun Tu* (One hundred horses, 1728) were representatives of this approach (Figures 2.10, 2.11). From 1736 onwards, when the Emperor Qianlong (r. 1736– 95), with whom he had a close relationship, was ruling the empire, Castiglione began to produce 'imperial portraits' which revealed his serious strength and innovative synthesis. The effect of chiaroscuro was softened in a more diffused Chinese space yet facial features,

anatomical accuracy, three-dimensional substantiality and an overall realism were rigorously maintained. Representative works here include *Qianlong Huangdi Chaofu Xiang* (Portrait of the Emperor Qianlong in formal court robes, 1736) (Figure 2.12), and portraits of the Empress and imperial concubines. From the late 1730s onwards, Castiglione's work began to incorporate large spectacles with the emperor and a whole entourage in various settings, projects which involved many of his Chinese students, such as the well-known *Wanshu Yuan Ciyan Tu* (Imperial banquet in the Garden of Ten Thousand Trees, 1755). He also made drawings for large engravings with many of his students producing the final work, which depicted victory campaigns of the Emperor Qianlong in the last decade of Castiglione's life.

As a whole Castiglione's painting followed an approach different from that of Jiao Bingzhen and Jiao's students. Whereas Jiao's approach was basically Chinese in the overall landscape composition, where European perspective was contained in a broad and aerial view, Castiglione's approach was substantially European in almost all aspects of Renaissance realism yet a Chinese preference for a softened and diffused illumination, for the use of lines and decorative surfaces, and for certain auspicious themes was fully incorporated. Castiglione's work also attracted interesting comments at the Chinese court. Although the Emperor Qianlong praised him for his skills of *xiezhen* ('depicting the real'), critics said that his work was indeed realistic yet it had no dynamic lines and strokes (*bili, bifa*), no vitality, liveliness and aura (*qiyun, shenyi*), qualities that Chinese artists regarded as of supreme importance.[32] This was in fact a continuation of the debate around Nian's book about the respective qualities of realism and subjective vitality (that is, of *zhen* and *miao*). Modern critics such as Yang Boda consider Castiglione's work strong in spiritual vitality and aura (as evidenced in the portraits), but would also agree that there were no brush strokes and powerful lines so important in the Chinese tradition. But Yang emphasizes that Castiglione's work is in the end neither 'Chinese' nor 'European', but a specific style that utilizes certain aspects of the two selectively.[33]

This leads to two observations. (1) Castiglione's work displays an East–West duality and eclecticism in taste and technique. Since artists and intellectuals in China in the following nineteenth and twentieth centuries remained in a situation similar to that of the 1730s in which one was caught between two persuasive cultures, this duality and eclecticism survived as main features of various intellectual and artistic practices. (2) Castiglione's East–West synthesis, on the other hand, was also a result of the power relationship he was embedded in with respect to the two emperors, especially the rigorous Yongzheng Emperor in the 1730s when the style was in its formative years. Yongzheng's specific request for an incorporation of Chinese themes and methods had surely had an impact on the artist.[34] Qianlong's favour and his request to depict spectacular scenes were surely also significant. There is evidence to show that Castiglione was not always willing to conform to these directives,[35] yet his contribution as a result was outstanding. In other words, both situational pressure and intellectual innovation contributed to the production of this cultural synthesis.

3 Western-Style Pavilions, 1747–86

One peculiar legacy of Castiglione, and of the Qianlong era, was the building of Xiyanglou or Western-Style Pavilions, a set of buildings and gardens in a quasi-Baroque style, in the Changchunyuan Garden to the north-west of Beijing from the 1740s to the 1780s. At the height of the Qing empire, when opulent villas and gardens were built around Beijing, the Changchunyuan Garden began to take shape in 1745. Between 1747 and 1751, a Baroque-style building (Xieqique) with a set of fountains was constructed.[36] Castiglione and Michel Benoist (Jiang

Youren) were possibly the designers for the building and fountains respectively. Historical records from here onwards are clearer. In 1752, nine sets of fittings were ordered to be placed inside the building. They included chandeliers, microscopes, large mirrors, curtains and sets of heavenly bodies (devices for astronomical studies). In 1753, Castiglione was requested to produce wall paintings of perspective views to be mounted inside the building. In 1756, Castiglione designed plans for buildings and gardens to the east of Xieqique, of which the emperor approved and requested construction that year. The Western-Style Pavilions were completed in 1783 at the latest. A set of twenty bronze engravings depicting the buildings and gardens, with the use of perspective and chiaroscuro, was completed in 1786. The project included Castiglione's students' drawings in Beijing and actual production in Paris coordinated by Michael Bourgeois (Chao Junxiu), before they were presented to Qianlong in 1786.[37]

The entire complex consists of a western section on a north–south axis of 350 metres centred on the building Xieqique, which was built first, and a long eastern section on an east–west axis of 750 metres designed by Castiglione.[38] On this axis, stretching from west to east, are two buildings (Haiyantang and Yuanyingguang), a large central fountain (Dashuifa), a few gates and a hill, and then a rectangular lake extending east (Fanghe) and finally a series of walls called 'Perspective Walls' (Xianfaqiang) at the eastern end. These walls created, for a viewer standing on the western side of the lake looking east on the axis, an illusion of a distant view of villages and mountains when realistic paintings were placed on the walls. Apart from Castiglione and Benoist, a few other Jesuits also participated in the design, yet there were no professional architects involved. The designs were not 'correct' but proximate imitations of Baroque and Rococo styles. The construction was carried out by Chinese carpenter-builders skilled in the local building tradition. The design as a result was a mixture

2.13 Northern elevation of Xieqique, engraving on paper, the second in a set of twenty leaves entitled *Yuanmingyuan Xiyanglou Tu* (Western-style buildings in the Yuanmingyuan garden), drawings by Yi Lantai and others, 1786.

2.14 Eastern elevation of Haiyantang, the twelfth in a set of twenty leaves entitled *Yuanmingyuan Xiyanglou Tu*.

2.15 Southern front of Dashuifa, the great fountain, the fifteenth in a set of twenty leaves entitled *Yuanmingyuan Xiyanglou Tu*.

of European and Chinese elements.[39] There were fountains, mazes, artificially trimmed plants, lawns, and masonry buildings with European scales and decorative details. There was the conscious use of perspective rules to create illusions of depth and distant views (at the eastern end, and also in the south-west). The axial links between large buildings with façades, and especially in a central, plaza-like space defined by façades around and across the central fountain, reveal another use of perspective-based design consciously or unconsciously. Yet these buildings used Chinese roof tiles, various building methods, and many decorative details, although the curved profiles for the roof outline were not used.[40] A set of twelve auspicious animal figures in the Chinese tradition was used to replace nude figures for a Western-style fountain (to the west of Haiyantang on the east–west axis) as nudity was not acceptable in China.[41] The twenty engravings of these buildings made in 1786 revealed these mixtures clearly (Figures 2.13, 2.14, 2.15 and 2.16). Further, as an essential part of the project, these engravings themselves were European in the use of perspective views, but also eclectic in the deviations from the 'correct' use of the

2.16 'Perspective walls' viewed on the axis across the lake, the twentieth in a set of twenty leaves entitled *Yuanmingyuan Xiyanglou Tu*.

technique where a more Chinese or aerial view was adopted.[42]

From the arrival of Ricci in Macau and Beijing in 1582–1600, to the beginning of the twentieth century, Western-style buildings were constructed in China in increasing quantity and with improving professional skills. These buildings appear to represent a preparatory phase from which 'modern architecture' in China, in technology (the use of reinforced concrete), function (the use of modern types such as railway stations, cinemas and banks), and style and form (the use of Beaux-Arts principles) developed. Yet the relations between these early Western-style buildings and 'modern architecture' in China await further explanation. If we look into these early Western buildings, we can find St Paul's Cathedral built after 1600 in Macau (and other churches and fortifications decades earlier), the 'Thirteen Hongs of Canton' (factories and offices operated by Europeans) in Guangzhou built after the 1680s, and churches in Beijing after 1605 (Nantang or 'Southern Church' for Matteo Ricci) and 1655 (Dongtang or 'Eastern Church') which were initially local in building method but were constantly rebuilt after 1700, 1800 and 1900 with increasing use of Western styles.[43] The Xiyanglou or Western-Style Pavilions of 1748–86 in Beijing was another major case in this early period. In terms of association with the imperial court of Beijing, which was the political and intellectual centre of China–Europe interactions after 1600, and in terms of Chinese internalization of Western influence, Xiyanglou stands out as the most critical of these cases (Figure 2.17). With this consideration in mind, we can identify characteristics of Xiyanglou that are significant for later developments:

1   The design was eclectic, with Western and Chinese styles used in a mixed manner. The use of 'Western Style' was a conscious choice; the adoption of some Chinese elements was also self-conscious. From this moment on, with increasing clarity and intensity, 'style' becomes a problem, to be consciously considered, selected, mixed and even manipulated for cultural and ideological purposes.

2   Construction methods for load-bearing brick and stone walls, and the associated patterns and details, as accumulated from the building of Xiyanglou, were recorded in *Yuanmingyuan Gongcheng Zuofa* (Construction methods of the Yuanmingyuan Garden), reserved for the imperial court.[44] It was the standard reference for Western-style buildings of the palace in the 1890s, which in turn became a style of 'latest' or 'modern' designs in Beijing after 1900 for shops, department stores, theatres, cinemas, railway stations and institutional buildings.[45] Eclectic and historicist designs with modern functions and building methods began to emerge from this moment onwards.

3   There was literal expansion of physical size of single buildings in Xiyanglou, and a parallel rise of the importance of single buildings as objects in spatial planning. Although there were walls dividing the complex, which was a Chinese tradition, these buildings were no longer part of a bounded courtyard and thus assumed a greater role as free-standing objects dominating the landscape. The front or façade of the buildings, now literally larger than that of conventional buildings in the local tradition, also assumed a greater importance in shaping space. Parallel to this and reinforcing this was the new awareness of a visual axis in the use of a perspective-based design. If the Chinese traditional use of axis was *organizational*, this new use of axis was intensely *visual*, making for a telescopic projection towards planes and façades as

2.17 Ruins of Xiyanglou: the northern side of the Xieqique building, photographed by Ernst Ohlmer, c.1870.

stage-sets. Subsequent 'Western-style' buildings in the 1890s and after 1900, with their increasing volume of the building and size of the façade, and the arrival of Beaux-Arts design principles in the hands of well-trained Chinese and overseas architects from the 1920s onwards, extended this Renaissance or perspective-based design into a more regulated and elaborated formal language.

From the 1730s to the twentieth century

In fact all three of these visual breakthroughs of the 1730s, Nian's book *Shi Xue*, Castiglione's paintings and the buildings of Xiyanglou, had important implications in modern China, and they are outlined here together.

1. After Nian's *Shi Xue* of 1729–35, another two books on the subject, *Huaqi Toushuo* (An illustrated guide to drawing) and *Toushi Xue* (a translation of Armand Cassagne's *A Practical Guide to Applied Perspective in Art and Industrial Drawing*, Paris, 1884), were published in 1898 and 1917 respectively.[46] In the first modern university curriculum published in China in 1902–3 (*Qinding Xuetang*

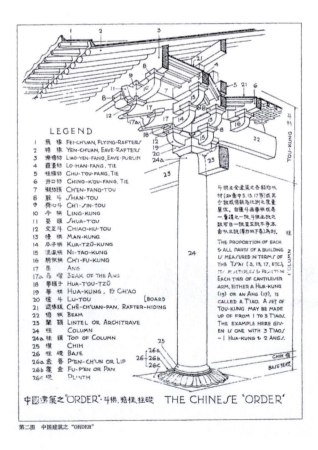

2.18 'The Chinese "Order"', one of the illustrations Liang Sicheng and his team completed by 1944 documenting traditional Chinese buildings in a 'modern' and 'scientific' language.

Zhangcheng, by the Qing government), and in the second National Curriculum published in 1912–13 (by the Republican government), scientific drawing was included for the disciplines of civil engineering and architecture.[47] When the university courses in civil engineering actually started in the 1890s, 'science of graphics' was taught as a subject. In the 1920s when the departments of architecture emerged, 'descriptive geometry' and 'perspective' were also taught, together with 'shades and shadows', 'water colour' and 'free-hand sketches', and 'design' and other subjects. In the use of scientific projection to describe Chinese traditional buildings, in 1931–44 Liang Sicheng (1901–72) with his colleagues and students produced for the first time in history scientific representations of Chinese ancient buildings using orthographic and perspective projections systematically (Figure 2.18). Nian's book of the 1730s was the first not only to introduce scientific drawings and projections, but also to absorb a scientific perspective in a cross-cultural setting. In this sense Nian and Liang are comparable in that the second develops a Renaissance gaze upon a Chinese world tinted with European assumptions, a situation encountered first in Nian in the 1730s. If in Liang we discover a use of Western scientific perspective by a Chinese mind and a projection of it upon a Chinese world of entities (traditional buildings) in association with European traditions ('order' and composition), then this was already carried out by Nian in the 1730s when Chinese utensils and a lantern festival scene were described in perspective drawings, along with Platonic solids and European architectonic objects (capitals and column bases). And, if in Liang we witness an implicit transformation of buildings as organic entities into that as solid objects, and a change from a phenomenal reading to a truthful mapping, then such transformations had also

2.19 'A galloping horse', ink on paper, by Xu Beihong, 1940.

occurred in Nian of the 1730s where 'lively' scenes were depicted in 'truthful' drawings.

2. In fine art, there is also a lineage extending from Castiglione's painting of 1715–66 to those after 1900 and in the following decades. If Castiglione had encountered a problem of how to chart a new path between European realism and the Chinese tradition of lines and strokes, between a 'truthful' and a 'lively' emphasis, then later artists faced the same issue and offered new possibilities. This is especially eminent in an academic and realist tradition following Xu Beihong (1895–1953) in the 1930s the 1940s, and into the Maoist era from the 1950s to the 1970s (when leftist political ideology further promoted artistic realism).[48] One of the paths opened by Xu in the 1930s to the 1940s and inherited in the following decades by modern Chinese painting was a new combination in which the Western realist tradition that emphasizes structure, volume, materiality, texture, chiaroscuro and light is combined with a use of dynamic lines and powerful brush strokes, thus resolving the *zhen–miao* problem encountered in Nian and Castiglione's time 200 years before. A comparison of Castiglione's painting of horses with Xu Beihong's approach to the subject reveals this clearly.[49] Xu's bold use of ink and brush strokes to depict a galloping horse, while anatomical structure and volumetric materiality expressed with chiaroscuro were precisely maintained, demonstrated a new synthesis of the Chinese and European methods to powerful effect (Figure 2.19).

3. In architecture, Xiyanglou of the 1740s to the 1780s had also raised a set of issues that early modern architecture in China had to deal with from the late nineteenth century onwards. There are two sets of issues here.

a   The first concerns the problem of 'style' and the choice and the mixing of 'styles' from Xiyanglou onwards. Once 'style' became a self-conscious problem, it opened up a freedom for manipulation but also an ongoing issue of concern and debate. In association with this were the rise of eclecticism

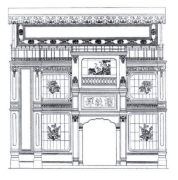

2.20 The Ruifuxiang Silk and Fabric Store, Beijing, built in 1893 and 1900.

2.21 The South Wing of the Ministry of Army (of the Qing dynasty), Beijing, built in 1907.

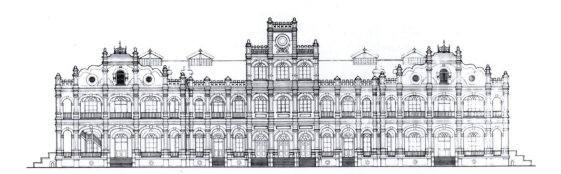

and artificial attempts at creating a national or regional style for a certain ideological purpose. From the 1890s to the 1950s, the situation in this sense remained the same. There were quasi-Baroque, Xiyanglou-style pleasure villas for the imperial court in the 1890s (such as the Qingyanfang, a boathouse, in 1893, and Changguanlou, a pavilion, in 1898).[50] There were shops adopting Baroque and Chinese details creating an eclectic urban vernacular after 1900 in Beijing (such as the Ruifuxiang Store and many other such shops and stores in the south of the city) (Figure 2.20). In the early attempt at modernization in the 1890s, after 1906 when a constitutional monarchy was declared, and then in the Republic of China from 1912, various modern buildings were built, including railway stations, ministries, banks, hotels, cinemas, theatres, hospitals, schools, colleges and prisons (Figure 2.21). Whereas the ministries and the railway stations tended to be Baroque, the banks and colleges often used Classical languages. 'Chinese styles' emerged first in missionary institutions (such as the Union Medical College and Hospital of 1919–21, and the Yanching University of 1920–6), then in public institutions for the Republican government, such as the National Beiping Library completed in 1931 (and many more in Nanjing, where the government was located between 1927 and 1937) (Figures 2.22, 2.23). This lineage then extends to the 1950s when style was once again an important issue, in a Cold War frame of thinking, defined by a socialist National Style in opposition to a capitalist International Style.

b Another issue Xiyanglou had opened up concerns the rise of objects and façades and the use of a perspective-based design (Figures 2.21, 2.22, 2.23). The use of load-bearing structures in Xiyanglou and in the 1890s and after directly contributed to this. The gradual use of steel and concrete since the 1910s had also contributed to the growth in size

2.22 The National Beiping Library, Beijing, built in 1931. Architect: V. Leth-Moller.

2.23 Mausoleum of Dr Sun Yat-sen, Nanjing, built in 1929. Architect: Lu Yanzhi.

of a single building. The use of chiaroscuro, perspective and orthographic projections in the Beaux-Arts descriptive language in design must have reinforced as well the concept of buildings as monumental objects with fronts or façades to be viewed on axes in some defined open spaces (mostly plazas and avenues). Since the basic design language in early modern China was framed in a Beaux-Arts design model, and since the descriptive language of the model was based on Euclidian geometry and Renaissance scientific projections including the use of perspective (as summarized in Gaspard Monge's *Géométrie Descriptive* of 1799),[51] and since the design of Xianglou had already adopted these elements in association with the visual change of the 1730s, the extension into more elaborate designs after 1900, and especially in the 1930s and 1950s in the use of objects and façades with optical axes, was inevitable.

It is important to note that, whereas buildings from the 1890s onwards became 'modern' in the technological and socio-political sense, Xianglou itself, built in the eighteenth century for the pleasure of an emperor, cannot be said to be modern in this sense. Yet one can argue that, before instrumental and socio-political modernization, there was already a visual and formal modernization in Europe and in China, which provided an epistemological basis on which modern buildings can be conceived. In this sense, Xianglou had encountered a formal and visual modernity the consequence of which can only be understood with long hindsight, and at a primary level of seeing and conceiving a building as such.

Symbolic forms between China and Europe

This brief history of the visual revolution after 1700 in China should bring about a few observations concerning European impact, different forms of rationality, and Chinese internalization and reorganization.

European impact

All the three products of visual revolution were associated with the use of geometrical rules of linear perspective as introduced in Nian's *Shi Xue* of 1729–35. Nian's book, in turn, extended Euclidian geometry as presented in Xu and Ricci's *Jihe Yuanben* of 1607 into a graphic description of vision one century later. That is, Nian's book was an extension of the Chinese learning of Western Renaissance sciences since 1600, including cartography and astronomy, in which Euclidian geometry proved essential. Nian's book also opened a path for further introductions of modern descriptive geometry and engineering drawing from the 1890s. If the various cultural manifestations of the visual revolution after 1700 were essentially manifested in Nian's book, then the real European impact here was the introduction of Greek geometry, Renaissance perspective, and the subsequent science of descriptive geometry.

This impact, on closer inspection, has two critical components: Platonic solids and Cartesian dualism. Xu and Ricci's translation of Euclid's *Elements* covered only the first six volumes on plane geometry in 1607, whereas the following nine volumes on numbers, three-dimensional geometry and five regular solids were translated into Chinese in 1857 (by Alexander Wylie and Li Shanlan). Yet, in so far as plane geometry prepares for the culmination in Platonic solids, the 1607 text laid down a basis on which the later emergence of forms of objects after 1700 can be anticipated. In Nian's book on geometric rules of linear perspective, in Castiglione's paintings with European realism, and in the Xiyanglou garden with its free-standing stone buildings, a three-dimensional object, a Platonic solid, is always there in different ways.

The second component here is a Cartesian dualist paradigm implied in the perspective setup. What had really 'arrested' the earlier Chinese tradition of vision, and turned it into a new way of seeing, is the fixing of the (monocular) eye on the viewing screen or the painting, and in a space between the viewer and the landscape of objects. If the earlier Chinese tradition had taught the artist to look across 'three distances', it had demanded the human subject to move and interact with the landscape. What the new setup is demanding is neither to 'move' nor to 'interact'. It frames a dualist split between the viewer and the world, between subject and object, with which a modern scientific attitude or posture can be formulated, which assumes a rational subject seeing, studying and controlling a world of material objects mapped in a pure, mathematical, universal and boundless space. Whereas Erwin Panofsky has referred this as 'symbolic form', prefiguring the Cartesian scientific worldview, Martin Jay has coined the phrase 'Cartesian perspectivalism' to suggest a Cartesian dualism and rationalism embedded in the framework of a linear perspective.[52] Robin Evans and Alberto Pérez-Gómez have also added detailed accounts of the Cartesian moment in the European architectural context.[53] If these observations are to be taken seriously, then the 1730s was the first Cartesian moment in early modern China in this specific sense.

Different rationalities

This European impact had certainly propelled China to develop a Cartesian and instrumental modernity in the following centuries. Yet, if we look into this transformation more carefully, we may conclude that this was not an enlightenment that brought China from a religious dark age to a secular modern rationality, but a specific transformation from one kind of rationality to another. Within the scientific and technological realm, as explained earlier, there was already a Chinese rationality in the use of grids for cartography, in geometrical studies as numerical problems, and in empirical and systematic observations of heavenly phenomena. The Renaissance sciences introduced into China in 1600–1723, therefore, provided a specific rationality based on Greek formal geometry, Renaissance mathematics, and the use of them to describe movement of objects in space. Similarly, in and after the visual revolution of the 1730s, the shift was also a specific transformation from one rational tradition into another. This can be observed in the area of painting, technological drawing, building construction and spatial planning.

In painting, the Chinese had a long tradition of depicting secular scenes of daily life and later on natural landscape of mountains and rivers. There was also an understanding of distances as perceived when one moves across the landscape in different directions. There was the use of rulers to depict buildings and constructed environment, in parallel projections. In technical drawing for building construction, precise line drawings depicting structures in orthographic and parallel projections were meticulously produced and complied, as evidenced in *Yingzao Fashi*, an official building manual of the Song dynasty (960–1279) published in 1066. In this historical context, what were brought into China in and after the visual revolution of the 1730s were a Greek formal geometry of pure spatial relations defined on planes and in three-dimensions, and the Renaissance use of this geometry to describe precisely a fixed monocular vision, and the subsequent modern descriptive geometry.

In building construction, the Chinese also had a long tradition of a system of building timber structures in which all small and linear members were measured with a standard unit based on the width of a part of a key joinery, with the unit itself ranged in a social hierarchical order (as prescribed in *Yingzao Fashi* of 1066). What the Western-style buildings of the 1750s and 1890s had brought into China was a load-bearing stone structure cased in Euclidian geometric forms as Platonic objects as well as in various specific styles. This precipitated a change from one rational tradition of small and meticulous articulation of timber structural members to another rational tradition with Greek geometric formulation of planes, façades, and three-dimensional volumes based on the use of bricks, stone and later reinforced concrete. The later introduction of a post-and-lintel structure in modern architecture, despite its similarity to the Chinese tradition, continued the articulation of 'solid' objects with increasing magnitudes in much of the twentieth century in most cases.

In spatial planning, the Chinese tradition involved a highly regularized use of axes and enclosures at a large scale. The palace complex and the city of imperial Beijing as formed in 1420 and expanded in 1553 displayed this quality clearly. The axis here however was organizational in that it acted primarily as a gigantic line of regulation passing through the entire ensemble, sometimes even the entire city, whereas its optical or visual functions remained secondary within enclosures. What the visual revolution of the 1730s had brought into China, as evidenced in Xiyanglou and other Western-style buildings of the 1890s and 'modern' buildings after 1900, was another kind of axis, one that is predominantly optical or visual, and local (compared with those long axes in imperial Beijing), in forming an immediate stage-set of façades and objects. The new axis regulates not the enclosing walls and courtyards of a larger complex, but large single buildings in the open space of an immediate or local urban stage-set. Objects, façades, visual planes or screens, articulated with optical axes, formulated an entirely different logic of space as a result of the use of Renaissance or Cartesian perspective. In this historical background, the change that occurred in early modern China was from one kind of rational planning to another: a change from an 'imperial' use of organizational axes regulating enclosed spaces (in courtyards and streets) to a 'Cartesian' use of optical axes articulating an open space (in the form of avenues and plazas) with monumental objects.

Chinese internalization and reorganization

Finally, let us consider the questions raised at the beginning of this essay: Can culture and science be separated in absorbing European influence in China? Can Westernization and modernization be separated in the process? In what ways have the Chinese been selecting, internalizing and reorganizing European influences? Parts of European development, religion, culture and science certainly had complex interrelations with one another. Their arrival in China was also interrelated as they were transmitted through human and institutional efforts, primarily that of the Jesuits. Yet there was an important period from the early to late Qing dynasty (1715–1840s) when, because of the rites controversy with the Church in Rome, Christian teaching was banned while sciences and associated cultural practices including painting and visual knowledge continued to be absorbed actively in Beijing with keen interest from the Chinese emperors. This situation reveals a possibility of separating certain cultural practices of a highly ideological content, such as Christianity, from the pursuit of empirical, objective, positivist (verifiable) knowledge with functional benefit, such as the sciences of astronomy and cartography. In any case, this separation was already achieved in the Qing dynasty to a significant degree.

But this history also reveals another face of the situation: while religious teaching was resisted, visual and stylistic culture continued to be absorbed along with Renaissance sciences. For example, when scientific devices for astronomical studies were fitted into the Imperial Observatory, visual documentation of them was made in engravings using perspective and chiaroscuro; when 'modern' buildings were introduced with new materials (glass, concrete), facilities (electricity), structures (bricks, concrete) and functions (railway stations, hospitals), they were also formulated in the Western styles modelled on Xiyanglou in the Baroque genre. Most importantly, when the Renaissance sciences of physics, astronomy and cartography were incorporated into China, they came with a 'style' of Greek thinking in the use of formal geometry, and the 'symbolic form' of Renaissance perspective and its Cartesian dualist split of subject and object. We are encountering here not only an architectural 'style' of social and technological modernity, but also a 'style' or 'symbolic form' of science and knowledge. At this moment, the separation of a biased culture and a positivist science appears impossible, at least at these historical moments. In other words, Westernization and modernization for a non-Western country such as China became one indivisible process. In historical reality as outlined in this essay, the symbolic form of geometry and perspective had arrived, been absorbed, and been exerting critical impact in China, with the further twist of the Western gaze adopted by Chinese intellectuals (from Nian Xiyao to Xu Beihong and Liang Sicheng) upon the Chinese world of things.

This leads to another facet of the history: although these symbolic forms of science and knowledge, between their cultural bias and positivist rationality, cannot be separated, they can nevertheless lend themselves to reorganization and hybridization in a new cultural and political setting. With the involvement of power and authority, of intellectual debate, and of cultural practice, hybrid visual forms and styles emerged in Nian's perspective drawings of a Chinese lantern festival, in Castiglione's painting of material objects submerged in a diffused illumination with the use of lines and surfaces, and in Xiyanglou's eclectic mixture, an approach which was much elaborated after 1900 in 'Western', 'Chinese' and 'modern' architecture. The essence of this historical transformation in visual culture, in the end, lies in a Chinese internalization of Greek geometry, Renaissance perspective, and modern methods of formal descriptions, thus opening up a series of hybridizations in which cross-cultural syntheses were attempted in search of a new symbolic form.

CHAPTER 3

THE ARCHITECT AND A NATIONALIST PROJECT

Nanjing, 1925–37

Although the history of modern China with wars and revolutions appears swift and chaotic, there were slow and stable progressions in nation building and modernization. China experienced foreign aggressions and partial colonization (from 1840), the decline and collapse of the Qing dynasty (1911), the rise of the Republic in 1912 that soon fragmented into northern and southern governments, a further fragmentation into areas ruled by local warlords and colonial authorities, a Northern Expedition in 1926 to unify China, a unification of central China under the Kuomintang or the Nationalist Party with its capital in Nanjing (1927–37), then Japan's full-scale invasion and China's resistance (1937–45), and a civil war between the communists and the nationalists (1945–9), before a People's Republic was established on the mainland in 1949 (and the Kuomintang's Republic on Taiwan). This was a torrential transition in which a large empire with a long tradition was shaken to the ground, with all the repercussions and radical changes that ensured. Yet against all odds, a new nation-state of China designed in modern ways emerged gradually. It appeared briefly in 1912, then in the Nanjing decade of the 1930s, and finally with greater stability after 1949. Industrialization, modern urban construction, the use of science and technology, the arrival of modern professionals, the development of a modern public society, all occurred with growing strength across these periods despite wars and interruptions. If we focus on the period before 1949, then the Nanjing decade (1927–37) is relatively speaking the most stable and constructive time, and deserves close observation. Focusing on this decade and extending further back, we witness two important currents of development: the emergence of modern city building and public space, and the arrival of Chinese architects for the first time in history.

First, through colonial domination as a result of unequal treaties, there were concessions as new cities or city quarters ruled by foreign powers chiefly in Shanghai, Tianjin and Hankou were built. Modern urban facilities, construction methods, transportation infrastructures, public places and institutions, and financial and administrative offices emerged one after another. In association with this, and resulting from other factors including large-scale urban migration, the arrival of technologies, and cultural–ideological trends in favour of modernity, progress, science and democracy, a public domain opened up gradually. It is found in urban and built space, printed press, the media of radio and cinema, telecommunication and transportation, and in the spread of public opinion and social movements through these spaces. A modern 'bourgeois' public sphere appears to have arrived, yet its qualities seem different from that in Europe. What was its special quality in China? What was the new quality introduced by the government of Nanjing in the 1930s? How was it designed and built in a spatial, visual environment? This, in turn, is related to the second development, the rise of Chinese architects in the 1920s and 1930s. What was the key role this profession played at that moment? What was its intellectual and critical agenda? How was it related to state authority, the Kuomintang Party and its government? In what ways did the profession contribute to the making of a new public space against the backdrop of the colonial urban construction that was there before?

Current scholarship on architecture of early modern China has uncovered a large amount of material and has also produced many analyses. The work is empirically substantial (as in the projects led by Wang Tan, Zhang Fuhe and Terunobu Fujimori), and sometimes well organized with an overall socio-historical understanding (as in Hou Youbin's writings),[1] and yet sometimes idealistic in exploring the intentions and design positions of the architects (especially Liang Sicheng). A social analysis of architects' design as situated in the specific historical moment, taking into account political factors and with a critical distance, is still lacking. Hou Youbin, in analysing factors shaping the 'Chinese Native Style' of the 1930s, complained that stylistic concerns were politicized then and thus 'unduly enlarged political effects of the images of the buildings'.[2] Hou at this moment closed this critical distance and moved into the scene to defend a disciplinary purity of architecture. Although as an architect one may support Hou's position, as an observer in a social and critical analysis it is important not to assume this purity and independence, but to read design as always already socially embedded and inevitably political. Adopting this perspective, this essay attempts to make a few observations on the currents leading to and culminating in the Nanjing decade, in order to understand the making of urban form and space, and the role played by the Chinese architect at the moment of its appearance, in the context of revolution and modernization in China before 1949.[3] The relationship between the architect and the Kuomintang Party, or the profession and state authority, in the domestic and colonial–international context, is a crucial concern. An institutionalization of knowledge in the local context, including a global transfer and local-historical production, in order for the Chinese architect to make a unique contribution at that moment, is another focus of the research.[4]

Background: cities and professionals before the 1920s

China's modernization was compelled by external forces rather than internal dynamics in the early stage. In urban construction, modernization occurred first in colonial concessions. As a result of constant defeat in wars with encroaching industrial powers, the Qing Chinese government accepted treaties which forced China to open its territories as 'treaty ports' for foreign trade, residence, civil construction, and further intrusion and control beyond the treaty ports in capital investment, taxation, industry, railway networks and the use of natural resources. From 1842 to the 1920s, there were some seventy-seven treaty ports established.[5] They centred on the south-east coast, along the Yangtze River and in north-east China. There were 'concessions' governed by foreign authorities in or next to existing cities; land leased for entire cities planned and built by Russia, Germany and Japan in the north-east; and foreign settlements in existing cities managed by Chinese authorities. The concessions were found chiefly in Shanghai, Tianjin and Hankou, where colonial authorities each owned a district; Qingdao, Dalian and Harbin were owned by Russia and Germany (and later by Japan in the 1930s and early 1940s); and foreign settlements existed in most other treaty ports along the coast and major waterways and railway lines. (The embassy district in Beijing can be added as a special case of a concession as it also attained autonomy inside the city.)

It is in these foreign settlements that we find the first attempts at modern urban building with a municipal authority governing the construction. Here we find the earliest introduction of modern urban facilities (gas, electricity, water), modern urban construction (roads, bridges, waterfronts), modern building types for public use (railway stations, department stores, hotels, banks), modern building technologies, Western classical and historicist styles, and an institutionalized control of building practice. In the urban areas governed by the Chinese, similar practice was adopted afterwards. Where concessions and Chinese areas existed side by side, the concessions grew larger and became the centre of the entire city, as in Shanghai, Tianjin and Hankou. Shanghai was the first city where concessions were established in 1843–5, and remained the largest in all aspects in the 1930s as a primary colonial–international city in China.[6] Established in 1843–5 and 1862 respectively, the International Concession (shared by the American and British) and the French Concession kept expanding and by 1915 surpassed the Chinese districts in total area and became increasingly the centre of the city as whole. Both concessions established a municipal Public Works Office for city construction in 1854–63.[7] Gas, water and electricity were supplied to the city in the 1860s to the 1880s.[8] Roads, bridges, banking of rivers, public transport systems with trams, telephone and telegraph services, and railway links to Nanjing and Hangzhou were introduced one by one. Whereas harbours and industrial plants were located outside, three separate Chinese areas surrounded the two connected concessions at the centre. In the core area along the Huangpu River was the administrative and financial centre; and perpendicular to the river front were east–west commercial streets with department stores, hotels, restaurants, and a race course to the west; beyond that were terraced and detached Western-style houses, as well as a Chinese–English hybrid, the *lilong* houses of various kinds. The International, French and Chinese areas maintained separate systems of public facilities such as the tram system, electricity and water supply, yet worked together as one hybrid international metropolis.

Here the 'public' sphere, in physical urban space, included parks and riverfronts; cinemas, cafés, teahouses and restaurants; as well as department stores and all entertainment facilities attached. Banks, offices, apartments, houses, railway stations, railway lines, harbours, factories and plants constituted a larger metropolis with thriving modern industry. Chinese industrialists, capitalists, bankers, small business owners, professionals, intellectuals, students and revolutionary activists lived along with foreigners in the concessions and elsewhere. Many of them, taking different political positions and playing different roles, engaged actively in discussions and social movements in support of Chinese national independence against foreign imperialism. They allied with different and changing ideological positions. They debated in cafés, classrooms and streets, and in the magazines and newspapers, and engaged in social movements facilitated in and by these spaces and printed media. Literature and cinema provided another sphere in which ideals, opinions and criticism were expressed. A bourgeois public sphere can be found here. A budding 'Chinese bourgeoisie' and a vibrant colonial–cosmopolitan urban culture were clearly visible.[9] Yet the political condition was unstable; the nation was fragmented; a unified and strong Chinese state authority was absent. A liberal society thrived in this unstable situation, in which a colonial setting, with all its political, economic and cultural power behind it, was in effect managing and partially protecting the metropolis. This social space was primarily built with modern Western technologies, with Western architectural styles, and was infused with Western cultures and traditions. A colonial backdrop to this public space was obvious.

The colonial cities in north-east China ruled by the Japanese in the 1930s and 1940s also went through modern planning and construction of the entire city. In other cities where concessions played a lesser role or where foreign settlements were found, modern urban building also took place with ideas, expertise and stylistic culture imported from Europe, but at a slower pace than in Shanghai. Beijing here is a good example.[10] Run by the Chinese, the late Qing government in its final years adopted reforms for a constitutional monarchy. In the 'new administration' of the Qing in 1905, a police department was established to look after municipal affairs including transportation and building construction. In the new Republican government after 1912, a Civil Affairs Office of the Capital (*Jingdu Shizheng Gongsuo*) was established in 1914 under Zhu Qiqian, which was responsible for urban building and management. This department carried out important modern urban development including the opening of imperial gardens into central urban parks, the opening of long avenues, the demolition of part of the city walls, the repair of a central city gate, the building of a railway line around the city, and many railway stations attached. Broadly speaking, from the late Qing to the Republican era, electricity (1905, 1919) and water (1910) were supplied to the city; streets were extended, widened and partly paved; more imperial palaces and gardens were opened to the public (including the front section of the Forbidden City being transformed into a museum). Arcades, department stores, shops and cinemas also emerged, in the old commercial areas in the south and the east, and increasingly around the embassy district in the south-east. Western styles were adopted in many ways. The most important included Peking Hotel (1903), the railway station at Qianmen (1906), and the schools of the Tsinghua College (1911–23). There were attempts to make a 'Chinese' appearance for the Peking Union Medical College and Hospital, and for the buildings at the Yanching University. Yet the overall modernization of city building, from building technology to stylistic influence, remained Western and was much influenced through missionary enterprises especially in education. Against this early modern urban setting was a new and liberal society opening up amidst a chaotic historical background. Students, intellectuals, professionals, small business owners, bankers, industrialists, reform-minded official-scholars of the Qing, and bureaucrats of the new Northern government all engaged in discussions and social movements in different ways and with different political alliances. In fact a Chinese bourgeois society was opening up in all Chinese cities through a network of telecommunication and printed mass media, and was spatially centred in large cities such as Shanghai, Beijing, Tianjin, Guangzhou, Hankou and Wuhan. A crucial condition of this liberal bourgeois society at that time was the lack of a strong national authority that could unify China and resist colonial domination of these major cities. The overall background and setting of this open society in the large cities remained colonial and Western.

If we look at the physical setting, in large cities such as Shanghai, we will find a mixed landscape of different styles, structures and spaces. Who designed and constructed these spaces and buildings? There had been British and French building companies operating in Shanghai since the 1860s.[11] The Chinese building teams in the modern sense, capable of building modern structures in brick and concrete, first emerged in 1880–3 (led by Yang Sisheng).[12] They worked and competed alongside foreign construction teams until the 1920s. From then onwards, and especially in the 1930s, in a different political setting when a Chinese national authority was partially established in Nanjing, the Chinese builders, now able to build large and high-rise structures in steel and reinforced concrete, almost completely dominated the market in Shanghai.[13]

Regarding the design of buildings, Chinese architects as a modern profession were absent from the scene until the early 1920s. From 1840 to 1920, Western-style buildings were designed initially by users with assistance from draftsmen. Soon professional draftsmen played a greater role in designing these buildings. The first Western architects appeared around 1860.[14] From 1900 onwards, foreign architects arrived and opened offices in large quantity, sometimes in collaboration with Western civil engineers.[15] Palmer & Turner (1911) and L. E. Hudec (1918) were among the most influential in Shanghai. The Chinese were first involved in an informal way: there were by 1910–13 a significant number of Chinese draftsmen opening design offices as architects.[16] These self-taught architects made certain contributions but were not trained to design in a creative way. Professional civil engineers, educated at civil engineering departments at universities instituted in China since 1896 or at universities in the United States and other countries, also designed buildings and even ran architectural offices in the 1910s.[17] Engineers provided designs of sound structures using existing types, but were not creative in formal design and spatial organization.[18] Before the arrival of the Chinese architect in the early 1920s, there were draftsmen, engineers and Western architects providing designs in China. The key question here is, when Chinese architects arrived for the first time in history, what role did they play as a new group of technical experts and self-conscious intellectuals at that moment, and in what political context did they play it?

The state and the profession, 1925–49

According to current research, two Chinese students went abroad in 1905 to study architecture – the earliest such attempt recorded – in Japan and England respectively.[19] By the 1920s and 1930s, however, large numbers of Chinese students returned after studying architecture in Japan, America, France, England, Germany and other European countries. While Japan was an important destination, the United States was the most popular compared with other Western countries. In the United States, it was the University of Pennsylvania that trained a majority of the Chinese students, but other schools such as MIT, Michigan, Columbia, Harvard and Illinois also received groups of Chinese students. Returning home, they soon established design practices. The first few architecture offices were set up in 1921, 1922 and 1925 by those returning from America (Lu Yanzhi, Zhuang Jun) and Japan (Liu Dunzhen, Wang Kesheng, Zhu Shigui, Liu Shiying), and more offices emerged soon after.[20] These architects not only established offices in design practice, but also initiated architectural education, formed professional bodies, and conducted research on native Chinese architecture. They established the first schools of architecture in 1923, 1927 and 1928 (with some ten more to follow in the 1930s and early 1940s); established the first professional bodies – the Society of Chinese Architects (*Zhongguo Jianzhushi Xuehui*) in 1927 and the Shanghai Association of Building Construction (*Shanghaishi Jianzhu Xiehui*) in 1931; published the first professional journals – *The Chinese Architect* (*Zhongguo Jianzhu*) and *The Builder* (*Jianzhu Yuekan*) – for the two associations from 1932; and also conducted the first modern scientific research on historical structures across China, which was carried out by the Society for Research in Chinese Architecture under Zhu Qiqian, Liang Sicheng and Liu Dunzhen from 1931 to 1944.[21] A comprehensive institutionalization of professional knowledge in the Chinese context was thus quickly established in these critical years. A careful analysis of the design practice, ideological alliances in the practice, the urban consequences of design, and the transfer and development of knowledge at this historical moment is now called for.

The young Chinese architects struggled in practice to obtain commissions.[22] Many finally developed through commissions by the Nationalist government in Nanjing from 1927 to 1937. In fact, as a whole, a major contribution of these Chinese architects during 1927–37 and 1945–9 was the design of a large number of public and government buildings in a 'Chinese Native Style' called for by the government from 1925 and persistently in the 1930s. There was a demand for such an approach from the party and the government; and there was a collaborative response from the architects. There was also a shared nationalist sentiment on both sides that facilitated such collaboration. In the end, the two appeared to have worked closely in the making of these nationalist monuments and a nationalist urban space defined by these buildings.

The two sides may be viewed separately first. On the architects' side, as part of the student body and new intellectuals with international awareness, critical views of their own tradition, and an urgent patriotic sentiment, the Chinese architects had complex relations with various ideas and movements in the Republican Revolution of 1911 and the May Fourth New Cultural Movement of 1919. A shared view was that Western science and democracy must be employed to cure the ills of the Chinese tradition in order to save and regenerate China, and Western colonial and imperialist aggressions must also be defeated in order to establish an independent China.[23] If there was a liberal end *and* a nationalist end to this spectrum of views, then there was a shift towards the nationalist position (and also a leftist and communist position) from 1919 to 1925 when all liberal democratic attempts seemed to have failed tragically. The nationalist sentiment was evident in the two journals *The Chinese Architect* and *The Builder*, and in the initiatives behind the Society for Research in Chinese Architecture. The editorial of the first issue of *The Chinese Architect* in 1932 made it clear that the mission was to 'integrate the strengths of Eastern and Western architecture, so that we may develop and carry forward native characteristics of architecture of our own nation'. The mission of the Shanghai Association of Building Construction (which published *The Builder*) was to 'study the disciplines of building and architecture, to improve construction practice, and to display and develop oriental architectural art'.[24] The purpose of the Society established in 1930 under Zhu Qiqian, and led by Liang Sicheng and Liu Dunzhen since 1931 in research, was closely associated with the nationalist current of the May Fourth Movement (promoted by Hu Shi and Liang Qichao, Liang Sicheng's father) that emphasized the need to 'study the national heritage' and 'the essentials of the national tradition'.[25] The research work, especially the discoveries made regarding Chinese architectural heritage, was a further support to the architects designing in the 'Chinese Native Style'. The research was therefore immediately political for the creative process of design. The publication of a ten-volume visual reference book on traditional Chinese architecture (*Jianzhu Sheji Cankuo Tuji*) in 1935–7, the staging of an exhibition of drawings and models of ancient Chinese architecture in Shanghai in 1936, and Liang's direct supervision of the design for the Central Museum in Nanjing in a Chinese native style (of the Liao dynasty) in 1935–6 all revealed a political agenda behind the research, which was to support the creation of a nationalist architecture.[26]

The architects' own statements provide other evidence revealing this support. Liang in his preface to a visual dictionary of Chinese architecture he compiled and published in 1935 said that he hoped 'Chinese architects may create new architecture for China . . . [and for that purpose] they should study the structure, organization, parts, proportion and balance of ancient Chinese architecture'.[27] Lu Yanzhi, the architect of the mausoleum for Sun Yat-sen, said that the aim was to interpret 'the spirit and ideals of Dr. Sun which seek to embody the highest of the philosophical thought of ancient China into the practical solution of life problems of the human race by methods developed through modern scientific researches', and hence the design was 'in accordance with Chinese traditions in planning and in the form', being 'apparent in its Chinese origin' but was also distinctively 'a creative effort in monumental construction of modern times'.[28]

On the side of the party and government in the 1930s, we may also extend the review to the earlier decades. The Republican Revolution of 1911, which elected Sun Yat-sen the Provisional President of the

Republic, soon handed its leadership to a northern military general and former Qing official, Yuan Shih-kai in Beijing. Yuan soon assumed autocratic rule in 1912 and declared himself the emperor of China in 1916. When his government collapsed in the same year China fragmented into a chaotic state in which each local region, city or district was ruled by a local warlord or foreign colonial authority. Sun Yat-sen's attempts to unify China as a modern, democratic republic from the south were a constant failure, until the mid-1920s. The success of the Bolshevik revolution in Russia in 1917 soon changed the course of the Chinese revolution. The Communist International helped establish the Chinese Communist Party in 1921 and also contacted Sun to support his nationalist and bourgeois-democratic revolution.[29] In 1923 an alliance of Sun's Nationalist Party with the Chinese communists and the Communist International was made. With the help of Soviet advisors, that is, with Lenin's theory and organizational politics, Sun's party and army were thoroughly reorganized in Guangzhou in the following years. In 1924 and 1925, the first congress of the Nationalist Party was held, which formulated a new revolutionary guideline for the party, a new army and a military academy were established and a party-directed military government was also formed. The alliance was broadly based, with the Chinese communists actively mobilizing the workers and peasants, a broad social basis not employed before, to support the Nationalist leadership.

The Northern Expedition of 1926 to fight the warlords and unify the nation was a great success. Nanjing and Shanghai were captured in early 1927 and, in 1928, much of southern, central and northern China was unified under Chiang Kai-shek and the Nationalist Party, with Nanjing as its capital and Shanghai its financial centre. Sun had already passed away in 1925 and the expedition of 1926–8 was led by Chiang. Chiang, however, in the early days of 1927 when Nanjing and Shanghai were captured, turned against the communists and workers' organizations, as well as the left-wing members of his own party.[30] Thousands of communists and associated individuals were disarmed, purged and executed, in his 'cleanse the party' campaign in early 1927. Chiang's government from 1927 onwards was socially elitist, and city-based, in alliance with capitalists, industrialists, bankers and professionals.[31] Without rural reform and progressive social transformation, his social agenda was to re-cultivate a Confucian ethics and its related hierarchical control. In the face of a serious challenge from the communists inland, the Japanese forces from the north-east (which had controlled north-east China after 1931 and were poised to advance southwards), his internal rivals, and demoralization inside the party and the government, Chiang also introduced fascist ideas from Italy and Germany.[32] His Blue Shirts, an elite organization, promoted absolute royalty to the party and the nation, and also carried out intelligence work and assassinations of opponents (communists,

Japanese, internal rivals, left-wing writers and journalists).[33] In the mid-1930s, he waged a New Life Movement which aimed to cultivate Confucian ethics of discipline and good conduct, as well as fascist ideas of royalty, order, revival of national culture, and a disciplined life style against liberal values.[34]

It is important to observe the ideological positions of Lenin, Sun and Chiang in order to understand the position of the Nanjing government of the 1930s. Lenin had a 'theory of imperialism' and an organizational politics of party dictatorship, both of which were introduced in China.[35] According to him, capitalism was reaching an imperialist age when it had to rely increasingly on overseas colonies for capitalist accumulation. Communists and workers of Europe therefore should ally with the nationalist and bourgeois-democratic movements in the colonies of the East, so that a global revolution against capitalism or imperialist capitalism could be organized. This theory provided a justification for communists' cooperation with bourgeois nationalists, and also gave a broader meaning to the Chinese nationalist revolution as part of a world-historical process. Yet a social or class revolution of the workers against the bourgeoisie to establish a communist-led socialism was not strongly promoted by the Soviets in China. What was emphasized in China at that time were the alliance and Lenin's organizational politics of party leadership based on a system of 'democratic centralism' which emphasized the absolute control of the party as the vanguard of the masses.

Sun's revolution aimed at national liberation, constitutional democracy, and social welfare for the people (in his 'three principles of the people').[36] The aim was to establish an independent democratic nation-state against imperialism, yet a social revolution (of the proletarians) against the bourgeoisie was not on his agenda. Sun's party also suffered from weak institutional control and a lack of revolutionary ideology embedded in social and military campaigns. Leninism changed all this. With the help of the Soviets, Sun's Nationalist Party acquired a rigorous centralism, and also a leftist inclination when workers, peasants and other groups of society were mobilized with the help of the communists.[37] This leftist dimension, however, was to a great extent purged by Chiang's government in Nanjing from the early days of 1927. A conservative, authoritarian, military-fascist rule was instituted in the 1930s.[38] In other words, what survived finally in the 1930s was Lenin's centralism, the practical politics of party dictatorship, with added Confucian and fascist values.

We should notice a shift from Sun to Chiang, a change from a broad alliance with a leftist tendency to a conservative authoritarianism. But we should also understand a consistency between the first and the second: neither of them was interested in social revolution against the bourgeoisie (industrialists, capitalists, bankers, small business owners, officials, professionals and intellectuals), and both were predominantly nationalist. In this sense, Chiang was extending Sun's nationalist revolution towards a conservative nation building.[39]

Chiang's cultural policy was consistent with his political position. In the face of leftist criticism amongst intellectuals and especially writers supported by the underground Chinese communists, and their formation of an 'Association of Left-Wing Writers' in Shanghai in 1930, the Nationalist government, in the voice of some anti-communist writers, declared a 'Manifesto for a Nationalist Movement in Art and Culture' the same year. In 1935 some leading professors in a party periodical also published a 'Manifesto for a China-based Cultural Construction'.[40] Interestingly, the nationalist cultural movement did not really happen in literature, but in architecture and urban construction. In hindsight, what really developed and remained influential in literature from the 1930s onwards was the critical works of the leftist writers based in Shanghai such as Lu Xun, Mao Dun, Tian Han and Ding Ling. The nationalist 'art and culture', in contrast, found its way into urban planning and architecture, especially in Nanjing in the 1930s, and also in other cities (Shanghai, Guangzhou, Wuhan and Beijing), in the hands of architects, planners and civil engineers such as Lu Yanzhi, Dong Dayou, Yang Tingbao, Tong Jun, Liang Sicheng, Henry K. Murphy and Ernest P. Goodrich.[41]

Here the key documents were the architectural competition guidelines in 1925 for a mausoleum for Sun Yat-sen, and the planning for Nanjing in 1929 and Shanghai in 1930. These documents called for a Chinese native style to be employed for the public and government buildings, and a construction of new urban spaces with landmarks bearing these Chinese features. Architects such as Lu Yanzhi, Dong Dayou, Yang Tingbao, Tong Jun and many others responded to the request with designs in close alliance with the requirements, and also by creatively adopting various formal solutions for each and every one of these projects. The mausoleum for Sun Yat-sen, proposed in 1925 and constructed in 1929, stood upon a platform on a large hill to the east of Nanjing, against which a great capitol of the government was also proposed in 1929 in the Capital Plan. In Shanghai a group of government and public buildings with Chinese formal features were completed between 1933 and 1935. In Guangzhou, Beijing and Wuhan, a few significant public institutions were also constructed in the style between 1929 and 1939. These monuments and the urban spaces they created stood as spatial materializations and visual manifestations of the nationalist cultural construction the government was calling for. We will observe these cases more closely later on.

The interaction between state government and the profession also occurred at an institutional level. The Chiang government employed a large number of professionals and former students returning from overseas studies in his many levels of state bureaucracy and associated organizations. Dong Dayou, a graduate of the University of Minnesota and Columbia University (1925, 1927), while running his architectural office in Shanghai since 1930, was employed as an advisor to the Planning Committee for the Urban Centre of Shanghai, as well as the head of an office supervising architects in the Shanghai municipal government. That he was responsible for so many key public and government buildings in the 1930s was related to his position in the bureaucracy.[42] Liang Sicheng, a graduate of the University of Pennsylvania (1927), a leading scholar in the Society for Research in Chinese Architecture since 1931 and also an architect responsible for a few buildings in Beijing in the 1930s, was employed by the Nationalist government in posts attached to the History and Language Research Institute (1932), Central Museum (1939) and Ministry of Education (1944). In 1947 he was appointed the representative of China for the design of the UN headquarters in New York. In 1948 he became an Academician of the Central Academy in Nanjing.[43] Ha Xiongwen, a graduate of Pennsylvania in 1932, was appointed to a section supervising urban construction (*dizheng si*) within the Ministry of Internal Affairs (*neizheng bu*) in 1937. In 1943, he was appointed the Head (*si zhang*) of the Office of Construction (*yingjian si*) in the same ministry, a position which made him a most prominent technocrat on construction in Chiang's government. He was a key figure in the making of building and planning laws issued and revised in these years.[44] Outside the category of 'Chinese architects', we can also identify key professionals that assisted with the party closely as technocrats: Henry Murphy as an architect, and Lin Yimin and Ernest Goodrich both as engineers, all educated in the United States.[45]

The government also exercised institutional controls upon design in the national Chinese style and on all aspects of construction. The competition guidelines for the specific buildings asserted a direct formal and ideological prescription as in 1925 and thereafter for some buildings of great symbolic importance. The 'plan' for city development for Nanjing and Shanghai imposed a framework of urban building and a general stylistic guidance. Committees were established under Chiang or other leaders of the party (such as Hu Hanmin and Dai Jitao) to work on these plans. Professionals such as Lin Yimin, Murphy and Goodrich and other Chinese and Americans were employed. Beyond this, there was also a hierarchical bureaucratic structure with which all construction in the nation could be supervised. Offices supervising construction at the level of county, city, province and the nation were established.[46] These were a Bureau of Public Works (*gongwu ju*) in each city (replacing the offices of similar functions of earlier regimes before 1927), a Department of Construction (*jianshe ting*) in each province, and the Office of Construction (*yingjian si*) in the Ministry of Internal Affairs at the national level (led by Ha Xiongwen since its inception from 1937 to 1949). Under this office, a national Building Law was published by the central government in 1938 (as well as the Urban Planning Law in 1939). This was by then the most comprehensive law governing practices concerning the architect, the builder, the assessment of private and public building, licensure, land use regulation, construction, illegal building, and conservation and preservation of heritage sites and structures.[47] Embedded in this bureaucratic and legal supervision of construction was a control of registration and the identity of the architect as a profession. It was first recognized as 'designers' (*sheji zhe*) in 1927 and 'industrial technician in architecture' (*jianzhu ke gongye jishi*) in 1929, and finally as 'design architect' (*sheji jianzhu shi*) in 1944 in a revised Building Law that included 'Regulations for Governing the Architect'.[48]

It is clear that, when the profession of Chinese architect emerged on the historical stage, it was quickly brought into collaboration with the Nationalist Party and the government from 1925 and 1927 onwards. The collaboration was both institutional and ideological. There was an employment of architects as technical experts in state bureaucracy. There was a top-down supervision of planning and construction. There were regulations governing registration and the identity of the architect (in a later period of formalization of the profession at a national level). There was patronage of some of these architects in developing their design profile and their nationalist design experimentation through this decade. There was, on the side of the architects, a certain readiness to cooperate with the authority. At this moment, they appeared 'conservative' compared with the leftist writers who constantly criticized the Chiang government and its Confucian and fascist values. In fact both the leftist writers and the nationalist architects represented two consequences of the May Fourth movement in the 1920s when Western-style liberal democracy proved to be a failure. If the nationalist position still carried a certain critical agenda, its target was foreign colonialism, not tradition, class or authority within. If we read the writings of Liang Sicheng and Lu Yanzhi, and observe the committed practice of these architects, we cannot fail to notice a certain political-critical position with a nationalist and patriotic sentiment. In so far as these architects and professionals were reflexive, and committed to a political course, there was a criticality here, even though the critique remained implicit and iconic. In this context, the critical thrust was in support of nation building, and national liberation and independence, against foreign colonial and imperialist aggressions. The object of critique was not authority, tradition or the status quo within society, but imperialism from without. This position may render their work 'conservative' and sadly sometimes in support of or in alliance with a fascist government. Yet Chiang's government appeared to be the only possibility in coastal and metropolitan areas at this moment for a strong Chinese state authority to arise. If this was a sacrifice, it was we may argue a willing sacrifice conditioned by a narrow historical environment.

The mausoleum and the planning proposals, 1925–30

Let us briefly review the first few moments when a nationalist ideology was translated into guidelines for urban and building construction. When Sun Yat-sen passed away on 12 March 1925, a Committee for the Affairs of Sun's Funeral was organized, which included some of the most important figures of the party such as Wang Jingwei, Dai Jitao and Zhang Jingjiang.[49] Attached to this was a Funeral Affairs Office that included Sun Ke and Song Qingling, Sun's son and wife, to represent the family. In April the committee and the office decided that Sun was to be buried according to his will on Zijing Shan or the Purple Hill on the eastern side of Nanjing, the city where in 1912 Sun was elected Provisional President of the Republic, the city that symbolized the beginning of his revolution. On 13 May the competition guidelines for the design of the mausoleum were finalized, and they were published two days later. Lu Yanzhi, a graduate of Cornell University (1918) who had established his office in 1921 in Shanghai, emerged as the first prize winner on 20 September.[50] Seven days later he was appointed the chief architect. Construction started in January 1926 but progressed slowly until late 1927. When Nanjing became the capital of the new Republic under the Nationalist Party led by Chiang Kai-shek on 18 April 1927, and after a party unification under Chiang in September, the committee was reorganized to include now all the top figures including Chiang, Wang Jingwei and Hu Hanmin. Chiang issued a decree to protect and facilitate the construction, which then accelerated the process. The main structure was completed in April 1929, and a grand funeral for Sun was organized on 1 June 1929, which was attended by Chiang and all major figures of the party together with a large crowd, when Sun's body was solemnly carried into the tomb (Figure 3.1).

3.1 Mausoleum of Dr Sun Yat-sen, Nanjing on 1 June 1929 during the state funeral for Sun Yat-sen. Architect: Lu Yanzhi.

3.2 Mausoleum of Dr Sun Yat-sen. View to the north on the axis in the 1930s.

The mausoleum was in fact a large memorial park with a 700 metre long path leading, northwards and upwards, to a monumental building on a high platform with majestic hills behind. This was largely predetermined by the guidelines. The guidelines requested that the mausoleum include a memorial hall and a tomb chamber.[51] The hall should adopt 'ancient Chinese forms with special and commemorative characteristics, or a creative new design based on the spirits of Chinese architecture'; the tomb chamber, open to the public and unprecedented in China, might adopt a Western style; the two should be on a plateau at 170 metres above sea level; an open space accommodating 50,000 people should be included in front; a long path leading down southwards might end at a point 110 metres above sea level; and all should be coordinated as one and built in stone and reinforced concrete. Lu Yanzhi's design responded to the requirement closely and creatively (Figures 3.1, 3.2, 3.3). The memorial hall adopted 'the roof of

3.3 Mausoleum of Dr Sun Yat-sen. Bird's-eye view to the north.

a Chinese palace', whereas the tomb chamber assumed the shape of a dome found in Western classical and neo-classical architecture (Figure 2.23).[52] The open space was provided and the long path marked the central north–south axis of the whole complex. The axial path had an avenue leading to a gate and a pavilion behind, then a stretch of grand steps leading to the hall and the tomb at a high platform at the end. The whole plan was also in the shape of a 'large bell', which alluded to Sun's last phrase in his will: 'to awaken the masses'.

A hybrid composition with Chinese and European elements can be found in the planning of the space, where a Chinese ritual passage (with an archway, a path, a gate, a pavilion with a stone tablet, a main memorial hall and a covered tomb placed in a sequence) and Western openness (tree-lined avenue with a straight visual projection and spatial accessibility, an open tomb, and a square for 50,000 people) were integrated.[53] Formally, Chinese styles (the roofs and other smaller details) and Western neo-classical shapes (the dome, and the massive four corners of the hall under the roof) were also integrated.[54] Sun's teachings and his key phrases were inscribed profusely throughout the buildings and inside the memorial hall. Sun's 'Outline of the Principles for the Establishment of the Nation' was inscribed on the eastern and western walls inside the hall; his 'Will', 'Final Teaching', and 'Speech to the Party', in the handwriting of Chiang and a few others (Hu Hanmin and Tan Yankai), were engraved onto the rear walls of the hall. Patterns of the emblems of the nation and the party were applied on the ceiling coffers inside the hall, and on the floor of the sunken altar inside the tomb chamber. After the grand funeral on 1 June 1929 attended by Chiang with a large gathering of the population, the site attained a supreme symbolic significance for the party and for Chiang himself.[55] All major rituals and celebrations of the party from 1929 to 1949 (except during the Japanese occupation of 1937–45) occurred here.

If the mausoleum was the first in the style promoted by state authority, then a large amount of buildings of this style with different design approaches soon emerged in the 1930s and the late 1940s.

3.4 Shanghai Municipality, Shanghai, 1933. Architect: Dong Dayou.

3.5 National Central Museum, Nanjing, built 1936–48. Architect: Xu Jingzhi, Li Huibo, with Liang Sicheng. Photo taken in 2001.

In a social and functional perspective, they included government ministries; memorial buildings and parks; other public buildings of a high symbolic significance (a party history exhibition hall, a 'great hall of the people', a national museum); public institutions dedicated to health, learning and art (hospitals, stadiums, gymnasiums, libraries, galleries); financial institutions (banks); and universities and research institutes. In geopolitical terms, the majority were located in Nanjing, and a group of public buildings built in 1933–5 was also found in Shanghai. Guangzhou, Wuhan and Beijing also had some of these national and public institutions (especially, a Memorial Hall of Sun Yat-sen in Guangzhou completed in 1931, a national library in Beijing in 1929, and a national Wuhan university built during 1929–39). In formal terms, these designs may be divided into a revivalist, a neo-classical, and an art deco position. The first followed closely historical forms (especially that of the roof) (Figures 3.4, 3.5, 2.22); the third employed a modern, abstract block on which Chinese decorative details were applied (Figures 3.6, 3.7, 3.8, 3.9, 3.10); while the second stood in between, with Chinese roofs often used creatively on abstract cubic volumes in a new composition (Figures 3.2, 3.11, 2.23). If the Central Museum (Nanjing, 1936–49, by Xu Jingzhi and Li Huibo with Liang Sicheng's advice) and the Municipality Building (Shanghai,

3.6 Ministry of Foreign Affairs, Nanjing, 1934. Architect: Tong Jun and Allied Architects.

3.7 National Art Gallery, Nanjing, 1936, Architect: Xi Fuquan, Photo taken in 2001.

1933, by Dong Dayou) are 'revivalist', then the Ministry of Foreign Affairs (Nanjing, 1931, by Tong Jun of Allied Architects), the Central Hospital (Nanjing, 1931, by Yang Tingbao of Kwan, Chu & Yang), and the stadiums and gymnasiums in Nanjing (1931 by Yang Tingbao) and Shanghai (1935 by Dong Dayou) can be seen as 'art deco modern'. On the other hand, Lu's Mausoleum of Sun Yat-sen (1929) and Dong Dayou's Library and Museum in Shanghai (1935) may be regarded as 'neo-classical' designs where Chinese roofs were employed in a new composition with abstract volumes, thus freeing the profile of the building from the restriction of the roof. Subsequent use of the Chinese Style in the 1950s and 1980s–1990s witnessed the second approach being developed further than the other two (for example in the Cultural Palace of Nationalities of 1956 and the Beijing Western Railway Station of 1996).

After the funding of Nanjing as the capital in 18 April 1927, a Committee for the Building of the Capital under Sun Ke, and an Office of Experts for Capital Design under Lin Yimin were established in early and late 1928.[56] The purpose was to develop a 'Capital Plan' (*Shoudu Jihua*) in 1929. Henry K. Murphy, an architect, and Ernest P. Goodrich, a planner and civil engineer, who were both American and had previously worked with Lin and Sun for the party in Guangzhou, were employed as special advisors for the office.[57] Other Chinese and American engineers and architects also served in the office. Murphy was also employed as the chief architectural advisor to the Nationalist government for the planning.[58] Murphy, an active architect who had already employed Chinese roofs and related styles on modern steel and concrete structures in the early 1920s for missionary universities in Beijing and Nanjing (and other colleges before), was in many ways a forerunner of this approach in formal design (although ideologically or in terms of nationalist sentiment his work belonged to a different category). Given his impressive work in this regard, Murphy was also invited to design a memorial complex (for Heroes of the Revolution)

3.8 Central Hospital, Nanjing, 1931. Architect: Yang Tingbao of Kwan Chu & Yang Architects.

3.9 Central Stadium, Nanjing, 1930. Front gate to the stadium. Architect: Yang Tingbao and Kwan, Chu & Yang Architects.

3.10 Central Stadium, Nanjing, 1930. Sports ground inside the stadium. Photo taken in the 1990s.

3.11 Shanghai City Museum, Shanghai, 1933. Architect: Dong Dayou.

to the east of Sun's mausoleum.[59] Murphy provided advice for the plan and had certainly supported the use of the Chinese native forms. However the document, the Capital Plan, was unmistakably a voice of the Chinese Nationalist Party. In this voice we can hear a principle in city building of that time: a hybrid synthesis of Western science and technology with Chinese culture and values. Sun Ke in his Preface says 'the capital was not only a centre of political order but also a centre of cultural life and excellence'; and the building of the capital should employ not only 'scientific principles developed in Europe and America' but also 'the excellent aspects of the artistic tradition of our nation'.[60]

3.12 Plan for the 'political centre' of the Republican government on the southern slopes of the Purple Hill in eastern Nanjing, a proposal made in 1929. To the east and west above the top are the Mausoleum of Sun Yat-sen and the imperial tomb of the first emperor of the Ming dynasty; to the west was a main avenue, Zhongshan Lu, passing the square site of an early Ming Forbidden City.

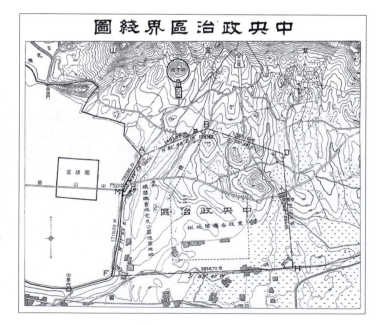

In the Capital Plan, after Chiang's handwriting of the book title, Sun's portrait and a script of his will, Sun Ke's preface and Lin Yimin's introduction, come twenty-eight chapters, with fifty-nine illustrations (maps, diagrams, plans, drawings), that deal with history, population growth, sites of the central and municipal governments, architectural style, roads, parks, railways, a harbour, an airport, water and power supply, housing, schools, industry, planning law, and finance. The capitol was planned further south of Sun's mausoleum on the southern slope of the Purple Hill (Figures 3.12, 3.13).[61] The forms of government offices and public buildings were required to adopt 'Chinese native styles', with various good features of 'ancient palaces' being included (Figure 3.14).[62] The planning of the road systems within the capitol and of the entire city followed a Beaux-Arts composition, then used in America and Europe, of diagonals in a grid of orthogonal lines. The capitol was compared with that in Washington.[63] Sketches of the capitol with all its buildings, of the city government centre, of major public buildings including a railway station, of main street intersections, parks and riverfronts were all included. History didn't allow the Nationalist government time to carry out all these ideas; and even within the decade and briefly afterwards (1945–9), government offices were built not in the designated area but elsewhere in the city for convenience. Some main axial avenues from the north-west to the east began to take shape based on planning, but that was very limited compared with what was proposed in the whole plan. The document of 1929, however, was in fact of a great importance in hindsight. It was not only a most elaborate argument for urban building with a Chinese native style, but also one that left its impact on a large group of buildings with a persistent use of the style in Nanjing and other cities in China of the period.

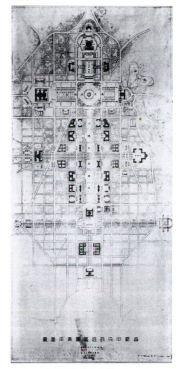

3.13 Layout of the 'political centre' of the Republic government. From north to south along the axis, congressional offices of the party, government offices of the state, and 'five houses and the ministries group' were placed in a sequential order.

3.14 A sketch of the congressional offices of the Kuomintang Party located at the top or northern end of the axis of the 'political centre'.

Shanghai's planning was consistent with that for Nanjing but in a different urban context. Shanghai was already the largest commercial port of China, with its urban centre inside the colonial concessions, a city ruled by foreign and Chinese authorities in separate areas. Not claiming the concessions, the government was attempting to build a new urban area that might surpass the old centre.[64] Upon the funding of Shanghai as a special municipality in 1927, Chiang and the city authorities began to plan its future. A new urban centre was proposed in 1929, one which was located well apart and further north of the old city of concessions (Figures 3.15, 3.16). Further north and closer to the Yangtze River was a proposed new harbour. The construction of the new city was to be 'more comprehensive and developed than the concessions'; and, with the new harbour becoming the biggest in East Asia, the new city area was to become the centre of the whole of Shanghai in the future.[65] These ideas went into the Shanghai City Centre Plan in 1930, and also the more developed Greater Shanghai Plan in 1930–1. American specialists in planning and civil engineering were involved in the design while the overall concept was largely devised by the party and the central government. As completed, the City Centre Plan included a plan for the centre with its districts (administration, commerce, residence), a road system plan (with radials, rings and grids), and a harbour–railway system plan. The first phase of the construction of this plan included the opening of the road system (in conjunction with the building of the harbour and railway lines), the claiming of the land, and the building of major public and government buildings.[66] The buildings were required to follow Chinese styles. Not satisfied with the competition entries for the design of the Municipality head office, the municipal authority asked Dong Dayou (who was then the advisor to the Shanghai City Centre Planning Committee) to revise the design in 1930. The construction started in 1931 and the Municipality Building was completed in 1933. Other major public buildings nearby in the new city centre, also designed by Dong, were soon constructed and were completed in 1935. They included Shanghai Library, Shanghai Museum and Shanghai Sports Complex (including a stadium, a sports ground and an indoor gymnasium). The formal approach of these works varied from 'revivalist' to 'neo-classical' and 'art deco modern'. Yet they all displayed a nationalist Chinese feature, all employed modern building technologies including the use of steel and reinforced concrete, and all were to accommodate modern and public functions. Unfortunately, after 1937 the war prevented further implementation of the city plan.

A nationalist public space

We can now make a few observations regarding public space, the role of the architect, knowledge transfer by the architect and the critical

3.15 A bird's-eye view of the Shanghai civic centre proposed in 1929–30.

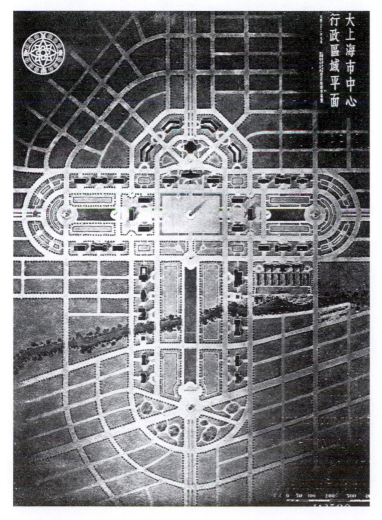

3.16 Plan of the Shanghai civic centre proposed in 1929–30.

3.17 Urban space in Nanjing of the 1930s defined by 'Chinese Native Style' architecture: aerial view of the east–west avenue Zhongshan Lu, with the Central Hospital to the west and a 'Lizhishe' government clubhouse (with a Chinese roof, 1929, by Fan Wenzhao) to the east, in 1935.

position it assumed in the Chinese context. Regarding public space that the planners and architects had created in the 1930s, we may observe a critical change at the threshold of the Nanjing government. The arrival of the Chinese architect in the 1920s and the beginning of assertions of the government on design and city building in 1925 (for the mausoleum) and in 1929 and 1930 (for Nanjing and Shanghai) were historical incidents that converged with each other. Together they created some landmarks and layouts of a new urban public space that may be qualified as 'nationalist'. This nationalist public space, with its

3.18 Nationalist architecture defining public space in the 1930s: Chinese delegates to the Berlin Olympics visiting the Sun Yat-sen Mausoleum before departure, 1936.

symbolic and spatial capacities, further developed a public social order that may also be termed as 'nationalist' (Figures 3.17, 3.18, 3.19). This may be explained in ideological, spatial and social terms.

1. Ideologically, this was the consequence of Lenin, Sun and Chiang's varying but consistent support for and constructions of national independence from colonialism and imperialism. Chiang's rule in the 1930s, accumulating the earlier ideological currents and adding Confucian and fascist ideas, as in the New Life movement, constructed this nationalist order in an authoritarian direction. Yet a cosmopolitan urban culture, with the new national pride and sense of Chineseness, survived and was in fact rather vibrant in artistic and literary culture especially in Shanghai.

2. In spatial layout and construction, the overall nationalist social order was pervasive in all cities and regions ruled by the party. Yet in the key cities and especially in Shanghai and most clearly in Nanjing, by 1937, there had emerged an urban landscape characterized at key locations by distinctively Chinese-style architecture and urban spaces in between these public landmarks. Of course the design prescriptions of 1925, 1929 and 1930 for the style, and for an urban construction with a distinctive Chineseness in style and in real politico-economic development, provided guidance for such a landscape to emerge. These prescriptions in turn were an implementation of the 'nationalist cultural reconstruction' in architecture and urban planning.

3. In social terms, a Chinese bourgeois space and society had already existed before 1927. Yet it was a temporary situation given the chaos that prevailed when China was fragmented and was managed by different local and colonial authorities. Without a strong national authority, open society remained fragmented and colonized and in danger of further disintegration. Hanging behind this open but uncertain society was a colonial backdrop, with strong industrial powers encroaching upon the country. The nationalist public space marked

by the buildings of the 1930s under Chiang's government, therefore, imposed a new layer of urban order and meaning, with a nationalist ideology for a new China resisting imperialist colonization. This new Chinese public space, in fact, was not only visual and symbolic (with the buildings established as landmarks), but also real and instrumental in governance and economic development. It was also manifested in a 'Chinese cosmopolitanism' (in Lee Ou-fan's term) especially in Shanghai, where literature, cinema and mass media attained a Chinese national subjectivity even as the city lived with and absorbed Western and foreign cultures in the 1930s and parts of the 1940s.[67]

A few more observations may be added:

1. *Spatial construction*. This nationalist public space and social sphere strongly emphasized the nation and state authority. This was inevitable considering that this was in the early years of a new government. But buildings and spaces for the public were also constructed. If we examine the Capital Plan of 1929, a complete civil construction of a modern city and national capital was accommodated. It included not only party, government and municipal buildings, but also commercial buildings, houses, schools, a railway station, an airport and other aspects of civil construction and industry. In the public buildings already constructed, we may note that these buildings of a Chinese nationalist style had a great capacity to accommodate large gatherings. While the Mausoleum of Sun Yat-sen had an open square that could accommodate 50,000 people, the Memorial Hall of Sun Yat-sen in Guangzhou (1931) had an auditorium with 4680 seats for public meetings. The Jiangwan Stadium in Shanghai (1935) had a capacity of 40,000 seats and 20,000 standing positions.[68]

2. *A nationalist bourgeoisie*. In so far as this was a bourgeois public society built and supported by the professionals, including architects, the critical position of intellectuals and professionals should be questioned. In the context as outlined in this chapter, the object of the critical thrust of the profession, or of those most committed in the group, was not the state, authority, tradition or the status quo. In fact, in a historical perspective of China at the time, there were hardly any 'state', 'authority', 'tradition' and 'status quo' left: they were in a chaotic and fragmented condition in danger of further disintegration. The object of critique, therefore, was not within but without: the colonial forces and imperialism. All committed intellectuals and revolutionaries, communist or nationalist, shared this common project. There was indeed communist and left-wing criticism of the Nationalist state, yet all were still united in the face of foreign invasion and imperialism. In this sense, European theorization of the 'bourgeoisie' and of its critical distancing from internal forces (state, authority, tradition, status quo) is not entirely applicable to China and other 'colonies of the East'.

In Europe, where modernization was internally driven and was not subject to external colonial invasion, the critical bourgeoisie and its avant-garde found its object of critique within society in a temporal progress. In China, however, during 1911–49 and perhaps over a longer period, the object of critique had to be upon external forces in a geo-political revolution against imperialism. Of course there were also internal critiques for social progress (by the left of feudalism, capitalism and the conservative bourgeoisie) in the Chinese revolution, yet it was the external critique of and resistance to foreign invasion and imperialism that unified all currents of the Chinese revolution, especially the communists and the nationalists. Not predominantly leftist, the critical thrust of the Chinese architect, at the moment of his emergence, was nationalist, sharing a common agenda with the government. If Western theorization of the bourgeoisie cannot entirely apply to China, then its theory of the critical and the avant-garde in architecture, articulated for example by Michael Hays and Peter Eisenman, must also be re-examined. We will come to this later.

3. *A hybrid modernity*. This nationalist public order, built in the 1930s with a Chinese agenda but also under the impact of the West and Western-induced ideas of modernization, was a hybrid entity unknown before. The Capital Plan of 1929 advocated a combination of 'principles of European–American science and technology' with 'the excellent artistic tradition of our own nation'. The reality was in fact more complex. Ideologically, the Chiang government was furthering Sun's bourgeois-democratic revolution which emphasized the importance of the 'people', yet there was also a fascist–military and a Confucian–hierarchical value brought in, with a Leninist institutionalization of party dictatorship. Physically and stylistically, the employment of modern civil engineering and building technologies was organized or given a form in the European neo-classical composition of a Beaux-Arts school then popular in the United States (brought to China by Western-educated Chinese professionals and Western, especially American, professionals such as Murphy and Goodrich). Integrated with that was the use of the 'Chinese Native Style' which, on close inspection, was a reinterpretation of a northern imperial tradition found in the palaces of Beijing of the Ming and Qing dynasties (1420–1911). That these different formal and constructive elements were put together in a convincing manner must be seen as a remarkable achievement of these earliest moments of 1925 and the 1930s.

The architect: a network of hybrid ideas and political agendas

So what exactly was the achievement, or contribution, made by the profession of Chinese architect at the earliest moment after its arrival on the scene? What role did it play and what contribution did it offer that had not been played and offered by other related groups of professionals? There were already draftsmen, civil engineers and Western architects practising in China before the arrival of Chinese architects. The contribution of the Chinese architect can be defined and assessed against the work of these professionals.

If draftsmen and civil engineers had reproduced existing building and structural types based on their experience and knowledge, the Chinese architects had created new designs in each and every case of these projects. What defines the Chinese architect against these professions in their work is *creative design* and *stylistic form*. Almost all of these designs were selected from competitions or careful consideration of many different and creative proposals and possibilities in each specific case. A technician or a scientist by training would not be able to systematically create a new design for a singular case, for the mausoleum of Sun Yat-sen for example, and carry the idea through to all details. In this sense, Chinese architects as *designers* had finally arrived in China in the 1920s, a few decades after the arrival of civil engineers. Second, in these designs, a stylistic form was given with which functions and structures could be organized into an operative and symbolic whole. Again only a trained architect would be able to provide such an organized and selected style or form, and to give this form to the whole entity with its social and technological requirements. In fact both 'design' and 'style' were the key themes emphasized by the Chinese architects to define their unique work and identity in their public discourse as found in the journal *The Chinese Architect* (1932–7).[69]

Among the foreign architects working in China, there were European and American architects who had already employed Chinese roofs and associated features on modern structures, for missionary colleges and hospitals in the 1910s and 1920s, before the arrival of the Chinese architect. Some Chinese architects such as Lu Yanzhi had also practised under Henry K. Murphy on the design of Yanching University in Beijing using Chinese styles in the 1910s before Lu began his own practice in 1921.[70] Many Chinese architects had either participated in or observed these earlier attempts. The design philosophy, a historicist attitude adopted from nineteenth-century Europe and taught in Beaux-Arts education programmes, was the same in these Western efforts and the Chinese architects' designs later on. The importance of these Western architects must be acknowledged. The division between earlier and later efforts was also blurred as some Western architects, especially Murphy, continued to make contributions after 1925 and 1927. Yet there was a difference between the two attempts. If we look into a formal profile produced in the 1930s as a whole, there was a comprehensive integration of several elements assembled only in the Nanjing decade through the Chinese architect as the agent of knowledge production and political enterprise. These included a neo-classical composition in a Beaux-Arts approach with a historicist attitude, a Chinese tradition adopted from northern imperial palaces found in Beijing, a far more confident and accurate use of traditional Chinese features and details, scholarly research on a wider Chinese building tradition as an input in design, and an anti-imperialist agenda of the government shared by Chinese society. The Chinese architect was in fact the only central figure that *integrated* these currents, through a comprehensive institutionalization of knowledge, in the Chinese context, with a global network of ideas and expertise, for the political agenda shared by state and society. This institutionalization involves an integration of a few crucial practices that may be listed below:

1   A creative design of form by the architect which gives a specific symbolic-formal organization to functions, structures and spaces.
2   The use of Baroque and neo-classical composition in a Beaux-Arts design philosophy imported from Europe and the United States, with a historicist attitude adapted into the Chinese context.
3   Systematic research into historical Chinese architecture and the transfer of these discoveries into design immediately, through the Society for Research in Chinese Architecture, as enacted by figures such as Liang Sicheng (Figure 3.20).

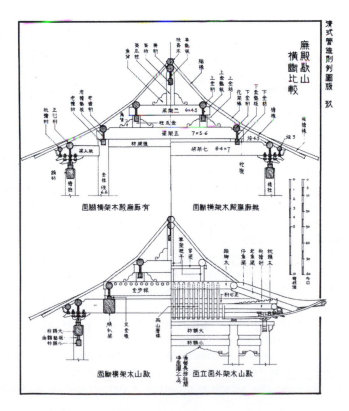

3.20 Research on indigenous Chinese buildings: plate 9 in Liang Sicheng's *Qingshi Yingzao Zeli*, 1934.

4   The establishment of tertiary education of architecture in 1923 and 1927–8 through which younger architects were produced who could further the task in the 1940s (and indeed in the 1950s and after as well).

5   Collaboration with a state authority that had a nationalist and anti-imperialist ideology, an authority that also had a mixed interest in Western scientific expertise, democratic ideals, Leninist centralism, fascist methods and Confucian values.

The simultaneous work of all these practices, integrated in a network of ideas and agendas with a global background, in a comprehensive institutionalization of the profession, with its production and its use of knowledge was the contribution made by Chinese architects, a contribution that differentiated them from all other groups. With this, they stood on the 'conservative' side in the spectrum of positions in the Chinese revolution, but constructed a nationalist urban order that was critical of imperialism and colonial domination.

A different kind of critical intellectual

If the nationalist attitude of the Chinese architects can be considered 'critical', then the meaning of critique in design practice has to be discussed here. Western sociology and architectural discourse, relying on Western European history of the past few centuries, have conceived of critique, arising from the progressive ideological politics of the intellectuals of the bourgeoisie, as a process that unfolds between these rising voices and an existing social order and authority (the *ancien régime*, modern bureaucracy, and capitalist market economy).[71] The critical space unfolds here within a social and national boundary (or in an international space in which a foreign power does not constitute part of the critical space). In the colonies or semi-colonies outside the Western world, however, for example in China, the critical space occurs both within and significantly without, across the national boundary. There was a social critique of tradition, class, feudal regime and bourgeois order, but there was a more pervasive nationalist critique and revolution against foreign domination imposed from outside. When it came to the nationalist agenda, the Chinese architects stood with state authority and national tradition. This poses a problem for whether they can be regarded as 'critical' in a Western framework. Michael Hays, using Mies van der Rohe as an example, considers a critical architecture to be 'resistant' and 'oppositional' towards certain authoritative order or culture, a design which also explores its 'own authorship' from the architects themselves.[72] Peter Eisenman also cites Piranesi, Ledoux, Le Corbusier and Mies van der Rohe as cases in which a critique of tradition, authority and status quo is attempted.[73] In the Chinese case, the architects do attain a certain level of authorship in design (especially through competitions). Yet they have not quite explored an individualistic 'own authorship' against social conventions. They have instead employed a native tradition, and have allied with state authority, against another 'tradition', 'authority' and 'status quo', the colonial domination in China.

If the Chinese case of the 1930s has a legitimacy and if these architects' work can be regarded as having a progressive ideological politics, then the Western theorization of the critical in sociology (as in Habermas) and architecture (as in Hays and Eisenman) may be developed, to include non-Western and colonial cases in which both social and national liberation constitute a critical agenda. In this new understanding, both the internal social critique for human liberation and the external geo-political critique for national liberation should be included as critical efforts. This entails a complex understanding of the critical in which a pure authorship can be 'dissolved' and allied with other social 'authors' as long as a real and progressive critique can be enacted. A privileged individualism must be identified and questioned. This new understanding may include a few facets:

1   It suggests that, as long as there is a real opposition or object of critique, a design may be considered critical, regardless of the condition and quality of the architect-author (regarding its autonomy or opposition in a simple sense).
2   The critical voice or author itself doesn't have to be on its 'own', distanced against the 'other', but can ally with others or other social forces and authors such as tradition and authority in certain conditions. The self–other dichotomy has to be dissolved in an embedded enterprise of the critical.
3   The purity of one's own authorship within the formal language of architecture should also be opened up, to include a social-realist conception in which a design with a use of conventions may also be critical in a certain context. A socially 'popular' design can be critical if it serves the population well for a progressive cause.

Modernism?

After the early 1930s, and also in the brief period of 1945–9 during a civil war when Nanjing was still the capital, an art deco modern and a pure modernist or international style emerged briefly in China. Certain European firms offered designs in art deco styles with modern inclinations in Shanghai and Tianjin (1934–8).[74] L. E. Hudec was a prominent architect in Shanghai who made a dramatic turn around 1933 towards an art deco and modern approach.[75] A translation of Le Corbusier's speech 'A new dawn in architecture' (given in 1930 in Moscow) was published in *The Chinese Architect* in 1934. His book *The City of Tomorrow* was also translated and published in 1936.

3.21 Hongqiao Sanitorium, Shanghai, 1934. Architect: Xi Fuquan.

3.22 Block A and B, apartments for American advisors, Nanjing, 1947. Architect: Tong Jun.

Various introductions and studies on Le Corbusier, Bruno Taut, Russian avant-garde and modernist urban planning were also published in *The Chinese Architect*, *The Builder* and *Xin Jianzhu* ('New architecture', from 1936).[76] The transition from an art deco modern to a purely international style occurred in many works designed by Chinese architects. The Chinese were not far behind Hudec and other foreign architects in China. Nor was there a long time lag between the arrival of the International Style on the world stage in 1932 (when the book and the exhibition titled 'The International Style' were opened to the public in New York) and its impact on Chinese architects in China. We can identify many designs that were in between art deco and modernism, such as the Grand Theatre (1933, by Hudec), Dahua Theatre and International Club (1935, 1936, Yang Tingbao), Wu Residence (1937, Hudec), Xinsheng Club and a residence for Sun Ke called Yanhuiguan (1947, 1948, Yang Tingbao). More importantly, we can identify a few that were distinctively modernist: Shanghai Hongqiao Sanatorium (1934, Xi Fuquan), Shanghai Maternity Hospital (1935, Zhuang Jun), Dong Dayou's own residence (1935), and Apartment Block A and B for the American Advisors (1946, Tong Jun) (Figures 3.21, 3.22). The Chinese have demonstrated a formal skill in adopting the new approach rather quickly. There was however a crucial lack of persistent individual research or experiment to develop modernism as a fundamental alternative to the idea of 'styles'. Modernism was treated as a stylistic option (for example in Dong Dayou's whole design profile); and in a design studio at a university it was a common practice in the 1930s and 1940s to divide students into three stylistic groups for the same design task: 'European classical', 'Chinese style' and 'International Style'.[77] Taking the Chinese scene of the 1930s and 1940s as a whole, there was not a substantial body of work in modernism, nor was there a thorough social-industrial development that propelled this change in design language at a technological level.

A few critical factors were at work that prevented China from producing a serious modernism at that time (and for a long time after). The overall socio-economic and political condition was weak and vulnerable, with a partially unified China lasting not more than ten years (1927/8–37) while the rest of China in the same period, and the whole of China in periods before and after, was in war and disarray. The overall economic and socio-psychological climate was not ready in China (compared with Western Europe, Japan and the United States at that time) for the architect to pursue an individualist experiment into inner knowledge of the discipline for a new course beyond the paradigm of 'styles'. Instead, they were serving many different clients, and significantly those of state authority and a national reconstruction project, with different styles on offer. A strong individualistic authorship was not possible, whereas survival of the profession and service to society and the client were more urgent requirements. Another reason behind the lack of development in modernism lies in a low level of industrialization and standardization. Steel, concrete and glass were not affordable enough for such a design development.[78] Nor was there a proper standardization in the production of materials and in design documentation and communication.[79] The real reason behind all this of course was the political weakness of the nation or state authority, which was unable to provide a peaceful environment for a long period during which economy and industrialization could take off.

It is interesting to note that modernism was also curtailed and suppressed after 1949 for ideological reasons, as communist China sided with Soviet Russia (against capitalism and the use of the International Style as a cultural expression of imperialism). This was in fact an extension of the overall difficulties of the nation struggling to emerge. Modernism as mass production of housing and as an efficient form for public buildings finally arrived in China in the 1960s and especially 1970s. Modernism as individualist experiments in search of a pure or internal disciplinary knowledge did not quite occur in China, despite some interesting cases, until the 1990s. It is not a surprise that countries included in Henry-Russell Hitchcock and Philip Johnson's exhibition in 1932 were European countries plus Japan and the United States, nations with a strong state authority and sustained economic development, in which formal experimentation and transgression against the styles of the past could be attempted (the Soviet Union may be treated as a special case in need of separate analysis).[80] In China, that moment only arrived in the 1990s.

Conclusion

Building construction was a business for artisans, not intellectuals or the literati of the official-gentry class in traditional China. This situation changed dramatically at the dawn of the twentieth century. In the 1920s and 1930s, the Chinese architect arrived as a new kind of professional, one that was both a technical expert and a reflexive intellectual, with creative design as a central task relating the work of the two together. This profession was soon called upon to collaborate with state authority for a symbolic and nationalist project to build a modern Chinese city and a Chinese public sphere. The profession, sharing the nationalist outlook and the same object of critique, which was imperialist colonial domination, brought forth both a system of Western disciplinary knowledge of the Beaux-Arts programme and historical scholarship on traditional Chinese architecture. In collaboration with planners, civil engineers, enlightened officials, new technocrats, American specialist advisors, and party and government leaders, a hybrid modern city with Chinese nationalist characteristics was designed and made to emerge in the 1930s, especially in parts of Shanghai and Nanjing. This modern project, in state structure and ideology, in city planning and building, in the architecture of public places and institutions, and in the urban public sphere, was characteristically mixed and hybrid. This new profession, at the earliest moment of development called upon to serve the nation, also displayed a specific criticality that should be observed. Its practice was not individualistic or experimental within the discipline, but collaborative with a national project. It was not critical or negative towards order and authority within, but towards colonialism and imperialism imposed from outside in the geo-political sphere. It was not 'avant-garde' in search of a better world that may arrive one day, but modestly and pragmatically bent on the urgent task of building a 'better' world, here and now, immediately. China has certainly changed a lot since then. But these special conditions and outlook still survive in many ways today. The Chinese case, being more socially embedded than autonomous, can prompt us to re-examine the meaning and possibilities of the critical in architecture and in social practice.

CHAPTER 4

A SPATIAL REVOLUTION

Beijing, 1949–59

Upon the inauguration of the People's Republic of China on 1 October 1949, symbols and images of various kinds were needed to represent the new nation. Architects who had practised in the 'Old China' and studied abroad, particularly in the United States, in a Beaux-Arts programme in and around the 1920s were called upon to serve the new Republic. They were now employed in state-owned universities and design institutes in a nationalization process. They were required to study Mao's writings and Soviet Russian examples, to reform their 'bourgeois' thinking, to adopt a 'proletarian' worldview and, in particular, to conceive a design approach suitable for socialist China. In response, these architects re-employed Beaux-Arts design methods, integrated American and Soviet influences, and created a Chinese 'national style' in the 1950s. The flag, the national emblem, and the Monument to the People's Heroes were designed early in the decade. Design theories were formulated in 1954 and 1958–9 with important buildings constructed at the two moments accordingly. In the first, Liang Sicheng articulated a Chinese version of 'socialist realism with national forms', which was reflected in the buildings of the time with Chinese features, especially the curved roofs. In the second, a more collective voice under the Party called for 'new styles for China's socialist architecture', which were manifested in a variety of forms, especially in the Ten Grand Buildings in Beijing in 1959. For the planning of the city, the basic concept was made around 1953 and 1954, under the Party's direction and with reference to the Moscow Plan of 1935 under Stalin. The Beijing Plan called for the administrative centre to be located inside the old imperial city, and for Beijing to be the political centre and industrial base of the nation, a city whose aim was, among others, to increase the 'efficiency of the working people's labour and production'.

Questions must be raised about the city of Beijing, formal thinking, and the role of Liang and the architect as a professional in such a political context. For the city, one would ask: What changes were being brought to this ancient imperial city and its traditional fabric? From a historical perspective, with the city having been an imperial capital before 1911, with decades of mutation in the twentieth century, and with the more radical transformation and destruction occurring in 2008, what was the major and perhaps strategic change being made to Beijing in the 1950s?

Regarding formal thinking, other questions must be raised: How was the idea of a Chinese 'national style' constructed? What were its sources and visual-formal basis? In what ways were tradition and 'Chinese architecture' conceived and invented? Which elements of this tradition were privileged? How were they composed to make a modern 'national style'? If the Kuomintang government in Nanjing in the 1930s had already made a comparable attempt, in what ways were these two moments, the Beijing of 1950s and Nanjing of the 1930s, related? In a global context, how were the Soviet and American influences employed together at this moment in Beijing? If the Russian and American models shared a common base in post-Renaissance Europe, what kinds of formal and visual conceptions were absorbed into China? Was there a 'Cartesian' way of seeing and forming being internalized in China?

For the role of the architect, questions here centre on the position of the individual and the profession in relation to state authority represented by the Party. How was the asymmetrical power relationship being imposed while still allowing the profession to contribute with its skill and knowledge in which 'Western' and 'bourgeois' forms were internalized in socialist China? How was the power–knowledge interaction being played out?

Liang Sicheng, a most prominent figure in the profession at the time, is the primary case we have to study first. Liang (1901–72) studied in the United States, at the University of Pennsylvania, from 1924 to 1927. Having established one of China's earliest architectural schools in Shengyang in 1928, he embarked on the first 'scientific' survey and documentation of ancient buildings across China from 1931 to the mid-1940s, with his wife and other colleagues in the 'Society for Research in Chinese Architecture'. He designed a few buildings in between, and advised on the design of Central Museum in Nanjing in the mid-1930s under the Kuomintang government. Arriving in Beijing in 1946 (and having visited the United States in 1947 representing Kuomintang China for the joint design of the UN Headquarters), Liang was actively involved with the Chinese Communist Party from 1949 onwards. His trajectory from here is a story we must observe in order to answer the question concerning the role of the individual and the profession.

Current scholarship on Liang has focused on the decades before 1949. Yet it was in the 1950s that Liang, now in his fifties, was most active in design thinking for the nation, and most involved with state authority and political ideology. Scholarship on Liang when it does touch on the 1950s tends to focus on ethical and biographic issues of his 'good' intentions and his tragic 'failures' under the powerful regime. Although these observations are important, it is arguably more illuminating if we are 'archaeological' in observing a social process in which forms and ideas were produced.[1] This chapter focuses on

Liang's trajectory not as a biographical narrative but as a path of social practice, in a social web of relations between intellectuals and the Party, in which national forms, as discourse, as formal language, and as constructed buildings and urban environments, were produced. In particular, this chapter explores a power–knowledge and political–epistemological nexus in which a certain formal-visual knowledge was employed for political purposes. The question here concerns specifically the Beaux-Arts model as it had travelled into China via Pennsylvania. It concerns not only design methods developed on the way through time and space, linking America and Russia with Nanjing and Beijing from the 1930s to the 1950s, but also a method of 'seeing' and representation adopted for the 'scientific' research on traditional buildings in the 1930s from which a modern architecture was conceived in the 1950s.

Starting with Liang's trajectory and following a development in the production of designs, forms, ideas and buildings, five critical moments can be identified. If the first three (1950, 1952, 1953) witnessed the making of the emblem, the monument and the plan of the capital, then the next two moments (1954 and 1959) saw two 'climaxes' in design theorization and building construction in Beijing in that decade. This study investigates key events and documents around these five moments in an attempt to explore the questions on Beijing, form and the architect.

The emblem, 1950

Being the head of architecture department at Beijing's Tsinghua University and a leading figure in the profession nationwide, Liang was invited to sit on many committees in Beijing from early 1949, including one for selecting the national flag and emblem in the preparatory meetings of the Chinese People's Political Consultative Conference. In the first full meeting of the Conference in late September, a People's Central Government, including Mao Zedong and Zhou Enlai as Chairman and Prime Minister, respectively, was elected, and decisions on the national anthem, the flag, the city as the capital, and a monument to the People's Heroes at Tiananmen Square were also made. The selection of the anthem and the flag was made on 25 September by Mao, Zhou and some sixteen advisors including Liang, out of some 200 entries for the song and 1500 proposals for the flag from a competition. While 'March of the Volunteers', written by Tian Han and composed by Nie Er in 1935, was selected as the national anthem, 'five stars', proposed by Zeng Liansong, was adopted for the national flag.[2] Liang worked overnight to draft the first measured drawings of the improved design for the flag on 25 September for the 'Opening of the Nation' on 1 October 1949. The decision on the emblem, however, was postponed as none of the entries in the competition was satisfactory.[3] Zhang Ding, from the Central Academy of Fine Arts, and Lin Huiyin, Liang's wife, from the architecture department at Tsinghua University, were each invited to submit their proposals with their teams from the two schools. Zhang provided a colourful design with the Tiananmen building viewed at an angle. Lin's proposal was abstract without the building and in three colours only (gold, red and jade white). After rounds of debate, Liang was invited by Zhou Enlai to join the design, and to lead with Lin the six-member team from Tsinghua for the design. The Tiananmen building, site of the May Fourth Movement of 1919 and of the 'Opening of the Nation' on 1 October 1949, was requested to be included on account of its symbolic significance. After rounds of resubmissions by the two teams, Zhou Enlai and the committee finally selected Liang and Lin's design on 20 June 1950. Mao approved the selection on 23 June and announced the decision on 20 September 1950.

The design included five stars in the sky above Tiananmen in a frontal elevation, which was encircled by gear wheels and grain ears tied with a ribbon at the base. All these were in golden yellow whereas the background or the sky was red, indicating an immense national flag all above. It described visually the new nation-state, a 'people's democratic dictatorship' led by proletarian workers and their vanguard the Communist Party (the big star), with a union of 'workers', 'peasants', 'urban bourgeoisie' and 'national capitalists' (the four small stars). The political content was expressed with Chinese characteristics in the careful use of the two colours. Throughout the process, Liang and Lin had emphasized an abstract, symbolic design in which 'China's artistic tradition' was adopted, so that there was a 'continuity of the old and new cultures of China' (whereas the other scheme was too colourful and descriptive). It responded well to the brief, which called for a design that should display 'Chinese characteristics' and 'characteristics of a government', and be 'solemn and splendid' (Figure 4.1).

4.1 National emblem (as placed on the Tiananmen building).

The monument, 1952

The decision to build a monument to the People's Heroes 'who sacrificed their lives for their country' was made in late September 1949. Mao wrote an epigraph for the monument. At 6:00 p.m. on 31 September, before the 'Opening of the Nation' next day, a solemn foundation-laying ceremony for the monument was held on a central point in front of Tiananmen, where Mao read aloud the epigraph and led the service for the whole company, the 576-member Political Consultative Conference including Liang. The design of the monument however proved complex. There were discussions on the form it should take from 1949 to 1952. Three types of design emerged after a competition: a form lying down on the ground, a group of human figures, and a vertical object or stele. In a debate on these schemes, Liang said that the monument was where Mao's epigraph or *beiwen*, that is, 'scripture on a stele' in Chinese, was to be inscribed. Liang argued that it should adopt the type of a stele, and that a Chinese stele (*bei*) would be more appropriate than an Egyptian obelisk or a Roman column.[4] After discussions involving Zhou Enlai, it was agreed that the design would adopt this typology, but also that the Chinese stele, being 'small and gloomy' and not 'heroic', be transformed and revolutionized. Zhou again invited Liang and Lin to lead the design. In May 1952, a team was organized in which Liang was responsible for the architectural design, whereas Liu Kaique and Fan Wenlan, a sculptor and a Party historian, were responsible for the relief sculpture and historical narratives to be represented. Zhou was involved in many decisions on the way including the exact point to locate the monument and the direction of the 'front' of the monument.[5]

The monument was completed in May 1958, at the centre of Tiananmen Square on the north–south axis. It stood 37.94 metres tall, with an architectural roof in the Chinese *wudian* style, and flat surfaces on the north and south in the *bei* tradition (Figures 4.2, 4.3). On the north and the south, the 'front' and the 'back' of the monument, were inscribed Mao's calligraphy 'Monument to the People's Heroes' and Zhou's handwriting of Mao's epigraph respectively. It had a double plinth and two terraces with Chinese decorative motifs. The lower plinth had ten relief sculptures arranged chronologically depicting a history of the Chinese revolution based on Mao's interpretation. While those on the east and west depicted 'democratic revolution of the old type' (1840–1918) and of 'the new type' (1919–49), those on the south and north depicted critical events of 1919 which divided the two periods, and of 1949 which ended the second phase. This narrative is to be viewed from the north first with its most recent revolution in 1949, which was exactly Mao's viewing position when he stood at Tiananmen and declared the 'Opening of the Nation' on 1 October 1949.[6] The relief sculptures were social-realistic in the nineteenth-

century European tradition but also Chinese in the use of lines and surfaces.[7] The entire monument, in fact, was Chinese in typology and certain details, but European or 'Western' in its heroic dimensions as one finds in an obelisk or a column in a large plaza. The change from a Chinese *bei* of some four to five metres to the monument at 38 metres, in a new square just opened measuring 500 metres east to west and 880 metres north to south, was a 'revolution' in spatial layout, at the heart of the old city articulated before by a different logic of space, that of enclosures and courtyards rather than openness and monumentality. We will come to this later on.

Beijing Plan, 1953

Although Liang played a major role in designing these national symbols, his influence on the planning of Beijing was limited. His reverence for the imperial capital and his idea of locating the new administrative centre to the west were at odds with the intentions of the Party. Whereas Mao wanted to see 'lots of chimneys' in Beijing, Zhou Enlai, standing on the Tiananmen looking south on 1 October 1949, said after the opening ceremony that this largest square in the world should also be the most beautiful, and that it should be the heart of the nation, with a monument, a history museum and a grand national theatre at the centre, the east and the west respectively.[8] In December 1949, various planning proposals for the city were debated. While Liang Sicheng and Chen Zhanxiang argued for a new centre to be outside the old city, proposals from Russian advisors (led by Barannikov)[9] and others from the planning committee (Hua Nankui, Zhu Zhaoxue and Zhao Dongri) suggested the political centre be located in the core area inside the old city.[10] Despite Liang and Chen's challenge to the Russian proposal, municipal officials clearly displayed their preference for the latter. In February 1950, Liang and Chen developed a 'Proposal for the Location of the Administrative Centre of the Central People's Government'.[11] Known as the Liang–Chen Plan, it proposed that the new centre be in the western suburb and argued for decentralization, clear zoning, balancing between development and preservation, and conservation of the imperial city on its north–south axis. Counterproposals by Zhu and Zhao were made in April. Active construction in Beijing, however, was ongoing in the central area, following effectively the Russian proposal which was in fact, as revealed later, based on Mao's message passed on to the Russian team via the municipal Party Secretary Peng Zhen.[12]

In 1952–3, two plans made by Hua Lanhong and Chen Zhanxiang respectively, under Liang's coordination, based on the idea of the new centre placed inside Beijing, were again sidelined for their lack of 'progressive' ideas.[13] To reach a better plan, the municipal government organized another team inside the Party to work in a building called Chang-guan-lou (in a zoological garden in western Beijing) which

4.2 Monument to the People's Heroes. Northern and southern elevations.

4.3 Monument to the People's Heroes at Tiananmen Square viewed from the south-west. Photo taken in 2007.

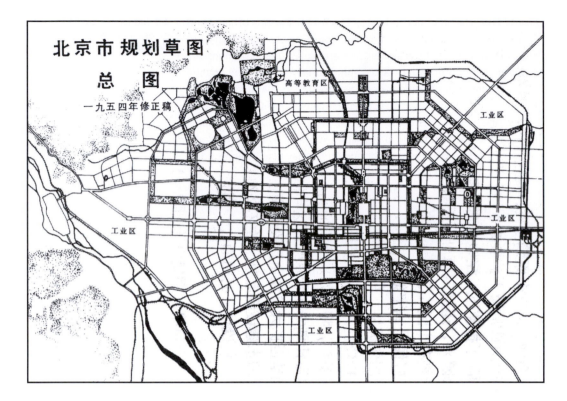

北京市规划草图
总　图
一九五四年修正稿

高等教育区

工业区

工业区

工业区

4.4 Beijing Plan 1953–4.

produced in November 1953 a decisive document, 'Draft Plan for Reconstruction and Expansion of Beijing'.[14] Known as the Chang-guan-lou Plan, it consolidated Mao's idea and the Russian proposal and laid down basic principles for Beijing to develop in the following decades, although new additions were also made in 1954, 1957 and 1958, and in the 1980s (Figure 4.4). Based on the Moscow Plan of 1935, it privileged industry and production. It stipulated that Beijing would be the political, economic and cultural centre, and also industrial base for the nation. It specified that the capital was for production, for the central government, and for the working people, and that it should strive to serve 'the rise of efficiency in the working people's labour and production'. It projected population growth and expansion of the city (5 million and 600 km^2 in twenty years) and areas for government, industry and education (at the centre, south-east and north-west respectively). It requested that the existing orthogonal streets be 'broadened, interlinked, and straightened', and the addition of ring roads around the centre and radial avenues extending outward, for efficient communications in all directions. While the major orthogonal avenues were to be 100 metres wide, the radial avenues and the ring roads with secondary roads were to be 60–90 and 40 metres in width respectively. Regarding preservation, it suggested that Beijing should develop from the historical past, preserve good elements, and eradicate restrictions of old layouts and patterns; and that preservation of heritage buildings should be assessed on a case-by-case basis.

Apart from a few cases (e.g. a curved road around the imperial garden at Tuanchen being successfully preserved in 1953), Liang's many suggestions were ignored.[15] Liang retreated as the decade moved on, which witnessed ongoing destruction of old buildings, roads, archways, city gates and walls to make way for the broad avenues and new buildings. Liang's 'conservative' attitudes were at odds with the revolutionary views of the Party, their destructive–constructive outlook for a new city and the nation, and their plan of an industry-led modernization in which 'efficiency' and 'production' were of most importance.

'National Forms', 1954

Despite this retreat on planning, Liang's influence on design thinking remained significant approaching the mid-1950s. Liang's writings and influence here coincided with the rise of construction activity, the spread of the use of Chinese roofs in prominent buildings, and a surge of national confidence. China achieved some success in these years in domestic and international affairs, despite a UN embargo in place since 1950 (after China joined North Korea in the war).[16] With Stalin's death in early 1953, China moved on actively to end the Korean War in late 1953. China played an important role in building 'principles of peaceful co-existence' with India, bringing peace to Indochina, initiating talks with the United States in Geneva, and at the opening of the Asian–African Conference in Bandung, Indonesia, in 1953 and 1954. On the domestic front, several campaigns including 'land reform' and 'suppressing counter-revolutionaries' established order and the reputation of the new government between 1949 and 1953. After a mild 'thought reform' programme, intellectuals, professionals and artists were organized into state-owned institutions. Private architectural firms were grouped into public companies and then state-owned design institutes by 1953. A General Principle for the 'new democracy' or 'people's democratic dictatorship', a transitional phase towards socialism, was established in 1953. The Principle specified that the task for China now was to 'industrialize the country, and to implement socialist transformations (of agriculture, traditional industry, capitalist industry and commerce)'. The first Five-Year Plan (1953–7) was made, which included 694 large- and medium-scale industrial projects, some of them with Soviet support, the most ambitious plan for industrialization in China at the time. The People's Congress, the Constitution and the State Council with its thirty-five ministries and offices were established in 1953 and 1954. Based on an earlier office of 1952, the Ministry of Construction was established in 1954. Liu Xiufeng (1908–71) was appointed the minister, and Wan Li,

Zhou Rongxing and Song Ruhe were appointed deputy ministers; all of them were Party members.[17]

There was in these years a culmination of discursive theorization and construction in Beijing, in which Liang played a crucial role. Liang visited Moscow and other Russian cities from February to May 1953. He had conversations with Arkady Mordvinov, then the president of the Architectural Academy in Moscow. Liang's writing on 'socialist realism' was clearer after the visit. The Architectural Society of China (ASC) (*Zhongguo Jianzhu Xuehui*) was established in October 1953. Liang was appointed deputy director, whereas Zhou Rongxing (1917–76), a deputy minister and Party member, was appointed director of the society: a vertical relationship that appeared in most organizations since 'old intellectuals' had to be supervised and reformed by the Party.[18] Liang was also appointed Editor-in-Chief of *Jianzhu Xuebao* (the Architectural Journal), which belonged to the society. Under Liang, the journal published its first two issues in June and December 1954.

Liang produced important writings in conjunction with the editing of the journal that year, amidst a rise in building activities and a spread of the use of Chinese roofs. The contents published in the journal in 1954 covered three areas of concern: ideology, historical research and design. More precisely, the contents were in three areas with three respective concerns: (1) an ideological argument for socialist realism demanding the use of national forms, (2) a study of traditional Chinese forms using historical scholarship accumulated before, and (3) an eclectic design method that recommended the use of these forms, which was reflected soon in design practice. Whereas articles in the first category in issues 1 and 2 were translations of writings from the Soviet Union, East Germany and Hungary (G. Minervin, A. Kovznezov, Walter Ulbricht, Kurt Magritz, Aleksandr Vlasov and Jozsef Revai),[19] those in the second were articles by Liang, Lin Huiyin and Mo Zhongjiang as architectural historians, and articles in the third category were explanations, working drawings and photos of actual designs under construction by the architects Zhang Bo, Zhang Kaiji and Chen Dengao. These two issues of the journal in 1954 demonstrated therefore another two dimensions: a geo-political alliance of China with Russia and Eastern Europe promoting national forms, and an immediate materialization of the ideas in designs and constructions in Beijing in 1954–5. The prominent ones published in the journal in 1954, all located in Beijing, were the Xijiao Guesthouse (later known as Friendship Hotel), Sanlihe Office Building, Beihai Office Building, and Dianmen Dormitories for the Civil Servants, respectively by Zhang Bo, Zhang Kaiji and Chen Dengao (for the last two).

Liang himself had written a lot in the past few years, in the most productive period of his life in design thinking. He had written a great deal in the 'ideology' area since 1950. In 1954 however, his writings had now expanded to include 'history' and 'design' issues in the new socialist-Maoist mindset. (1) There were eight pieces in the first area from 1950 to 1954, yet it was the last one, the speech in 1953, published in 1954, that was the clearest and most influential. (2) In the second or 'history' area, Liang published three pieces: a book completed in 1944 entitled *Zhongguo Jianzhu Shi* (A history of Chinese architecture) and two articles in issues 1 and 2 of the journal. Among these, the article in the first issue, 'Characteristics of Chinese architecture', was most concerned with how to use historical forms for design in socialist China. (3) In the third or 'design' area, a pamphlet by Liang, 'Architecture of the Motherland', summarized and integrated the two key texts in the ideological and historical areas. Because of the clarity of these texts in 1954 and Liang's institutionalized position then, these three texts (the speech, the 'characteristics' article and the pamphlet) claimed a leading position in each of the three areas of the discussion. The third text, integrating the ideological stance and historical knowledge, was most significant in defining design thinking in China in the mid-1950s (Figure 4.5).

The first was his speech 'On socialist realism in architectural art and on the study and use of national heritage', delivered at the opening of the ASC in 1953 and published in *Xin Jianshe* (New Construction) (no. 2, 1954).[20] Liang used the ideas of Mao, Lenin and Stalin, and Soviet examples including Moscow's metro stations, for a socialist realism with national forms in China. The argument was that political and ideological confrontation with bourgeois capitalism in countries like China also involved a nationalist, de-colonizing and anti-imperialist element. It therefore required cultural and artistic expressions in China and other similar countries to adopt a 'national style' rather than the 'International Style' from the capitalist, colonialist and imperialist West.

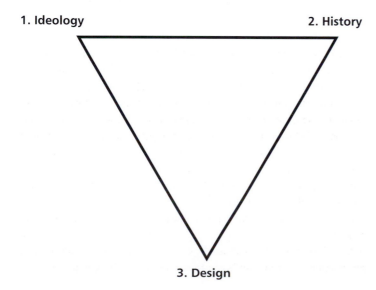

1. Ideology   **2. History**

3. Design

4.5 A triangular structure in Liang's writings as culminated in 1954. 1. 'On Socialist Realism...' (speech 1953, article in *Xin Jianshe*, 2, 1954) + 7 articles (1950–3). 2. 'Characteristics of Chinese Architecture' (*Jianzhu Xuebao*, 1, 1954) + *A History of Chinese Architecture* (book, 1954) + 1 article (*Jianzhu Xuebao*, 2, 1954). 3. 'Architecture of the Motherland' (with 2 sketches) (pamphlet, 1954).

The second was the article 'Characteristics of Chinese architecture' (*Jianzhu Xuebao*, no. 1, June 1954).[21] Liang outlined nine features of the Chinese building tradition, an account that privileged the roof and the related elements. Liang said that these features formed a 'grammar'. He than indicated that these forms could 'transcend the limitation of materials', that there was a 'translatability' in them that would allow them to be used with different materials, structures and typologies.

The third, the pamphlet titled 'Architecture of the Motherland', was published also in 1954.[22] Liang asked how to adopt traditional forms without mimicry. Liang quoted Mao's idea of 'selective inheritance', one which 'discards feudalist garbage and absorbs democratic essence'. Liang then provided two principles and two sketches to illustrate his interpretation of this idea in a design process.[23] One sketch depicted a group of buildings three to five storeys high at a street intersection, the other a group with a central tower thirty-five storeys high (Figure 4.6). In both, Chinese roofs were used, along with certain decorative motifs and a neoclassical approach to massing. The first principle stipulated that traditional forms with the associated grammar could be used whatever the size and height of a building one was designing, that is, 'translatability' was used here. For the second principle, Liang said, in developing a national form, an 'overall silhouette' was most important, whereas 'proportion' and 'decorations' were second and third in the order of importance.[24]

Liang was not necessarily a teacher who supervised all these designs with Chinese roofs in 1954–5. Given his endorsed position and his textual output, he was in fact the theorist of the movement. In this sense, his thinking and his geo-historical trajectory are significant for analysing an epistemological basis of these designs that emerged in the mid-1950s. What are the sources of these ideas? Stalinist classicism from 1932 to 1954, marked by Boris Iofan's Palace of the Soviets in 1932 and reflected in the materialized projects including the metro stations (from 1932) and the 'Tall Buildings' (1947–54), was certainly important, given Liang's visit to Moscow in 1953.[25] The scale of the Tall Buildings, revealing Russian traditions in great 'silhouettes', certainly opened Liang to new possibilities. The interactions between Chinese architects and Russian advisors (Mukhin, Asepkov and Andreev) in Beijing in 1953–4 contributed further to the Russian influence on Liang.[26] The use of realism in art and architecture for a leftist politics was also encouraged in this connection, although this was already explored in fine arts in China before and theorized by Mao in his 'Speeches at the Seminar on Literature and Art in Yanan' in 1942, in which he also used one of Lenin's writings of 1905 ('Organization and Literature for the Party').[27]

There were also 'Western' connections, which were less acknowledged in the 1950s, but in fact had a longer tradition in

a

b

4.6a, b Two sketches of 'imaged buildings' in Liang's pamphlet *Zuguo de Jianzhu* (Architecture of the motherland), 1954.

China. Liang's later self-criticism in 1958 and 1959 acknowledged this 'dark' truth. Liang said that the ideas in 1954 were similar to that of the 'palace style' in Nanjing in the 1930s for the Kuomintang government, which in turn was based on the Beaux-Arts eclectic design philosophy established in nineteenth-century Paris.[28] Liang also said that his historical research in the 1930s and early 1940s was based on Fletcher's *History of Architecture*, which he studied at the University of Pennsylvania in the 1920s.[29] It is well known that Chinese students returning to China during and after the 1920s, and especially those from the United States, were educated predominantly in Beaux-Arts programmes. The importation of eclecticism from nineteenth-century France and Europe into China via the United States and by other routes,

4.7a, b Main Hall of Sanhuasi Temple, 1060, Datong and Wooden Pagoda of Fuguangsi Temple, 1056, Yingxian, Shanxi; ink renderings made in 1934 by Liang and assistants, published in Liang, *Zhongguo Jianzhu Shi* (A history of Chinese architecture), 1954.

a

b

山西應縣佛宮寺釋迦木塔

for the design of Chinese national forms, as tested in Nanjing of the 1930s and developed in Beijing in the 1950s, is a well-known story, although mutations on the way must be noted, especially those from the 1930s to the 1950s, an issue to return to a little later.

What is more intriguing is a deeper concept of space and form being imported, from Fletcher to Liang, and from historical research to design. If we trace a trajectory backwards in time we will be able to find this out. The tripartite theory made in 1954 by Liang involved a 'history' part and one of the key texts in this area apart from his 'characteristics' essay was his book *Zhongguo Jianzhu Shi* (A history of Chinese architecture) published in 1954. This manuscript with its drawings and renderings was in fact completed in 1944 (Figures 4.7, 4.8, 2.18).[30] These drawings and texts were based on his surveys and documentation from 1931 to the early 1940s. And this first systematic 'scientific' research on historical buildings in China, in its methods of representation, was based on Fletcher's methods, including its line drawing plates, that Liang learned at Pennsylvania in the 1920s. If Fletcher had started his first systematic line drawings for his 'world architecture' in 1901, then scholars have also pointed to his forerunner J.-N.-L. Durand, who made the first systematic line drawings for cross comparisons in 1801–19 (Figure 4.9).[31] Since Liang and his team used linear perspective drawings, ink washes, pencil sketches, techniques of chiaroscuro, plates of line drawings for universal comparisons across time and place, and also orthogonal projections in plans, elevations and sections, it is not difficult to trace the origin not only to 1901 and 1801–19, but also to a whole realistic and rationalistic representational tradition since the Renaissance when linear perspective was formalized.[32]

What is important here is that amongst many routes of transferring 'modern' Western ways of seeing into China (from Nian Xiyao of 1729–35 onwards; see Chapter 2), we find a specific moment of the gaze casting its visual rays through Liang directly onto the traditional Chinese buildings in 1931–44. The drawings and renderings of 1944, in effect, were not 'neutral' representations of Chinese buildings, but 'symbolic' ways of seeing these buildings (to borrow Erwin Panofsky's term), which turned these soft, embedded, perforated buildings into solid, isolated, heroic objects.[33] Through Liang's eyes, Chinese buildings were made to re-emerge in a new light framed by a modern Western *perspective*. When these works were published in 1954, Liang's design imagination in the two sketches was in a better position to be supported. The modern gaze and representation of the Chinese buildings of the past offered a basis on which an imagination of a modern Chinese building was attempted. This perspective was then immediately transferred into design practice which witnessed actual buildings of large scale completed in the mid-1950s.

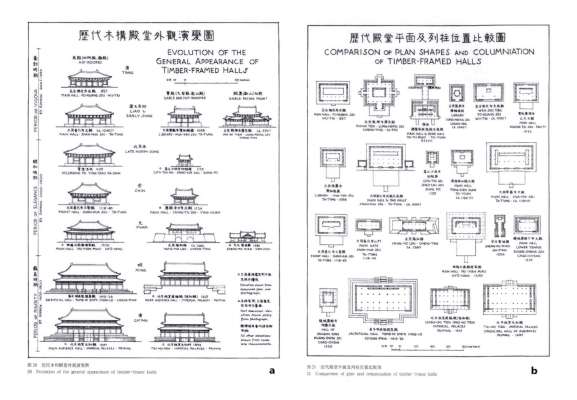

4.8a, b Two plates for comparative studies on 'Chinese architecture', 1943–4, by Liang and assistants, published in Liang, *Zhongguo Jianzhu Shi*, 1954.

A basic epistemological perspective, a Cartesian dualism of objects versus subjects, and a Cartesian gaze on a world of objects in an open, infinite, mathematical universe, were then localized and absorbed into a Chinese political–cultural production.[34] In this process, a modern subject, as a rational being behind the gazing eye upon the world of material objects, was constructed. Through recursive productions, this way of seeing informed the making of forms as objects, which then reconstituted the modern subject as reflected on and symbolized in these objects. And, if these objects assumed a national style, then they reflected, symbolized and represented a national collective subject, which was of course the People and the Republic of new China.

There were therefore three lines of development being localized into the Chinese politico-cultural context in 1954: the Soviet influence in 1953, the American Beaux-Arts design method from Pennsylvania via Nanjing of the 1930s now reaching Beijing, and the American–European method of visual representation applied to historical research on Chinese buildings in 1931–44 and now resurfacing in 1954 for creative design thinking at this moment. These developments 'intersected' in Liang and integrated in his theoretical discourse marked by the three texts and especially the third one with the two sketches, and most distinctively the one with the thirty-five-storey tower with Chinese roofs. This was the moment in history when the

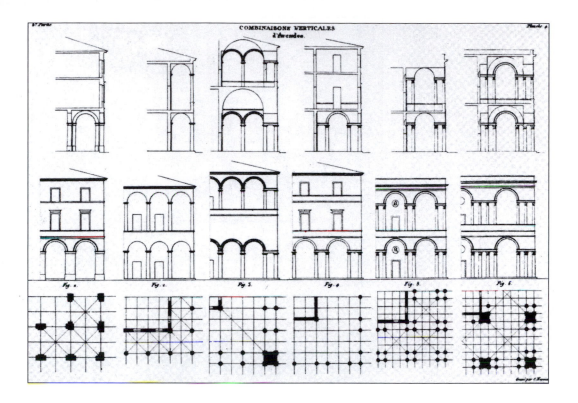

three lines, hitherto separated and 'growing' on their own, conjoined. Within the Chinese context, thanks to the new insight gained from Russian influences and from historical representations completed in 1944–54, the outlook of Chinese architects, including Liang, in Beijing of the mid-1950s was different from that in Nanjing of the 1930s. It was more open and comprehensive. The sketches of 1954 and the buildings completed then would have been unthinkable in the 1930s in terms of physical scale, vertical profile and formal flexibility (Figures 4.10, 4.11).

4.9 Designs for arcades, in Jean-Nicolas-Louis Durand, *Precis des leçons d'architecture*, vol. 2, 1819.

Interlude

Khrushchev's criticism of Stalin in late 1954, late 1955 and early 1956, first on his classical architecture and then on his statecraft, had a great impact in many countries.[35] Opening up a space for anti-Stalin movements in Poland and Hungary in 1956–7, it also encouraged the Chinese Communist Party to open itself to criticism in the 'One Hundred Flowers' movement in 1956 and early 1957. It also provided an opportunity for Mao and the Chinese Communists to depart from both Stalin's and Khrushchev's positions on many issues. Mao outlined an industrialization model different from that of Stalin ('On the ten great relationships', 1956). Mao articulated a sympathetic reading of

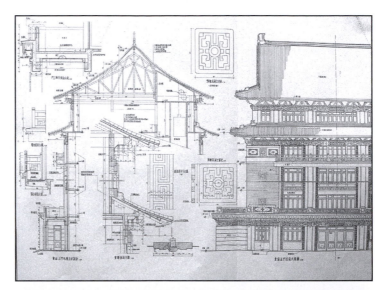

4.10 Working drawings for Xijiao Guesthouse (Friendship Hotel) by Zhang Bo, in *Jianzhu Xuebao*, 1 (1954), 46.

4.11 Cultural Palace of Nationalities, Beijing, 1959. Architect: Zhang Bo. Photo taken in 1996.

the anti-Stalin criticisms ('Contradictions within the people', 1957). China disagreed with the Soviet Union in succeeding years on other issues. In the architectural profession, there was an immediate following of Khrushchev's position, but then a gradual distancing from Soviet influences in search of a new formulation. Liang was much criticized in 1955 following the Soviet criticism of Stalin. An editorial in the *People's Daily* criticized wasteful practice and 'revivalism'.[36] The publication of the *Journal* was terminated (until August 1955). Both Party officials and Liang himself made self-criticisms in 1955. In the following year, however, different opinions could be aired in open debate. The opinions of Polish architects visiting China at the time, who praised modernism and suggested that both Stalin's classicism and Khrushchev's industrialization were 'extremes', were fully published in the first and second issues of the *Journal* of 1956.[37] Later in the year, in the August to December issues (fifth to ninth), Chinese architects discussed how to move on from the impasse left by the Soviet experience as both modernism (of Western capitalism) and the national style (of Stalin's classicism or socialist realism) were 'wrong'. Dong Dayou and Zhang Kaiji aired their views against doctrines and extremes. But it was Yang Tingbao who had the clearest and most daring voice in the December issue regarding especially Liang's position. Yang said 'national form' was necessary; even the 'big-roofs' (as Liang's ideas were nicknamed) could be used sometimes if the surrounding buildings were in that style; the key point was to develop a design that was 'socialist' and 'realist', and that Chinese architects should strive to create 'new national forms'.[38] There were surely discussions behind the scenes between Party members and perhaps with the architects as well (it is known that Zhou Yang, an art theorist of the Party, defended 'national form' in the mid-1950s).[39] In any case, by early 1957, the Party finally made its official position clear: 'we oppose revivalism, but not ideas of national form . . . we should develop new national forms that are not disconnected with history' (Zhou Rongxing's speech in February published in the March issue of the *Journal*).[40]

'New, Chinese, Socialist': the Ten Buildings and the Square, 1959

Arising from a mixture of factors, including a deepening of criticism of the Party inside China and an increasing tension with the United States over Taiwan (despite China's constructive efforts since 1954), a radical attitude erupted in Mao and counterattacks started both internally and internationally.[41] In China, Mao launched the Anti-Rightist Campaign against the critics in June 1957, a radical, assertive leftist position that Mao never abandoned in the following years and decades (and that culminated in the tragic Cultural Revolution in 1966–76). In international affairs, China argued with the USSR on many issues, leading to further disagreements and the Soviet Union's withdrawal of advisors and aid projects thereafter. China had worsening relations with the United States, fuelled by China's fire attack on Jinmen Island under Taiwan's rule in August 1958, America's escalating deployment in the region, and Khrushchev's further displeasure with Mao. China also had conflicts with India relating to border issues from August 1958. Within China, the swift success of 'socialist transformation' by 1956, and the successful completion of the first Five-Year Plan by 1957, together with the earlier rise of international influence and now a tense international environment, all made Mao ambitious and assertive in the final years of the decade. In this context, in 1958 Mao launched the 'Great Leap Forward' and a movement to develop 'People's Communes', intending rapid progress for China.

The profession came again under great political stress. The *Journal* dedicated three issues in 1957 and three in 1958 to Anti-Rightist criticism. Chen Zhanxiang and Hua Langhong were condemned as 'rightists' and wrote self-criticisms in the November issue of 1957. Although Liang was spared this time, he (along with Liu Dunzhen) also made self-criticisms in the November issue of 1958. The storm, however, was roaring forward, in a more 'constructive' manner. There was a rise of discursive and building activities once again in the final years of the decade. Liang, however, was no longer at the centre as in 1954. Replaced by Party leaders in the discursive formulation of design thinking, Liang was gradually sidelined in these years. This direct domination of the Party in design thinking was related to the fact that design theorization coincided and was associated with the national political project of the Ten Grand Buildings in 1958–9.

Wan Li, Deputy Mayor of Beijing, in a mobilization meeting for the architects and related professionals and officials on 8 September 1958, announced that 'national celebration projects' would be built to celebrate the tenth anniversary of the Republic in 1959, 'to test the level of productivity achieved in socialist China . . . and to answer with actions and facts . . . those who doubt that we can build a modern nation'.[42] Wan Li said that these designs could be bold; 'big-roofs' could be used; other approaches should be explored; the buildings should not be limited to one style. Zhou Enlai, in November 1958, in defence of a Western–classical composition adopted for the two largest buildings on the two sides of Tiananmen Square, said that as 'proletarian internationalists' we should be open-minded, and be prepared to adopt good ideas from anywhere, whether 'past or present, China or other countries' (*gujin zhongwai*).[43]

The square was an integral part of the national celebration projects, but was also an independent monument to the new republic, attracting the close attention of Mao Zedong and Zhou Enlai after 1949. Both, standing on Tiananmen on the opening days of the People's Republic, commented on what should be on the vast square stretching to the south.[44] In late 1958, when the design was finalized, Mao and Zhou's words were closely followed. Mao demanded that Tiananmen Square reflect a nation that had a long history, a great land with rich resources, and a large population; that it be able to accommodate one million people; and that it be the largest in the world.[45] Mao further demanded that the east and west edges of the square start with the two ends of an open court in front of Tiananmen (500 metres apart) and extend all the way down (across a distance of 880 metres) to the city wall and city gate in the south.[46] Zhou Enlai's idea specified the layout further: with the Monument to the People's Heroes at the centre, to the east and west of the square should stand a museum of history and revolution, and a great hall of the people, respectively.[47]

Design discourse continued in 1959. When the designs for the Square and the Ten Buildings were settled and constructions on the way, a conference on 'Housing Standards and Issues of Architectural Art' was organized, and was attended by all prominent architects and related Party officials in Shanghai from 18 May to 4 June 1959. Issues of form and design were thoroughly discussed and Liu Xiufeng, the Minister of Construction, made the final speech outlining effectively a theory of architecture and design from the Party's perspective. In the June, July and August issues of the *Journal*, Liang's speech was published first, followed by the speeches of nine other prominent architects (Liu Dunzhen, Ha Xiongwen, Chen Zhi, Zhao Shen, Wu Liangyong, Wang Tan, Dai Fudong, Jin Oufu and Chen Boqi, in the order of appearance in the publications). In the October–November issue, when the Ten Grand Buildings were completed, and their drawings and photos and related texts were all included, Liu's ten-page essay was published. Whereas Liang's talk was short, Liu's treatise was extensive. If Liang rephrased the accepted ideas of the time, Liu provided effectively a Party theory of design and architecture with the new official position that had emerged in 1957 and was now confirmed and evidenced in the grand buildings of Beijing. Titled 'Creating new styles for China's socialist architecture', it included a historical review of the decade, a six-part theory of design, and his recommendations for the architects.[48] Regarding design, Liu said we should 'research, study, critique and inherit traditions . . . and innovate and create ceaselessly'; the result should be those developed from the Chinese tradition, made with modern materials and technologies, and with good elements absorbed from 'past and present, China and other countries' (*gujing zhongwai*); they should be in 'new styles, new forms, that are Chinese and socialist'.[49]

The actual design and construction since late 1958 reflected these ideas clearly. Some thirty-four design institutes in Beijing and more than thirty architects and specialists nationwide were called upon to provide proposals for the Ten Buildings.[50] The list of the buildings slightly changed as some projects were postponed and others included. Based on some 400 initial proposals, the designs were finalized in October and construction soon started in late October in 1958. Totalling 673,000 m², the Ten Buildings were all completed and ready for use by September 1959, in time for the grand national day celebration on 1 October 1959. The event was presided over by Mao, Liu Shaoqi and Zhou Enlai, and attended by Khrushchev and leaders of socialist and communist parties from eighty-seven countries, a grand celebration also attended by 110,000 people in the Square and a 700,000-person parade along Changan Avenue.[51]

1   One central idea reflected in these buildings was the use of 'all good elements' from 'past and present, China and other countries'. Whereas four buildings used Chinese roofs on selected parts atop the building, two used Western–classical compositions

with long colonnades, one used a spire reminiscent of Russian features, and the remaining three used flat roofs and planar compositions. Although simple and 'modern' elements can be found in the last three, decorative Chinese motifs can also be found in them and in other buildings. The two with Western compositions, the Great Hall of the People and the Museum of Revolution and History, on the two sides of the square, also employed Chinese elements (the central bay being larger, yellow tiles on the long cornice, and other details).[52] These buildings reflected the new theory formulated since 1956–7: they were no longer restrictively 'revivalist'; 'national forms' were used and interpreted in a more flexible and complex manner; other 'good elements' were included so not all of them were purely 'Chinese'; a few were also partly 'modern'. None of the designs however were 'modernist' given the criticisms of modernism and bourgeois capitalist theories in the early 1950s. Zhang Bo, once a student of Liang, and the designer of the Cultural Palace and co-designer with Zhao Dongri of the Great Hall of the People, said that these designs were still 'eclectic' and were effectively based on the 'translatability' theory Liang articulated in 1954.[53] Liang's tripartite synthesis of political ideology, historical forms and eclectic design, in fact, survived unconsciously in Liu Xiufeng, Wan Li and Zhou Enlai's discourse. The so-called 'good elements' were treated in fact as historical styles in an eclectic manner; and the relationship between historical forms and new designs remained the same as in Liang's and the Beaux-Arts design philosophy that had been localized in China for decades already.

2   Another major idea implied in the theory but consciously used in the design was the 'grand' size of the buildings and their urban dimensions. The breakthrough of 1959, in fact, lies in this aspect. This was best reflected in the two buildings the Great Hall and the Museum, and in Tiananmen Square in between. Based on some eighty-four plans and 189 elevations, the schematic design of the Great Hall was finalized on 14 October 1958 by Zhou Enlai.[54] It was based on Zhao Dongri's design, with the floor area triple that in the initial brief when functional needs and the scale of the place around the site were carefully reconsidered. After this, the square could be finalized in its precise dimensions, and with this, the Museum on the opposite or eastern side of the square could then be designed as a balance to the Great Hall on the west. As completed, the Great Hall, 171,800 m^2 in total, contained a 10,000-seat auditorium and a 5,000-person banquet hall. It measured 174 metres east to west and 336 metres north to south, with a long flat roof at 40 metres, and a row of 20 metre-high columns on the east facing the square (Figure 4.12). On the opposite side, the Museum, with similar and smaller dimensions,

maintained a perfect balance (Figure 4.13). In between was the square measuring 500 metres east to west and 880 metres north to south, which was defined by the two buildings east and west, and the Tiananmen building and the Zhengyangmen gate tower on the north and south, and then the Monument to the People's Heroes at 38 metres tall at the centre.[55] On the north runs the east–west Changan Avenue, 80 metres wide between kerbs or 120 metres wide between walls, whereas on the south the square was linked to other quarters on a north–south axial street. Although the square can accommodate some 500,000 people, half of what Mao demanded, it followed Mao and Zhou's ideas closely in Zhao's design.

In Zhao Dongri's words, the Square was 'open and broad', 'vast and splendid', 'reflecting the revolutionary and combative

4.12 Great Hall of the People, Beijing, 1959. Architects: Zhao Dongri, Zhang Bo and others.

4.13 Museum of Chinese Revolution and Chinese History, Beijing, 1959. Architects: Zhang Kaiji and others.

4.14 Central Beijing. **a**: Before 1919. **b**: In 1959 (Building 3 was added in 1977).

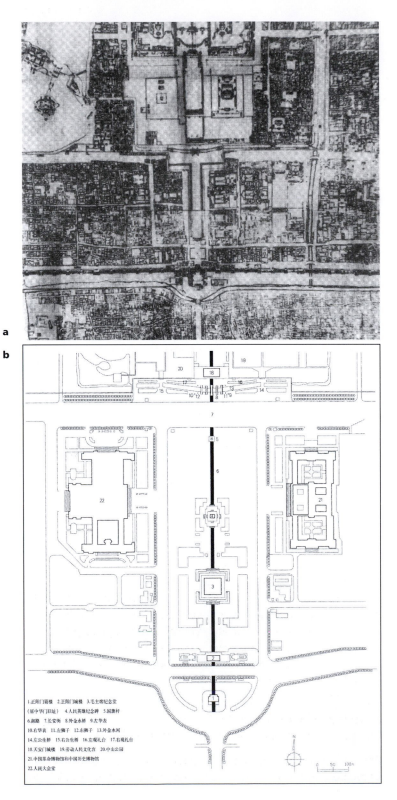

a

b

spirit of the Chinese people', accommodating functions of an unprecedented magnitude, and challenging the limits of 'feudalist layout', 'bourgeois architectural theory' and the scale of all existing squares.[56] This area of Beijing had already been gradually penetrated by new roads since the 1910s. Further clearing occurred in 1949, 1955 and 1958. By now in 1959, much of the city walls and gates around had been demolished, especially the gates and archways on the two sides of Tiananmen on the east–west avenue, the two long red walls running north–south, and a small gate connecting the walls at the south. The final clearance in 1958–9 was a culmination of these radical 'revolutions'. A new space with a logic of openness and object-based monumentality had now arrived and was inserted into an old imperial urban fabric with a spatial logic of alleyways, courtyards and walled enclosures (Figure 4.14). The Square as it emerged in 1959 marked a radical shift from one space to another, from the past to a future yet to be fully articulated. Since this spatial revolution was not total, that is, old urban fabric still survived to the north in the imperial palace and in the surrounding sea of old textures, the historical revolution in fact remained as a spatial rupture or discontinuity. Unresolved, the situation of 1959 initiated further battles and conflicts to come in the following decades with new intensities between these two types of space, with their different charms, reasons and ethical possibilities.

3 Despite this confrontation exposed in 1959, there was a consistency between the Square and the imperial palace as part of the old fabric in the north behind the Tiananmen building (Figures 4.15, 8.5). A Chinese sense of scale and horizontality survived and extended to the south across the entire square. Zhang Bo, contemplating the unprecedented height–distance ratio of 1:12.5 (40 m:500 m) on the east–west section of the square, realized that there was also a horizontal composition in the imperial Forbidden City so that sky and horizontal lines were of primary significance, a pattern that surely reappeared in the square.[57] Zhou Dongri, in describing the Square stretching east, west and south in the endless avenues, also said that it absorbed an 'excellent and superb form-and-propensity' (*xingshi*) of the imperial palace and imperial parks developed over centuries at the north, and that the Square extended 'a deep distance on the north–south direction in a Chinese tradition'.[58]

A space of the state, 1949–59: achievements, problems and possibilities

At the end of the first decade of the Republic, a comprehensive landscape of symbolic forms of the new state was constructed. It included not

4.15 Tiananmen Square viewed from the south, Beijing, 1959.

only iconic symbols such as the emblem and the Monument, but also formal architectural language such as 'national forms' and 'new styles', as well as urban planning schemes, infrastructural and building constructions, and finally the urban centre of Beijing at Tiananmen Square. Situated in a historical perspective, the achievements, legacies and problems of this landscape in political and formal terms may be observed.

1. In political terms, we can identify two issues. First, what was achieved here was surely a space of the nation-state on a symbolic and socio-spatial level. In so far as the state was a 'People's Republic', great gestures were made to involve the 'people' of the nation (in the collective design process, in the scale of parades and ceremonies, in the size of the space), in order to constitute a socialist public in spatial terms in the urban design but also in symbolic expression and in real social practice. But can this space and society accommodate new practices? What happens if the public or the people begin to employ the space for new purposes that have not been programmed or not happened before? Incidents that occurred afterwards especially in the more liberal but also uncertain times of the 1980s revealed this problem vividly. They demonstrated an unresolved definition of the public and public space of China as a whole and of this square in particular.

Second, as a symbolic landscape of the nation-state, it was a space of objects and, with this, a realm of constructed 'subjects' and subjective identities. These were national collective identities, the 'People' of the Republic and the Chinese nation. They included the five 'stars' or classes or groups of the people under the leadership of the proletarian workers and the Party as the vanguard. But can this space and society accommodate new identities of the people? What happens if the composition of the people evolves, overlaps and mutates, with more urbanites and professionals, more 'urban petite bourgeoisie', 'capitalists' and other social groups emerging? What happens if the groups also multiply or fragment into 'individuals'? How are these new subjectivities to identify themselves in this space of the People's Republic? History has witnessed these developments in the post-Mao period after 1976 and the political turbulence that ensued. In other words, how to rearrange and redefine space and society so that new identities can be accommodated remains an issue for the square and for China as whole.

2. In formal aspects, two issues should also be raised. First, what was achieved here in this symbolic space of the state was a 'national form'. This form on the one hand was hybrid and international, and on the other involved the basic conception of a space of objects. In this latter aspect, it opened up a landscape of heroic objects with openness and monumentality alien to the traditional Chinese urban fabric of dense and small enclosures. Because of this, it opened up a conflict

4.16 Central Beijing on the Changan Avenue in 2002.

between the two spaces that was not resolved then and is still ongoing with new intensity in the conditions of the 1990s and today.

Second, this was not a generic landscape of objects, but a specific one in a horizontal profile around the centre of Beijing as it emerged and was defined in 1959. Later developments maintained this low and horizontal skyline in consistency with the square and ultimately with the imperial Forbidden City at the centre. In this sense the square of 1959 had established a modern Beijing as a horizontal city of horizontal objects, which is now more pronounced in 2008 as new landmarks have been added within and around the second ring road (Figure 4.16).

Beijing, form and the architect

With these observations in mind, questions raised at the beginning of this chapter concerning Beijing, formal production and individual architects can be answered. For the city of Beijing, from the historical perspective of a traditional city ending its imperial status in 1911 and undergoing transformations in the twentieth century, the 1950s and especially 1959 were decisive moments, when the old city was qualitatively altered and a new mode of space, a space of modern objects in a horizontal profile, a 'European' substance in a 'Chinese' composition, was established. A pattern of modern Beijing was established in 1959 which became clearer in the following decades, including the active 1990s and the early twenty-first century. A trajectory of urban spatial change in Beijing from 1911 to 2008 via 1959 can thus be traced.

Regarding the production of national forms or the national style, there were Chinese as well as Western and Soviet sources. Various Chinese elements were employed: the selected colours, the decorative motifs, the specific types such as the stele, the prominent features including the roof, the outlines and proportions of an ancient building, and a more hidden use of scale and horizontality. These elements were identified and reorganized through a subjective and creative practice. In particular, the core body of these sources, the grammar of 'Chinese architecture' with nine features centring on the roof, was based on Liang's historical research from 1931 to 1944 as employed in 1954. The tradition of 'Chinese architecture' was *created*, through not only a new method of 'seeing' in historical investigation and representation (1931–44) but also a political use in the making of the national style (1954). Through this epistemological–political transformation, historical sources were *made* to become 'national' forms, for a modern 'nation-state' of China then under active construction.

The separate entries of Soviet and American models and their integration in Beijing in the 1950s were significant at many levels. Liang's visits, writings and sketches in 1953–4 constituted the moment in history when these lines of influence conjoined. In particular, post-Renaissance or classical 'modern' ways of seeing and representing, of conceiving forms and objects, were brought into China in urban and architectural production in 1953–4 through these communist and capitalist influences, in design and in historical research. The sketches of 1954 and the designs of the mid- and late 1950s were therefore more open and generous than the mindset of Nanjing of the 1930s. The 1950s inherited the 1930s but also added new perspectives not attained before.

Finally, we have to consider the role of the architect in relation to power and authority in such an environment. Discussion here has to be situated in the narrow historical corridor that China was passing through. Given the overall disintegration of imperial China, the weakness of a capitalist-bourgeois regime sliding into fascist dictatorship in the 1930s while facing a powerful Japanese invasion, and a growing hostility between capitalism and communism worldwide in the following decades, a radical communist revolution in China before 1949 and its ongoing assertive stance afterwards seem inevitable. In this context, a 'proletarian dictatorship' under the Party appears also to have been inevitable. In such a context, there was no room for architects to think with individual and professional autonomy. To locate the centre to the west for conservation of the old city (as in the Liang-Chen Plan), to develop modernism for a more abstract expression of Chinese culture (as in Hua Lanhong's Children's Hospital, Beijing, 1952), to explore abstract, critical and independent positions opposing mainstream practice (as the young Chinese have been doing now since the late 1990s), were historically not possible. The architects and the Party had entered, as it were, a binding 'contract' from which no one could escape. What should be appreciated is that, despite all that, the architects had offered their skills and knowledge for the political task of representing the new Republic. They found a special terrain where 'old' skills could be employed. They employed a 'Western' body of knowledge in a classical or nineteenth-century stage of modern architecture, and developed a national style for a modern nation-state in China. Modernism and critical practice were not possible in the 1950s, yet a classical stage of modern architecture in China, in historical hindsight, had now reached its greatest manifestation in Beijing by 1959, in a relentless power–knowledge contract that dominated the country at that time.

CHAPTER 5

THE 1980s AND 1990s

Liberalization

The quantity and efficiency of design practice in China today are impressive indeed; but are there interesting and persistent design positions emerging from this practice? How to locate and analyse them in the context? In this chapter I would like to outline a historical and international context in which new design currents and positions, especially those of the new generation, can be located and examined. I find it necessary to view the rise of the positions historically, so that they can be comprehended in the immediate context of contemporary China and, significantly, in a longer history of modern architecture in China. According to my observation, a modern tradition had already been formed before the opening of the contemporary era, a backdrop that must be included for a study on contemporary design positions.

Since modernization in China was driven by external or Western forces rather than internal dynamics at the earliest moments, 'modern' and 'Western' architecture cannot be historically separated in China. The earliest moments of modern, Western architecture in China may be found in the mid-eighteenth century when Western-style buildings, eminently the Xiyanglou (literally 'Western-style pavilions') at the Changchunyuan garden in Beijing brought into China large-scale masonry constructions and issues or problems of 'style'. After 1840, colonial settlements in treaty ports across China opened up a new stage in which historicist and neo-classical architecture of European origins were introduced. The end of the Chinese empire in 1911 and a fragmented nation in the following years opened up a new phase when Western designs and construction methods were introduced. The use of Chinese roofs on modern structures was first experimented with by Western architects for missionary institutions (universities and hospitals) in China, to facilitate a localization of Christian missions. The formal language then 'leapt' onto a new project.

Chinese students, after studying architecture in Japan, America and Europe, returned and established design practice from the early 1920s. The first nation-state of China, under the leadership of the Kuomintang or Nationalist Party, was established in 1927 with Nanjing as its national capital. Modern 'scientific' architecture in combination with 'native Chinese style' was promoted by the government and embraced to a considerable extent by the Chinese architects, an alliance that produced a substantial group of 'Chinese style' architecture in

Nanjing and other cities in the 1930s. As a group or socio-historical phenomenon, this is the first moment or first production of a 'Chinese' and 'modern' architecture, with the Beaux-Arts design philosophy the Chinese students had absorbed from their overseas education, a design model that was then also prevalent in the more advanced countries where they had studied, and especially in the United States.

After the Second World War and the civil war, the People's Republic of China was established in Beijing in 1949 under Mao Zedong and the Chinese Communist Party. After a few years of Russian influence the 1950s saw a second wave of this formal language under a different ideology: 'Socialist Content with National Form'. Socialist functionalism, more efficient and economic, gradually dominated the country in the 1960s and 1970s. There was also a short period when a political expressionism emerged in the early 1970s after the Cultural Revolution, in which large sculptural forms such as stars and red flags were applied to many public buildings. All this came to an end in the late 1970s. Mao passed away in 1976; after that Deng Xiaoping assumed leadership in 1978, and then introduced reform and open-door policies. The following decades, the 1980s and 1990s, saw a dynamic transformation driven by market reform and modernization, resulting in urbanization on a grand scale and intensive building construction throughout the country, turning China into the largest building site in the world today.

Against this historical background, 'contemporary China' may be best defined as post-Maoist starting from 1976, a turning point in the gradual transformation of China from a Marxist–Leninist–Stalinist vanguard to a secular market economy. It is also important to identify a modern tradition in architecture formed before 1976. The legacy of this tradition in post-1976 China, the continuations of and the revolts against it, must be comprehended so that current design positions can be contextualized.

An international perspective is also needed. China has not been 'isolated' in the world history of modern architecture. China was historically a recipient of Western (and of Japanese and later on Russian) influences in the process of developing its modern architecture. This has been the case since, at the latest, 1840, when China was partially colonized, when foreign architects practised in China after the 1860s, and when Chinese after studying abroad (notably in the United States) returned and imported the Beaux-Arts system in practice and education beginning in the 1920s. After 1949, the Soviet Russian influence contained elements of Beaux-Arts eclecticism. At the same time, the education system established in the 1920s exerted deep influences after 1949 in basic design philosophy despite the ideological shift towards socialism. After 1976, overseas influences from the West (and Japan and parts of Asia) entered China once again. Many Chinese went and are still going to these countries to study. Foreign and Western designs and theories are introduced and studied. Despite the dramatic historical change and the overall success of China in building a modern economy and nationhood on the world stage, China has been and still is 'behind' the West. A linear and progressive perspective is therefore necessary in reading modern Chinese architecture against the historical development of modern architecture in the West.

A modern tradition before 1976

In China, architecture as it developed up to 1976 can be summarized in three streams.[1] The first involves the use of Chinese roofs and decorative details on modern structures for modern functions (Figure 5.1). After initial experiments by Western architects for missionary institutions such as Henry Murphy's Yanching University Campus (Beijing, 1926), Chinese architects produced many buildings in the 1930s under the promotion of the Nationalist Party in Nanjing. The primary example must be the spectacular Mausoleum for Dr Sun Yat-sen by Lu Yanzhi (Nanjing, 1929). In the 1950s, under the Communist Party in Beijing, architecture of socialist realism or 'Socialist Content with National Form' was promoted. The eclectic design method was employed again for more buildings, often at a larger scale, in the capital and elsewhere. The Friendship Hotel by Zhang Bo (Beijing, 1956) and some of the Ten Grand Projects such as the Palace of Nationalities and the Beijing Railway Station (by Zhang Bo and Yang Tingbao respectively, 1959) are the primary examples. In some important cases, such as the two Grand Projects to the east and west of Tiananmen Square, that is, the Museum of Revolution and History and the Great Hall of the People (by Zhang Kaiji, Zhao Dongri and Zhang Bo, Beijing, 1959), Chinese roofs were not used but decorative motifs were applied extensively. All these buildings, from the 1910s to the 1950s, were designed by architects trained in a school with Beaux-Arts influences outside of

5.1 China Art Gallery, Beijing, 1962. Architect: Dai Nianci. Photo taken in 1997.

China, most notably in the United States (especially at the University of Pennsylvania), or in a school in China which adopted a predominantly Beaux-Arts approach (especially at the Central University of Nanjing from 1927–8 onwards). The Beaux-Arts approach allowed the use of a religious or imperial style as a classical language in an eclectic synthesis with modern steel and concrete structures for public and state functions, thus turning a classical tradition into a national and public language. The National Style thus developed in these decades is therefore a Chinese version of the neo-classical architecture produced around the world after its development in Europe in the eighteenth and nineteenth centuries.

The second stream is the political expressionism that occurred for a short period around 1970. As a consequence of radical campaigns of the Cultural Revolution, popular and literal icons such as large portraits of Mao, characters of revolutionary slogans, and sculptures of red flags, red torches and the 'revolutionary masses' in a socialist-realist genre were applied on or around the buildings, as in the Yangtze River Bridge (Figure 5.2), Chengdu Exhibition Hall and Changsha Exhibition Hall (1968, 1969 and the early 1970s). The last such design may be the Memorial Hall of Chairman Mao to the south of Tiananmen Square completed in 1977. This trend first emerged in the buildings of Tiananmen Square by 1959 where literal icons were applied. Since this expressionism started from and also ended in Tiananmen Square (1959 and 1977), and the icons were the added-on elements such as the roof and the decorative details, and since the architects were of the same generation who had first used the Chinese roof and details, this was methodologically an extension of the Beaux-Arts tradition in China, an extension that had acquired a more popular and realist tendency in the 1970s.

The third current includes aspects of modernism that emerged in China from time to time but never quite blossomed at a critical

5.2 Yangtze River Bridge, Nanjing, 1968. Architect: Department of Architecture at Nanjing Institute of Technology. Photo taken in 1997.

and experimental level. Ladislaus Hudec's Grand Theatre and the Wu Residence in Shanghai (1933 and 1937) and Dong Dayou's own residence in Shanghai (1935) were art deco with modernist treatment of walls, roofs and windows. Xi Fuquan's Hongqiao Sanatorium in Shanghai (1934) and Yang Tingbao's few buildings, including the Yanhuiguan villa (Nanjing, 1948), were modernist with art deco traces. Tong Jun's Apartment Blocks (Nanjing, 1947) were arguably the most thoroughly modernist. Yet modernism had never been quite absorbed in China in the 1930s and 1940s for many reasons but perhaps essentially because of a backward economy and a weak government, and finally the war in the 1940s. In the early 1950s under the Communist Party, when socialist realism had not yet reached a dominant position, functionalist modernism with formal innovations was experimented with, as in the important cases of the Children's Hospital by Hua Lanhong (Beijing, 1952), the Peace Hotel by Yang Tingbao (Beijing, 1952) and the Teaching Hospital by Feng Jizhong (Wuhan, 1954)

5.3 Children's Hospital, Beijing, 1954. Architect: Hua Lanhong.

5.4 Apartment Blocks for Foreign Diplomats, Beijing, 1973–5. Architect: Beijing Municipal Institute of Architectural Design.

(Figure 5.3). They were criticized as architects were soon requested to adopt socialist realism with the Chinese national style. In the 1960s and 1970s, functionalist modernism became prevalent in large-scale public buildings such as airports, stadiums, gymnasiums, exhibition halls, department stores, some apartment blocks and, at a crude and rudimentary level, all public housing designs (Figure 5.4). This may be regarded as a type of socialist modernism, as it was rational and functionalist with a clear idea that architecture was to serve the masses and the state.

Among these cases, there were only a few moments when architecture might have developed into an individualist, experimental and autonomous discipline. The early modernism in Shanghai and Nanjing in the 1930s and late 1940s and the modernist designs in the early 1950s displayed such a possibility. However, on account of fundamental problems (a backward economy, a low level of industrialization, lack of a strong government, international hostility and ideological control), a favourable social environment was not available and such opportunities for critical experiments were quickly closed off. The rest of the development, that is, the mainstream design practice before 1976 in China, ensured architecture the position of a servant to society and the state. In the case of socialist modernism, architecture was to serve large, public, collective functions. In the case of the National Style including its political expressionism, architectural form was determined from 'outside', from the need to adorn styles and icons upon the buildings, to be viewed as images accessible to the population. It is an architecture of decoration, an architecture of social and socialist realism. The ideas or content expressed though these images concerned grand narratives of the nation, its grand tradition, its heroic revolution and its glorious future. The Sun Yat-sen Mausoleum of Nanjing in 1929, and Tiananmen Square of Beijing in 1959 may be considered the extreme moments of the National Style representing the nation-state of China. On the grand and steep steps of the first, or across the vast and dry landscape of the second, the Chinese people may feel greatly inspired and deeply moved for the great cause of revolution from which a modern nation will arise, yet they may also witness a desert with no concern for existential beings or persons. Existential beings or persons have to be as it were disciplined, chastised and even sacrificed so that the spectacle of a grand nation can be staged. There were historical and perhaps cultural reasons for such a tough and grand space to be made in modern China, yet a person-based, humanistic critique must also be raised.

In the modern tradition thus developed, as in the mainstream before 1976, there was no concern for architecture as an autonomous discipline with its internal disciplinary knowledge. There was no concern for the art of building-in-itself, the analytical, tectonic relations in the use of material and the method of construction. Nor was there a concern for space or the spatial experience of the person. Along with these was a lack of concern for a grounded or personal being and its reading and experience, or a lack of concern for spatial experience meaningful to the visitors or users as existential subjects. This, in turn, was related to an overall lack of liberal social space in the decades of revolution for national independence and socialist campaigns.

In Europe and the United States in the eighteenth and nineteenth centuries, and in many other countries thereafter, neo-classical architecture based on the Beaux-Arts design principles were used to represent the modern nation-state.[2] This is the case not only in the capitalist, bourgeois nation-states, but also in the socialist, proletarian countries such as the Soviet Union. In other words, the ideological division was less important, whereas a certain design language, capable of transforming traditional styles into the image of the nation and the state, served for all kinds of modern republics whether socialist or capitalist. Since this architecture represented the earliest or classical phase of modern (bourgeois or proletarian) state and society, it can be regarded as the 'first modern' in architecture. If this is the case, then it can be argued that modern architecture in its first or classical phase had been localized and by 1976 fully established in China through decades of use and development of the National Style.

After 1976: a social landscape

The radical change in China seems difficult to explain. Yet, if we observe closely, the desire to modernize the nation has been a central goal throughout China's modern history despite various interruptions. The resurfacing of this goal, together with changing conditions inside and outside the country, ensured a gradual although turbulent transition from a radical vanguard of Marxism–Leninism in the earlier decades of the twentieth century to the 'socialist market economy' of the 1990s. The aging of Mao, the disasters of the Cultural Revolution, the rise of the technological and defence capabilities of China, the conflict with the Soviet Union, the opening dialogue with the United States, besides other factors, contributed to the easing of confrontation with the West in the 1970s, and a general trend towards openness and pragmatism thereafter. With Deng Xiaoping assuming national leadership in 1978, the 'four modernizations' programme and the reform and open-door policies were introduced, initiating a long process of transformation. In hindsight, the process may be regarded as involving two phases, the 1980s and 1990s, with 1989 as a dividing point. The first decade was characterized by grand idealistic debate with a profound uncertainty, and a successful rural reform but an increasingly difficult urban reform with rising corruption. The conflict between the need for further privatization and the need for social stability, between corruption and social critique, and between a neo-liberal/conservative elite and a rising social critique based on ideals of equity and 'democracy' voiced by students, erupted in the late 1980s and culminated in the tragic violence at Tiananmen Square in 1989. The 1990s started with stronger state control and a further opening up of the market economy after Deng's speech in 1992. The neo-liberal and neo-conservative package was further implemented with apparent ease and success. The 'socialist market economy', now fully installed, allowed a liberal market economy to prosper alongside or within the strong centralist state under the Communist Party. This package has delivered an apparent social stability together with a staggering economic growth rate, which has been continuously the highest in the world. Yet underlying problems, notably income disparity, environmental pollution and the neglect of social welfare, are accumulating at the same time.

A different society and state have emerged. Ideologically, there has been a shift from the radical Left of the 1960s to a 'central' position of the late 1990s with a mixture of socialism, statism and market capitalism, in a neo-liberal and neo-conservative combination. Marxist indoctrination in all spheres of life up to 1976 has now given way to the open, secular, non-ideological and materialist culture of the 1990s. The package of a strong state with an open market economy secured an efficient process of production, which employed cheap resources inland and exported goods to the world, an efficient turnover cycle which has attracted ever more foreign direct investment (FDI) (by now China's FDI is one of the largest in the world). The sustained high growth rate thus achieved, in turn, brings about increasing income disparity and environmental degradation with their threats to stability and development, but also an expanding middle class and an emerging civil society with an ambivalent attitude towards the government.

The speeding up of communication across socio-geographical space is an important factor. Some time in the early 1990s, space inside the nation and between the nation and the world was dramatically compressed, with a much faster infrastructure of communication networks installed, for the surging flood of ideas, capital, goods and human movement to travel across this space. Airports and seaports have been built or upgraded, while highways have quickly emerged, extended and interlinked into regional and national networks. Mobile phones, broadband internet and other facilities of information technology have emerged dramatically and have been quickly embraced by the population. All these contribute to the speeding up of communication and of the cycle of production and profit-making.

The result for the building industry is brutal and demanding: the task is to build the largest amount of floor area in the shortest time, to house the fast-expanding commercial and production spaces and the fast-growing urban population, and also to cater for exuberant property development and market speculation. This has entailed a process of demolition of parts of old cities. The result, as we see it today in many Chinese cities, is a scene of exuberant skylines of high-rises above a 'thousand plateaus' of demolition and construction, surrounded in turn by a sea of roads, car traffic and human movement.

The city is expanding in all directions, with increasing densities and physical magnitude, in a rush to accommodate some 15–17 million new members of the urban populace each year. Speed and scale are the two crucial factors. With the scale of urbanization, cities are growing into city regions in various directions. With the speed of development, there are eruptions of demolition and construction on sites unevenly distributed in or around a city, a rising sharp disparity in socio-economic statuses and material quality, a new juxtaposition of urban and rural textures (urban quarters in rural settings and vice versa) and a radical difference between spaces and urban quarters often in close proximity. This brings about a new 'city' or urban–rural landscape of extreme difference and heterogeneity.

For architects, China now provides the largest market. Under pressures for speed and quantity, Chinese architects are possibly the 'busiest in the world', being some 2500 times as efficient as an American architect, as estimated by Rem Koolhaas.[3] Design has been fully computerized in the 1990s, enabling architects to design quickly (but also to replicate designs easily). In 1994–5, a registration system was re-established after four decades of absence, allowing architects to obtain licensure and establish private practice. In the past ten years, private design firms and studios have mushroomed, adding a significant new dimension to the profession. Foreign architects entered the scene in the early 1980s. In the late 1990s and especially after 2001 (when China joined the WTO and won its bid to host the 2008 Olympic Games) the number has increased significantly. While large commercial firms have established branch offices in China in the 1990s, small and 'edgy' architects mostly from Europe have won competitions in recent years. As the market opens up, competition becomes intensive for everyone, with a tendency for large firms or star architects from abroad to win the largest commissions. At the moment, there are state-owned design institutes, private ateliers, international architects and, importantly, hybrid and shifting combinations among them. Collaborations between Chinese and foreign architects are commonplace now, which facilitates a process of learning from architects from abroad for the Chinese architects. There were criticisms of overseas architects taking the best commissions in China, yet the government clearly has larger concerns for China in the context of global economic practice and global image. It is clearly committed to fair rules of international competition as well as China's and Beijing's images on the world stage. In this situation, as far as architectural ideas and innovations are concerned, there are in principle no barriers in China: any idea may be realized somewhere in China, as long as the conditions are favourable.

There has been at the same time a change in the social position of architects in China. If they were free professionals in the 1920s, 1930s and 1940s but requested to serve the state to develop a modern national image for public buildings, if they were then 'nationalized' from the 1950s to 1976 in socialist China into state-owned design institutes working collectively for society, they are now once again professionals with great freedom. This freedom was already available in the 1980s, and was finally institutionalized in 1994–5 with the new registration system for practising architects. They are now increasingly market-oriented, whether working in private offices or in state-owned design institutes. They are moving out of the sphere of influence of central authority in both design ideas and financial support. This is particularly true for the young and middle-aged architects leading private offices or autonomous units inside the institutes. With the support of the market, they are gaining a relative independence from the state. What is the effect of this on their design ideas? This connection between design ideas and the newly obtained social space in the market economy is critical and deserves further discussion.

After 1976: architectural currents and positions

Against an overall background of designs of mixed qualities, and against a very disparate urban landscape with crude use of icons and forms, there are nevertheless important streams emerging in the 1980s and new currents in the 1990s.[4]

Among three design streams in the 1980s, the first may be called 'neo-National Style'. There was a wide range of approaches from straight revivalism to creative use of traditional Chinese elements with Post-Modern influences. Dai Nianci (Guest House, Qufu, Shangdong, 1985), Zhang Jinqiu ('Tang-dynasty' hotel complex and Historical

5.5 Western Railway Station, Beijing, 1996. Architect: Zhu Jialu. Photo taken in 1997.

5.6 Fragrant Hill Hotel, Beijing, 1982. Architect: I. M. Pei. Photo taken in 1997.

Museum, Xian, 1988 and 1991) and Zhu Jialu (Western Railway Station, Beijing, 1996) can be regarded as the leading architects in this respect (Figure 5.5).

The second stream may be described as 'modern vernacular'. Instead of employing Chinese roofs of the imperial tradition as in the National Style, a regional, vernacular language (including pitched roofs, traditional window patterns, wall textures in vernacular houses) is employed in a design which is also consciously modern or abstract. I. M. Pei's Fragrant Hill Hotel (Beijing, 1982) was the finest example although it may be regarded as an exception as it was designed by a Chinese-American with a very different formal trajectory based in the United States (Figure 5.6). Denton Corker Marshall's Australian Embassy in Beijing (1982–92) also reinterpreted walled compounds in traditional Beijing in a modern and abstract language. In the works designed by the Chinese, brick walls are often used, and the design tends to be more iconic with Post-Modern influences, and sometimes more neo-classical or late modern in massing. In this sense,

5.7 Meiyuan Memorial Museum, Nanjing, 1988. Architect: Qi Kang.

5.8 New Library at Tsinghua University, Beijing, 1991. Architect: Guan Zhaoye. Photo taken in 1997.

5.9 School of Architecture at Tianjin University, 1990. Architect: Peng Yigang. Photo taken in 1997.

this approach is also related to a late modern formalism with heroic massing and axial layout revealing in fact a legacy of the Beaux-Arts principles. Examples include Qi Kang's Meiyuan Memorial Museum (Nanjing, 1988), Wu Liangyong's Juer Hutong Houses (Beijing, 1992), Guan Zhaoye's New Library at Tsinghua University (Beijing, 1991), Liu Li's Yanhuang Art Gallery (Beijing, 1991), Shen Sanling's School of Theological Studies (Beijing, 1999) and Cui Kai's Fongzeyuan Restaurant and Foreign Language Press (Beijing, 1995, 1999) (Figures 5.7, 5.8). The late modern end of this approach can be found in Peng Yigang's architectural department building at Tianjin University (Tianjin, 1990), Bu Zhengwei's terminal building at Jiangbei Airport (Chongqing, 1991) and many memorial projects by Qi Kang, as well as those of a younger generation such as Xu Weiguo and Hu Yue (Figure 5.9).

The third is the International Style for high-rise hotels and offices, a relatively anonymous phenomenon which has significance in China historically, as its arrival in the 1980s marked the arrival of commercial

5.10 Great Wall Hotel, Beijing, 1983. Architect: Beckett International. Photo taken in 1997.

modernism on a large scale and in quantity. The Great Wall Hotel by Beckett International (Beijing, 1983) is one of the earliest International Style buildings to be built in Beijing after 1976 (Figure 5.10). Today the trend continues in which commercial modernism incorporates cultural icons, such as the Jinmao building in Pudong (Shanghai, 2000), designed by Skidmore, Owing and Merrill with East China Architecture Design Institute (ECADI). Among designs by the Chinese the earliest examples after 1976 include the White Swan Hotel by She Junnan (Guangzhou, 1983) and International Hotel by Lin Leyi (Beijing, 1987). These last two examples also share traits with a heroic, late modern formalism as identified in Peng, Bu, Qi, Xu and Hu above.

These three streams have continued in the 1990s and today, although they are also mutating and encountering criticism especially in the case of the neo-National Style. In the dynamic design practice of the late 1990s, two new currents have emerged. One is the use of neutral, abstract forms for the largest projects currently under construction in China. This may be regarded as 'super-modernism', which extends modernism to a larger scale and often with a dynamic, post-rational and sublime aesthetic as a consequence of 'deconstruction' in the West.[5] In China's socialist market economy, the state is actively leading the projection of an image of progress and modernization on the global stage with instant visibility and market consequences. To produce marks of distinction in global media and for global competition, and also in relation to the 2008 Beijing Olympic Games (and the 2010 World Expo in Shanghai), state and municipal governments have proposed to build large-scale cultural facilities in Beijing, Shanghai and Guangzhou. Through design competitions, many European architects with portfolios in the new and radical modernism of the 1990s won the commissions. If the Grand Theatre in Shanghai (1998) by Jean-Marie Charpentier with East China Architecture Design Institute (ECADI) was a forerunner, more projects are now under

5.11 National Grand Theatre, Beijing, 2007. Architect: Paul Andreu. Photo taken in 2007.

construction or have recently completed in Beijing. These include the new headquarters of China Central Television (CCTV) by Rem Koolhaas (with ECADI), the National Olympic Stadium by Herzog & de Meuron with China Architecture Design and Research Group (CAG), and the National Grand Theatre by Paul Andreu, among others (Figure 5.11).

At the same time, a modernism on another scale is developing. Around 1996–7, a new current not seen before in China emerged, and it has been expanding in recent years.[6] This is a tectonic modernism that comes from Chinese architects of a younger generation. Exemplified by the works of Yung Ho Chang, Liu Jiakun, Wang Shu, Cui Kai and many others emerging more recently, such as Tong Ming, there is a persistent interest in tectonics and in 'architecture in itself'. This includes a minimalist treatment of materials, an analytical opening of tectonic relations, and a focus on space and spatial experience with a careful use of light, texture and space in between. In an attempt to challenge the mainstream tradition formed in the 1970s, the idea here is to search for an autonomous architecture that may resist 'external' demands and the burden of modern Chinese tradition. As we have reviewed above, such an attempt to explore a purist, experimental modernism with an individual's own research focus, briefly attempted from the 1930s to 1980s in some limited cases (Xi Fuquan, Tong Jun, Yang Tingbao, Hua Lanhong and Feng Jizhong), had never really occurred as a consistent phenomenon in China's modern history until the late 1990s. Who are these architects? Under what social circumstances are they developing their ideas and what are their propositions?

Autonomy as a progressive and critical force in China

Born in the late 1950s or early 1960s, and now in their mid- or late forties, they were the first generation of architects educated in China after the Cultural Revolution.[7] They entered universities from 1977–8 onwards, and received a liberal education in post-Mao China, where books and journals from outside and Chinese translations of polemical texts from abroad became available on campus. With the opening of the country to the outside, some also went overseas to study (mostly in the United States, Europe and Japan). Some also practised and taught there before returning to China.[8]

Many of them are running their own private offices. Others work in semi-autonomous units in state-owned design institutes. Their design practice is market-oriented and market-based. With a liberal education, a cosmopolitan outlook, and importantly the support of the market, they are gaining relative autonomy from state authority in design ideas and financial support. This autonomy in turn is tolerated by the authorities in the socialist market economy. In such conditions, these architects are free professionals. They are part of the new and growing middle class who are market-dependent and who are also enjoying, and helping generate, a liberal civil and public sphere. The more vocal of them also share a more critical voice through a network of architects, artists, writers and critical intellectuals. The liberal socio-economic space now available to the architects, and their independent and sometimes critical design ideas, are interrelated in this historical environment.

In terms of their social engagement, they are gaining a position as well as an important social space. (1) They have attained a degree of autonomy. (2) They are asserting a level of authorship as some of the best of them write, lecture and publish arguing for their own ideas and approaches. (3) They have their own discursive space, which includes university classrooms, traditional media such as journals and books, and importantly a public space on the web (abbs.com.cn and far2000.com). (4) There is an international space in which they collaborate directly with architects from abroad for projects inside China, and more recently on projects abroad as well. (5) For the more influential in the generation, there is an international audience for their ideas and designs through forums and exhibitions organized by cultural institutions around the world and especially in Europe. (6) There is also a tolerance of them by state authority, and a degree of support from property developers which has facilitated innovative formal breakthroughs (but also purchased the design as symbolic capital for branding in the market).

In terms of their design ideas, the central proposition is the need to claim an 'architecture in itself', an autonomy of the discipline, from the overwhelming demands of society and the state in modern China as accumulated by the 1970s.[9] The focus is on an autonomous disciplinary knowledge within architecture, which included a purist treatment of materials, an analytical exposure of construction or relations between parts of a construction, and a sensitive design of space and spatial experience with close attention paid to light, texture, small space in between, and the aura of spaces in the experience of residing in or visiting the building. The underlying concern here engages with a personal subjectivity in an immediate existence. Starting in the late 1990s, in such works as Yung Ho Chang's Book-Bike Store (Beijing 1996), Liu Jiakun's Hedouling Studio (Chengdu, 1997), and Wang Shu's Chenmo Studio (Haining, 1998), the purist and tectonic modernism today also expands to an abstract regionalism and perhaps a critical urbanism. But the overall agenda remains that of an analytical and critical architecture in the Chinese historical context. The agenda as Chang has expressed it is to subvert the Beaux-Arts tradition accumulated by the late 1970s, which has been continuing today with many Post-Modern variations.[10] The agenda, in other words, is to challenge the decorative realism in the Chinese modern tradition that was based on external demands for external images, with a new architecture of autonomy based on internal disciplinary values.

If we pause here for a moment and compare the new approach with the Beaux-Arts-based National Style, there is indeed a progressive agenda to surpass the modern Chinese tradition.[11] In almost all aspects, the current new architecture opposes and is subversive of that tradition. Whereas the National Style is an architecture designed from 'outside' in political dependence and in design process, the new architecture is explored from 'within' in search of social and formal autonomy. Whereas the first is an architecture of realism in the sense that it serves the popular taste, the new architecture insists on a design of abstraction that resists popular appropriation. Whereas the first is primarily semantic and expressive, the second is syntactic and relational. Whereas the first expresses grand narratives of the nation-state and its classical or imperial tradition to the masses, the second unfolds quietly a minor narrative of a local context, tradition or a specific theme, in the immediate spatial experience of the person.[12]

There is a variety of design approaches among these architects. Cui Kai and Li Xinggang, for example, are each leading a semi-autonomous unit in the state-owned institute China Architecture Design and Research Group (CAG).[13] Although market-oriented they typically receive large and public commissions, a condition which requires flexibility rather than polemics. Cui Kai's recent works (leaving behind Post-Modern influences) are therefore modernist with a proper image for public institutions (China Academy of Urban Planning and Research, Beijing, 2003, Conference Centre of Foreign Language University, Daxin, Beijing, 2004) (Figure 5.12). Li Xinggang's designs, although also restricted and still evolving, display a tendency to break away from rational modernism yet at the same time incorporate concerns for tectonics, space and environment. Zhang Lei is also leading a semi-autonomous design office attached to Nanjing University.[14] His modernist design, with elegant proportions, tends to be rational and

5.12 China Academy of Urban Planning and Research, Beijing, 2003. Architect: Cui Kai.

controlled, as is the work of Zhou Kai and Tang Hua (each leading his own design office). Although there are important differences between them, Zhou's, Zhang's and Tang's modernism tend to be universal and formal. They also share a heroic trait in the use of large scales, which is perhaps a legacy from the past. They form a contrast to Ai Weiwei and Wang Shu, who are among the most individualistic (methodologically) and subversive or critical. Wang Shu's exploration of tectonics and abstract narratives of form, material and construction is one of the earliest in this generation, along with Yung Ho Chang and Liu Jiakun. His interior renovation of Chenmo Studio (Haining, 1998), a series of cubes called 'Eight Lamps' (Hangzhou, 1997), an interior design of a pub with an exhibition hall titled 'A Room with a View' (Shanghai, 2000), and the Library of Suzhou Wenzheng College (Suzhou, 2000), are a series of spectacular transformations of the cube, in an attempt

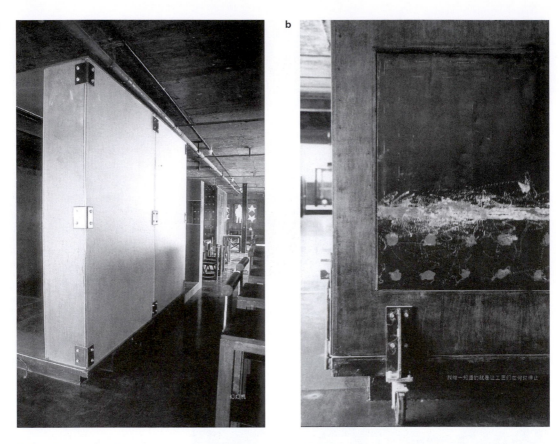

5.13 'A Room with a View' (bar and gallery), Shanghai, 2000. Architect: Wang Shu. **a:** A 'slide projector' and a 'camera box' as two transitional spaces. **b:** Detail of the 'camera box'.

to combine analytically modernism and the Chinese garden design tradition (Figures 5.13, 5.14). His work displays a 'combination of Chinese literati tradition with a European bourgeois modernist aesthetics', a characteristic common to some in this generation but arguably more dramatically expressed in Wang.[15] Wang's recent research and design continue the path with a stronger use of the Chinese intellectual and urban–rural tradition, and a clearer critique of the contemporary urban condition in China and Asia generally.[16]

In terms of both sensitivity and experience, Yung Ho Chang, Liu Jiakun and Wang Shu are arguably the most challenging and representative of this group, with Cui Kai on a different path in association with the state-owned design institute, Ai Weiwei again on a different, more subversive and artistic path, and Qingyun Ma exploring an urban architecture. Liu Jiakun and Yung Ho Chang form a good comparison and a good introduction to the group. Whereas Chang was educated in China and then in the United States and also practised and taught there, and had been lecturing there at times while based in Beijing from 1995 to 2005 (and more recently has assumed a professorship and the position of head of architecture at MIT since late 2005), Liu was entirely educated in and is practising in China. Whereas Chang is

based in Beijing (and since late 2005 between Beijing and Boston), Liu Jiakun is based in Chengdu, the capital of an inland province, Sichuan. Liu is well known for his artists' studios and galleries in the rural setting outside Chengdu, such as Hedouling Studio (1997) and the Buddhist Sculpture Museum (2002) (Figures 5.15, 5.16). The use of material, of skylight, of space in between, and the making of a tactile aura based on local building traditions are convincing as a place-based tectonic modernism that breaks away from the National Style. Liu says it is important to appreciate one's own limited condition, its locality and its tradition, and to explore them as positive 'resources' for creative design.[17] His 'low-tech' strategy involves a calculated employment of local building technologies to express the cultural richness of the region. He also argues that the primitive vernacular of the region and early modernism in Europe of the 1920s can be regarded as two

5.14 Library of Suzhou Wenzheng College, Suzhou, 2000. Architect: Wang Shu.

5.15 Hedouling Studio, Chengdu, 1997. Architect: Liu Jiakun.

5.16 Buddhist Sculpture Museum, Chengdu, 2002. Architect: Liu Jiakun.

'beginnings', with which a new design approach can be developed.[18]

Yung Ho Chang, on the other hand, first explored a series of intellectual themes that were cross-cultural, before developing a

5.17 Book-Bike Store, Beijing, 1996. Architect: Yung Ho Chang.

5.18 Morningside Mathematics Building, Beijing, 1998. Architect: Yung Ho Chang.

5.19 Villa Shizilin, Beijing, 2004. Architect: Yung Ho Chang

specific position in the context of China. Thanks to his education in the United States, for a decade while teaching in the States (1985–96) he explored issues of programming, temporal experience, narratives in cinema and literature, and the use of installations as a means for design research. A few themes recurred in his works, such as bicycle-based mobility, cinematic experience, linear perspectives, the camera box and the Chinese landscape scroll. His Book-Bike Store (Beijing, 1996), Pingod (apple) Sales Centre and Gallery (Beijing, 2003) and Villa Shizilin (Beijing, 2004) revealed a persistent study of these themes. In the last two buildings, for example, 'perspective boxes' are inserted into the structure (an old industrial structure in the first, and the walls of a purpose-built country club in the second), functioning as entries, window-rooms, a stage-platform and semi-open courtyards. Topologically transformed roofscapes are also used to relate to the profiles of the mountains visible nearby. Across these designs, however, is a latent position that becomes clearer in his formation of a design

5.20 Father's House, Xian, 2003. Architect: Qingyun Ma.

position in China. From the very beginning (the Book-Bike Store) and in these three buildings as well as others by Chang, materials and relations between parts of the building are exposed and displayed (Figures 5.17, 5.18, 5.19). The ideas or themes of the design are expressed not through iconic decorations but through tectonic and spatial relations. In his article 'Basic architecture', he argues that what is needed in China is a 'basic architecture', one that is based on elemental ideas of a 'building' (*fangwu*, *jianzao*) rather than styles, added-on decorations or external ideologies, as found in the Beaux-Arts tradition of the earlier decades and the Post-Modern historicism of the 1980s and 1990s.[19] Architecture must be understood as 'architecture in itself', pure and autonomous, as a basic tectonic, in a concerted employment of materials, construction, form and space.[20]

Recently, a regionalism and a position critical of market capitalism in the city are also emerging.[21] Qingyun Ma's Father's House (Xian, 2003), Yung Ho Chang's Villa Shanyujian and Villa Shizilin (Beijing, 1998, 2004), Wang Shu's Villa-15 (Nanjing, under construction), Liu Jiakun's many designs and the designs of some emerging architects (such as Tong Ming's work, Suzhou, 2004) can be viewed as examples of the first (Figures 5.20, 5.21). Chang has made it clear that, in the face of today's urban chaos and rampant construction with minimal concern for quality, order and specificity of individual buildings, a critical architecture is needed.[22] It is important to explore autonomous issues of architecture, to resist the capitalist tendency of the market ('to insist

5.21 Dong's House and Restaurant, window details, Suzhou, 2004. Architect: Tong Ming.

upon autonomy is to be critical of capitalism') and, when possible, to engage with the client-developer for social and public interests ('the third approach' that is both research-based and participating in the market). Liu Jiakun, explaining his urban architecture strategy, has made a similar point, about the need to protect the discipline and its internal values as well as public space and its interest, through an engagement with the client at the earliest stage of brief preparation.[23] Qingyun Ma, in his North Bund urban renewal proposal (Shanghai, 2002), also suggests an incremental process that sustains a dense urbanity against the idea of quick clearing and the use of object typology for pure profit demanded by the developer.[24] All of these indicate a new awareness: although it is important to critique the legacy of the nation-state from a liberal perspective, it is also important now to critique the rising capitalist forces from a social and public viewpoint. In both cases, it should be noted, the emphasis on autonomy and disciplinary knowledge within the object of architecture has served as a basis for a critical position.

The most important development here is not any one of the specific positions of these architects, or necessarily the quality of some of these designs at the moment, as both are evolving. The most important development here, it seems to me, is the historical rise of social and economic autonomy of this profession in post-1976 China, which allows them to claim a cultural, formal autonomy in architecture from the excessive demands of the state before 1976. This search for autonomy in design both politically and formally, following the logic of the design discipline that deals with the art of making and building, perhaps necessarily requires the adoption of a pure and a material-constructive approach, which can be found in the tectonic modernism explored before and notably in Europe of the 1920s. The appearance of this formal language in China in the late 1990s, so over-used in the West and yet so fresh and 'sharp' in this country in the 1990s, is therefore understandable.

What is happening therefore is the beginning of a localization of experimental modernism in China. In other words, after a long delay of some four decades from the 1940s to the 1980s, when China was trapped in the 'first modern', the Beaux-Arts neo-classical architecture, the process has now quickened in the final years of the twentieth century and the beginning of the twenty-first, accelerating forward as it is propelled by economic growth and social liberalization, towards the 'second modern' (modernism). In such a rushing ahead, in an ongoing synchronization with development in the West, Chinese architects are also being brought to confront the 'third modern' (or super-modernism) with a sublime aesthetics and sometimes post-Cartesian or complex rationality, a new chapter that is now awaiting close observation.

CHAPTER 6

CRITICALITY IN BETWEEN CHINA AND THE WEST, 1996–2004

That China is producing a large quantity of buildings with an alarming speed is well known in the world, thanks partly to Rem Koolhaas's characterization of the 'Chinese Architect' in the book *Great Leap Forward*.[1] What is unclear to the outside world, however, is an intentionality developed within China. There is by now a long tradition of modern architecture in China in which ideas and visions are expressed. This history of intentionality is also mutating. Whereas for decades it was a collective expression directed by state authority, there is now a tendency in which one finds individual positions opposing mainstream practice. There is an expanding group of architects in China whose designs involve self-conscious strategies that resist or transcend certain mainstream conventions. This deserves close observation.

Parallel to this is an unprecedented opening of dialogues between Chinese and overseas architects from Europe, the United States, Japan and parts of Asia. Amidst and behind this is a longer story of the relationship between China and the Western world (with Japan and parts of Asia in between). If this relationship has been one-way from the West to China in the project of Westernization and modernization, there are now signs of a two-way communication of ideas and energies between the two. In other words, there are now influences from the West to China *and* China to the West, each engendering certain effects in a specific direction. What are these effects? What are the roles of Yung Ho Chang and Qingyun Ma, each having been educated in the United States before practising in China? What is the effect of Rem Koolhaas in the West after his studies of China and parts of Asia?

This chapter explores ideas and incidents that may help illuminate these developments: (1) the emerging 'critical' designs in China, and (2) the arising exchange of ideas in specific directions between China and the Western world, which seems to precipitate a criticality in China and a post-criticality in the West. This chapter argues for a proposition that a 'symmetrical' tendency has occurred in the past few years: while there has been a flow of influence from China (and Asia) through figures such as Rem Koolhaas who are supporting a post-critical argument in the West, there has also been a flow of ideas from the West through Chang and Ma that are facilitating a rise of criticality in the Chinese context.

Methodologically, this chapter argues for a geo-global and cross-cultural perspective in which a study on China or a country in the West is incomplete until the investigation is 'externalized' in a global space of co-presence. This approach has two requirements. (1) It demands a study of China's development with reference to the West (and parts of Asia). It is assumed that what is happening to China now is the result of a long process of modernization, a powerful force which had travelled from Europe via different routes to the Asian continent since the early twentieth century if not earlier. This *historical* asymmetry necessitates a methodological preference for reading European and American theories in a study of non-Western cases such as China. For example, to understand current China, it seems helpful to read studies on nineteenth- and early twentieth-century Europe, in which there were developments of a market economy, bourgeois liberalism and purist architecture. This is by no means a confirmation of Euro-centrism. Rather, it may help deconstruct the universal supremacy of any theories if and when they are historicized and localized in their temporal and geographical context.

(2) This geo-cultural and global perspective also requires an acknowledgement of Asia and in some cases China, or an 'outside' beyond the West, when a certain Western theory or discourse is studied. Since the 1960s and through the following decades to the present, the world is becoming interdependent, and influences from Asia (initially Japan) to the West can be identified. The more recent years have witnessed an intensified discourse on Asia and China as sites of instrumental architecture for urbanization and modernization in the Western media and in theorists' discourse as in the case of Koolhaas. Yet the current debate on post-criticality, which sees Koolhaas as a leading figure, ignores the geo-politico-economic 'outside' where Asia is playing an active role. This chapter argues that China, Asia and a materialist 'outside' spreading across the world must be included for a study on the West in general and on or for the post-critical debate in particular.

This chapter starts with a reading of Peter Eisenman and Rem Koolhaas, to discover different Western perspectives on practice and Asia. It then moves on to George Baird, Michael Speaks, Robert Somol and Sarah Whiting to explore recent arguments for post-critical pragmatism, and suggests that the 'external' perspective is missing and sites of 'Singapore Songlines' and 'Pearl River Delta' must be taken up as challenging cases if Koolhaas is regarded as leading the post-critical, as suggested by these scholars. The chapter then shifts to the other side of the story, the opposite flow of influence. Here the chapter moves on to China, and identifies the rise of purist architecture with a degree of criticality, in the historical condition of contemporary China, in which Western influences play an important part. The chapter concludes with an observation on an in-between space where a third position is found.

Peter Eisenman: critical architecture as 'transgression'

Peter Eisenman published an essay entitled 'Critical Architecture in a Geopolitical World' in 1995.[2] Eisenman identifies the rise of geo-politics since the 1970s, replacing the old class-politics of communism versus capitalism. With this change, Asia became more independent while the West experienced a lack of resources to support its own critical architecture. Nevertheless, in the West, a long tradition of the critical and a mechanism to produce critical discourse still remain. In Asia, Eisenman believes, building construction is active but the idea of a critical architecture is not accepted, nor is there a mechanism to produce critical discourse and practice, nor is there a critical tradition as in the West. Architecture in contemporary Asia, for example in Jakarta, Kuala Lumpur, Singapore, Bangkok, Seoul and Shanghai, as cited by Eisenman, is conservative, 'accommodating' the forces of the state and the market. Western architects themselves, while working in Asia, according to Eisenman, adopt an 'accommodative' approach in the spirit of the new conservatism.

For Eisenman, a critical architecture as developed in Europe since the late nineteenth century is 'transgressive', not 'accommodative'.[3] It originated from critical thinking in the late eighteenth century by Immanuel Kant and Giovanni Battista Piranesi. The critical concerns 'that condition of being which speaks of the possibility in being of knowledge'.[4] It explores the possible in being and in being of knowledge. It critiques the status quo, and searches for a possible future. The critical is then related to the avant-garde. Historically, the critical was part of the ideological struggle of the rising bourgeoisie. It was part of the revolutionary politics of new social groups emerging with the capitalist market economy. This 200-year project, however, was exhausted around the middle of the twentieth century, according to Eisenman, as geo-politics and the media revolution superseded the classical politico-economic system. A media-based concept of architecture, exploring the iconic, presence and conditions of the body, should be investigated if the critical in architecture is to be revived. In relation to Asia, Eisenman adds that self-reflexivity of the critical tradition is compatible with the national independence movement of the former colonies in Asia after the 1960s. Eisenman implies that a critical architecture thus understood should be and can be developed in Asia.

Other scholars such as Michael Hays have also defined aspects of critical architecture in the Western tradition.[5] 'Autonomy', 'resistance', 'opposition', 'subversion' and a 'distance' from the existing order are the important aspects of the critical, which are consistent with the more forceful, vectorial idea of 'transgression' in Eisenman. What distinguishes Eisenman's essay, however, is the use of the idea of the critical *outside* the Western context, a move which compels him, it seems, to trace the history of the critical concisely and precisely in early modern Europe, in the rise of liberalism, capitalism and industrialism, from 1760 to 1960. If Asia and China now in particular are engaged in modernization with elements of liberalism and capitalism as originated in early modern Europe, then Eisenman's definition of the critical in that historical context is a crucial point of reference. Perhaps there is an underlying sociological relationship between the market economy, liberalism and critical architecture, although the tradition and political culture of a region or a country such as China may add significant layers of modification, an issue I will return to in the next chapter ('A Global Site and a Different Criticality').

However, there are points to be contested. First, Eisenman doesn't seem to be serious about practice as an active force itself that can transform the critical mind. The critical posture somehow has been formed long ago in Europe and its business now is to project itself onto the outside and the non-Western world. Forces of modernization and urbanization, travelling to new geo-cultural sites, engendering new shapes of design practice, are not taken up seriously. Second, the site of Asia is treated passively. Characterized as 'the Pacific Rim and the Muslim world', and exemplified by a list of the cities cited above, Asia is treated evenly and generally. Asia is blank, flat and passive, just like the realm of practice, which is also treated as a passive backdrop, on which the critical spirit is to issue its force of transgression. Is there a different position in this regard, one that takes up the site of Asia and the realm of practice actively?

Rem Koolhaas: beyond the critical

Also in 1995, Koolhaas published 'Singapore songlines' in his and Bruce Mau's *S, M, L, XL*.[6] This is a differentiated reading of Singapore, Southeast Asia and aspects of Japan from the 1960s to the 1990s. The article starts with a criticism of indifference in the West toward Singapore's success in economy, mass housing and the creation of a new city. This indifference reveals, apart from colonial arrogance, a loss of touch with the 'operational' and the 'making' of the city, according to Koolhaas. The article describes the destruction of the old fabric and the creation of the new city, under a government that is authoritarian, efficient and developmentalist, a leadership that has delivered mass housing, basic welfare and a surging economy. Despite mainstream practice being practical and instrumental, there is also a critical voice in Singapore led by William Lim and Tay Kheng Soon, as recognized by Koolhaas. This, in turn, is related to avant-garde architects emerging from Japan in the 1960s led by Kenzo Tange, the first non-Western critical voice in history as described by Koolhaas.

At the heart of this transfer of critical energy and the making of the city in Singapore is a materialization of the idea of megastructure envisaged by Kenzo Tange and explored by Fumihiko Maki, after earlier explorations in Europe. Through a cross cultural transfer, the idea of megastructure, originating in Le Corbusier, Team X and the Smithsons up to the 1960s but then discredited in the West, was re-interpreted and materialized in Asia. The master form, or the collective form in fact, worked in that it captured and intensified the dynamic, congested life in the Asian city. On account of demographic pressures and the speed of urbanization, these heroic modern forms acquired vitality and a new life from Asia from the 1960s. Koolhaas, writing in the 1990s, aimed to absorb these ideas and energies. The ideas of the collective and meta-forms in particular resurfaced clearly in his recent Book City and CCTV projects in Beijing.

If these two articles of the mid-1990s can be used as an indication at all, Eisenman and Koolhaas seem to adopt different, almost opposite, approaches to Asia and practice. If the first is passive and indifferent to the realm of practice in general and the forces of urbanization and modernization in parts of Asia in particular, the second clearly is open to them, and intends to absorb ideas and energies from them.

In hindsight, this article by Koolhaas is the first in a series of investigations on parts of Asia continued in the following years, in *Mutations* (2000), *Great Leap Forward* (2001) and *Content* (2004). Koolhaas asks the persistent question about the status of Western critical theory in the face of challenge from contemporary Asia throughout these studies, although the empirical focus has moved on to the more variable, complex cases of China including the PRD (Pearl River Delta) region, Beijing and other cities. Koolhaas states:

> today it is clear that modernization is at its most intense in Asia, in a city like Singapore or in the Pearl River Delta. These emerging cities teach us about what is in the midst of happening . . . To renew the architectural profession and to maintain a critical spirit, it is important to be aware, to observe these emergent conditions and to theorize them . . . so that conclusions can be drawn.[7]

Issues of history and context and of tabula rasa are discussed where Asia provides stimulation for reassessment of certain positions held in the West after the 1960s. In *Great Leap Forward*, Koolhaas contrasts the presence of excessive urban production (in Asia such as in the PRD region) and the absence of a universal, plausible theory of urban condition and urban production, a wrenching situation that cries out for a new theory. The book, a preliminary study on the PRD, thus ends with a glossary of some seventy new terms, which represents 'the beginning of a conceptual framework to describe and interpret the contemporary urban condition'.[8] In his latest book, *Content*, Koolhaas's outlook remains as in 1995 on Singapore: 'Our narrative on China is ungenerous and uncurious. . . . But . . . the situation is richer . . . [involving] a triangulation of huge danger and huge potential. . . . The future of China is the moment's most compelling conundrum'.[9]

There is a consistent outlook on Asia as observed from the West. Koolhaas's research, in these cases, is an interested, sometimes very close, reading on parts of Asia. It is a process of learning from Asia, in order to absorb challenges from the frontier of urbanization and modernization, so that Western theories and critical thinking may be reformed. It is important, says Koolhaas, 'not to oppose two situations – the European and the Asian, the eastern and the western – but to establish parallels so that conclusions can be drawn'.[10] There is a cross-cultural perspective here but with a specific vectorial movement: an Asia-to-West or China-to-West flow of ideas and energies for a reform of Western thinking. There is also a specific type of ideas and energies absorbed into the West: the pragmatic, the operative, the making. Further, if the purpose is to 'renew . . . a critical spirit', then the move here is not to eradicate the critical tradition altogether, but to find a new critical position where pragmatic urgencies can be internalized. In this sense it is not different from Eisenman in purpose, but the difference in approach is significant.

From criticality to post-criticality: in Europe and America

There is already a history of ideas beginning with the late 1990s in America and Europe that explores a new pragmatism, as found in John Rajchman, Joan Ockman and Michael Speaks.[11] George Baird's recent article '"Criticality" and its discontents' may serve as a guide to the argument in its latest shape.[12] Baird outlined recent voices that had argued for an alternative to the now overpowering and constraining tradition of the critical or 'criticality' in the West, including Rem Koolhaas, Michael Speaks, Robert Somol and Sarah Whiting. Rem Koolhaas is the first in recent times, according to Baird, to emphasize efficacy above criticality, social and practical understandings above formal and ideological positions. Baird cited a statement made in 1994 by Rem Koolhaas as an early voice opposing the critical: 'The problem with the prevailing discourse of architectural criticism is the inability to recognise there is in the deepest motivations of architecture something that cannot be critical.' This is certainly consistent with Koolhaas's interest in effective practice and, a point to come to a little later, regions outside the West such as Asia.

Speaks, Somol and Whiting were also cited as important voices of this move. Somol and Whiting's article 'Notes around the Doppler effect and other moods of modernism' identifies two positions that have evolved since the 1970s: the 'critical' project argued for by Peter Eisenman and Michael Hays, and the 'projective' practice exemplified by Rem Koolhaas.[13] Whereas the first concerns autonomy, process and critique, the second explores force, effect, product and possibilities. Whereas the first operates on the logic of signification, of the sign and index, the second functions on the basis of the 'diagram' and 'abstract machine', which are not semiotic or transcendental in essence as proposed by Deleuze and Guattari.[14] Somol and Whiting are arguing that the architectural discipline has been absorbed and exhausted by the project of criticality. It is time now to explore alternatives such as the projective approach.

Michael Speaks, in two articles on 'design intelligence' in 2002, argues for a radical change in the profession.[15] It is not enough, according to Speaks, just to develop a theory of pragmatism; it is more important to explore new forms of practice and investigation. Abstract truth and stylistic concerns now have to give way to little truths and the 'chatter of intelligence'. Practice and research, in turn, have to adopt supple, dynamic, open ways of engagement with realities. Again, Rem Koolhaas's OMA and AMO are cited among other offices and research programmes as examples that are engaging the world in a mobile and 'intelligent' manner. (The offices cited include Field Operations, Greg Lynn FORM, FOA and UN Studio; and the research institutions MVRDV, AA's DRL, the Berlage Institute and Harvard GSD).

Having reviewed these new voices, George Baird concludes that there is now a move from 'criticality' to 'post-criticality', to a 'post-utopian pragmatism'. This is certainly a timely and insightful observation on a transformation now unfolding in Europe and America. However, if we follow Baird's argument a step further, a crucial aspect is missing. Baird's entire discussion concerns the crisis of the critical and the transformation into the post-critical *in* the academic and professional circles *in* the Western world. But what is the *external* background? What are the global, politico-economic conditions today that are affecting if not engendering transformations that have surfaced as voices for the post-critical in the academic, professional circles? Baird may be intuitively aware of an outside world that is propelling this change, since both Koolhaas and Speaks are interested in the 'outside' or externality. But this externality has not been identified and explored.

In the context of the present discussion, two interrelated senses of externality are crucial behind the change that must be highlighted: the politico-economic condition outside the profession, and the geo-cultural regions outside the West, especially Asia including China. Increasingly these two externalities are interrelated. Baird's assessment, insightful within an interior, misses this layered, material and geo-cultural outside, especially Asia. And it is in Asia today that practice and pragmatism are reaching their extreme intensity. My argument is that it is this intense practice and pragmatism that are providing some of the impetus to the West for a transformation through mediating figures such as Rem Koolhaas. If Koolhaas is really a leading example of post-critical practice, and if Koolhaas has indeed been absorbing energies from Asia into the West, then this move to post-criticality in the West must have been engendered, partly at the least, by the storms of urbanization and modernization in Asia. This has a few implications.

The current move to post-critical pragmatism in the West and the recent studies on Asia and China in the West represented by Rem Koolhaas are interrelated in the real geo-global space of the world. In this interregional, cross-cultural space, figures such as Koolhaas are absorbing currents and flows from China/Asia for a transformation of Western critical thinking. Further, moving in between regions and cultures, at least between the West and China, Koolhaas assumes not only a connecting agent but also a third position external to both, a position that may enable him to be critical and 'transgressive' to certain traditions in both.

It also means that China, on its way to become an economic superpower, may for a period act as the largest exporter of the impetus that is effectively 'post-critical'. Certainly much research is needed to explore this in-between space where, as it were, China awaits Deleuze, that is, intense practice in China resonates and dramatizes the 'diagrammatic' pragmatism envisaged in the West. At this stage, it may not be too far-fetched to say that this impetus is effectively 'projective', 'pragmatic' and 'diagrammatic' in Somol–Whiting and Deleuze–Guattari's sense, and that this impetus will continue to flow to the West and the world, in the current and possibly historic shift to post-critical pragmatism. This is perhaps the context in which Koolhaas's book *Great Leap Forward* should be understood, as an indicator in the history of ideas and theories in architecture.

Great Leap Forward captured a particular situation in China, which is paradoxically rather unfamiliar to the Chinese at their first encounter with the book. Many in China are surprised at what they see when opening the book, even though the content is discovered to be objective. This is the brutal and materialist force in China captured in the book, which is so taken for granted in China that it is no longer recognizable *within* China. It is identifiable only to the observers from outside or those who have used conditions outside (for example, in Europe and America) for comparison. Koolhaas, standing outside China (and outside the West), therefore benefits from the view of the double other, and offers a unique narrative fresh to the Chinese and challenging to Westerners. At the same time, precisely because of this externality, the landscape observed is distant. The internal condition, especially the intellectual efforts of the Chinese, needs to be observed closely.

In China

China's move from a Marxist–Leninist vanguard to the current position of a socialist market economy is complex.[16] There are numerous moments of transition and crisis. Basic points in time, however, can be marked. If 1976–8, when Mao passed away and Deng Xiaoping resumed the leadership, represents the beginnings of a post-Mao, post-communist era, then the year 1989, when the Tiananmen Incident occurred, may serve as a point dividing the 1980s and 1990s, and the two stages of Deng's reform. It is clear now that, whereas the 1980s were besieged with radical ideological debate and a profound sense of uncertainty, the 1990s opened up a confident path of development in which an open market economy led by a strong central authority proved workable, problems notwithstanding, in delivering general social stability and fast economic growth.

From this perspective, the single most important factor in shaping Chinese society today is arguably the introduction of the market economy, which is now increasingly dynamic if not rampant. Along with this goes the emergence of a non-ideological, pragmatic, liberal and urbane civil society with a rising and expanding middle class. The Chinese 'bourgeoisie', re-emerging on the mainland, at this stage includes entrepreneurs, developers, managers and small business owners, as well as market-based professionals such as architects. Around 1994–5, the professional registration system was re-instituted after four decades of absence, and private offices mushroomed across the country. There are now state-owned design institutes, private offices, and mobile hybrids straddling both. All of them, despite the variety in shape, are essentially market-oriented. In a situation not entirely dissimilar to Europe as described by Eisenman, the blossoming of the market economy is now bringing about the rise of liberal, critical positions, and the opening of a critical distance between individuals and mainstream conventions and their various forms of power.

At this juncture, the first generation of Chinese architects of the post-Mao era, receiving education after 1977–8 with Western and international influences, some having studied in America, Europe and Japan, emerged in the late 1990s as a new voice in the history of the architecture of modern China. Adopting purist and tectonic modernism, they are making a breakthrough in a country that has been dominated by decorative social realism originating from the Beaux-Arts tradition imported around the 1920s (Figure 6.1). Alongside this is a rising self-consciousness of their own design positions, in a society that is more tolerant and in need of critical or progressive voices. Some of the most influential figures of this generation include Yung Ho Chang, Cui Kai, Liu Jiakun, Qingyun Ma, Wang Shu, Ai Weiwei, Zhang Lei, Zhou Kai, Li Xinggang, Tong Ming, Deshaus (Liu Yichun, Zhuang Shen, Cheng Yifeng) and Urbanus (Zhu Pei, Wang Hui, Meng Yan and Liu Xiaodu).[17]

Together they share characteristics that should be noted. (1) They have attained a relative autonomy and freedom from the state in design conception and financial support. (2) They oppose the mainstream Beaux-Arts tradition evolved up to the late 1970s and the

6.1 Friendship Hotel, Beijing, 1956. Architect: Zhang Bo. Photo taken in 1997.

Post-Modern popular commercialism of the 1980s and 1990s. They advocate tectonics and a search for internal disciplinary autonomy in the hope of transcending the dominant social realism of twentieth-century China. (3) There is a hidden ideological position, which opposes the ideology of the leftist state up to the late 1970s, the grand narrative of socialism expressed in the Beaux-Arts language. This 'rightist' position is also shifting to an emerging new 'left' that is arising to oppose the new capitalist forces in the market economy. (4) They assume 'authorship' in that they write and articulate their own individual design positions. They also have a discursive space of their own. This space includes press, media, exhibition venues, and digital sites (abbs.com.cn, far2000.com). Significantly, this discursive space also migrates to overseas institutions such as universities and exhibition centres/events (Aedes in Berlin, Centre Pompidou in Paris, Biennales in Venice), extending a network society of communications across national borders. (5) Within China, despite recurrent difficulties, there is toleration by the state and support from the market for the 'transgressive' designs emerging from these architects (such as the developer SOHO China's 'Commune by the Great Wall', Beijing, 2002), even though that support itself is a marketing effort for icons of distinction.

Yung Ho Chang, Liu Jiakun, Qingyun Ma

Looked at more closely, these architects are different from each other. Cui Kai for example leads a semi-autonomous unit in a state-owned institute, the China Architecture Design and Research Group (CAG). There is less room for polemics and more demand to serve different and often large, public clients. His purist modernism, although transgressive to the Beaux-Arts tradition, tends to be correct for these public institutions. Wang Shu, on the other hand, who studied in

Nanjing and Shanghai, and teaches in Hangzhou in the same region, explores a more individual, autonomous position in which purist modernism is combined with the Chinese literati tradition found in this region in the late imperial period (in painting and in landscape garden design). Let us now examine more closely Chang, Liu and Ma.

Yung Ho Chang studied in China (Nanjing Institute of Technology, 1978–81) and the United States (Ball State and UC Berkeley, 1981–4). Professor Rodney Place, who had studied under Robin Evans and taught at the AA School in London in the late 1970s, taught Yung Ho Chang at Ball State in the early 1980s. His influence on Chang has been important, as Chang has acknowledged.[18] After practising for a few years, Chang taught at four universities in the USA for a decade (Ball State, Michigan, Berkeley and Rice). Conceptual thinking, spatial programming, temporal experience, life-world narratives (as in cinema, literature and painting) and the use of installations for design investigation were the focuses of his teaching. He became a licensed architect in the United States in 1989. After a few years of shuttling across the Pacific he established his own Atelier FCJZ in Beijing in 1994 and settled there in 1996, starting a new life of practice and teaching in China. He became the professor and head of the Graduate Centre of Architecture at Peking University in 1999, and frequently lectured at universities in the USA and around the world. During this important period (1994–2004), he produced nine interiors and renovations, twelve new buildings, twenty-one installations (some of which are exhibitions), six book monographs and numerous articles in Chinese and English. The installations and exhibitions are mostly in Europe and the United States.

Judging from this range of work, he may be considered a theory-based architect. Although the buildings he designed are limited in number, they are research-oriented. Viewed over time, they expand in scale with an increasing ease in the innovative use of building technologies. What is consistent in these works is an emphasis on the exposure of materials, on spatial experience and relationships with the outside, and on a studied theoretical theme. A few themes he has explored in the past resurface in different ways as persistent topics of research, such as bicycle-based mobility, cinematic experience, the perspective box and the camera, and the use of European techniques in late imperial Chinese painting. His Book-Bike Store (Beijing, 1996) uses large bicycle wheels, steel frames and translucent glass walls to create an urban station for the mobile public in the Chinese city (Figures 6.2, 6.3). His Pingod (apple) Sales Centre and Gallery (Beijing, 2003) is a renovation of an old industrial structure with 'camera' boxes punched into the structure as entries, meeting rooms and a stage platform (Figure 6.4). His Villa Shizilin (Beijing, 2004) explores perspective openings and topologically transformed roofscapes, to engage with a surrounding forest and the undulating profiles of the mountains at a

6.2 Book-Bike Store, street front, Beijing, 1996. Architect: Yung Ho Chang.

6.3 Book-Bike Store, interior on the ground floor.

distance (Figure 6.5). In his essays, we find a clear explanation of the positions behind these designs.

The initial polemic for Chang is the need in China for a 'basic architecture', one that is based on the rationale of 'buildings' or 'built structures' (*fangwu*, *jianzao*) rather than external styles, decorations and ideological prescriptions, as we find in the Beaux-Arts-based designs of the earlier decades and the Post-Modern historicism of the 1980s and 1990s. Chang says 'architecture must be understood as architecture in itself', pure and autonomous, as basic tectonics, in a concerted employment of materials, construction, form and space.[19] Furthermore, according to Chang, in the face of today's urban chaos, and rampant construction with no concern for order and quality, a critical practice is needed. While size, quantity, speed, chaos and replication are the norm, a critical architecture according to Chang should explore smallness, order, quality, slow and careful design, and the singularity of each project.[20] At the same time, he also questions the tendency in the West to separate autonomous design thinking from commercial practice.[21] He argues for 'a third approach', one which involves a 'critical participation' whereby research and critique are embedded in design practice in the real marketplace. In this regard, he emphasizes the need to retain autonomous values of architecture so as to resist elements of capitalism, *and* to engage with client-developers on 'fundamental issues' to serve society at large.[22]

If Chang's work is concept-based with Western influences, Liu Jiakun's designs are regionally grounded, especially in the use of materials. Liu was educated in China, in Sichuan Province in the south-west (Chongqing Architecture University, 1978–82). After fifteen years of practice in government design institutes with sojourns in Tibet and Xingjiang in between, he established his own office in 1997 in Chengdu, the capital city of the province. As of 2004 he had completed some eighteen buildings and a few installations. Liu is famous for his design of artists' studios and galleries situated in rural and natural surroundings outside Chengdu, such as Studio Hedouling (1997) and the Buddhist Sculpture Museum (2002) (Figures 6.6, 6.7, 6.8 and 6.9). His urban projects include the Red-Age Entertainment Centre, where a large-scale red metal frame encases an old multi-storey building (Chengdu, 2001). Another urban project is the Department of Sculpture at Sichuan Academy of Fine Arts (Chongqing, 2004). Large and bold massing and local materials are used. The scale and verticality of massing, as well as the opening of large holes and courts high above, respond well to the humid climate and the vertical urban landscape of Chongqing between rivers and mountains.

Liu's writings explain his ideas clearly. In 'About my work', Liu says it is important to understand the location of one's practice.[23] Situated inside China in the south-west, subject to various limitations, it is important to appreciate the region's condition and tradition, and to turn them into positive 'resources' for a creative design. Liu divides his work into 'rural' and 'urban'. For the first, a 'low-tech' strategy is adopted. Owing to limited budgets and the rudimentary construction skills of rural builders, it is important to explore a vernacular language. This language, although 'rough', can be expressive of a regional culture with a long history as well as of the particular taste of the Chinese literati tradition in painting (the deliberately non-academic, non-professional approach that allows a freedom from formal techniques). This strategy,

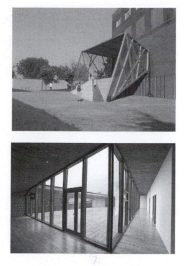

6.4 Pingod (apple) Sales Centre and Gallery, Beijing, 2003. Architect: Yung Ho Chang.

6.5 Villa Shizilin, Beijing, 2004. Architect: Yung Ho Chang.

6.6 Studio Hedouling, side entrance, Chengdu, 1997. Architect: Liu Jiakun.

6.7 Studio Hedouling, interior, Chengdu, 1997. Architect: Liu Jiakun.

6.8 Buddhist Sculpture Museum, side view of the entrance, Chengdu, 2002. Architect: Liu Jiakun.

6.9 Buddhist Sculpture Museum, interior, Chengdu, 2002. Architect: Liu Jiakun.

according to Liu, can be useful to regions and countries backward in technology but rich in culture and tradition. For urban projects, Liu says that there is no longer any restriction in the use of technology and material. However, the danger is for architecture to degenerate to the status of a slave of commercial interest, providing only a superficial play of forms. The strategy here should be an active engagement with the client to explore programme planning at the earliest stage, in order to introduce public and urban considerations and to gain a position from which to protect the autonomy of architectural design.

In another article, 'March on to the beginning', Liu explains his work with international references.[24] He says that, in hindsight, his work explores an 'architecture of resistance'. It shares with Paul Ricoeur the concern to synthesize ancient traditions with modern civilization, a statement which implies a sympathetic reading of Kenneth Frampton's critical regionalism. However, the synthesis here is carried out on Liu's terms. For him the pristine, rustic vernaculars and the abstract, minimalist early modern architecture share comparable qualities. These are the two 'beginnings', regional and modern, from which design in this region can develop, an idea that is evident in his buildings.

Compared with Liu and Chang, Ma is relatively new to the scene, yet his work is now opening up a new dimension in China, a kind of reflexive urban realism often in alliance with the municipal government. Ma studied at Tsinghua University in Beijing and the University of Pennsylvania (1989–91). He practised in New York, returned to China, then went back to the United States to teach and practise in Philadelphia, and finally settled in Shanghai to open his own office, MADA s.p.a.m., in 1999. Along with those of other Chinese architects such as Chang, Liu, Wang Shu and Ai Weiwei, his works were exhibited in Berlin and Paris (2001, 2003). In December 2003, he was one of the 'ten vanguards' around the world in the *Architectural Review*. In

February 2004, he staged a solo exhibition 'MADA s.p.a.m. on SITE' at Aedes, Berlin.

Ma acknowledged the influence of Alex Wall on urban design strategies when they collaborated in competitions in Philadelphia. Alex Wall, in turn, had previously collaborated with Rem Koolhaas. During Ma's deanship at Shenzhen University (1996–7), he assisted Koolhaas in the investigation of the Pearl River Delta, and was the commentator on the research work in *Great Leap Forward*. Ma is also the strategic advisor for OMA's design for the CCTV headquarters in Beijing.

The statements and buildings from Ma's office conjure up a socially conscious, urban-oriented design position. According to him, all designs should be research-based, each within its particular circumstances. Design is a 'reflexive platform' for 'an argument between ideas and realities'. Design must engage with the city. It should actively participate in the explosive urban transformation unfolding in China today. Megastructures are possible and necessary in China. A 'scaleless architecture' is possible as a concept which encompasses interventions from a small house to large-scale urban renewal. Architecture, however, should be a means of critique of social, urban problems in contemporary China.[25] Like Chang, Ma also noted the separation in the United States between 'theory' and 'practice', for example between critical design teaching at universities and commercial practice outside. He emphasized that in his practice in China critical thinking and commercial practice have to be integrated.[26]

One of the largest urban redevelopment studies carried out by Ma's office is the North Bund renewal plan (Shanghai, 2002–4), covering a site of 180 hectares. Introducing a system of 'cuts' and 'glues' at regular intervals, the idea is to preserve the energy and life of the existing neighbourhood with a human scale, in between the larger 'green cuts' of retail and cultural facilities. The intention is to retain the fabric for a long-term, piecemeal development with the support of the municipal government and private investment, and to resist the idea of clearing and the typology of large objects based solely on profit for the developers.[27] Urban concerns are central whenever possible, even where the scale is small, as exemplified by his Edge Park attached to a classical Chinese garden in Qingpu (Shanghai, 2004). Sandwiched between a private, traditional garden and a public, modern mess of ugly structures, the linear park articulates a dialogue between old and new, classical and modern, serene and brutal, which is dramatized by the corner pavilion where concrete and wood structures are folded onto each other (Figures 6.10 and 6.11).

In between China and the West

To summarize, the starting point for these architects is the idea of a 'basic architecture' or 'architecture-in-itself', as Yung Ho Chang

6.10 Edge Park, viewed across a river, Qingpu, Shanghai, 2004. Architect: Qingyun Ma.

6.11 Edge Park, the corner pavilion, Qingpu, Shanghai, 2004. Architect: Qingyun Ma.

first proposed, a claim for the autonomy of the discipline, against the demand to dress up for external purposes (social, ideological, historical, commercial). Following that are two emerging positions: an abstract regionalism as in Chang and Liu Jiakun (and in some of Wang Shu and Qingyun Ma's projects), and a socially concerned urbanism as specifically addressed by Ma (and also in Chang, Wang and Cui and others more recently). The analytical depth in 'architecture-in-itself' as displayed here, as a group or consistent historical phenomenon, is not found before in modern China. The transgression of the decorative realism of the Beaux-Arts tradition and the recent Post-Modern historicism has never been so clearly and self-consciously articulated in writing and in built works. There has been no critical distance or relative autonomy attained before. Nor was it possible to claim autonomy in the Socialist–Maoist time, when architects worked in collective institutes, or earlier still in the short-lived, semi-colonial capitalism of the 1920s and 1930s, when architects had no sustained economic support for the freedom that is now available. With the market economy established and a civil society opening up in China, these architects now have a socio-economic basis upon which to assert their voice and authorship. International exposure is another support for the rise of the critical voice in the profession.

Observing this new criticality in China carefully, one finds a Western influence. Directly or indirectly, figures such as Koolhaas, Frampton, Alex Wall, Rodney Place, Robin Evans and many others are found in their designs and writings. The fact that some of them have studied and practised in the West before returning to China is an important geo-cultural condition in which a vectorial move can be found. Here, besides specific contents, it is 'theory', reflective thinking, depth and autonomy of design (and of architecture-in-itself), and the idea of distance and resistance to external pressures, that are transferred into China by these architects. This flow of criticality from the West to China is also assisted by other efforts such as the study and translation of Western books as initiated by the late Professor Wang Tan and other professors such as Luo Xiaowei since the late 1980s, and recent studies on tectonics (including Frampton's texts) by Wang Qun, Peng Nu and others.

At the same time, there is also a filtering process. As Chang and Ma both acknowledged, the separation between 'theory' and 'practice' in the West is not suitable to China. There is a subtle move here: although the idea of critical autonomy is absorbed, there is no need for excessive or absolute autonomy that negates practice or pragmatic considerations. At this moment, there is a relative advantage for the Chinese architects in fending off excessive negation and the 'burden' of critical architecture in the West, which have 'exhausted' the discipline, as Baird, Speaks, Somol and Whiting have pointed out.

6.12 A construction site in China in Rem Koolhaas's essay 'Pearl River Delta' (2000).

Chang and Ma are therefore standing somewhere in between China and the West, like Rem Koolhaas, although coming from the opposite direction.[28] Being external to both worlds, they can be critical and transgressive to certain conditions in both. At the same time, they are mobile global agents importing and exporting ideas in between. They are each responsible for the traffic of ideas in a certain direction. If Koolhaas is absorbing the vitality of production and pragmatism in the frontier of urbanization from China to the West (Figure 6.12), enacting a move from criticality to post-criticality in the West, then Chang and Ma are absorbing criticality from the West into China, engendering the rise of an autonomous, critical, discursive architecture in China. In other words, there is a 'symmetrical' exchange of energy between the two worlds at the moment, a situation that is likely to develop further. With these considerations in mind, it is reasonable to expect a further integration between China, Asia and the West, and a re-synthesis of theory and practice in the discipline.

**COMMENTS FROM G. BAIRD, Y. H. CHANG,
P. EISENMAN, L. LIU, M. SPEAKS AND OTHER
ARCHITECTS/CRITICS: A CONVERSATION**

When 'Criticality in between China and the West' (*Journal of Architecture*, 10, issue 5, November 2005) was translated and published in China (*Shidai Jianzhu: Time + Architecture*, 91, issue 5, September 2006), comments from architects and critics in China and the United States were invited and published with the paper in the same issue of *Shidai Jianzhu*. Five of them are reprinted below. A review of all the eleven comments, written in late 2007 and published here for the first time, is included afterwards.

1 George Baird: 'The Criticality Debate: some further thoughts'

In his thought-provoking text 'Criticality in between China and the West', Jianfei Zhu makes reference to an essay I published in the *Harvard Design Magazine* in 2004: 'Criticality and Its Discontents'. In that text, I noted the pivotal role that had been played in the emerging debate over criticality by Rem Koolhaas. Indeed, I noted that Koolhaas has frequently been cited as a key figure in the development of the so-called 'post-critical' position that has recently been posed as a theoretical and a professional alternative to criticality for architects. But I also pointed out how easy it is to find statements from Koolhaas over the past decade or so that seem to dissociate him quite significantly from any clearcut endorsement of the 'post-critical'. In his subsequent text, Jianfei Zhu has developed an extended commentary on Koolhaas's role in China in recent years. And his argument has the effect of dissociating Koolhaas from the so-called 'post-critical' even more decisively than my own did. This short text is a further commentary on Jianfei Zhu's and my own readings of Koolhaas's relationship to criticality on the one hand, and to China on the other.

Subsequent to writing 'Criticality and Its Discontents', and subsequent to reading 'Criticality in between China and the West', I have had occasion, together with a group of students from the Harvard Design School, to undertake a systematic review of a large group of Koolhaas's published texts from 1972 through to the present.

In our ongoing discussions of these texts, my students and I noted, as many others have also done, how criticality on the one hand, and efficacy on the other, tend to present themselves as alternating poles in his thought. We noted also how his polemical – even journalistic – prose style leads him to give great latitude to his own propensity for rhetoric. In any given text, we found ourselves concluding, he is likely simply to let his rhetoric loose, allowing his conclusions to lead where they may, for the sake of the rhetorical effect itself, quite possibly at the same time producing at least latent contradictions with the observations of others among his own writings.

But then we thought we also began to perceive other, less obvious patterns. We noted, for example, that the characteristic tone of voice that typified the earlier writings – declaratory, mythologizing (in a fashion that is surprisingly reminiscent of the prose style of Le Corbusier, Koolhaas often comes close to referring to himself in the third person) – has significantly shifted in more recent times. Nowadays, as often as not, his tone is more personal, and more personally engaged. For example, we were fascinated by the potential significance to be gleaned from a sustained comparison of two of his well-known texts: 'The Generic City' from 1994, and 'Junkspace', first published in 2000.

Each of these texts is well enough known in its own right; we, however, grew increasingly curious in regard to the decisive difference of tone between them. By and large, 'The Generic City' exudes the impersonal, declaratory confidence of the early Koolhaas. 'Junkspace', on the other hand, could hardly be more personal. We even began to ponder the extent to which it could be described as a rant. Since the subject material of the two texts is relatively similar, this struck us as a tonal discovery of some importance. Where the first text seems largely to present a series of observations in regard to the generic urban phenomena that are largely affirmative in tone, the second one is much more critical – sometimes even of the same phenomena. Here again, we at first suspected that we should read the two texts as tonally heterogeneous riffs, each one playing out a certain stance for the sake of seeing where it would lead.

But then we found ourselves reaching more extended conclusions. It began to seem to us that relatively few of the most recent texts exude the declaratory early rhetoric at all. In this regard, we began to suspect that there has, in fact, been yet another fundamental shift in Koolhaas's basic theoretical position, and that the publication of 'Junkspace' is the earliest available evidence of this. Koolhaas has, after all, acknowledged that his position shifted at the end of the 1980s from one we might call 'neo-modernist' to a more avant-gardist one. We now suspect that there has been another shift of position, as yet unacknowledged by him, occurring in the late 1990s or early 2000s. Since, as I noted in my own criticality text, he was one of the first in the 1990s to publicly resist the constraints of Eisenmanian criticality, it would not surprise me to find him nowadays increasingly rediscovering the appeal of the critical, be it in Europe, or China, or America.

In this sense, then, I am further convinced that Jianfei Zhu's reading of Koolhaas's stance on criticality and on China is a correct one. Indeed, it is my view that Koolhaas's stance on China, and Jianfei Zhu's insightful reading of it, will feed provocatively back into the Western world in the days and months and years ahead.

George Baird is the Dean of the Faculty of Architecture, Landscape and Design, at the University of Toronto, and the Principal of Baird Sampson Neuert Architects Inc., Toronto, Canada.

2 Yung Ho Chang: 'Criticalities or What the West Meant for Me'

Initially, the Great Cultural Revolution in 1960s China prepared me for critical thinking. However, I acquired a better understanding of criticality while studying and working in the United States or generally the West; thus, for me, what constituted criticality had perhaps a lot to do with the West I was experiencing or how it was defined at a given moment:

Criticality 1

The first West that I encountered upon arrival in the United States was European Modern Art, from Marcel Duchamp's visual art work to Flann O'Brien's novels to Chantal Ackerman's films. Within such context, criticality is about conceptual propositions or the ways in which an individual may construct the question 'why' and the answer 'how' specifically for an issue. It is critical in the avant-garde tradition since it does challenge the status quo as well as conventions.

Concept brings about a distrust of authorship and has developed in many instances an interest in process. In my case as an architect, that in turn leads to an extensive research component in my design practice and therefore a singular, complex, mixed activity of design-research.

Since the contemporary version of conceptual thinking was originated from art, it has lent architecture naturally to interdisciplinarity. By the same token, notions in Asian art, such as the non-perspectival pictorial spaces in Chinese landscape scrolls, may also shed light on the design of built environment. With the help of a conceptual frame of mind, the cultural boundary is crossed. Open and inquisitive, conceptual thinking is postmodernism beyond formalism. It encourages experiments with ideas other than with forms.

Criticality 2

The second West for me has been American academia, in which a left-wing political position is the norm and social concerns are of paramount importance in almost any scholarly pursuit, including of course architecture. To be critical is, for the American intelligentsia, to establish one's social-political agenda. In other words, criticality carries on the Marxist legacy: it is a critique of capitalism.

Specifically in architecture, an agenda-driven practice would prioritize urban and environment issues, such as public space and/

or sustainability. Although, from time to time, I was exposed to or was even caught in between a debate between design and social responsibilities, I came to believe that an architect contributes to society through design.

However difficult, there are ways to take initiatives in developing and pushing the social content of an architectural/urban project; one possibility is for the architect to be involved in the stage of programming, which is increasingly happening at least in young market economies like China.

Criticality of this nature has also made me rethink the socialist past of China. In the 1960s, I grew up imbued with the Marxist ideology that became so dogmatic and extreme that it defeated its own purposes in the end. Yet, today, a total dismissal of that history and an unconditioned embrace of market economy seem to be just as dangerous. The challenge is to balance public and private interests. It is something that can only be achieved by the society as a whole and in the collective effort of achieving that architects should participate actively.

Curiously, this criticality takes on a modernist standpoint. It may appear to be at odds with a postmodernist one or Criticality 1 but I believe a true postmodernism is inclusive.

Criticality 3 or Materiality

The architectural milieu in the West has had its own definition for criticality, that of an autonomous architecture and that of making. I do not think this particular criticality contradicts the previous two, since either conceptual thinking or a social agenda has to be manifested in physicality to have an impact on the way people live. Space, form, material, tectonics are the building blocks of ideas and attitudes. That is to say the three criticalities have to work together to produce a thoughtful architecture. Or, if Criticalities 1 and 2 take me away from the specificity of making buildings and cities, the third one, as it is supposed to do, brings me surely and firmly back to architecture.

Yung Ho Chang is the Professor of Architecture and the Head of the Department of Architecture at Massachusetts Institute of Technology and the Principal of Atelier Feichang Jianzhu (FCJZ), Beijing, China.

3 Peter Eisenman: 'Contro lo Spettacolo'

> The spectacle is the sun that never sets on the empire of modern passivity.
>
> Guy Debord

Today, across cultural practices, the distracted viewing of the surface has replaced the reading of depth. This is abetted by the media, which stages the appearance of reality as a spectacle. The spectacular is linked to the contemporary inundation of information, which proselytizes the new and demands the continual production of new imagery for consumption. The images sought by the media are circulated instantaneously, virtually and seamlessly.

The media's search for fantastic imagery, as well as the precedent set for architecture by the 'Bilbao effect', perpetuates an increasing need for the spectacular in the form of ever more precious forms of novelty. These shapes – mutations of their own mediation – are the spectacles of today. Seductive renderings of impossible buildings are their own graphic reality, fuelled by a voracious need for publicity. These images are the narcissistic death rattle of a discipline lost in the tidal wave of image-dependent media. In staging the appearance of reality as spectacle, media induces passivity. The more passive the audience, the more necessary spectacular imagery becomes. It is a vicious cycle in which architecture today is more than ever implicated. In such a context, today's subject, now rendered passive, is truly in danger of losing the capacity for close reading. Where is architecture's critical resistance to this process of loss? The crisis of the spectacular demands a call for a new subjectivity, for a subject removed from the passivity induced by the image and engaged by form in close reading.

Peter Eisenman is the Principal of Eisenman Architects, New York, and teaches architecture at Yale University, Princeton University and Cooper Union, USA.

4 Liu Jiakun: 'An Open Letter to Jianfei Zhu'

I must apologize for the delay in replying. I have read the article several times. In my opinion, it is an important article that reflects an important time. Although I have tried several times to write a response to the article, I am not satisfied, because often my writings have been recapitulations of my personal practice and experience rather than theoretical articulation. Since time is running out, I have decided to write this letter as a response instead.

Metaphorically speaking, 'exchange' can be conceived of as crossing fingers of two open hands. However, over the years, my personal experiences of 'exchange' with colleagues from abroad tell otherwise; instead of two open hands, there is one opening and the other closed. Therefore, it is more like a kind of overlapping, or even merely a shadow cast of one hand on the other.

We know far much more about them than they know about us. This can be seen in many aspects. They are often so surprised when we mention some of the latest authors or popular DJs in the West. Their surprise was quite shocking to me as well. The situation is so asymmetrical; before we know it, everything from the West has already permeated our daily life and yet their knowledge about us still looks like storms from far away. These foreign friends, mostly professionals, are sincere and interested in the East and China. However, because of a 'time lag' in cultural transmission, or because we are changing too fast, I often feel that they are coming back from the future we are chasing to talk to us about our past. Sometimes I think we architects, riding on the epic surge of China, begin to emerge on the architectural scene; yet in fact, as individuals, we have nothing much to be proud of. What happens if China is not the 'largest construction site in the world', not the 'experimental ground for architects from around the world'? To quote from the movie *Isabella*, 'It is not that I look down upon you, it is that I can't see you.'

After years of exchange, I am now familiar with Western ways of reading. If you follow their political correctness and use a few key words, you will be easily recognized; this is a technique that we all tacitly understand. Of course, these popular topics are not inappropriate; they are at least a compensation for the loss of common values and shared beliefs. I do the same, but I have my own doubt and inner resistance. My personal experience tells me that Chinese reality today should not be described with that set of discourse; but how to describe this reality, I am not very sure myself. Some of my more honest descriptions seldom capture their attention, yet what they are interested in [are actually less important; these words] are not fabrications but I feel somehow I am not really true to myself. This is not their problem: everyone recognizes what they are familiar with, like catching one's name amidst a noisy crowd in a street. The problem is that this situation can foster a generation of Chinese architects who use pirated Western standards to describe and deal with Chinese reality.

Although we take a lot of photos, we do not learn much from exhibitions. Yet if we walk about and especially visit those architectural offices we often learn a lot. The unselected normal buildings, the actual urban condition of a building familiar in the magazine, the daily routine of foreign architects . . . these true relations between background and representation often bring about a lot of enlightenment to me. The most important result of an international communication is a clearer view about myself and a demystification. Technological basis, theoretical domination and a system of critique in the Western world make their ideas well grounded and fully rationalized. But if we insist on equality between cultures, these theories and techniques should not be automatically universalized. Whatever your background, everyone starts with daily operations. The true advantage of those master architects lies in their social basis; these original forces prior to academic theorization provide a capacity superior to that of others.

Where is our advantage? Of course we have abundant opportunities for practice, but with a lot of problems which also excite our Western colleagues. Both opportunities and problems are a huge and a special resource. In London, after the lectures by you, Yung Ho Chang and teacher Isozaki, my lecture was titled 'Coping with Reality'. It was about 'small truths' embedded in an 'effective practice'. The lecture didn't really talk about my works, but the relationship between works and reality, about a realistic attitude, and a method of employing potentials from reality; it apparently aroused much interest, and was perhaps enlightening to many. One architect said that there was always a presence of a concrete reality and a concrete region behind every project I showed in the lecture; he said it was perhaps an 'expressive realism'. I actually think I didn't start with the idea of expressing a reality. Rather, real problems as a background of these designs were so great that they inevitably left behind their traces in my works. I don't consider internationalization every day as it is around us all the time; nor do I concern locality always as I am living in it day and night. Establish firmly a sense of reality in building practice in China now, focus on problems closely, observe and analyse various kinds of resources carefully, employ existing conditions to deal with these problems. These issues themselves will have already defined a 'Chineseness'; these developments will naturally move forward and secure a 'contemporaneity'; and if you have some creativity in resolving these problems, an 'individuality' will also emerge inevitably. These are the aspects of a basic method I adopt.

It's time. It seems chaotic now, but the age of youth is always chaotic; indeed there are disappointing things happening around, but if these continue to happen despite our complaining, it must be because there are greater forces and rationales at work. One shouldn't complain about one's own time. An old poem runs like this: 'we are living in the third world on the other side of the sun / no one tells us what we should do'. A century of Chinese revolution has finally reached this chapter, and I feel very lucky to be a Chinese architect in such a historic time. I sincerely hope that you and those you mentioned in your article will take advantage of this historic opportunity and unique resources, assume the responsibility to establish a system of discourse based on contemporary Chinese practice, so that when we work at home we have our own sense of direction, and may bring our own fresh soil when floating overseas, so that we are no longer isolated carrots washed clean by others.

Liu Jiakun is the Principal of Jiakun Design Studio, Chengdu, China.

5 Michael Speaks: 'Ideals, Ideology, Intelligence in China and the West'

There are many things to agree with in Jianfei Zhu's important and timely essay, 'Criticality in between China and the West'. For the sake of brevity and clarity, however, I want to focus on a few things with which I disagree and which form the basis for raising a different set of concerns than those he raises. Let me begin by suggesting that the distinction between critical and post-critical architecture – made by Robert Somol, Sarah Whiting and George Baird, and on which Zhu's essay depends – is a misleading one that too often reduces complex realities to static ideological categories. Such a reduction occurred at a recent conference at TU-Delft, in the Netherlands, devoted to examining the implications of the post-critical for European architecture. Organizers and indeed many participants assumed that the conference would prove to be a debate between the two ideologies, between those who support 'criticality' and those who support 'post-criticality'. No such thing occurred, in fact, because those identified as post-critical (including me, Stan Allen, Somol and Whiting) offered no post-critical agenda or ideology. And that is because there is none. Whereas criticality may very well be considered an ideology – one that demands above all else adherence to the idea that architecture must be critical of and resistant to the market – the post-critical is an assertion that ideology in general, and the ideology of criticality in particular, is no longer relevant in the contemporary world. Indeed, it would not be inaccurate to say that the ideology of criticality has encouraged vanguard architects in the West to reflect on and criticize rather than actively engage the market-driven world that has arisen in the early twenty-first century. What thus unites all those identified as post-critical is nothing more than the belief that the critical project that dominated vanguard architecture in America and Europe from the 1970s to the 1990s is now bankrupt and that a new set of practices are emerging all around the world, including, and especially, in China.

Unfortunately, this same ideological reduction occurs in Zhu's essay, where, for example, he opposes the ideology of Western criticality to the ideology of Chinese pragmatism, an essentially post-critical (and therefore post-ideological) embrace of the rapacious market conditions that now prevail there. Zhu suggests that Western-educated architects such as Yung Ho Chang and Qingyun Ma have imported the ideology of criticality to China as a way to resist the market while Rem Koolhaas, among others, has imported Asian pragmatism to the West in an effort to circumvent the dead ends of criticality. His essay, in fact, focuses on this 'cross-cultural', ideological approach. I am not an expert on contemporary China, and so cannot speak with any authority about what is now occurring there. What I can say, however, with some greater sense of certainty, is that architecture and design practices in the West are today being transformed by the very same forces of global – not Western – modernization at work today in China. No longer commandeered by the West, global modernization operates at different speeds and with different intensity around the globe. This means that transformations in design practice are taking dramatically different forms in China, where the market is nascent, and in the West, especially in America, where the market is more mature, though no less dynamic. Static ideological positions cannot be imported from one situation and applied to another to hasten or retard these processes; nor do they allow one to explain one situation by reference to another. The real situation is thus much more complicated than these ideologies suggest. Whereas architects such as Chang and Ma may view criticality as a necessary condition for developing autonomy *within* the market, Peter Eisenman and other Western adherents to the ideology of criticality believe autonomy is possible only *outside* the market. Indeed, China's burgeoning market economy is precisely what makes it possible for practices such as Chang's and Ma's to break from the ideology of social realism and distinguish themselves from the Post-Modernism of the 1980s and 1990s and from more overtly commercial practices operating in China today. Criticality and autonomy are different in the West and in China even though the globalizing forces of modernization that are transforming each are the same: for Chang, Ma and other emerging architects in China, criticality offers autonomy *from* ideology while for many of those in the West criticality offers the autonomy to be *bound* by ideology.

Similarly, although it is undeniable that Asia in general and China in particular have had a significant impact on the thinking and practice of Rem Koolhaas, it is not the case that Koolhaas has imported Asian pragmatism or any other ideology to the West. Nor is it the case that any such importation leads to the emergence of the 'post-critical'. If anything the various positions identified as post-critical have arisen from within the West as attempts to argue for new, affirmative practices more suited to the challenges issued by global modernization. Koolhaas figures prominently in accounts of the 'post-critical', whether in Europe, America or in Asia, because he and his office are practitioners of an affirmative, global modernism tethered neither to the naive *ideals* of Modernism nor to the negative *ideologies* of Postmodernism. Let us remember that Koolhaas provided one of the most important critiques of the ideals of Modernism while at the same time offering one of the most powerful alternatives to the ideologies of Postmodernism. In his first book, *Delirious New York: A Retroactive Manifesto for Manhattan*, published in 1978, Koolhaas chronicled the pragmatic Modernism of Manhattan which needed no manifesto or ideals to be enacted or built, only the 'Culture of Congestion', the grid and the elevator. The implicit critique of the architectural manifesto (which Koolhaas retroactively writes for Manhattan to show that the manifesto is irrelevant) is an explicit critique of Modernist ideals, those Western, Enlightenment principles which were to guide modern architects into the rationally planned future they foresaw. That, of course, was not to occur. Nonetheless, *Delirious New York* is consistent with a number of Western critiques of the ideals of Modernism during the 1970s and 1980s, including those of Post-Modern historicists such as Robert Stern and Charles Jencks, Critical Regionalists such as Kenneth Frampton, and Deconstructivists such as Eisenman, Bernard Tschumi, Mark Wigley and others. These various architects and critics sought to replace the ideals of Modernism with the ideologies of a diminished, hypercritical Postmodernism that had lost faith in the Enlightenment project that Modernists sought to continue. Although each of these ideologies posed as a rival to Modernism, none offered anything more than negativity and half-truth to replace the affirmative ideals that defined the early twentieth (and last Western) century. What is significant, and different about Koolhaas, however, is that while he recognized the limitations of Modernist ideals he did not seek to replace them with Postmodernist ideology. Rather, in *Delirious New York* he chronicled and learned from the historical processes of modernization that created Manhattan, as he would later chronicle and learn from the processes leading the present and then future of global modernization in Singapore and China.

Global modernization calls for global modernism freed from Modernist ideals and Postmodernist ideology. Koolhaas, and indeed a number of others, have begun to forge such practices driven instead by intelligence, by practical design knowledge generated through continuous speculation about and engagement with the real world. Perhaps the most important feature of such practices is their approach to research which is never driven by the desire to *discover* universal (Modern) or repressed (Postmodern) truths but instead by the practical necessity to *produce* plausible, actionable truths used to intervene in and transform the city and the world. These practices have thus collapsed the distinction between abstract theory (ideals/ideology) and practice, preferring to treat research as a form of design and design as a form of research that increases the practical intelligence of each office and of the architectural profession as a whole. Moreover, I would say that it is intelligence and not ideology that connects Koolhaas and other Western practices to the work of Yung Ho Chang, Liu Jiakun, Qingyun Ma and a number of emerging architects in China. Chang and Ma, like Koolhaas, have used research, publications and exhibitions and even built projects as means of producing design knowledge or intelligence. It would seem that such intelligence rather than ideology is required in the volatile market reality of contemporary China where distinctions between what Zhu, quoting Chang, calls 'autonomous design thinking and commercial practice' seem irrelevant. Liu Jiakun's subtle approach to this market, for example, where vernacular and modernist idioms are treated as equally legitimate strategies, is better explained as a practice driven by intelligence than by reference to Kenneth Frampton's ideological assertions of 'critical regionalism'. But it is Qingyun Ma and his office MADA s.p.a.m., whose very name foregrounds strategic thinking, that are most clearly driven by intelligence rather than ideals or ideology. Ideals (universal truths) and ideology (hidden truths) give the solution to problems in advance, that is, in the form of the problem itself. Intelligence, on the other hand, requires analysis, experimentation and collaboration between client and designer without preconceptions or solutions given in advance. Everything is open to speculation. Design problems, then, are created not discovered. This is precisely how MADA s.p.a.m. explains its design approach on its website: 'Problems are amorphous. Therefore, we never take a problem, we find a problem. We set off to discover, distil and define problems.' MADA s.p.a.m. defines design problems through an active research/design approach that redefines architecture as 'a form of knowledge gained through experiment and readjustment', a practice, I would suggest, of design intelligence, not design ideology.

Michael Speaks is the Dean of the College of Design, the University of Kentucky, Lexington, USA.

6 Review and response

The debate organized by *Shidai Jianzhu: Time + Architecture* at Tongji University Shanghai in 2006 included eleven commentaries in response to my paper 'Criticality in between China and the West'.[29] The critics were Zheng Shiling, Li Xiangning, Li Hua, Peng Nu, Zhou Shiyan and Zhu Tao, as well as the five authors whose comments have been reprinted above. To facilitate substantial discussions in the future, it would be useful to give a short review and an initial response where necessary from my perspective.[30]

6.1

Zheng Shiling's comment, 'A transformation in contemporary architectural criticism', provided a summary of key figures and their positions in Western architectural discourse and related areas of philosophy in the past few decades and further back.[31] He concluded that other disciplines such as philosophy and cultural studies now had to play a greater role in architecture, and that 'ideological critique' and 'introspection' were of great importance today. Zheng's picture was broad, which opened up a space for further debate. Zhou Shiyan's comment, 'Speaking air into the air', was far more critical.[32] She challenged the possibility of 'communication' she identified as a crucial idea in my article, as well as the role of the critic implied in my writing. What I had identified in my article in fact was not a full 'communication' per se between China and the West, but a certain pattern of interflow between them. Regarding the role of the critic in the author, I suppose I was writing my article as a 'critical historian' rather than a 'critic' of current design practice in a literal sense. To criticize these Chinese architects in any straightforward sense, upon the qualities of their designs for example, something Zhou seemed to imply I ought to do, was not my purpose. What was intended, instead, was a critical understanding of these architects as a historical phenomenon.

6.2

Li Hua's 'Extending a critical space: questioning the categories of China and the West' was a much closer and more careful reading.[33] She showed an appreciation of the 'third perspective', the 'external' viewpoint beyond a local Chinese or Western outlook I identified in some of these architects in the article, and an 'externalization' strategy I adopted as a research method. Li Hua however thought that I had overlooked the asymmetrical relationship between China and the West (a recurrent theme in these comments that I will come back to later on), and had used categories of 'China' and the 'West' simplistically. She employed Edward Said's critique of the use of the Orient and the East as a basis for her criticism; she argued that New York, Singapore and China's PRD (Pearl River Delta) were just new cases for a constant interest in Koolhaas; she also argued that in the Robin Evans–Yung Ho Chang, Frampton–Liu, and Koolhaas–Ma interrelations there were non-linear processes of influence in which new discoveries and reforms of earlier ideas took place. My response is that (1) though the China–West relationship has not been and still is not symmetrical, that shouldn't prevent us from seeing a moment of symmetry that had occurred for a while; (2) categories such as 'China' and the 'West' are artificial constructs yet they can be useful, although an ongoing critique of categories must be kept alive; (3) Koolhaas had indeed kept a consistent interest in modernization from the United States to Asia and China, yet a geographical leap into China and Asia in general remained important given that many had been often limited by these geo-cultural distances; (4) the Evans–Chang and other such relations I identified involved indeed non-linear and complex interactions in which 'misuse' did occur in creating new ideas and new designs in the new contexts.

6.3

Peng Nu's comment, 'Critical architecture and architectural criticism', made three observations.[34] (1) There was a critical architecture in

China in the 1990s; however, the momentum should be revived now, given that tectonic purism in Chang was becoming a token or style and that Ma's practice had embraced the market economy fully. (2) Cross-cultural dialogue was not possible in an absolute sense yet in practice it can be effective in that energies can be absorbed from others. However, regarding the 'third perspective' identified in my article, Peng showed her reservations. (3) There was an idolization of star architects in China largely driven by media and popular demand, a situation that required a stronger critical voice from the critics or architectural intellectuals, which was lacking today and for which the current debate was an indispensable point of departure. I share with Peng the urge to encourage a sustained criticality in design practice, a further questioning of the external or the third space outside any locality (yet I believe it is possible and indispensable), and a critical reading of the relationship between media and design discourse, and her call for a strong and autonomous criticism.

6.4

Li Xiangning's comment, 'Dialogue with the other', described a lack of understanding of China in the West in the current 'China fever' spreading worldwide.[35] A persistent focus on a few architects and an overall disapproval of massive constructions betray this misunderstanding on the part of the Western audience. Li Xiangning described an 'expedient tactics' employed in China that had catered for building with quantity, speed and efficiency, in a socio-political and economic environment today that was shifting so fast that permanent values in architecture were irrelevant. Li then came back to the issue of misunderstanding and suggested that the real difficulty in cross-cultural communication between China and the West was how to let the West or the world understand China as a whole in its specific realities. For Li, the purpose here was not to confirm a similitude in style or quality, or that China can also export something to the West, but to secure mutual respect and understanding. The debate between criticality and post-criticality, according to Li, was 'totally not applicable in China'; 'nor would Western interest in China bring about any real influence in the West'. I appreciate Li's point on understanding China as a whole in its complex realities, and his identifying of an 'expedient architecture' beyond a few individual architects. Yet a total gap imposed by Li between the two worlds appears to be too artificial. The shifting patterns of mutual influence between China and the West (and other regions) in human history are just too abundant to be ignored. I do appreciate Li's frustration at Westerners' misunderstandings of China, yet mutual influence continues regardless; we cannot retreat from this but are all obliged to observe and understand, and even facilitate in a constructive direction. In the case of the debate on criticality and post-criticality, my interest was not to encourage an application of the positions in China, but to explore a methodological space in which China and the West can be debated upon *together* on one platform (despite the differences), for which that particular controversy may serve as a point of departure.

6.5

Zhu Tao's comment, 'The criticality debate in the West and the architectural situation in China', had two main propositions.[36] First, in contemporary China in the face of ecological degradation, capitalist greed and rising income disparity, what was needed was not a theoretical debate on post-criticality but a tangible critique of social practice in architecture. Second, Tao separated formal and social criticality, and called for the Chinese to engage with the latter in the face of current challenges. In both we hear a leftist voice in Tao that should be supported. The 'neo-left' voice in the Chinese intellectuals and the architects, however, had already emerged, and was clearly identified in my paper (in all the three cases I studied, that is, Chang, Liu and Ma, and also in these architects as a whole). How to forge a critical practice today in the rampant market economy is a common task we have to share, not in a narrow, either–or mindset with a few Maoist slogans, but a comprehensive collaboration in which both formal and social critical practice, and both urgent critique and careful historical and critical scholarship, must be included.

Tao had three particular contentions with my article, concerning post-criticality, Koolhaas and megastructures, and this generation of Chinese architects. (1) For post-criticality, Tao questioned if this had now become the Zeitgeist of the West. I was instead concerned not with anything conclusive or clear-cut but with an ongoing debate in which certain proponents such as Koolhaas can be both 'critical' and 'post-critical', as Baird and I had identified. (2) Regarding Koolhaas and China, Tao raised a few specific questions. He questioned how Asian or Chinese pragmatism was exported to the West. In my understanding, Koolhaas's writings, speeches and exhibitions circulating in the West on China and Asia were crucial acts of this export, besides media coverage in the professional publications in the West on Asian countries and especially on China now. Tao questioned if Asian pragmatism in general and a heroic modernism in the use of megastructures in particular, as studied in Koolhaas, were relevant to the urban design practice in the West today. In my understanding, Koolhaas was testing ideas on the one hand, and also seriously believing in 'bigness' with capacities to accommodate increasing size and density of conurbations in the global trend of urbanization. That in turn should not contradict lessons learned from Jane Jacobs since the 1960s, yet a conservative ethos arising since must also be highlighted. (3) Regarding the Chinese architects, Tao questioned exactly what was so 'critical' in them, contending that they were engaged in a 'generic practice of language' rather than a 'particular critique of language' in a contemporary China where 'anything goes'. Tao's reading here is general and contemporary, not historical, and also Western–universal rather than locally based. Although a purist formal language may lose its criticality in China today from around 2005–6, the historical journey I described involved the architects breaking away from the decorative traditions of the Beaux-Arts and Post-Modern influences, gradually in the 1980s and 1990s, and then decisively since 1996, with the rise of the new generation educated since 1977–8, the beginning of the post-Maoist era. The breakthroughs in 1977–8 and 1996–7, some two decades apart, mark critical moments in the history of design in current China. If one looks into this history, one will appreciate a specific critique of language *in the Chinese context* in these architects such as Yung Ho Chang, Liu Jiakun and Wang Shu during 1996–2000 and soon after.

6.6

The next five comments, from Baird, Chang, Eisenman, Liu and Speaks, have focused more on the criticality debate, but issues of asymmetry and misunderstanding between China and the West continue to surface as a concern. George Baird, whose initial article ' "Criticality" and its discontents' precipitated much of the discussion in my writing on the issue, has provided a further reading on the central figure, Rem Koolhaas.[37] Baird emphasized that, despite the fact that Koolhaas had been cited as a key figure by the post-critical theorists, Koolhaas's own statement can also lend support to a critical position. Baird reminded us that he had pointed this out in his initial article, and that my subsequent article has also recognized this. Baird then moved on to identify, in Koolhaas's writings from 1972 to the present, not only a tonal shift in recent years but also a positional evolution. With this, Baird argued that Koolhaas had made two crucial shifts, around 1990 and then 2000: first from a neo-modernist to an affirmative avant-garde, and then from the affirmative position to a new outlook that appeals to criticality. In this perspective, 'The generic city' (1994) and 'Junkspace' (2000) can respectively illustrate an affirmative and a critical stance (as well as a change from a declaratory to an engaged tone). In Koolhaas's 'Pearl River Delta' (in *Mutations*, 2000), I also found a relaxed and engaged discussion on his project and on the forthcoming book *Great Leap Forward* (2001). Here in 2000, in what is apparently a speech he delivered to a Western audience, he displayed a certain frustration at comprehending and a critical view of urbanism and architecture in Asia ('we find this kind of habitat a bit sinister, rather strange . . . So, in Asia, there is a crisis of architecture and urbanism).[38] Interestingly, he still insisted on reading and theorizing these cases, in order to 'renew the architectural profession and to maintain a *critical* spirit'.[39]

6.7

The title of Yung Ho Chang's comment, 'Criticalities or what the West meant to me', revealed a Western influence of criticality on China through him as I had identified in the essay.[40] But, interestingly, this Western criticality also interacts with a Chinese Maoist past. Chang made a reference to the Cultural Revolution of the 1960s which prepared him for critical thinking, and then late in the article he said that today a total dismissal of the Maoist past for a full embrace of the market economy must be resisted. In his writing, this re-appreciation of the socialist past was associated with a leftist political position he recognized in Western academia. He in fact identified three criticalities he had absorbed from the West: conceptual art, leftist ideology, and the materiality of the autonomous object in architecture. This substantiated our understanding of a Western criticality being brought into China through him and this generation. But what made these ideas 'critical' in China was the arrival in or encounter with the local historical condition, such as the idea of autonomy against the Maoist Beaux-Arts tradition, or the leftist criticality against the current rampant market economy. Further, in my reading, there had been a development in adopting Western criticalities in the Chinese context in Chang. Whereas Chang had always focused on the first criticality, his third criticality in material autonomy emerged (or re-emerged) only when he arrived in China in the early 1990s to confront a pervasive practice of decoration in the Beaux-Arts and Post-Modern traditions. His second criticality in the leftist, Marxist outlook also became relevant only after China, where his practice has been based, turned increasingly capitalist beginning in the late 1990s. Chang is a case to illustrate how China and the West, or Chinese practice and Western discourse, have been closely intertwined.

6.8

Peter Eisenman's comment, 'Contro lo spettacolo' or 'against the spectacle', described a prevalent phenomenon in cultural practice today, the saturation of images, replacing depth with surface, rendering reality as spectacle.[41] Aided by media and information technology, the world of surfaces and images is now spreading everywhere. Architecture, with the 'Bilbao effect' as the precedent, is much implicated here. In this world of the spectacle, fantastic images 'proselytize the new' and facilitate a demand for endless production of the new and the spectacular. These images induce a passivity in us, which in turn demands ever more fantastic images or spectacles in a vicious circle. Eisenman identified this as a crisis in today's subject, a situation which, according to him, called for a critical resistance in architecture, and a new subjectivity 'removed from the passivity induced by the image and engaged by form in close reading'. The pertinence here lies not just in the spectacular being built in China actively with a prevalent use of digital rendering in conjunction with politico-economic efforts to increase visibility in the market, but also in the Western architects closely engaged in such a construction, especially the star architects thanks to a symbolic capital attached to their status. Yet images and spectacles themselves, including mediated visibility, a century-old phenomenon, with its own 'depth', do not seem to be a problem on their own. Although a critique in Debord and Eisenman is necessary, it remains unclear why 'surface' cannot be or has not always been part of reality in depth. Similarly, one can also ask why 'passivity' and 'close reading', 'images' and 'form' (in depth) have to be either–or alternatives. Is it possible to imagine a subjectivity that is immersive *and* reflective, embodied *and* critical, 'induced' *and* 'distanced', in a mobile, relational and comprehensive form of existence. I assume that a new reflexivity has to be built in relation to the conditions and possibilities provided by media and informational technologies, and a widened and intensified market economy.

6.9

Liu Jiakun's 'Open Letter' brought us back to the issue of communication and asymmetry between China and the West.[42] Liu explained difficulties in cross-cultural communication in a few aspects: the asymmetry of knowledge in the two directions ('we know more about them then they know about us'), the use of established 'key words' for communication which do not quite reflect one's actual situation, and the major difficulties of describing the Chinese situation in an indigenous discourse. Regarding the first observation, I agree with Liu in this and assume that things can only change slowly. For the second point, I suppose the difficulties lie not in a gap between public speech and private experience, but between Western international concepts and Chinese indigenous experience. I believe this gap can be bridged only through tentative efforts. I think the gap can be bridged at times for certain projects of communication (but that is not to assume that a full and thorough communication is attainable). This leads to the third observation made by Liu, which was also identified by Li Xiangning, the difficulties in describing China as a whole in China's own terms or with an indigenous discourse. Liu's final sentences in the letter expressed a hope that I establish a system of discourse based on Chinese practice. I see my current work, as in this book, as an attempt to describe China with sufficient references and terms rooted in China's own history and unique condition. But I also see modern China since 1840, if not 1700 or earlier, as an international narrative in which China cannot be described without external reference to other nations, especially Western and European nations, on account of a politico-economic asymmetry that had altered China subsequently.

Despite the difficulties Liu expressed in communication with overseas colleagues, he has also highlighted benefits he experienced. This included a clearer view of oneself through communications as mirror reflections, and a demystification of the images of star architects through a closer observation of their real working conditions, which strengthened Liu's own conviction of the importance of certain original forces in dealing with reality prior to academic theorization. This led to Liu's statement about his working method: if one is able to focus on problems in reality and utilize local resources creatively in China, then a Chineseness will surface naturally. These observations in Liu confirmed that communication, although frustrating at times and involving a deep asymmetry not to be removed soon, can still be beneficial in effect. It reveals a certain effect from outside upon the Chinese inside, but also, in his outlining of his method, an adoption of an international experience to strengthen a position that had been indigenous always. In Liu's work we see in fact an 'expedient architecture' that remains 'formal' and 'critical' in China.

6.10

Michael Speaks's comment, 'Ideals, ideology, intelligence in China and the West', brought us back to the debate on criticality, in which cross-cultural communication still surfaced as a problem.[43] Denouncing a reduction of the debate into 'static ideological positions' in the current discussion, Speaks offered a definition of post-critical thinking as a belief that criticality, which had been influential in the West from the 1970s to the 1990s, was now bankrupt. Further, according to him, the ideology of criticality which encouraged architects to reflect and criticize rather than actively engage with the market was no longer relevant in the twenty-first century. What was emerging, according to Speaks, were new practices worldwide, including China and the West, that were affirmative, in a constructive relation with global modernization. Not satisfied with the idea that 'static ideological positions' could be brought into other regions to hasten or retard certain processes, Speaks adopted another perspective to explain developments outside the West such as in China: the 'same global modernization' spreading worldwide which different regions experienced at 'different speeds and intensities'. With observations I had made in my essay, Speaks developed a neat comparison between China and the Unites States: whereas autonomy secured criticality *inside* the market in China it did so (as in Peter Eisenman) *outside* the market in America, and whereas criticality allowed the Chinese architects to move away *from* Maoist ideologies in the West it achieved its position by aligning architects *with* leftist ideologies. I find this comparison interesting but in need of further explanation. In my observation, the first contrast is a deeper phenomenon which is perhaps related to cultural and philosophical traditions in Europe and China (where a dualistic/confrontational and a relational/synthetic thinking had developed respectively, a point I will explore at the end of the next chapter). The second contrast appears more of a temporary phenomenon: the move away from Maoist and socialist ideologies in China was at its clearest in the 1980s and early 1990s, and leftist voices are certainly on the rise today (yet a return to the Maoist system seems impossible). But in this second contrast there is still an element of the first: behind the retreat from radical Maoism is a surfacing of a deeper Chinese sensitivity that tends to be non-positional or non-ideological, more comprehensive, and more willing to engage with practice and material production, in the form of Deng Xiaoping's pragmatism. In the European tradition, on the other hand, the tendency appears to be in favour of a committed, clearly defined position and an engagement with a transcendental/metaphysical discourse. It is precisely this pragmatism and a mobile and 'general' subjectivity in the Chinese tradition, in my view, that allowed the Chinese in the post-Mao era to move in between opposing ideologies of 'communism' and 'capitalism'. An aspect of this, in relation to Chinese traditions and the search for a new criticality, will be explored tentatively at the end of the next chapter.

Speaks's strategy of adopting a framework of the same global modernization with different local speeds and intensities allowed him to comment on China and the Unites States with ease. With this, he turned to Koolhaas and argued that Koolhaas, though having studied Singapore and China, had not really imported any Asian pragmatism into the West. Rather, it was developed within the West in Koolhaas's quest for the implications of global modernization, which had brought him to New York first, and then Singapore and China. Speaks's next important observation was his identification of a certain form of knowledge in design practice today worldwide with a post-critical and affirmative perspective. This is not 'ideals' or 'ideology', but 'intelligence', a practical knowledge of 'small truths' developed on the way, itself always open-ended, and speculative. Speaks has a clear framework here: whereas Modernism was affirmative with naïve 'ideals' about universal truth, and Postmodern criticality was negative with 'ideologies' to critique and repressed truths to uncover, contemporary post-critical practice is affirmative with practical 'intelligence' of small truths collected on the move, itself open-ended and worldwide in scope.

I appreciate Speaks's adoption of the framework of global modernization with different local intensities, one in which China and the United States, or Asia and the West, and other regions can be included. I also appreciate Speaks's identification of an Asian or Chinese pragmatism *as* post-critical and post-ideological in his passing statements (which was exactly what I was arguing for), an observation that methodologically brought China, Asia and the West onto one platform of discourse, which was what I wanted to facilitate and bring about as well. What I cannot agree with, however, is Speaks's reduction of others' ideas, and the critical and post-critical thrusts I identified in my article, into 'static ideological positions'. Speaks says 'static ideological positions cannot be imported from one situation and applied to another to hasten or retard these processes; nor do they allow one to explain one situation by reference to another'. Static positions certainly cannot be moved around, by definition. But what was transferred from one geo-cultural location to another, as I identified between China and the West, were complex and soft ideas circulating all the time (as in the case of transfer of ideas from Robin Evans to Rodney Place to Yung Ho Chang, or from London to Houston to Beijing). Further, given that there had been circulation of ideas and influences as I had identified, an explanation of one region with a reference to the other appears not only workable, but also necessary and important. Speaks's own statements had testified this: whether Koolhaas had imported ideas from Asia or not (and I think there is no need to focus on semantics), he had certainly travelled from New York to Singapore to China in his research, published these studies in the West and returned to Beijing with his designs, which had certainly been reported, discussed and criticized in the West. The shuttling in space and in mind is just too abundant to be ignored. In another note, if there had been real impact across the Atlantic in the past which necessitates an explanation of one region with a reference to the other, then there is no reason why it is not happening across the Pacific, and across other geo-cultural gaps and spaces. In any case, to 'externalize' one's observation and to move out of one's own geo-cultural locality as a method of observation is a main proposition I made in the paper.

In Speaks's writing, there is a special way of avoiding the 'horizontal' reference of the other that still allows him to discuss the other, China and the West for example. If his and my approaches are both noted, then there are two ways of 'moving' around and out of the West methodologically: the one adopted by Speaks assuming a global modernization with different local speeds, and the one I attempted in which horizontally there were flows of ideas and energies circulating around. One is a top-down view that bypasses geo-cultural movements, the other is a horizon on and above the earth taking account of messy movements of ideas, things and energies. The two methods perhaps have to work with each other.

What concerns me most is Speaks's suggestion that post-critical thinking and practice, exploring pragmatic intelligence on the go in the market, are not 'ideological'. I suppose by 'ideology' we mean an ethical position one takes that has some real socio-political consequences. If that is the case, then contentions can be raised. Speaks's statement is that either these architects identified by him are not ideological, or the outlook he argues for is not ideological. In the first case, I suppose all approaches adopted by a self-conscious architect are ideological. In the second, the outlook or attitude Speaks is arguing for, I think, cannot be value-free or completely non-ideological either. Ethical and political position has to be (re-)defined and has always already been defined in one's materialized action regardless of one's own statement. One cannot remain completely non-ideological. Yet a post-critical attempt to move away from the criticality of the 1970s to the 1990s in the West, to identify a negative burden, and to open the profession up, in order to engage with socio-economic transformations, is entirely understandable. What these post-critical voices including Speaks are searching for, and what is really needed if one is to critically engage with global modernization, is perhaps *another ideology or criticality*. It is 'non-ideological' in Speaks's terms (that is, it is disassociated from the negative ideology of the West in the late twentieth century), yet it remains ideologically committed to *a broad, secular, humanistic and ecological ethics*. Perhaps the debate we are witnessing today is a sign of a larger shift taking place in human history from one ethic to another. It is perhaps an evolution of subjectivity, and of political ethics, from a dualistic, oppositional and negative to a relational and affirmative formulation. It is a development from a resolute ideological positioning to a modest, open-minded and constructive ethic which appeals to a general humanism. In my view, Chinese and Asian cultures can add important contributions to this evolution, a point I will explore tentatively at the end of the next chapter.

CHAPTER 7

A GLOBAL SITE AND A DIFFERENT CRITICALITY

As China becomes the largest construction site in the world today, three issues are arising in relation to this development. One concerns a 'symmetrical' exchange between China and the West as I have identified. It seems important to develop this observation further, to capture a larger picture of design practice in China and a growing international discourse on China. Both historical and geo-global perspectives must be employed. It is an ongoing reading that I should like to pursue further. The second issue concerns the position of 'critical architecture' for China and elsewhere. China and other parts of Asia have certainly provided cases for an instrumentalist viewpoint that can lend its support to a post-critical argument as Koolhaas's studies have already attested. Yet this 'China' and 'Asia' refer to a pragmatic practice in these countries, not the new critical 'avant-garde' I have also identified. There are both critical and instrumental practices overlapping and interrelating here. A crucial question therefore remains. Do we need critical architecture in China and elsewhere, in the face of a generic contemporary instrumentalism in these countries, and in the world at large with a neo-liberal ideology of globalization? If the answer is yes, and if post-critical thinking is also persuasive in transcending a negative criticality in the West, then what kind of new critical architecture should we adopt? Are there signs we can identify in China today which are relevant for the search of this different criticality? This will be explored as a continuation of my observations on the 'symmetry' and the Chinese 'avant-garde'.

The third issue concerns China's current politico-economic development and its likely position in the capitalist world or 'the capitalist world-system' in Immanuel Wallerstein's term. Current observations have identified a trajectory in China that is neither 'communist' nor 'capitalist', but a third path in which the state plays a synthetic leadership role which does not subject itself to the market capitalism promoted by neo-liberal voices, especially in the United States. In different perspectives, Tu Wei-ming, Peter Nolan, David Harvey and Satoshi Ikeda have all identified signs of a new development towards a post-capitalist world-system in which China plays an important role. What does that mean for the architecture discipline? If that implies a new ethics and cultural aspiration, what is its implication for 'critical architecture'? Can 'criticality' be recomposed, to absorb not only Western ideas but also those that do not postulate notions of autonomy, negation and transgression?

I would like to deal with these issues continuously. I will first describe the 'symmetrical' exchange in a historical and geo-global perspective, and then move on to discuss issues of critical architecture and China's third way or middle path with its implications for architecture.[1]

A moment of symmetry

According to Immanuel Wallerstein, a capitalist world-system emerged around 1450–1500 when Europe acquired the Americas as its colonies, in which Europe and the Americas assumed the position of 'core' and 'periphery' respectively in production, economy and political domination.[2] By the end of the nineteenth century, this system had expanded to cover almost the entire world with vast areas of colonies as periphery and the advanced nation-states as its core, in which there existed a global division of labour and a hierarchy of importance in production, finance and politico-military power. Using this theory and its terminology, China around 1900 was at the periphery after many defeats, a loss of land and resources, and having been transformed into semi-colonies since 1840. In an ambivalent relationship with the West or the core states, China was the victim of this aggressive capitalist modernity, yet Chinese still looked to the West for ideas and knowledge for self-strengthening, modernization and social progress. While Western architects were practising in China, Chinese students went to study architecture in the advanced nation-states including Japan, the United States and countries in Western Europe. What they learned was predominantly a Beaux-Arts system of design well developed in Europe before and in full swing in North America in the 1920s and 1930s. A flow of ideas and disciplinary knowledge from the West into China can be clearly identified. Today, China appears to be moving into a core position in the world, or converging with the core states in many aspects of the world-system. The Beaux-Arts system is no longer the dominating design paradigm; design and construction are now a much internationalized enterprise; the speed and scale of urbanization in China are generating an astonishing landscape of ongoing building sites and a strange new urbanity of immense quantities; the commitment to international practice and the need to raise profiles in the world have also attracted almost all influential architects worldwide to design and build in China; an international discourse on China is also arising while some overseas architects and theorists are speculating on implications of the development of China and Asia. With such a landscape unfolding in and around China, there appears to be a flow of images and impacts from China to the West and the world at large. Yet the flow of influence in the old direction, from the West into China, remains active in new conditions: while Western and other overseas architects are active in China, Chinese students continue to flock to the classical core states, the advanced countries, to study architecture as before. What is really happening here in contemporary China in a historical and international perspective? An accurate description of a crucial 'moment' is necessary, a moment I described as that of symmetry between China and the core states, in a fluid, ongoing history that had not witnessed such a moment before or after. In my argument, a moment of symmetry has just occurred around 2000. The interrelation between China and the West or the core states has perhaps already moved on beyond this moment since new developments have already emerged. Yet this moment has to be grasped and recorded.

Modern architecture in China before 1976–8, that is, before the arrival of the post-Mao era, included two main traditions: a Beaux-Arts-based historicism and a socialist modernism. The first is arguably the more predominant. It was based on the education system established in the late 1920s, largely imported from America through the Chinese architects educated in the United States in the 1920s and after (although those educated in Japan and Europe also played a role). Its primary features are the use of historical images and styles upon modern structures, and that of symmetrical compositions in some cases. Evident from the 1920s to the 1990s, its primary climax was in the 1930s and 1950s with direct support from the state authority in Nanjing and Beijing respectively. It may appear with the use of a curved Chinese roof resulting in a dramatic profile or a flat roof with a modern look but with Chinese, sometimes Western and other cultural-traditional decorative motifs. The use of political icons at the end of the Cultural Revolution around 1970, and a resurfacing of the use of Chinese roofs under Post-Modern influence in the 1980s and 1990s are two of its variations. The decorative legacy in fact continued in the last decades of the twentieth century in disguise in other directions (as in regionalism). The second main tradition employed a version of modernism for the design of public institutions and mass housing in the 1960s and the 1970s. It was largely an economic and rational solution rather than an ideological adoption like the national styles of the 1930s and 1950s, or the result of a formal research and disciplinary inquiry by individuals as one finds in Europe in the 1920s and thereafter. Given the social conditions, there have been no opportunities for architects to engage in individual experiments with autonomous formal possibilities. With some exceptions (such as Xi Fuquan, Tong Jun, Hua Lanhong, Yang Tingbao and Feng Jizhong in the 1930s, late 1940s, early 1950s and after), the primary contribution of the Chinese architects before the late 1970s had been design for the nation and the public with a stylistic historicism and an economic modernism. In the Maoist period (1949–76), design was even more 'collective' as both the client and the profession working in the design institutes belonged to the collective public, and individual authorship in design was thoroughly abolished.

The reform and opening-up since 1978 under Deng Xiaoping brought China into a new era. The post-Mao era, already three decades old now, may be divided into two periods, the 1980s and the 1990s including the early years of the new century. If the first introduced rural reform and partial urban liberalization with a limited opening to international investment, the second has completed urban industrial reform and has established a 'socialist market economy' with increasing openness to international commerce and cultural participation, especially from the late 1990s onwards. In design, the 1980s is characterized by two related contributions on the part of the Chinese architects: a late modern formalism, and a decorative vernacular or regionalism, sometimes with a mixture of the two (which I have termed 'late modern with new vernacular'). Professors and senior architects educated before 1977–8 were the main force. Wu Liangyong, Guan Zhaoye, Peng Yigang, Xing Tonghe, Bu Zhengwei and Cheng Taining were some of the most influential figures. But Qi Kang's large quantity of designs in the 1980s from his design and research institute at the Southeast University of Nanjing is arguably the most substantial representative of these architects. The 'late modern' designs (such as Chai Peiyi's International Exhibition Center, Beijing, 1985, Peng Yigang's School of Architecture at Tianjin University 1990, Xing Tonghe's Shanghai Museum 1994, Bu Zhengwei's Jiangbei Airport Terminal, Chongqing, 1991) are abstract, heroic, volumetric and often symmetrical. Classical compositions and a national or collective heroism well developed in the Beaux-Arts-based tradition in the Nationalist and socialist periods before 1976 can be clearly identified. The new vernacular (such as Qi Kang's Meiyuan Memorial Museum, Nanjing, 1988, and Guan Zhaoye's New Library at Tsinghua University, Beijing, 1991) uses bricks and pitched roofs with other decorative details also added. Once again, the stylistic historicism of the pre-1976 periods survived here in the hands of senior architects who had already been active in those earlier times. Apart from these historical lineages, there were also horizontal or international influences here: the brutalism and late modernism of the 1960s and 1970s, and the Post-Modernism of the 1980s and after. The 'late modern' and 'new vernacular' of the 1980s in China, after all, were attempts in a new post-Mao era, by the senior Chinese architects who studied in the Maoist period, to modernize design language and to synchronize with Western international developments.[3]

The 1980s also witnessed the arrival of overseas architects in limited numbers. The prominent examples would be I. M. Pei's Fragrant Hill Hotel in Beijing (1982), Denton Corker Marshall (DCM)'s Australian Embassy in Beijing (1982–92), and Kisho Kurokawa's Sino-Japanese Youth Centre (1990). Formally, these designs were in a range between late modernism and Post-Modernism, yet each design was distinctive with strong formal integrity. Conceptually, they were 'dialogues' with Chinese traditions. If Pei's Fragrant Hill Hotel used iconic and decorative elements to engage with southern Chinese vernacular and scholarly gardens, and if Kurokawa's Youth Centre employed Japanese and Chinese cultural icons with a modernist language, then DCM's Embassy used a more abstract or purist modernism, with an abstract version of Post-Modernism (axes, walls, layers, panels, square wholes), to interpret a walled-compound typology found in imperial Beijing. These interactions with China, however, remained isolated cases of intellectual dialogues, not quite a full participation in the local scene yet.

For the 1990s and after, the major contribution is the arrival of a new generation of Chinese architects on the national and international stage. Educated in the post-Mao era at the universities from 1977–8 onwards, with teaching programmes open to Western and international influence, and some of them having studied abroad in the advanced countries, and having already experimented with ideas and designs in different settings, these architects 'suddenly' emerged around 1996–2000 with a purist and experimental modernism based on individual research as never seen before in China. The key characteristic of these architects is their individual authorship of design, and their experimentation with internal disciplinary knowledge and methods, in the areas of tectonics, space and experience. In so far as their focus is upon these internal or autonomous ideas of architecture, and their intention is to challenge and transcend mainstream decorative practice in the Beaux-Arts modern tradition, its variations in the post-Mao 1980s, and its current popular and commercial tendencies, these designs are 'critical' in their historical context. The emergence of these architects is part and parcel of the social and politico-economic liberalization of China in the 1980s and 1990s, the emergence of a civil society and a middle class (in relation to but increasingly separated from a parallel capitalist bourgeois class), and the opening of the design practice (with the registration system installed in 1994–5). Although the situation is evolving, in the earliest years from 1996 to 2000 and soon after the crucial architects include Yung Ho Chang (Book-Bike Store 1996), Liu Jiakun (Hedouling Studio 1997), Wang Shu (Chenmo Studio 1998, 'A Room with a View' 2000, Suzhou University Library 2000), Cui Kai (Extension to Foreign Language Press 1999, Convention Centre of Foreign Language Press 2004), and Qingyun Ma (Father's House 2003, Winding Garden, Qingpu, 2004).

Another contribution or crucial development of the 1990s and now is a 'flood' of international participation in China or, more precisely, an emergence of a sea of interflows in design practice between Chinese and overseas architects for projects in the country. This situation turns China into a 'global' construction site in many ways. The scale of urbanization, the quantity of construction and the amount of foreign direct investment (FDI) are all among the largest in the world. Since

1994, FDI has increased dramatically to cover ever more areas of China beyond the former Special Economic Zones. After 2001 when China joined the World Trade Organization and won its bid to host the 2008 Olympic Games, the architects of major projects were selected through international competitions. These processes attracted ever more architects from around the world to participate in China, and also 'star' architects mostly from Europe to design prominent buildings of national significance.

It is important to note that, in historical perspective, the post-Mao era, now three decades old, is the longest and most politically stable period in the timeline of all periods in a turbulent modern China since 1911 or even since 1840. It is also the longest period of being open to the outside, and of a sustained market economy and technological and industrial modernization in China since the late nineteenth century.

The last development identified above, the 'flooding' or the interflow of overseas and Chinese architects working alongside or together in China today, is in fact a summary description of the entire scene in the

7.1 A 'mega' project: National Olympic Stadium ('Bird's Nest'), Beijing, 2008. Architect: Herzog & de Meuron with CAG (China Architecture Design & Research Group). Photo taken in November 2006.

country now: all architects and their different design positions now and from the past are contained here. To observe design practice and thinking in contemporary China in historical and global perspectives, it is important now to examine this overall sea of interflows. Upon closer observation, four types of designs can be identified: a generic background, the megaprojects, the medium projects, and the small projects. The generic background is what one sees in most cities in China today: a hybrid landscape of high-rises and super-blocks, often of commercial functions and large housing developments, designed by Chinese architects from state or private offices as well as overseas design companies of various sizes and design orientations. All stylistic 'isms' can be found here but Post-Modernism and International Style loom large on the skyline. Buildings of earlier decades of all qualities with fragments of still earlier historical fabrics coexist in a most heterogeneous landscape at lower altitudes across the urban ground. Against this backdrop are three groups of influential or controversial designs.

The first are the 'megabuildings', those large landmark projects of municipal and national significance, such as cultural facilities in large cities and especially those for or associated with the Olympic Games in Beijing (and the World Expo in Shanghai). The clients are public, mainly city or state government or their subordinate organizations. The architects are predominantly Europeans (from the UK, France, Germany, the Netherlands and Switzerland among others). And prominent examples include Rem Koolhaas's CCTV buildings, Herzog & de Meuron's National Olympic Stadium (Figure 7.1), Norman Foster's Extension to the Beijing Capital Airport, and the structural engineers behind all three, Arup from England.

7.2 A 'medium' project: Culture Center, Shenzhen, 2006. Architect: Arata Isozaki. Photo taken in December 2005.

7.3 'Small' projects. **a**: 'Bamboo
Wall' house, Beijing, 2002.
Architect: Kengo Kuma. **b**: Book-
Bike-Store, Beijing, 1996. Architect:
Yung Ho Chang.

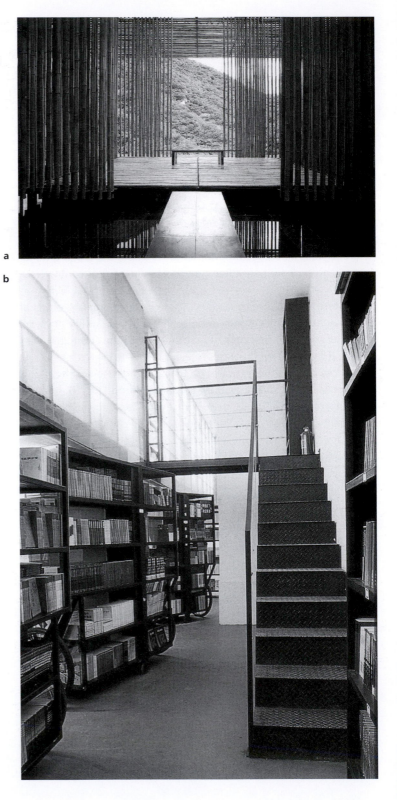

a

b

The second are the 'medium buildings', most notably cultural facilities and substantial housing developments. The clients are mixed; they can be public or private, that is, government agents or property developers. The most prominent architects come from a variety of Western countries but the most noted among them are arguably the Japanese, as in the case of Riken Yamamoto's Jianwai SOHO housing towers (Beijing, 2003) and Arata Isozaki's Cultural Centre (Shenzhen, 2006) (Figure 7.2).

The third are the 'small buildings', small in terms of scale and function, not impact and significance. They include offices, studios, houses and villas. The clients here are typically private. The eminent architects for these designs are Chinese and international. Among the overseas architects, the national origins are global, yet the Japanese architects (besides Korean and other Asian architects) are again among the most influential. Kengo Kuma's designs, the 'Bamboo Wall' house in the collection of model villas in a 'Commune by the Great Wall' outside Beijing (2002) (Figure 7.3a), and his recent Z58 office in Shanghai (2006), are among the most distinctive. Another crucial example is Office dA (Monica Ponce de Leon and Nader Tehrani) from Boston, USA, with its design for a 200 m² gatehouse in Tongzhou outside Beijing (2004), a small project that displays rich interlays of skin and structure, material and space. The Chinese architects here are the 'breakthrough generation' identified above, including Chang, Liu, Cui, Ma and Wang and increasingly some younger architects such as Tong Ming (Figure 7.3b). Whereas the main agendas for these Chinese architects are material texture, tectonics, details, space, light and experience, in relation to a personal, vernacular or traditional life-world resisting modern traditions and mindless designs, the agendas of the overseas architects at this end, operating at another level inside the Western trajectory in 'deconstruction' and 'neo-modernism', share the same critical interest in materiality, tectonics, space and experience. In fact Western and Japanese architects operating at the larger scales, such 'edgy' or reflective architects as Isozaki, Yamamoto, Herzog & de Meuron, and Koolhaas, remain tectonic or post-tectonic in a more radicalized form of a new modernism. The common theme here is identifiable, and should be further emphasized. Here should be noted the phenomenon of 'group design', whereby architects from China, Asia and around the world are invited to design, for example, a villa each for a property developer to showcase new ideas in design and life style, such as the 'Commune by the Great Wall' (outside Beijing, 2002) for the developer SOHO China, and the ongoing CIPEA (China International Practice Exhibition of Architecture) in Nanjing by another developer. These are crucial venues in which common yet different thinking amongst the Chinese and overseas architects can rub against each other, which certainly provides a window to observe and learn for the Chinese (and everyone else).

7.4 Publications on China. **a:** Cover of *2G: International Architecture Review*, 10 (1999): a special issue titled 'Instant China'. **b:** Cover of *Alors, la Chine?*, Paris: Pompidou Centre, 2003: exhibition catalogue. **c:** Cover of *Architectural Record*, 3 (2004), with a special section on China.

These three prominent groups of designs, the large, the medium and the small, are in fact productions of 'symbolic capital', for marks of distinction in the local, national and international market.[4] They are collaborations between the architect and the powerful client, private or public, to mark a sign of distinction or symbolic supremacy for a commercial body, a municipality, or the nation, in a competitive market and a fluid mass culture of images at different levels. At these levels, a formal capital in design is employed for cultural, social and commercial visibility needed for the developers or the municipal and national bodies. The resources of the profession, especially the reputation of knowledge and its practitioners the architects, are collaborating with the resources of these political and commercial authorities: a joint venture that enhances the effective power of both systems of resources. That the world's most prestigious professional honour, the Pritzker Architecture Prize, was given to Foster, Koolhaas, and Herzog & de Meuron in 1999, 2000 and 2001, who were soon the designers of China's largest national landmarks of 2008 (the airport extension, the CCTV building and the national stadium) from 2001 onwards, reveals clearly this collaboration at the highest international level.

Yet this situation should not prevent us from appreciating these moments of participation and openings of possibilities. First, not all commercial and political authorities are always suppressive: they can be progressive or suppressive in a humanistic judgment depending on the specific historical case. Against a colonized past and a highly regimented Maoist period, the post-Mao political and economic reform in principle and in this particular history is progressive and liberating for the Chinese nation (despite the increasing problems that must be dealt with as well). Second, there is a dialectical relationship between power and design we cannot deny. While design serves political and commercial powers, a politically supported opening-up and a financial or material basis also allow design knowledge to develop and to be materialized.

In this respect, a lot of design thinking and experimentation are happening in China with architects and their ideas crossing the national borders in this sea of exchange, thanks to this politico-economic opening. Here we can identify primarily two currents moving in opposite directions: a flow of impact from China to the West and the world; and a flow of impact from the world and the West into China. In the first flow of influence, it seems that China as a whole exerts a certain impression upon the world and Western professional circles. Here ideas of a pragmatic attitude of efficient design and building to serve a large society in active modernization offer a window or scenario for rethinking some of the established ideas in the West in the aftermath of the postmodern critique of instrumental modernity in architecture (and in other disciplines). In the opposite direction, it seems that it is primarily the quality of design with reflexivity and radical architectonic ideas from Western and some Asian architects, especially the Europeans and Japanese, that had the most effect upon China. Here tectonics, purism, critical design and concerns for the public (with its social democratic values) are among the most distinctive in terms of Western influence on the Chinese scene. Let me now examine the two flows of impact more closely.

The flow of impact from China to the West and the world is mediated through three channels: a discourse on China in professional media in the West distributed worldwide (such as forums, exhibitions and special issues of magazines), a focused reflection on China by individual architect-theorists exemplified in Koolhaas, and the increasing actual participation and design of buildings in China as reported in the West. In the first, since *AA Files* (36, 1996) and *2G: International Architectural Review* (10, 1999) (Figure 7.4a), there has been a stream of special issues on Chinese architecture in *A+U*, *Architectural Record*, *AV Monographs* and *Volume* (in 2003, 2004, 2004 and 2006 respectively). Special exhibitions have also been staged on the subject mostly in Europe, such as those at Aedes Berlin, the Pompidou Centre in Paris, the Architecture Centre in Rotterdam, and recently the 15th Architectural Congress at the Architecture Centre in Vienna (in 2001, 2003, 2006 and 2007 respectively). Impressive catalogues were published with these events (Figure 7.4b). Forums and lectures such as at the Royal Academy of Arts in London and the 15th Congress on 'China Production' in Vienna (in 2006 and 2007 respectively) added unique opportunities to introduce the Chinese scene. This public discourse on China in the West and world imparts a central impression which may be best summarized in the words on the covers of the relevant issues of *2G* and *Architecture Record*: 'Instant China', 'China . . . builds with superhuman speed, reinventing its cities, from the ground up'. Behind these headlines were magical skylines of soaring towers (Figure 7.4c). This imparts an imagination of China and also, if and when taken seriously, a window onto another reality of an instrumentalist architecture for active modernization.

The focused reflection on China by architect-theorists so far may be best exemplified by Koolhaas. We can identify a sequence of statements or propositions that overlaps with observations on China and Asia in Koolhaas's writings. Here we are encountering possibly the most serious theoretical reflections in the West today on a real or effective architecture for active modernization, using China and other parts of Asia as its primary archive and laboratory. In the 1995 book *S, M, L, XL*, four articles, on 'urbanism', 'bigness', 'Singapore' and 'the generic city', are particularly relevant (Figure 7.5a). In 'What ever happened to urbanism?', Koolhaas says that we must dare to be 'uncritical', to accept the inevitable urbanization across the world, and to explore an inevitable design thinking that facilitates this new material condition.[5] In the second article, Koolhaas argues that an architecture of 'bigness',

7.5 Koolhaas's publications. **a:** Cover of the book *S, M, L, XL*, 1995. **b:** Cover of the book *Mutations*, 2000. **c:** Inside cover of the book *Great Leap Forward*, 2001.

7.6 Images used in Koolhaas's writings. **a:** 'Singapore songlines' in *S, M, L, XL* (p. 1062). **b:** On Pearl River Delta of China in *Mutations* (p. 317) and *Great Leap Forward* (p. 197).

a

b

with its maximum quantities, can disassociate itself from the exhausted artistic and ideological movements in Western architecture, and 'regain its instrumentality as vehicle of modernization'.[6] In the third article, Koolhaas uses Singapore as a convincing reality outside the West, to explore 'the operational' and 'city-making' in architecture, ideas that had according to him long been forgotten since the 1960s in the West, ideas that may bring us in the West back to a heroic and functioning modernism of magnitude and capacity, for urban and socio-economic transformation (Figure 7.6a).[7] In 'The generic city', Koolhaas challenges the ideas of identity and regionalism in full swing in the 1980s and 1990s and encourages a recognition of a universal modern city found everywhere, one which has been much criticized in the West, yet positively embraced in Asia ('Asia aspires to it . . . Many generic cities are Asian').[8]

In *Mutations* (2000), Koolhaas publishes a speech, 'Pearl River Delta', which summarizes some of the ideas behind the forthcoming book *Great Leap Forward* (2001) (Figures 7.5b,c, 7.6b). Koolhaas is apparently providing a rationalization for a focus on Asia, possibly to the Western audience to which the speech was given. Koolhaas observes that modernization has its peaks of intensity in different locations, and that, whereas it had been in Europe and then the United States, 'today, it is clear that modernization is at its most intense in Asia, in a city like Singapore or in the Pearl River Delta'.[9] These Asian cities can teach us about what is happening now. 'To renew the architectural profession and to maintain a critical spirit, it is important to . . . observe these emergent conditions and to theorize them'.[10] In *Great Leap Forward*, Koolhaas describes that Asia is now in a relentless process of building, on a scale unseen before, in a maelstrom of modernization that destroys existing conditions and creates a new urban substance.[11] A new theory of urbanism and architecture is needed, and the seventy terms identified at the end of the book to describe the Pearl River Delta of China may serve as a beginning of this new theory.[12]

This focused observation on China by the architect-theorist, published in the West, is then related to the third channel of influence on the West, the actual participation of design and building in China by the Western and overseas architects that are instantly reported in the West. Koolhaas of course won the competition for the new China Central Television headquarters (CCTV) in 2002, to be completed in 2008 (Figure 7.7a). The commissions to Western and overseas architects for stadiums, gymnasiums, grand theatres, airports, museums, expo buildings and the less famous but more pervasive large-scale housing developments are part of this impact upon the West that at least implicitly suggests an instrumentalist architecture of scale and bigness for active urbanization and modernization. Perhaps in the end the CCTV building and the National Olympic Stadium will remain as the lasting beacons for this alternative architecture of quantities engaged in social and material progress (Figures 7.7a,b,c).

7.7 Construction sites. **a:** CCTV
building under construction,
September 2007. **b:** National
Olympic Stadium ('Bird's Nest')
under construction, November
2006. **c:** National Grand Theatre
under construction, March 2007.

a

b

c

This trend, best reflected in Koolhaas, has been picked up in another theoretical debate, on 'post-critical' pragmatism as argued for by Robert Somol, Sarah Whiting and Michael Speaks, and as observed by George Baird in the past few years, in a discussion that has relayed between the United States and parts of Europe (especially in the Netherlands).[13] They have identified a discontent with the critical tradition that has controlled and exhausted the profession in the West by now, a trend towards pragmatism, of 'diagrams' and 'effects', a trend already exemplified in Koolhaas according to Somol, Whiting and Speaks. Although they have identified Koolhaas, they have not acknowledged a crucial geographical site or theoretical laboratory that is Asia and China in Koolhaas's thinking, or any site in terms of a real world-historical development in modernization.[14] There are, however, more important issues to be raised. That these post-critical theorists have not picked up a geographical site itself is perhaps less of a problem when we confront another issue: the possibility of a new criticality emerging from this crossing onto new sites. For at a theoretical level, a central issue remains about the composition of a new criticality to be proposed, one that may absorb the post-critical yet remain socially committed and progressive. If China is indeed in the grip of a most intense instrumentalism in architecture and yet if there are indeed public and socialist ideas to safeguard and disciplinary criticality to maintain and develop, then will there be new patterns of criticality emerging here? Are there clues and possibilities we can pick up in China as a site of theoretical reflection for the formulation of a new criticality? I will provide a preliminary discussion at the end.

7.8 Gatehouse of an art centre, Tongzhou, Beijing, 2004. Architect: Office dA (Monica Ponce de Leon and Nader Tehrani). **a:** Interior. **b:** Exterior.

a

b

a

b

In the opposite direction, there is also a flow of influence from the West and the world into China. Here we can identify two agents with which this impact was realized. The first was the Western and some Asian architects providing quality designs in China; the second was the Chinese 'breakthrough generation' educated in the post-Mao era, which is represented by Chang, Liu, Cui, Ma and Wang among others, that emerged from 1996 onwards. While the first brought Western ideas into China, the second was also an agent of Western ideas as these architects had studied in the post-Mao education system open to international influence and some leading members of them have also studied in the West.

The Western and overseas architects here provided 'large', 'medium' and 'small' projects, such as the CCTV building, the Stadium, Jianwai SOHO housing development, the 'Bamboo Wall' house, the 'Z58' office, Shenzhen Cultural Center, and the Tongzhou gatehouse (by Koolhaas, Herzog & de Meuron, Yamamoto, Kuma, Isozaki, and Office dA of Boston), as identified above (Figures 7.8a,b, 7.9a,b). In the Western architectural context, these architects come from a time of 'new modernism' and 'deconstruction' that attempted to transcend historicist Post-Modernism in the 1980s and 1990s. Their own interest

7.9 Z58, office headquarters, Shanghai, 2006. Architect: Kengo Kuma. **a:** Street front. **b:** Rooftop water pavilion.

7.10 Designs by Yung Ho Chang. **a:** Book-Bike-Store, exterior, Beijing, 1996. **b:** Morningside Maths Centre, Beijing, 1998. **c:** Villa Shizilin, Beijing, 2004. **d:** UF Soft Research & Development Centre, Beijing, 2006.

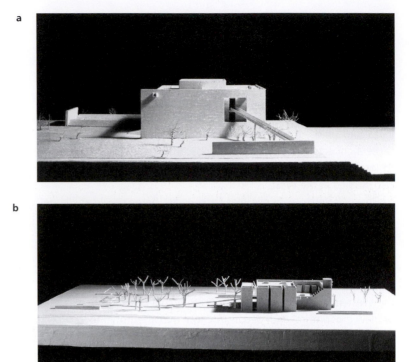

in purism and tectonics, though in a more radicalized shape, coincided with the local Chinese agenda to transcend Beaux-Arts historicism and the mindless popular commercialism. The well-established critical approach with form, autonomy, authorship and reflexivity in the West has certainly been much appreciated in China by those interested in transcending the local mainstream traditions.

The second agent, the Chinese, in fact have all sorts of relations with these overseas architects, perhaps most tangibly through work on the Commune by the Great Wall, the CIPEA, the book *Great Leap Forward*, and the various collaborations.[15] Having studied in an open education system after 1977–8 and having studied abroad in some cases, they have made critical transgressions in China by emphasizing autonomy, tectonics and reflexive authorship. The earliest crucial examples include those emerging in and after 1996: Yung Ho Chang's Book-Bike Store, Morningside Mathematics Centre and Shizilin Villa (1996, 1998, 2004) (Figure 7.10), Liu Jiakun's Hedouling Studio and Buddhist Sculpture Museum (1997, 2002) (Figure 7.11), Cui Kai's Extension to the Main Office of and Convention Centre for the Foreign Language Press (1999 and 2004) and his recent 'Desheng Up-town' office complex (2005) (Figure 7.12), Wang Shu's Chenmo Studio, 'A Room with a View', Wenzhen College Library of Suzhou University, and Xiangshan College of China Academy of Art in Hangzhou (1998, 2000, 2000, 2005) (Figure 7.13), and Qingyun Ma's Central Commercial District of Ningbo, Zhejiang University Library in Ningbo, Father's House in

c

7.11 Designs by Liu Jiakun. **a**: Studio Hedouling, design model, building completed in 1997, Chengdu. **b**, **c**, **d**: Buddhist Sculpture Museum, Chengdu, 2002.

d

Xian, Shopping Maze of Wuxi, and the Winding Garden of Qingpu (2002, 2002, 2003, 2003 and 2004) (Figure 7.14). New architects are also emerging in recent years, such as Tong Ming (Dong's House and Restaurant, Suzhou, 2004) (Figure 7.15).

All of these architects write clearly to explain their design approach: whereas Chang and Ma had a stronger theoretical basis (having studied in the United States), Liu and Wang explored their ideas with a stronger reference to Chinese traditions interlaced with Western ideas and concepts, and Cui Kai's writing reveals directly his working strategies in a Chinese reality of design in institutes for large clients (Figure 7.16). For the more reflective with Western methods, both Ma and Chang had a strong thematic focus for each project, although Ma seems to have a stronger urban emphasis whereas Chang explores a more cultural and experiential theme in specific cases (Figure 7.17).

Chang's writings, in historical observation, were the earliest to

7.12 Designs by Cui Kai. **a, b:** Extension to the Foreign Language Press, Beijing, 1999. **c, d:** Desheng Up-town office complex, Beijing, 2005.

mount a clear challenge to the Chinese modern traditions using autonomy as his primary critical category. He thus represents a critical thrust of this generation at this moment. In 1998, in his article 'A basic architecture' (*Pingchang jianzhu*), Chang argues for a non-discursive architecture based on a pure tectonic logic of building and its intrinsic poetic (of the steps, the columns, the walls, the openings,

the skylight, the courtyard etc.), for which he cites the works of Mies van der Rohe and Giuseppe Terragni as exemplars (Figure 7.17a,b).[16] In the article 'Learning from industrial architecture' (2002), he argues that, once meaning is removed, architecture is an entity in itself, pure and autonomous.[17] Chang here argues for a basic architecture that is not dependent on another reality, for example a representation of a social ideology imposed from outside, but an intrinsic system on its own, one which may have the capacities to transcend the Beaux-Arts modern tradition in China of 'fine arts' and 'decorations' and its recent Post-Modern and other variations. Chang recommends the Bauhaus system as an alternative to the decorative and the 'fine arts' traditions. In his more recent writings in 2004, his 'bourgeois' and 'rightist' position for an autonomous architecture against decorative expressions of ideology of the Maoist Beaux-Arts tradition has shifted to a leftist viewpoint opposing 'bourgeois' capitalism. In 'The third

7.13 Designs by Wang Shu. **a:** Chenmo Studio, interior, Haining, 1998. **b:** Wenzheng College Library, Suzhou University, Suzhou, 2000. **c:** Xiangshan College, China Academy of Art, Hangzhou, 2005. **d:** Xiangshan College Phase II, 2007.

7.14 Designs by Qingyun Ma.
a: Library of Zhejiang University, Ningbo, 2002. **b:** Father's House, Xian, 2003. **c:** Wuxi Shopping Maze, Wuxi, under construction as of 2003.

attitude', he advocates a position that is neither a pure critical research nor a commercial practice, but a 'critical participation', and that it is important to emphasize autonomy as a means to oppose and critique a rising capitalism.[18] In 'The next decade' (2004), Chang reveals that he would combine research and service to society, focusing more on urban strategies, with concerns for the public domain.[19] Although there is a shift in the object of critique from the Beaux-Arts tradition to a new capitalist aggression in China, the emphasis on autonomy (in a critical participation) remains a central method for a reflective and critical agenda. The important development here is not so much a mature critical architecture well developed in China in these architects, but the *emergence* of a self-conscious critical intention clearly written and well demonstrated in the built works in 1996–2000 and after in the *history* of modern Chinese architecture. This is surely a breakthrough in the historical context, as I have identified in 'Criticality in between China and the West' (2005): the emergence of a purist architecture with a level of criticality, as reflected in these architects' employment of tectonics, autonomy, individual authorship and reflexive experiment.[20]

If we combine the two observations above, that is, if the flow of impact from China to the West and that from the West into China are related together as simultaneous developments occurring around 2000 in opposite directions, a symmetrical exchange is clearly in sight. While China is absorbing a 'criticality' from the West, the West is absorbing a 'post-criticality' from China. Whereas the first may be best

7.15 Design by Tong Ming. Dong's House and Restaurant, Suzhou, 2004. **a:** Exterior. **b:** Interior.

represented in the Chinese architects of Chang's generation and his writings, the second is best represented in Koolhaas and his writings. Whereas in the first what has been absorbed in China was in surplus in the West, that is, notions of rigor, discipline, internal disciplinary knowledge, autonomy, reflexivity and critical authorship, in the second what has been acknowledged in the West was in surplus in China, that is, examples of instrumentalist architecture, built with efficiency, offering quantities and capacities, for a large society engaged in active urbanization and modernization. Historically, if the first occurred precisely in 1996 and 1998 (when the Book-Bike Store and 'A basic architecture' by Chang appeared), the second occurred in 2000, 2001 and 2002 (when *Mutations*, *Great Leap Forward* and the CCTV design by Koolhaas appeared). The second trend can also be pushed back to 1995 when *S, M, L, XL* was published, in which 'Asia' and 'Singapore' had been studied (if we see China as part of the modernizing Asia in Koolhaas). The second trend can also be extended to 2004 when the post-critical discourse has 'arrived' in the West as summarized by Baird's 'criticality' article that year (followed by the Chinese response in 2005 and 2006). It can also be extended further to 2008 and after when these major landmark buildings by the Western architects in China are completed. If one is to be strict, the symmetrical moment in fact occurs most clearly, or in its earliest historical freshness, between 1996 and 2002.

What makes this symmetrical exchange occur is a stark difference between the two worlds when they opened to each other, or when they opened to each other to such a point that an interflow between them started to occur, which happened in the late 1990s. The stark contrast between the two made a natural exchange of energies between them in which what is in surplus is naturally exported to the other side. When the two gradually merged into a larger and hybrid whole, which is now happening every day, the exchange will be replaced by new patterns of communication. It is important to note that instrumentalism

7.16 Writings by Chinese architects. a: Cui Kai, *Gongcheng Baogao: Projects Report*, Beijing, 2002. b: Wang Shu, *Sheji de Kaishi: The Beginning of Design*, Beijing, 2002. c: Liu Jiakun, *Cishi Cidi: Now and Here*, Beijing, 2002. d: Tang Hua, *Yingzao Wutuobang: Building Utopia*, Beijing, 2002.

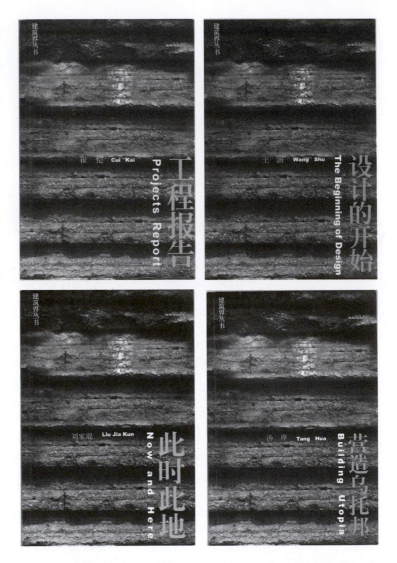

in architecture, although at its most intensive now in Asia, has also occurred before in the United States and in Europe at the high tide of capitalism and industrialization in the nineteenth and early twentieth centuries. Even at the present, post-critical thinking arises in the West from a neo-liberal free market economy and technological revolution occurring in these countries (but also everywhere else including Asia and China). On the other hand, criticality, though well developed in the European tradition and more so in architecture since the 1960s in the postmodern critique of instrumental modernity, can also be found in Asia and China in the past and in its modern history. And even within this generation, in Chang, Ma and Cui, and particularly in Liu and Wang, Chinese intellectual sources are also actively used so that their criticality is not entirely Western either. Further, in terms

a

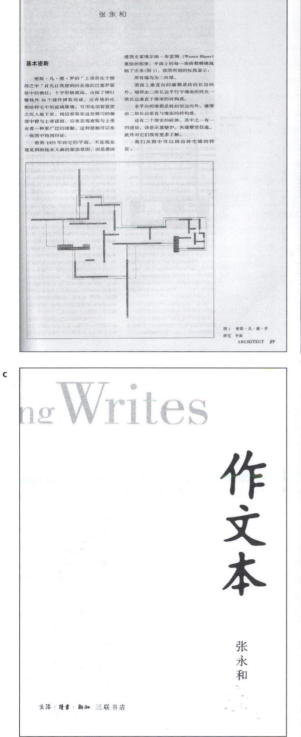

b

c

d

7.17 Writings by Chang and Ma. **a:** Front page of Yung Ho Chang's 'Pingchang jianzhu' (A basic architecture) in *Jianzhushi: Architect*, 84 (1998), 27–34. **b:** Yung Ho Chang, *Pingchang Jianzhu: For a Basic Architecture*, Beijing, 2002. **c:** Yung Ho Chang, *Zuowenben: Yung Ho Chang Writes*, Beijing, 2005. **d:** Qingyun Ma, *MADA on SITE*, Berlin, 2004, a catalogue of Ma's solo exhibition at Aedes Berlin.

of direction of impact carried out by certain 'agents', there are also new developments. While Koolhaas and the Chinese architects have been talking to the Western and Chinese audiences respectively, facilitating an impact from the other world, they have also shifted to new audiences as well: Koolhaas engaging with the Chinese audience concerning Beijing while Ma and Chang, now teaching in the United States, are initiating new programmes with 'Chinese' influences.[21] In a word, the initial symmetry I identified is a tendency in the exchange between the two worlds at a particular moment.

In a fluid history unfolding today, new trends are emerging that are sure to confuse and replace this symmetry. One of these new trends in China is an increasing interest in the indigenous Chinese intellectual and cultural traditions, and a use of this long historical resource to mount a critical architecture. This poses a new problem worth investigating: in the ongoing debate concerning the critical and the post-critical now moving across the Pacific to Asia and China, are there non-Western intellectual resources to be employed in this project of searching for a new criticality? Are there signs in China and in the discourse concerning China that can be identified and explored further for a new formulation of criticality?

Criticality

According to Wallerstein, the capitalist world-system has core nation-states, which have been shifting in membership and geographical location. This system, according to Wallerstein, though having evolved since 1450–1500 with a repeatable pattern of cycle and movement, may not survive and may go through structural change in the new environment today given the ecological limitations of the planet.[22] If we adopt this theory, many questions can be asked. If China is moving closer to the status of a core state, how will it relate to classical core states such as the United States? Will China bring about a significant change to the world-system? And, since this system may mutate significantly, in which direction will this occur and what is the likely impact of China on this mutation?

David Harvey has observed that Chinese state authority, with a long-term communist commitment to social equity, has displayed determination to lead and supervise, and not subject itself to, the capitalist class in China and the flow of commerce and finance into the country from the international market dominated by the US economy.[23]

Peter Nolan has also identified tendencies in China to develop its own 'third way' (which is neither bourgeois-capitalist nor proletarian-communist), so that it may resolve social and ecological crises and maintain stability and relative fairness, while resisting a totally free market economy and its global practice as promoted by the United

States.[24] Nolan indicates that, by making it work in China out of necessity for survival and development, China is also likely to offer a solution to capitalism at large, which always had its own contradictions, long since identified by Adam Smith. What China can offer is not only a few rules but a whole moral philosophy developed in its tradition. According to Nolan, China has a long tradition of a social, ethical and comprehensive 'third way', which included a pervasive yet non-ideological state, a method of enabling and controlling the market, and a moral philosophy of duty, relationship and interdependence which allows the state to supervise the market in an organic social environment.

Satoshi Ikeda, with his observations on China's tradition, its current performance in 'market socialism', and the world-system dominated by the US-led neo-liberalism, has also made similar observations to Nolan's.[25] According to Ikeda, with a long tradition and with its current behaviour, the Chinese state today is neither bourgeois nor proletarian; it does not subject itself to the demands of capital yet is able to attract global capital and sustain growth. In this way, China may break away from the fate of other, smaller Asian countries, and attain a core status outside, or at the least not subordinate to, the US-led market economy. With this, there may emerge a China-led post-capitalist world-system, one which does not uphold neo-liberalism and the bourgeois ideology of the free market and endless accumulation as absolute rules, one which employs a neutral and pervasive state to balance concerns of development, society and ecology, one which can secure better 'bargains' for the populations of the periphery or the 'third world' in the global politico-economic order.[26]

The key issue here is a pervasive and non-ideological state in a Chinese tradition of organic interrelationships in social and ecological ethics, a notion that escapes Western categories in social theory as developed in the past few centuries within the Western world. When state, market and society are related in ways different from that found in the modern Western world, then all other Western categories including notions of the critical, such as 'resistance', 'transgression', 'autonomy', and 'avant-garde', may not be applicable in China either without significant modifications. Today we can identify indications of a pervasive and non-ideological state emerging in China that is neither capitalist nor communist in the classical sense. Almost all policies implemented in post-Mao China explore this new path that moves in between the apparent contradictions. If the state is pervasive and organically embedded in society, and if the market economy is also organically situated in society in a subordinate relation to the state, and if cultural and critical practice is also socially embedded, then the entire composition of a critical architecture will also have to be relational, organic or embedded, rather than confrontational or oppositional. The contemporary Chinese political system is sure to evolve with the introduction of more market democracy, political participation and effective jurisdiction, yet the Chinese tradition of relational ethics, already providing a middle path through Western categories and oppositions in the post-Mao era, is likely to remain and to bring about a new social system. In such a context, criticality has to be defined as a relational practice.

Glimpses of these developments can be discerned in architecture. The new CCTV headquarters in Beijing designed by Koolhaas is an interesting case. This can be observed in three aspects. (1) Regarding the role of *the state* and *television service*, multiple and 'contradictory' functions are performed here. The client, China Central Television and the national government behind it, is playing a multiple and pervasive role in a society that also receives it this way. While the broadcasting service represents the state voice, it also represents a domestic mass culture and society with a popular basis, as well as a national image worldwide. And while it functions as informational windows on China and the world, it also disseminates moral teaching and cultural leadership for the population. (2) The *building* also functions in complex ways. In the iconic landmark of CCTV, we witness a representation of a new nation, its collective aspiration, and a new state leadership. The building promotes the city and the nation in a global capitalist market and visual media, yet it still functions as a socialist-collectivist work unit within. (3) The *historical condition* for the emergence of this design also reveals a complex situation. The building ensures a political and pragmatic employment of a landmark, yet it also allows and supports a subversive architectural idea to be materialized. While a radical design is materialized, it also serves to symbolize a nation in radical transition. The situation confuses classical categories of the 'critical' as negative and distanced with that of the 'conventional' as instrumental to society or social functions. In a 'critical facilitation' here, a radical form supports and is supported by social and political agents. Further, it has occurred at a crucial historical moment when the agents are actively engaged in material and social transformations.

Amongst Chinese architects, there has always been an employment of indigenous ideas for a critical architecture in this generation (Chang, Ma, Liu, Wang, Cui). Liu Jiakun and Wang Shu are exemplary of this. Wang's recent theorization of a critical project, 'thinking by hand', 'to reconstruct life-world amidst collapsing modern cities in China', employs more indigenous ideas in the intellectual tradition and the pattern of rural–urban environment from China's past.[27] These increasing appropriations of Chinese ideas may introduce further a holistic and organic viewpoint into critical reflections.

Regarding the mode of critical practice, another three aspects must be noted. First, these architects have always been working in a local Chinese manner in which a critical social positioning cannot be entirely autonomous and confrontational. The autonomy I identified above was a relative and relational autonomy. They were gaining relatively more autonomy than in the past, and the autonomy achieved today remains embedded and relational. An entirely confrontational and negative criticality in the Western tradition cannot be applied here in this organic social setting with its long tradition. Second, in both Ma's and Chang's writings, one can identify a distancing from a certain Western practice of a critical design opposing commercial practice. Both have said on different occasions that there was a separation between 'theory' and 'practice' in the United States, a situation the Chinese architects cannot and should not follow.[28] What the architects should do, according to them, was a critical practice embedded in reality. Liu Jiakun has also theorized his ideas of involving the client in planning at the earliest stage, to protect autonomous concerns for form and public space. Wang Shu and Cui Kai's work also displays active dialogue with the client for their new or critical ideas. Third, Chang in 2004 has particularly framed this as 'the Third Attitude', one which did not separate research and practice, critique and participation, one which integrated the two in what he termed a 'critical participation'.

If we observe conceptualizations of relevant categories in Western social theory and in architecture, we do find a model of thinking based on 'confrontation' between concepts and between social positions or categories (which in turn is related to an Aristotelian tradition of confrontational dualism).[29] For example, in Jürgen Habermas's theory of 'civil society', the concept is defined in a clear, distinctive and oppositional confrontation with 'state authority' and 'market capitalism' (or 'capital').[30] For him, in order to restore a life-world of social communities and a democratic civil society, we need to establish a 'dam' to prevent the flooding or aggressive invasions of state and capital, or rational bureaucracy and market capitalism. To actually move on to promote and protect civil society (which inevitably employs aspects of capital and authority one way or another), one then has to 'corrupt' the theory somewhat as the theory does not allow a more organic and relational perspective for such a compromise. In another example, Peter Eisenman's theory of the critical and the transgressive is also clear, confrontational and uncompromising: 'the critical as it concerns the possibility of knowledge was always against any accommodation with the status quo'.[31] Again this theorization itself does not allow a relational perspective to emerge, even though a relational 'compromise' or 'corruption' always happens when a 'critical' building, when constructed, allies itself with power, resources and capital one way or another. If this moment of being uncritical is internalized in a new critical project, then we have to look for a new formulation. For this, a non-Western philosophical tradition may offer useful insights. According to many studies, for example in Tu Wei-ming's writings, China and East Asia are providing alternative approaches to modernity and capitalism, bringing with them organic and relational ethics found in traditional moral practice such as in Confucianism.[32] This, in turn, is related to a general Chinese philosophy of duality represented by forces of *yin* and *yang* being mutually related and transformative rather than exclusive and confrontational.[33] A political consequence of this is a relational civil society between state and society which escapes a dualist, confrontational conception of the 'public sphere' in Habermas according to a recent debate.[34] In this tradition, state, society and market had worked in a network of social relations in formal and informal ways. More importantly, this networked and relational practice had been theorized and culturally and morally internalized in a long tradition. In such a tradition, a pervasive, benevolent, moralistic but politically non-ideological state coordinates market and society, in which a transformative thrust, a 'critique', unfolds in relation to others or other forces.

Given all these considerations, we may identify two likely contributions coming from China in the near future. As China attains more influence, it may, as identified above in the symmetry, export an instrumentalist architecture of quantities and capacities that loosens or disentangles the rigor and restrictions of 'critical architecture' disseminated from the classical core states of the Western world. This pragmatic and 'junk' architecture of magnitude may be more useful for the populations of the periphery or even the middle class and 'working people' everywhere else. Another possible contribution is a reform of the idea of the critical by bringing in a 'relational' perspective, so that the agenda is no longer critique as confrontation or negation of the opposed other, but critique as participation with and possible reform of the related other, including agents of power, capital and natural resource, in an ethical and organic universe.

CHAPTER 8

BEIJING, 2008

A history

China has been going through radical transformations for three decades by now, as a consequence of Deng Xiaoping's reform beginning in 1978. A market economy has been established; large foreign capital has been attracted into the country; and massive exports have been flowing into the world. Rural and urban reforms have dismantled the Maoist planned economy, liberalized society and production, and triggered freedom and mobility for the population, as well as the 'largest mass migration to the cities the world has ever seen'.[1] Some 12 to 19 million people have migrated to the cities each year since 1980, which has created by now some 530 million urban residents, 40 per cent of the national total, a trend that is expected to continue for some time.[2] Massive infrastructure and urban architectural projects, ranging from dams, bridges and highways to new towns, housing developments and civic buildings across the country for the past three decades, have changed the landscape fundamentally. It has created a new urban–rural habitat that is promising and inspiring on the one hand (for a new modern way of life with a higher standard of living on a larger scale), and threatening and destructive on the other (to historical fabrics and ecological balance, with national and global consequences). In the realm of architectural design, overseas architects have joined the process since the 1980s. In 2002, there has been a dramatic arrival of Western architects to design some of the largest pieces of civic architecture in China, many of which have been completed in Beijing in 2008.

In terms of the larger picture of state–society–market relationships, we should also note that behind this opening-up and active participation with the global economy and cultural production there lies the crucial role of central government. In many ways, and surely from 1989–92 onwards, the Chinese state authority has entered a resolute relationship with market and society whereby, with strong management of society, an open and dynamic market economy was encouraged to grow, which in turn converged with the interests of global capital for investment, itself fuelled by neo-liberal policies in the UK and the United States since the late 1970s.[3] The state is leading the nation in opening-up and integration with the world economy, ensuring a 'joint venture' in neo-liberal economic practice between China and the West. In this perspective, the entry into the World Trade Organization and the success in bidding for the 2008 Olympic Games in 2001 marked a threshold of this state-led integration of China into the world. At this juncture, if there is a tangible symbol representing this historic moment, it has to be Beijing or the urban and architectural 'form' of the city as emerging in 2008. A close reading of this form can reveal a lot about China in transition.

Of the three urban regions in mainland China's three deltas, Beijing, Shanghai and Guangzhou (and Hong Kong) are considered the leading cities in each. Yet Beijing clearly stands out from the others in that it has inherited a classical Chinese culture directly and physically, as it was the national capital in the Yuan, Ming and Qing dynasties for some 800 years. Beijing was the imperial capital from the late thirteenth to the early twentieth century, and has been the capital of the People's Republic since 1949. With three decades of modernization, with intense land speculation by global capital, and with intensified efforts towards setting out a modern metropolis since 2001, Beijing is the only city in China where living classical Chinese tradition confronts directly the latest modern designs and developments. This situation is now displayed in 2008 when the latest modern infrastructures and megabuildings are completed alongside the imperial palace and a large imperial urban profile with a 600- to 800-year history. Before focusing on this form and moment in 2008, let us first briefly review a history of urban development in Beijing in the past three decades.

Three decades, three phases

After Khubilai Khan established the city of Dadu in 1283, in 1420 Emperor Zhu Di of Ming China, maintaining the same north–south axis, modified the city into Beijing, which witnessed an extension to the south in 1553.[4] The configuration of this city as marked by axes and city walls then remained, surviving the 1911 Republican Revolution, the founding of the People's Republic in 1949, and the Cultural Revolution in the 1960s and 1970s. This shape is now marked by the trajectory of the second ring road and a series of spaces on the central axis (Figure 8.1). What have survived include the overall urban configuration; the central north–south axis; the palace at the centre; the surrounding hills, parks, lakes and temples; areas of old urban fabric populated by *hutong* alleys and courtyard houses; parts of two city gates; and some very small sections of city walls. City walls and gates were gradually demolished since the 1910s. In the 1950s and 1960s, they were mostly erased along with many temples and arches to make way for broad avenues and large buildings constructed since 1949. The celebration project for the tenth anniversary of the People's Republic in 1959 marked a major breakthrough in this destructive-constructive effort of Maoist China. It included the completion of the 400,000 m^2 Tiananmen Square and the Ten Grand Buildings by 1 October 1959, the National Day of the year. The 1960s were quiet

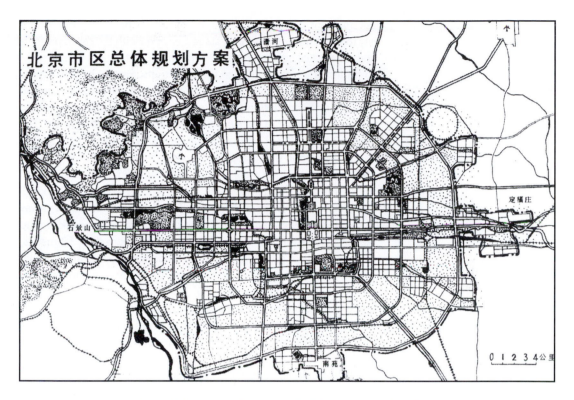

北京市区总体规划方案

8.1 Beijing Plan of 1982.

in construction, and Mao's Cultural Revolution reached its apogee in 1966–9. China's return to a path of economic construction and opening-up to the West started in the early 1970s, when China joined the UN and China–US relations started to improve. Economic and public modernism in architectural design, already having emerged in the 1960s, grew into a prevailing practice in the 1970s. There was also an indication in 1975 that Beijing would become a 'new, modernized, socialist city'. However, a thorough turn in policy and ideology towards modernization was impossible until Mao died in 1976 and Deng assumed leadership in 1978.

There are three phases from here onwards, each taking about a decade, with 1989/92 and 2001/2 as two turning points. In the first (1978–89/92), leaving behind the Maoist planned economy, the new practice was a 'commodity economy with planning and market regulations'. Foreign investment began to flow in. Hotels, offices, shopping malls, housing developments, and cultural and exhibition centres were built. Large housing districts, subway extensions and the second and third ring roads were completed in the late 1980s in Beijing. The quantity of construction per year for the city rose from 4.5 to 7 and 10 million square metres from the late 1970s to the mid and late 1980s.[5] It was against this 'invasion' of intense building that conservation of historical Beijing emerged as an urgent issue. In the planning regulations of 1980–3, the policy for swift economic development, for engaging with overseas collaborations and for the city to be on the 'international' stage coincided with the call to preserve and inherit Beijing's image as a 'renowned, historical, cultural city'.[6] To protect the historical urban centre with its imperial palace, a large horizontal urban architectural complex, one of the largest ever and the only one surviving in China today, the initial restriction imposed was on the number of storeys a new building nearby could adopt. The Beijing Plan in 1982–3 stipulated that buildings in the 'old city', that is, within the second ring road, could only be four to six storeys high.[7] In 1985, the control was more precise: the height limits in areas around the palace, the royal temples and lakes were set at 9, 12, 18 and 45 metres gradually as the building site in question moved further away from the centre. In 1987, the regulation became more restrictive: no building inside the second ring road could be more than 18 metres, except those along the ring road, the Changan Avenue, and another avenue further south (the Qiansanmen Avenue) which can be at 30 and 45 metres maximum. In 1990, some twenty-five historical areas inside and around the centre were specified as zones for protection.[8]

On the political and economic fronts, China's reform entered serious difficulties late in the decade, when urban reform for state enterprises and price reform were followed by widespread corruption, inflation and relative decline in income for many. There were deeper issues unresolved, such as the model of economic development, the role of the state and the forms of freedom and democracy China should adopt then. The Tiananmen Incident of 1989 dramatically exposed these crises or, more precisely, the radical difference in the answers to these questions from different parties of the society, especially central government and the student bodies, and also between and within the intelligentsia, the reform-minded new 'bourgeoisie' and the population at large.[9] The ending of the incident with the use of force by the state, tragic as it certainly was, gave China time and space for swift economic development in the following decades, yet profound problems have to be resolved at some point in the future.

The second phase (1989/92–2001/2) was characterized by ongoing strong rule by the state and a more radical opening-up of the economy to market practice and global investment. After Deng's speech in his tour to southern China in early 1992, 'market economy' in socialism or 'socialist market economy' became the set policy in late 1992. Reforms that had stopped in the late 1980s restarted, this time leading to success and social stability. Urban land can now be rented for speculation and development with overseas capital. Beijing in the 1990s witnessed a development more intensive than that in the 1980s. The quantity of construction per year had increased to between 11 and 12 million square metres (rising to 20 million and later 30 million after 2000).[10] The invasion of massive buildings in the centre, the breaching of height restrictions, and the destruction of old courtyard houses and urban fabric were now happening at a greater pace. The Oriental Plaza and the Financial Street, which should both have been 45 metres maximum, reached 68 and 116 metres in height, as a result of aggressive demands for profit by the developers.[11] The protection of historic Beijing was once again called for with increased urgency and intensity. The Beijing Plan for 1991–2010, as set down in 1992–3, specified that Beijing be an international city 'open in all aspects', ready for the Olympics and for the fiftieth anniversary of the People's Republic (in 1999), and that it become a 'modernized international city of the first rank' in the period from 2010 to 2050. The plan then specified that the 'renowned, historic, cultural city' of Beijing must be protected, at the level of buildings, urban areas and the whole urban framework at the centre of the city. Ten aspects of the framework of historical Beijing were specified for protection including the north–south axis, the orthogonal pattern of streets and alleys, the horizontal profile of the city defined by the imperial palace at the centre, the river and lake system, and the visual corridors between key points across the city.[12] In this ongoing battle, various conservation regulations were made in 1997, 1999, 2001 and 2002. That in 2002 specified thirty areas of protection inside the old city. In 2004, the number was increased to thirty-three, which claimed 29 per cent of the total area (besides the palace ensemble) inside the second ring road.[13]

From 1978 to 2008, three plans for Beijing were made, in 1982–3, 1992–3 and 2004–5. They were ongoing articulations of consistent principles. The policies to develop high-tech industry and a tertiary or service economy while removing production industry to elsewhere, to reduce population growth and concentration inside the city (now already at 15 million), to 'green' the city and to raise ecological qualities of the city, remained the same. In particular, the emphasis on developing a modern city and the need to protect the 'renowned, historical, cultural city' went hand in hand with increasing intensities. What was discussed in the first two plans but with more emphasis in that of 2004–5 was the idea of a 'greater Beijing region' with two axes, two development bands, and multiple urban centres, in a region beyond the conventional scope of 16,800 km², to cover 70,000 km² which included the neighbouring cities. Another newly emphasized idea was a 'humanistic' city and a 'habitable' city to be cultivated in Beijing.[14] Both new ideas indicated a near saturation of major constructions inside inner Beijing: it was time to explore outer areas and to articulate a humane and liveable urbanity inside. Yet another priority was coming upon Beijing at the same time.

The successful bid to host the 2008 Olympic Games, and the entry into the World Trade Organization (WTO), in July and November 2001 respectively, marked the beginning of a new or the third phase of development. China's long march into the WTO from 1986 to 2001 reflected a protracted reform aimed at adoption of a market economy and a gradual integration with the world economy which was, in its own history, going through a process of globalization. It was a journey of China *and* the West, for both to accept each other with open market regulations. The entry secured two-way trade across Chinese borders and China's participation on a level field on the world stage. It 'accelerated China's pace of building a market economy opening to the outside, and its effective participation in economic globalization'.[15] Apart from causing an increased volume of trade, the staging of the 2008 Olympic Games in Beijing provides a window to showcase China's commitment to open trade and international rules. The Action Plan in 2002 specified that the preparatory work for the Games is 'open to the nation and the world in all aspects with international regulations and modern standards'. It is to 'raise the level of openness in all aspects of the city of Beijing, and to display to the world a new image of the nation after reform and opening-up'.[16]

This plan is important as it reveals to us key principles behind the building of Beijing as it appears in 2008. According to the plan, the strategic conceptions include the theme of 'New Beijing, Great Olympics'; the organization of the Games based on 'green', 'science and technology' and 'humanism' principles; and a commitment to showcase images of a 'renowned, historical, cultural city', and to build the city as highly modernized by 2008 with a 'framework of a large, modernized, international metropolis'. It also specifies that the event is organized with the whole nation, with modern methods, and with open policies 'in all aspects'. Regarding sports facilities, one of the principles was to create 'classics in sports architecture'. There are 'one centre' and 'three other zones', the first being the Olympic Green on the northern section of the extended central axis, and the other three being located in the west and north. In the central Olympic Green are three primary buildings, the National Stadium, the National Gymnasium and the National Swimming Centre, to accommodate 80,000, 1,800 and 1,700 spectators respectively (besides another ten sports buildings in the Green, fifteen in other areas of Beijing and five outside). Regarding ecological environment and infrastructure, the plan proposes extensive greening of the city with 'green barriers' between urban areas. The infrastructure projects include four subway lines, light rails around the city, a speed train to the airport, a second highway to the airport, the fifth and sixth ring roads, and an extension to the Capital Airport. The plan also includes the construction of a 'social environment'. It requires the making of a cultural setting including the opening, closing and torch relay ceremonies; the building of 'modern cultural facilities' in the city such as Grand National Theatre, China Central Television (CCTV) headquarters, Capital Museum and National Museum; and the protection and display of the 'renowned, historical, cultural city' of Beijing with its axis, the palace city, the urban framework, the great imperial parks nearby, and the Ming-dynasty Great Wall further outside.

To comprehend the 'form' of Beijing in 2008 as a symbol of China in transformation, a study of the following aspects may provide useful insights: a subjectivity expressed in the symbolic form of the city, conservation practice of the city that revives an imperial grandeur displayed in a horizontal profile, ways of representing China in Beijing in 1959 and 2008, and the political position of state authority at this historical juncture.

A symbolic form

While architects educated before 1978, often based in state design institutes, have continued to play a leading role in most of the public and commercial projects, younger generations educated after 1978 began to assume important roles with more exposure from the mid-1990s onwards. With their autonomous studios and greater access to international ideas, they have brought a purist modernism with regional sensitivities into China, as manifested in the works of Yung Ho Chang, Cui Kai, Liu Jiakun, Wang Shu, Qingyun Ma and many others. Overseas architects entered the scene in the early 1980s as well. Foreign investments in the 1980s and 1990s brought in designs from outside as overseas architects were often appointed by the investing parties. Parallel to this is a smaller stream of 'avant-garde' architects invited by the Chinese with domestic capital, which has produced a series of interesting buildings. Starting with the Fragrant Hill Hotel in 1982 by I. M. Pei, the recent ones include villas of the Commune by the Great Wall (such as that by Kengo Kuma), the gatehouse of an arts centre in Tongzhou (by Office dA of Boston) and Jianwai SOHO (by Riken Yamamoto), from 2002 to 2004. If the first was a blend of modernism with iconic historicism, the later ones were predominantly modernist, with tectonic and sometimes regionalist sensitivities. This then overlapped with, and therefore supported, the interests of the Chinese, especially of the post-1978 generation. In this way, collaboration between them, as in the case of the Commune by the Great Wall (Beijing, 2002) and China International Practice Exhibition of Architecture (CIPEA, Nanjing, ongoing) where Asian and international architects were invited to design with the Chinese, has been a contribution to the local profession in design practice.

From 1998 onwards, however, a wave of greater magnitude has arrived. State investments for large public buildings, sports facilities and infrastructural projects were organized; and the architects for these projects were selected through international competitions. The first such competition was for the Grand National Theatre in 1998–9. The process was lengthy but the design commission was awarded in July 1999 to Paul Andreu of Paris. It was constructed accordingly beginning in 2001 and completed in 2007. After Beijing's success in bidding for the Olympic Games in 2001, the next two years witnessed a series of international competitions. In 2002, the competitions for the Olympic Green, the Wukesong Sports Centre and the new CCTV headquarters were organized, and the commissions were awarded to Sasaki Associates (USA), Burckhardt & Partner AG (Switzerland) and Office for Metropolitan Architecture (Rotterdam) respectively. In 2003, competitions for the National Stadium, the National Swimming Centre, the Capital Museum and the Capital Airport extension were won by Herzog & de Meuron (Switzerland), PTW Architects (Australia), AREP Group (France) and Foster & Partners (United Kingdom) respectively. In 2004, the design for the extension to the National Museum was awarded after an international competition to Von Gerkan, Marg & Partners (Germany).[17] Construction started on one after another. All these offices, in the process, collaborated with Chinese architects to gain advice concerning building methods and cultural sensitivities in China. Many also worked with the British engineering firm Arup for structural designs.

What is emerging in Beijing in 2008 is a special landscape for which the Chinese state has invited the most suitable architects around the world to design the landmarks of an 'open, modern, international city' of Beijing, as 'new images of the nation after reform and opening-up'. This landscape is surely a spectacle with great symbolic capital, a spectacle of great marks of distinction, which will showcase Beijing and China in the global media with its pervasive and instantaneous circulation of images. It may 'induce passivity in today's subject' (according to Peter Eisenman) and become economic capital and political power on its own (according to Guy Debord). Yet concrete historical conditions should be carefully observed as well. These buildings, in fact, are themselves symbols and material components of a real socio-economic and political transformation in the city and in China. In this sense, these buildings represent a moment in China's own history in modernization and integration with the global community. Further, the form adopted in these buildings reveals a dynamic spiritual quality and a national subjectivity. The meaning or content of this 'subjectivity' should be assessed against two backdrops: (1) a global setting in which China's relations with the core powers of the world or the West play crucial roles and (2) a historical background in which China's struggle for national self-strengthening and modernization since the late Qing dynasty is another important factor.

If we observe the process in which the buildings are conceived, designed and constructed, we have to say that they are results of collaborations between China and the West (despite ongoing conflicts at a certain ideological level). It is a collaboration of certain Western formal conceptions with Chinese political and socio-economic conditions at the dawn of the twenty-first century. It involves a 'marriage' of a new and radicalized modernism, facilitated by computer and other technologies in the West, and a socio-economic and technological modernization of China, both occurring since the late 1970s and yet not interacting with each other until recently. Further, this is not a passive meeting but an active interaction. While the radicalized modernism from the West fits China so well now, the socio-economic forces in China have also materialized and magnified ideas of radical modernism of the West.

Out of these landmarks, the CCTV buildings and the National Stadium perhaps require analysis first. Although both display the latest Western experiments in tectonic and formal language developed since the late 1970s, the Stadium is particularly astonishing in its seamless integration of new structure, material, form and space on such a scale, as facilitated by new material science, CAD programs and local building capacities (Figures 8.2 and 8.3). The CCTV buildings, on the other hand, reveal a specific formal-critical inquiry in modernism (in association with constructivism) first explored in the 1910s and 1920s in Russia and in Europe, then revived after 1976–7 and manifested in 1988 in Western Europe and North America (Figure 8.4). If we review Mark Wigley's statement on 'Deconstructivist Architecture', an exhibition in New York in 1988 where the CCTV designer Rem Koolhaas was one of the architects included, the text reads exactly like a footnote to the CCTV buildings completed some twenty years later. Wigley says:

> The frame is warped . . . The structure is shaken but does not collapse . . . These buildings are extremely solid. The solidity is just organized in an unfamiliar way, shifting our traditional sense of structure. Though structurally sound, at the same time they are structurally frightening.[18]

In Koolhaas's own writing on 'Bigness' in 1995, his words also read like a footnote to or a sketch of the building in 2008:

> Bigness is . . . a hyper-architecture. The containers of Bigness will be landmarks in a post-architectural landscape . . . generated through superhuman effort'.[19]

The 1988 event, and the 'Bigness' of Koolhaas of 1995, were part of an overall evolution of formal-critical architecture in the West, along with the arrival of late capitalism, the post-Fordist ('flexible' and 'globalized') economy, network society, and information and computer technologies. In form or in the language of design, what has really developed from the discourse of 1988 and 1995 is perhaps a way of seeing, symbolizing and facilitating a Deleuzian thrust, a raw materialist dynamism for modernization and evolution found everywhere today. What is most interesting here as reflected in Beijing, however, is not that it is a Western development on its own, but a meeting of a radical West with a wild East, or of a radical modernism of the West encountering modernizing Asia with its 'bigness' and 'frightening' force for real transformation.[20]

8.2 National Olympic Stadium ('Bird's Nest'), Beijing, 2008. Architect: Herzog & de Meuron with CAG (China Architecture Design & Research Group). Photo taken in September 2007.

8.3 National Olympic Stadium seen across the roof of National Aquatics Centre ('Water Cube'), both under construction in late 2007, Beijing. Architect for the Aquatics Centre: PTW Architects with CCDI (China Construction Design International).

This collaboration in formal design and building construction, further, is perhaps a symbolic expression of another convergence, in the same global evolution, of neo-liberal practices adopted since the late 1970s in China and in the West, especially in the UK and USA as David Harvey has clearly identified.[21] This is not to say that the two worlds will continue to converge into one, and that China will be another entirely 'Westernized' nation. Unlikely as this is to happen, and with the possibility that China is moving in a new direction beyond classical categories (of communism and capitalism), this meeting in 2008 has nevertheless marked a closer interrelation of China with the West and other nations worldwide. As a complex interaction, it surely involves closer interdependence (as these landmarks and the recent global economy testify) as well as at times intense ideological dispute with different values and interests involved (as the Olympic torch relay in France and the USA revealed in early 2008).

In the perspective of China's own modern history, this borrowing of a radicalized modernism from the West, while displaying a closer integration with other nations of the world, has also expressed a level of modernization and national strength that China has attained in a long struggle in recent history. This history can be extended back to cover the past three decades of reform and opening-up after 1978, and also a longer history of 170 years since 1840 when China was attacked and shaken to the ground and self-strengthening efforts were made with extreme difficulties from the late Qing dynasty to

the post-Mao era. In this sense, the 'frightening' dynamism and its sublime 'bigness' in these buildings represent the large and dynamic transformation China has been undergoing in the recent past and in its entire modern history, united with a central theme of national survival and development. With this dynamism and magnitude, and the change or the success achieved in China, these buildings then inevitably express a pride and confidence of the nation, and a hope of what can be achieved in the next era. We might add that the dramatic events in the months before the opening of the Olympic Games, notably the talk of boycott amongst some in the West, and the devastating earthquake in Sichuan and the massive relief effort that followed, enhance further the heroic narrative of the nation struggling and developing in the world, and achieving a greater determination, and also a greater ease and confidence, as a result.

As they are the landmark of the historical rise of China, these buildings as they emerged in the Beijing of 2008 may also signal a climax and the end of a certain era and the opening of another. At a literal level, the space left for monumental landmarks in Beijing will quickly diminish. The direction of development in Beijing, as the Plan of 2004–5 indicates, will be increasingly about aspects of a humanistic city including ecological and habitable qualities, rather than grand projects and heroic changes. A micro, internal and intensified urbanity at a human and walkable scale is likely to be emphasized. At a national

8.4 New headquarters of China Central Television (CCTV) under construction in September 2007, Beijing. Architect: Rem Koolhaas/ OMA with ECADI (East China Architectural Design & Research Institute).

level in its overall socio-economic development, a raw and dynamic transformation in China's drive for modernization for the past three decades has also come to an end, as various new policies launched in recent years have indicated. With a socially and ecologically conscious leadership on the rise, a refined social and economic system emerging with rules governing labour, rural development and public welfare, and an increasing concern for research, quality and design, the moment of 2008 may be remembered as the close of the first and the beginning of a new era in China's long march to modernization.

The horizontal versus the vertical

Beijing may have undergone two waves of modernization, the 1950s and the present time from 1978 (intensifying after 1992) to 2008, in a Maoist and a market-socialist programme respectively. Yet the intensity of the first cannot be compared to that of the second. And it is in the current market-oriented modernization that heritage is under serious threat of a full-scale erasure. As noted above, it was in the early 1980s, when open-door programmes were adopted, that conservation became a serious policy. Although there were difficulties, as witnessed for example in the building for Oriental Plaza, the conservation effort has been escalating to face the challenge, as evidenced in the plans of 2002 and 2004–5, thanks to the effort of intellectuals, social activists, and municipal officials and state bodies and agencies. This is an ongoing resistance on the part of society and the state to protect tradition, culture and national identity against market capitalism and global homogenization even though China's reform aims to attract foreign investment.

Beijing as it stands now has survived with its grand palace at the centre and imperial parks, hills, lakes and various crucial visual links on axes, in a horizontal profile visible in the city centre (Figure 8.5), while large modern buildings are being constructed around the centre and further outside. In this sense, an imperial Beijing is now *reinvented*. When tall buildings are kept at bay outside the second ring road, and when large modern buildings inside the ring road are required

8.5 Hall of Supreme Harmony at the centre of Beijing on the north–south axis built and reconstructed since 1420.

to stand shorter at 9, 18, 30 and 45 metres, the imperial palace at the centre acquires a new grandeur not visible before.[22] Further, this is an expression of the power of a horizontal landscape against the strength of a vertical metropolis. As visible today, the horizontal city of an imperial tradition has managed to 'control' the vertical capitalist metropolis at a distance and with height limits. Beijing thus imparts a certain Chineseness in this horizontality across the whole urban landscape. Looked at more closely, this Chinese or 'imperial' grandeur is articulated with a large system of the horizontal centre with surrounding lakes and hills, the ancient Bell and Drum Towers, the axes linking the centre to the gates and the Temple of Heaven in the south, the Western Hills further away, and the Ming-dynasty Great Wall further in the north-west. This system is then articulated with later and recent structures, Tiananmen Square with its buildings made in 1959 (and also 1977), the large monuments added to the west and east (the Grand National Theatre in 2007 and National Museum in 2010), the east–west Changan Avenue with massive but horizontal buildings on the two sides, and the entire Olympic Green and its great horizontal structures on open fields in the northern section of the central axis. Even the CCTV headquarters outside the ring road has a horizontal–vertical articulation instead of a conventional vertical skyscraper. Almost all major landmarks in Beijing now are horizontal in a certain composition. In this way, an imperial city of horizontality with its north–south axis, first appearing in 1283, then articulated in 1420, now survives in 2008 with a powerful modern interpretation.

It must be added that ideas of a horizontal space and imaginations of a great or immense universe were closely interrelated in a Chinese order of things that, as symbolically and visually conceived, exists between 'earth' and 'heaven'. This is clearly visible in a horizontal scroll painting or an urban architectural construction, for example in the scroll depicting Emperor Kangxi's return to the palace of Beijing, or a cross-section on the axis and the overall layout of the city itself.[23] Given that the modern metropolis of Beijing has expanded from an area of 62 and then 324 km^2 to 16,800 km^2, and that a new 'greater Beijing region' is to cover a territory of 70,000 km^2 with many cities nearby, this horizontality is now acquiring a geographical dimension across the land, in a mixed urban–rural habitat on a vast scale.

1959 and 2008

As a government-led project to represent the nation in Beijing, the building of ten grand monuments and Tiananmen Square in 1959 can be compared with the building of large cultural and sports facilities for the Olympics in 2008. There are differences and consistencies that can be noted. In 1959, the occasion was a celebration on the national day (1 October) of the ten-year progress of a Maoist Republic defining

8.6 Tiananmen Square seen from the south-east. Photo taken after 1977.

8.7 National Grand Theatre, Beijing, 2007, viewed from the south-west, with the Great Hall of the People completed in 1959 at the back defining the western edge of Tiananmen Square.

itself against Khrushchev's USSR and the imperialist capitalism of the USA in the Cold War era. In 2008, on the other hand, the occasion is China's hosting of a celebrated cultural and sports event participated in by nations worldwide, when China as a market socialist economy is engaging with almost all countries around the world. In 1959, architectural forms were employed for a political critique, when a National Style with tangible Chinese features was adopted to oppose modernism or the International Style, seen as aesthetic instruments of capitalist imperialism. In 2008, modern forms largely imported from the capitalist West are adopted to express the progress of the nation after opening-up, which reveals a retreat in the ideological critique or confrontation, but also an advance in national, economic and technological development, with the buildings themselves acting as symbols in a homogenizing global market and media culture (Figures 8.6 and 8.7).[24]

In 1958–9, the Ten Buildings and Tiananmen Square were designed in a decorative Beaux-Arts language with literal Chinese details and Chinese roofs. The Chineseness was tangible on individual buildings, yet conservation of the historical city was largely ignored. The architects were all Chinese, and the constructions were completed in eleven months, between October 1958 and late September 1959. In 2008, the operation was more open. The forms are modernist in a new or radicalized manner; the architects are mixed in nationality and are predominantly European as selected through international competitions; the Chineseness is abstract as found in the horizontally projected roofs in many buildings and in the overall horizontality of the cityscape in the centre (besides other innovative design ideas), when heritage conservation of the historical city also becomes a crucial concern with renovation and preservation projects implemented. There are more than 20 projects this time although the list is open-ended. Constructions typically take some four to six years to complete. The scale and the investment are much larger. There are also significant infrastructure projects going on this time, most notably the extension to Capital Airport by Sir Norman Foster of the United Kingdom, 'the single largest airport expansion project the world has ever seen, as well as the fastest ever built'.[25]

In both cases, however, there are consistencies. In the 1950s and in current China, the state authority is leading the national modernization project whether it is defined as 'socialist' or 'market socialist'. In both 1959 and 2008, the state is organizing the event with nationwide collaborations. In both, the great landmarks are expressions of a modern China for international visibility, although, to be sure, the meaning of being modern and the condition of that visibility have changed greatly. Further, after decades of transformation, the Chinese state and nation have displayed a greater ease now than in the 1950s, when the world itself has become more integrated as well.

State, market and society

The state–market relationship is crucial in the making of Beijing of 2008. On the one hand the Chinese state is opening actively to international capital. On the other, it retains a certain power when necessary to limit international investment and resist the invading homogenization of the global economy. The real cases are complex and many concerns can be raised. The key issue here, however, is the retaining of a political superiority above capital and market, which is fundamentally important. It makes further actions in heritage protection, in building an ecological urbanity and in socio-physical liveability structurally possible, as evidenced for example in the EcoCity of Dongtan and other urban models put forward in the Shanghai Expo of 2010. If the Chinese state continues to develop in this direction, towards a synthetic or comprehensive position that can consider collective and long-term interests of people above pure economic interests while still being able to attract global capital and sustain development, then a new state–market relationship will emerge with credibility and even influence beyond China.

At the same time, the state–society relationship must also be noted. The Chinese state is certainly concerned with the long-term wellbeing of the population. However, what can be observed in the recent past is often a monopolistic alliance of the state with large capital, and with international systems of cultural production. This reduces space for small and local practice. The problem here goes beyond the design professions such as the architect, in a larger area of social life where fair distribution of wealth and greater space for participation and expression are in need of further improvement. What forms of political 'democracy' China is to adopt remains a question unlikely to be decided for a long time to come. Yet issues of economic and social democracy, of public welfare, of relative equity and justice, of rational controls for long-term environmental sustainability, are what China has to deal with immediately. Various policies issued recently for public welfare, labour practice, environmental control and 'socialist new villages' are positive signs in this direction.

Though the future of China is hard to predict, all the signs one can identify in the post-Mao transformations and in the Chinese political tradition seem to point to a new system emerging in China that is neither 'communist' nor 'capitalist' in the classical sense, a new polity in which a pervasive state authority rendered in a Chinese ethic of duty coordinates society and the market economy, a national authority that can sustain growth and relative equality without subjecting itself to either capitalism or radical liberalism. A crucial dimension here is the generic, the synthetic, the comprehensive, the 'non-ideological', which define a new system beyond classical ideological categories made in the West in the nineteenth century in social theories.

In this perspective, the buildings that arose in Beijing in 2008 do reveal signs of a new practice emerging. While representing the rise of China from an agricultural empire into a modern industrial republic with a combination of Western and Chinese traditions, these buildings, and their production in the political and cultural context, specifically reveal a synthetic approach. They reveal a synthetic polity that combines liberal and collective interests, and a synthetic aesthetic that is modernist, mass-based, 'heroic' in scale and capacity, and hybrid in cultural content.

CHAPTER 9

GEOMETRIES OF LIFE AND FORMLESSNESS

A Chinese urban tradition

After three decades of fast development, China today faces urgent problems accumulated in the recent past. These include expanding income and social disparity, the loss of public goods such as a clean environment and social welfare (housing, health and education), and the destruction of historical urban fabric. In the last instance, it includes not only the demolishing of physical courtyard houses and lanes, but also the erosion of an overall urban public space with humane, habitable, accessible and green qualities. Although current government policies aim to correct the one-sided development, with many regulations issued forcefully to protect the environment and aspects of social fabric and public service, critical knowledge for urban design in the Chinese context is, however, still missing. For example, there has been a call to make Beijing 'humane' (*yiren weiben*) and 'habitable' (*yiju*), yet a body of critical studies that is both empirical and critical, historically founded and practically normative, is hard to find. How to reconstitute a habitable city for the public and the majority with humane and ecological qualities? How to imagine a new urban public space of these qualities that is modern yet suitable for China? How should modern Beijing evolve with useful legacies from its ancient past and cultural tradition? Can traditional Beijing with a 500-year history teach us anything critical and constructive today? Can we situate the discourse on Beijing in an international context so that the project contributes to a global dialogue and debate? To offer a preliminary answer to these questions, I will first employ European theorists' reading of Chinese and Asian urbanities as mirror reflections on the Chinese situation, before turning directly to traditional Beijing, on which I will make four observations.

Henri Lefebvre has made a differentiation between 'conceived' and 'lived' space: a dominant space of rational knowledge and political ideology, and a dominated space of direct experience of life with desires expressed through images and symbols.[1] Although Lefebvre tended to see this as a universal difference, he also shifted to a relativist viewpoint. Whereas he believed that there was a distinction of the two and a domination of the first over the second in Europe especially since the Renaissance, he questioned if such a distinction existed in Asia and China since a different writing system was adopted there. According to him, since the Renaissance, in European cities, a dominant space of the conceived, represented in the use of the perspective (the gaze and the logic of visualization), the high façade, the front of the buildings as objects and the long avenues leading to them, was clearly different from and in a superior relation to a dominated space of a medieval and religious texture in a life-world of the city (ego, bed, bedroom, dwelling, house, square, church, graveyard, and the symbolic figures of devils and angels, heaven and hell).[2] Lefebvre then questioned if such a distinction existed in Asia and China. The Chinese characters, being different from alphabetic writing, acted as a crucial sign in Lefebvre's thinking, pointing to another possible world without such a distinction (Figure 9.1). 'It is indeed quite possible', argued Lefebvre, 'that the Chinese characters combine two functions in an extricable way, that on the one hand they convey the order of the world (space–time),

9.1 Calligraphy by Zheng Banqiao (1693–1765).

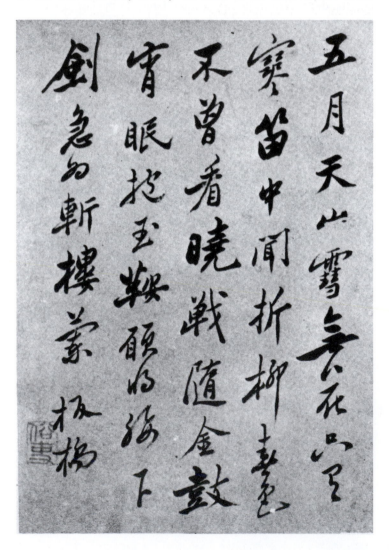

while on the other hand they lay hold of that concrete (practical and social) space–time wherein symbolisms hold sway'.[3]

Lefebvre did not move on to observe Chinese urban space as he did European cities. If we push this argument further, we will arrive at this reading: Chinese cities do not have such a distinction but combine the two spatial orders, the conceived and the lived, where the perspective and formal geometry do not dominate but instead merge with a messy world of actual life and its religious and anthropological expressions. If we turn to observe a real historical city in China, such as imperial Beijing (1420–1911), we do find a spatial pattern of this kind, being different from that in a Renaissance European city. Without a bright and frontal order of public space dominated by the logic of visualization or perspective, that is, without an optical and public centre defined by high façades, squares and long straight avenues, historical Beijing is a dense world of compounds, streets and lanes, with the palace enclosed and hundreds of temples as local civic centres scattered across the city and further into the rural areas, with webs of streets linking them together. Yet the whole city is geometrically well organized. A total rational order and a localized world of actual daily life with religious expressions are combined. Without the telescopic perspective employed for open urban space, the Chinese city has no domination of the optical, visual and formal over the lived and the religious–anthropological such as one finds in a Renaissance city (Figures 9.2, 9.3, 9.4).

There are two important issues in such a Europe–China comparison: the way contraries or binary poles ('conceived' and 'lived') are dealt with in the two traditions, and the problem of urban layout as a reflection of a worldview or epistemological framework in the two traditions (the city as a reflection of how its inhabitants see the world in the tradition in which the city was formed).

Regarding these two issues, François Jullien offers crucial observations. In his comparison of Chinese and Greek/European philosophical traditions, he makes an extensive study of the approach to binary poles or contraries in Aristotle and in ancient China.[4] Jullien argues that both cultures have identified contraries as the basis for change yet the two traditions deal with the interrelation between the contraries differently. Whereas the Greek conceives the binary poles as exclusive and confrontational (as formal categories), the Chinese regards the contraries as mutually related and transformative. Without formalizing the contraries, that is, seeing them as formal *and* material at once, *yin* and *yang* (or any binary poles) are not mutually exclusive but interacting with each other ceaselessly. This relational approach to contrariety in China explains various aspects of socio-cultural practice in which China often adopts a middle path between conceptual poles identified in European terminology, from the conceived–lived contrast in the past to the communist–capitalist categories at the present. Indeed, Chinese characters or square words are abstract signs *and*

9.2 *View of an Ideal City* by an artist in the School of Piero della Francesca, c. 1470.

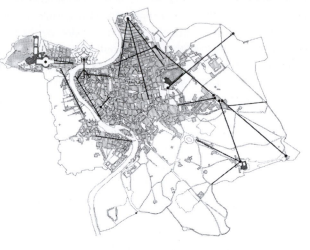

9.3 A map of Rome in the eighteenth century, showing streets opened up by the Popes since the fifteenth and sixteenth centuries.

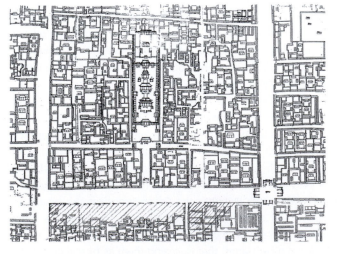

9.4 A map of Longfu Si Temple and the urban texture around, Beijing, 1750.

concrete images; it is a conceived writing system *and* a lived enactment of the body and person in writing. The urban layout in historical Beijing also includes both a geometrical regularity *and* a scattered life-world of religious and anthropological expressions.

Regarding the issue of city as an epistemological layout, Jullien's study is illuminating as well. The analogy of knowing to seeing is employed to help extend epistemological effort to visual experience in painting in his studies, which in turn may also be extended to urban experience in our analysis here. According to him, whereas the European approach to knowledge includes a panorama of things, a top-down gaze upon a world that can be organized homogenously, the Chinese approach to knowledge involves not a total perspective but a series of views from one situation to another, as on a journey, through which relations between views may be sketched in, like a meandering path in the mountains in a Chinese landscape painting.[5] These two images of epistemological approach in fact also correspond to urban layout in a Renaissance city and a historical Chinese city such as Beijing respectively. If the first is constructed with the logic of the perspective aiming at comprehending a totality, the second is built with changing views of long and shifting journeys linking one locality to another. If the first is optical, formal, centric with the logic of the gaze, the second is invisible (always 'behind' and 'around the corner'), localized, corporeal and experiential. If the first is immediately grand and heroic, the second is visually humble and horizontal, small in any locality yet large in an endless unfolding of the local.

This brings us to Roland Barthes's reading of Tokyo with again a comparative reference to the Western cities. Among his many observations on Tokyo in his *Empire of Signs*, two appear most relevant here. The first concerns an empty centre and the second a spatial logic that requires the intense labour of a journey. For the first, Barthes suggests that all Western cities have a centre, a site of fulness and 'truth', for spirituality (churches), power (offices), money (banks), merchandise (department stores) and language (agoras, cafés and promenades).[6] In Tokyo however, one encounters a paradox: it has a centre but it is 'empty' in that the central area of the city is an enclosed imperial palace that is invisible to the outside. City life takes permanent detours and returns around a centre, a subject, a truth that is 'empty'.[7] For the second, Barthes talks about difficulties in finding a place in Tokyo because of a numbering system for postal addresses which is unclear or inconvenient to outsiders.[8] The observation here, however, concerns not just the postal address, but an entire spatial layout of the city that is localized and demands corporeal labour and experience in order to read and understand.

> The city can be known only by an activity of an ethnographic kind: you must orient yourself in it not by book, by address, but by walking, by sight, by habit, by experience; here every discovery is intense and fragile.[9]

Historical Tokyo or Edo in fact shares comparable spatial qualities with southern Chinese capital cities such as Nanjing and Hangzhou. They all had imperial palaces enclosed and the geometrical layouts of the enclosures were all irregular because of topographical conditions (rivers, lakes, hills). Beijing (and other northern capitals such as Changan and Bianliang) had a more regular or geometric layout in the shape of the enclosed palace on a flat land. Yet the *topological* pattern of an enclosed imperial palace with a dense street layout and active localized uses remains consistent between these northern and southern cities. Beijing, Edo and some other cities in the region are comparable in this sense. Roland Barthes's two 'European' or comparative observations on Edo can be borrowed to describe historical Beijing. Imperial Beijing is a city of an 'empty' centre in that central areas are invisible or, more precisely, they display only partial visibility of the invisible, the long walls, trees and city moats surrounding the forbidden centre. Second, historical Beijing is visually forbidden or empty yet pervasive in a local dispersion: it is a city that can be discovered only through walking and localized experience that is 'intense and fragile'.

We have highlighted a local, corporeal, experiential characteristic of historical Chinese cities such as Beijing. In relation to a Chinese approach to contrariety and a conceived-and-lived quality of Chinese writing identified above, we have also realized that there is a synthetic or relational middle path in the Chinese tradition in the city in which a conceived geometry and a lived space of concrete life, corporeal experience and religious–anthropological expressions are closely combined. It seems that, compared with the European Renaissance tradition, a sphere of the lived, local and informal is more closely internalized with the conceived, total and formal in the Chinese cities so that the overall urbanity reveals more clearly an organic world of liveliness and formlessness.

It is important to note that, in Lefebvre's theory, lived space, being related to a life-world of energies and desires with religious and artistic expressions, contains revolutionary potentials, which can be employed to challenge a conceived world of abstractions and rationalities of power and knowledge in modern state, market capitalism and technological systems. Lefebvre's Marxist and postmodern agenda against instrumental modernity is clear in his own writings. Relating his ideas to the tradition in China, however, should not lead us to conclude that there is anything leftist or revolutionary in the Chinese tradition itself. The relevance in my borrowing of his ideas here lies in possible potentials of a tradition as a critical resource to correct a one-sided modern development. The relevant potency of the Chinese tradition here is a balanced, synthetic, relational approach which may help correct the abstract and the instrumentalist in modernization. For the task of reconstituting a humane and habitable urbanity for the public today, the structural tolerance of the lived, local and informal in the Chinese urban tradition seems particularly important. For a closer reading on historical Beijing, four observations can be made.[10] Three concern spatial qualities of the city, and the last the Chinese revolution that conditions our learning from the past today: (1) nature, (2) scale, (3) formlessness and (4) historical gap and continuation.

1

In historical Beijing, built fabric and natural landscape were closely interrelated. There were urban and rural areas coexisting inside the city wall (especially in the Outer or Southern City); there were extensions of urban functions outside the city walls, especially the numerous temples scattered in the hills and mountains around Beijing; there were also large areas of natural landscape (lakes and hills) inside the Imperial and Palace City at the centre of Beijing (Figures 9.5, 9.6). In this last instance, we also witness a coexistence of regular geometry of built fabric (walls and courtyards of the palaces) with an irregular geometry of nature (especially the six lakes meandering through the city). Without a dualistic confrontation between humans and nature in the basic cosmological outlook, the Chinese have developed one of the longest histories of appreciating nature and landscape in the world.[11] This is manifested not only in the urban layout with a synthesis of contraries (urban–rural, natural–artificial, regular–irregular), but also in other forms of cultural expression (poetry and painting) and in philosophical discourse as well (Taoism, Confucianism and Yin–Yang cosmology).

For the problems confronting us today, what can be learned here includes (1) an ecological ethic in the layout of human habitat in which nature takes primacy and human agency is considered relational with respect to nature, and (2) a specific pattern of eco-urbanity in which

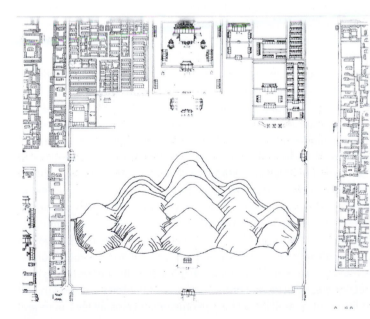

9.5 A map of Jingshan Hill on the central axis, part of a series of imperial gardens in central Beijing, 1750.

9.6 Jingshan Hill with a pavilion at the top, and the pagoda of the 'Northern Sea' (Beihai Park) behind, viewed from the east in central Beijing in the 1990s.

landscape, rural conditions, a juxtaposition of nature and artificial urbanity, and an intermingling of regular and figurative geometries can be actively utilized.[12]

2

In the ancient city of Beijing, there was a coexistence of compositions at different scales, as most clearly evidenced in and around the imperial palace where large-scale courtyards coexisted with smaller-scale compounds. At the largest scale, the whole of Beijing was strictly organized with axes and references to the four cardinal points; at the smallest scale, minute houses, courts and gardens were also well regulated with compositions relating to these axes and primary orientations. According to Wang Guixiang and Wang Qiheng the Chinese teaching in design emphasizes a coexistence of *dazhuang* (the large and sublime) and *shixing* (the appropriate), that is, a large composition and appropriate local forms and spaces.[13] The idea is also expressed in the word *xing* (shape or form of a smaller scale) and *shi* (tendency and propensity of a lager scale). For example, a well-known Chinese teaching says 'consider forms at a distance of 100 feet, and a dynamic lifeline at a distance of 1000 feet' (*baichi weixing, qianchi weishi*). This coexistence of compositions at different scales can be considered a case of fractal geometry with self-similar patterns recurring at all scales as we find in clouds and in plants and vegetation.[14] The design here in Beijing is an intuitive implementation of this natural or organic logic into an artificial and geometric urban architectural construction (Figures 9.7, 9.8, 9.9). It is interesting to note that, whereas fractal geometry captures natural forces of growth and additions of quantity, Euclidian geometry concerns instead pure and static forms and proportions.[15] It is also important to note that, while Euclidian or Greek geometry has focused on pure form and formal relations, ancient Chinese studies have emphasized geometric shapes containing numerical or quantitative problems.[16] In other words, the 'fractal geometry' of imperial Beijing is not a geometry of form and proportion, but a geometry of number and quantity. It includes a compositional logic of growth, addition and proliferation, a spatial logic of the 'more'.

The lesson here includes recognizing a non-formal geometry of quantity and substance which permits external additions and internal intensifications. A concrete message here is that a megabuilding or large urban structure is not a final condition, but an initial stage to which external additions of equal or larger frames and internal smaller frames and spaces can be included. When forms of '100 feet' and a dynamic propensity of '1000 feet' are all included, a rich human construction can be expected which has not only large-scale accommodative capacities but also micro spaces at a local human scale. Large and small are not contradictory but can be related, each playing its own role.

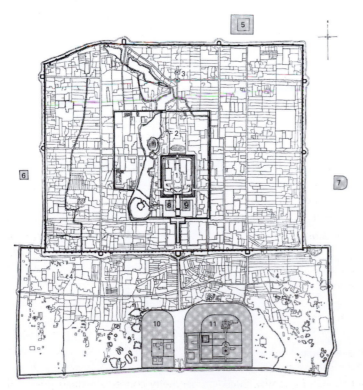

9.7 A map of imperial Beijing, 1553–1911.

9.8 A map of central Beijing showing the Forbidden City and the approach in the south and Jingshan Hill in the north, 1644–1911.

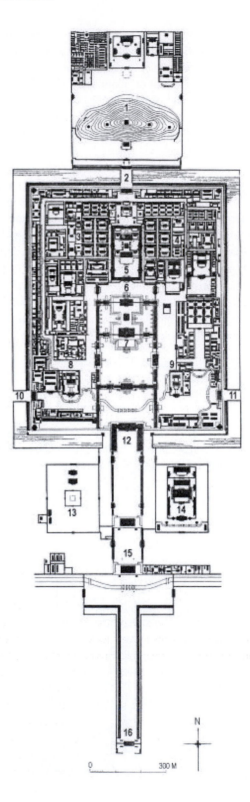

KEY
1. Perspective Hill
2. Martial Spirit Gate
3. Western Palaces
4. Eastern Palaces
5. Central Compound (emperor and Empresses residence)
6. Gate of Heavenly Purity
7. Hall of Supreme Harmony
8. Hall of Martial Grace
9. Hall of Civic Glory
10. Western Flowery Gate
11. Eastern Flowery Gate
12. Meridian Gate
13. Altar of Land and Grain
14. Temple of Ancestors
15. Gate of Heavenly Peace
16. Gate of Great Qing

N

0   300 M

9.9 An aerial view of central Beijing from the north in the early twentieth century.

3

In historical Beijing, one will not find a centre of 'truth' as Roland Barthes has identified in Western cities, or a conceived rational space of the perspective that Henri Lefebvre has found in Renaissance European cities. Unlike a Western city after the Renaissance, without central squares, broad avenues, high façades and the visual logic of the gaze, the traditional city of Beijing unfolded with a different logic of space. It had a total geometry of the entire city rigorously implemented, yet it also had a pervasively localized space of a life-world of social communities with their religious and anthropological expressions. This city of life was extensive, with scattered local centres such as temples (Figure 9.10), and was interconnected with webs of streets and lanes which channelled endless journeys that led to these localities. This composition included a geometry of magnitude and quantity. It also included a dispersed texture or field of local societies and communities, with their daily life and festive expressions unfolding around temples, teahouses, restaurants, guildhouses and various shops along streets, in a constant and flexible use of space by the population (Figure 9.11).

9.10 Temples as centres of local society scattered in and beyond the city of Beijing, 1644–1911.

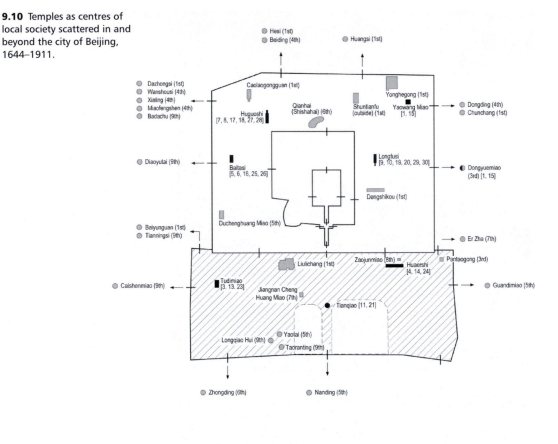

KEY

● Temple and fair sites opened monthly [with the date of the fairs]

◍ Temple, fair and pilgrim sites opened for annual worship (with the month in which they were visited).

▨ Areas of concentration of guild halls, theatres and theatre-restaurants.

9.11 Street scenes of Bianliang (Kaifeng), the capital of the Northern Song dynasty (960–1126): sections of scroll painting *Qingming Shanghe Tu* by Zhang Zeduan (active 1101–1124).

Built 'forms' were not solid and distinctive, like tall stone architecture in the European cities, but low-rise, soft and layered (with timber, stone, brick, tiles, bamboo and wooden fences, curtains of signage etc.) with shifting social activities (commercial, religious, everyday). Form as a pure, clean and distinctive shape of objects such as one finds in the European cities was 'dissolved' by these features: (1) a domination of horizontal structures (small and grouped), (2) enclosure of significant buildings (palaces, government offices, temples) by courtyard walls, (3) a soft surface of built forms along public/commercial streets, (4) weak or multiple programming of spaces (a temple was also a commercial focus accommodating monthly or yearly festivals and other functions), and (5) constant and flexible use of space by the population (a house compound can be turned into a temple, a teahouse or restaurant can accommodate theatres, not to mention the more amorphous use of streets and other outdoor spaces).

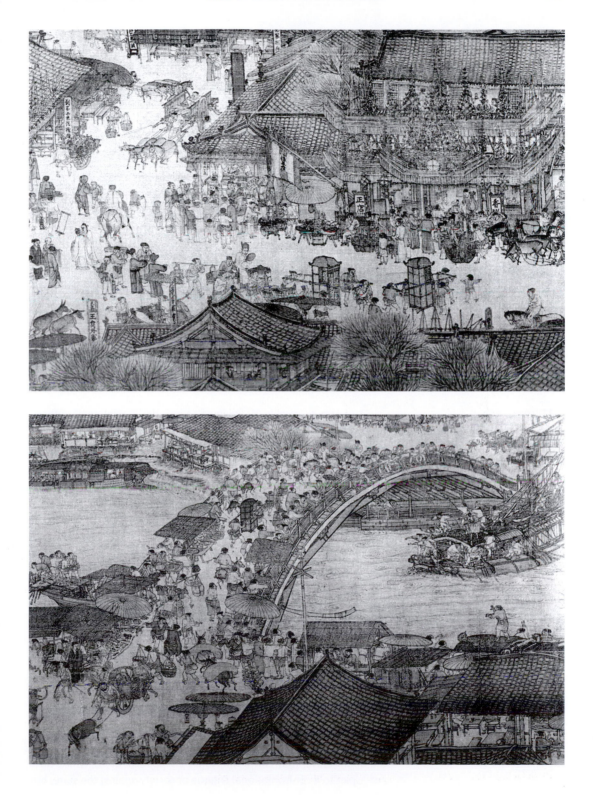

9.11 (*continued*).

At a socio-political level, Beijing also included a relational synthesis of a total geometry of the formal state and a dense texture of local informal society with its transactions. Sociologists such as Philip C. C. Huang have uncovered a relational and informal mediation between formal organization of the state and local informal communities (which resolved two thirds of all legal cases according to one empirical study of the late Qing dynasty).[17] In such a situation, moral and political order was secured neither by the tyrannical state nor by the critical civil society in confrontation, but through relational mediation between state and society, and between formal regulations and informal socio-personal interactions with a shared culture.[18]

There are several aspects we can adopt for today's design practice and social critique. (1) To accommodate the lived or a dynamic life-world for social communities, urban and architectural design can be conceived as a construction not of a formal object, but of a field or texture with scattered local centres or intensities. Adopting a geometry of quantity that is fractal and formless, energies and intensities can be added both internally and externally in an extensive field.[19] (2) Weak and multiple programming can contribute to a liberal accommodation of informal use of space and its underlying forces and potentials. (3) Such a design of the informal, with a geometry of the formless and the quantitative, may contribute to a new political ethics which does not aspire to a confrontational critique of society against the state, but a relational criticality in which a progressive agenda is implemented in an embedded practice involving 'others', that is, many different agents and forces.

4

The above three observations on historical Beijing and the lessons we identified require a qualification if they are to be useful today. Historical and modern Beijing, or imperial and modern China, cannot be simply equated: revolution and modernization have occurred separating us today from the past. Regarding modernization in the urban world, the scale and fabric of the city today have been much altered. Constructions are larger in scale and more vertical, that is, more three-dimensional and object-oriented; and the fabric has been torn apart and remade with formal geometries of a scale even larger than in Renaissance and nineteenth-century European cities. The past three decades witnessed an explosion of this city which had already emerged in the early modern (1910s–1930s) and socialist (1950s–1970s) periods. The use of ideas learned from historical Beijing therefore has to be distilled to deal with the problems we are facing today. The idea of this geometry of substance or quantity, of extensive texture, of local intensities, of informal use and liberal programming, may be especially useful today to re-humanize the object and formal geometries so dominating in modern and contemporary Beijing.

Regarding the Chinese revolution, we must understand that radical and profound changes have occurred separating the present from the past. If we examine these revolutions closely, we realize that a central theme and a major consequence, regardless of ideological positions and despite the turbulent changes, is the rise of the 'public' in modern China. There was already a public with the arrival of the modern press and urban facilities in the 1910s–1930s. Yet it cannot sustain itself without a strong national state or sovereignty protecting it from foreign domination and supporting it within. After 1949, a public was established, but it was collectivist and regimented. The radical leftism of Mao from 1957 to 1976 brought this collectivist uniformity into chaos. Today the public is mutating into a liberal and individualized society, yet Western-style checks and balances through a transparent press and an independent legal system are still missing: a horizontal liberal civil society is burgeoning yet a vertical mechanism critical of the state (which is needed if such a transformation is to happen) is lagging behind. What is clear so far is that the 'people's democracy' that Mao and the Communist Party were promoting from 1940s onwards is not radically different from the 'bourgeois democracy' the Nationalist Party explored and experimented with.[20] In historical hindsight, and as evidenced now in both Taiwan and mainland China, the left and right of the Chinese revolution are converging in a common liberalization of the public.

Regarding the shape of a liberal and democratic public, a central question remains about the form or institution this public in mainland China is to take. Will a free press, an independent legal system and multi-party elections, or certain aspects of these practices, ever become established in China? Given the path already travelled by the Chinese in the twentieth century, political institutions with Western sources are likely to be further adopted, with Chinese modifications. What is likely to emerge in China is a combination of liberal and democratic institutions with relational and informal practice. In the recent debate on 'civil society' and 'public realm' in relation to China, scholars have already highlighted the specificity of the Western model and a relational ethics in China's past in which a powerful 'third realm' had played a critical role between state and society.[21] With the weight of the tradition, it would be impractical not to expect this Chinese ethic to re-emerge and assert its capacities for a harmonious and functioning society. It is also important to note a tendency towards social democracy rather than a 'strong' capitalist liberalism in present-day China. Within the Communist Party, there are voices against the Leninist legacy; there are debates that reveal a preference for European-style 'social democracy' as an alternative to 'Soviet communism' and 'American capitalism'.[22] On the outside, the Party under its new leadership has been active in 2006 and 2007 in rebuilding public goods (including a clean environment and social services) and social equity and justice, in an effort to contain market aggressions and single-minded developmentalism, while leading and managing a sustained development at the same time.

We may conclude that it is now historically possible, and politically progressive, to envisage a new public domain with a relational ethics and an organic urbanity, in the Chinese tradition of the synthetic that cultivates the local and the informal, in a city of nature, quantity and formlessness.

CHAPTER 10

TWENTY PLATEAUS, 1910s–2010s

Visualizing history

Architecture may be studied as a single object of an architect's design or as part of a continuous built environment in a socio-spatial setting. In the first instance, buildings are appreciated as isolated monuments in an abstract professional discourse such as architectural history, in which the design of the object attains a discursive and symbolic significance above that particular socio-spatial context. In the second, however, that isolated significance is no longer relevant whereas an overall social continuum and socio-spatial practice in that context are of paramount importance. Both approaches are of course important. Of those adopting the first approach, and in the area of modern Chinese architecture, we can identify three groups of studies: those on *jindai* or 'early modern' Chinese architecture (from 1840 or 1911 to 1949), those on modern Chinese architecture of the twentieth century with a focus on the post-1949 periods, and those in contemporary design forums on today's practice in relation to certain theories. If the first is represented by the collaborative work of the Chinese and Japanese led by Wang Tan and Terunobu Fujimori since the mid-1980s, the second may be best represented in Zou Denong's *Zhongguo Xiandai Jianzhu Shi* (A history of modern Chinese architecture, 2001), whereas the third includes various discussions amongst architects and students at conferences, in magazines and on websites such as <abbs.com. cn>. If we put them together, we will find artificial historical divisions framing their discussions and also separating their observations from each other. Whereas the first does not concern itself with the complex relations leading into the post-1949 periods (or earlier intellectual currents before 1840), the second implicitly privileges the Maoist period of 1949–78 and a government perspective, thus ignoring a recent individualist development in post-Mao China. The third, on the other hand, as unfolding among individual (especially young) architects and students, is predominantly non-historical: it operates in an assumed freedom of possibilities without a historical perspective and is sometimes at a loss when a normative position in design is to be defined. How to transcend these biased and limited views? How to break down these historical and methodological barriers or divisions? The problem therefore is as follows: Can we establish a *general* framework of all significant design currents or positions in modern China? Can we, as a first step towards this purpose, develop a general map or chart of all these important design positions in twentieth-century China?

This is a project I have been working on for a while.[1] The result is a chart that covers all design positions in mainland China from the early twentieth to the early twentieth-first century (Figure 10.1a, b).[2] Here design position is defined as a specific approach with which ideas and ideologies are manifested in completed projects and buildings at a certain historical moment. This position is defined as one that stands out beyond conventional designs in the built environment because it is 'significant', 'interesting' or 'problematic' in a design and social history. And a design position can be selected as such if it has one or more of the following features: it is new or controversial in formal terms in a specific or national-historical context, dominant in socio-cultural status because of a dominant political ideology involved, or reflected as a sustained phenomenon in a group of buildings or as a single building that has led thereafter to a group of buildings.

These selected positions, manifested in projects and buildings, are considered as 'monuments' with a discursive and symbolic significance in the discourse of architectural history and the related socio-political history. The research here intends to capture intensive historical moments at which a specific group of designs with a shared position and ideology emerged. These moments are thus both historical (representing a temporal point or area) and critical (for capturing a formal and socio-political topic or problem in design). In so far as they are moments of intensity in the production of ideas, designs and buildings, these topical points or areas are referred to as 'plateaus'. Borrowing from Deleuze and Guattari, historical moments of intensity are likened to features of a geological landscape in which concentration of force results in the rise of a topological profile that is rare, extreme and critical.[3] The intention here in this research is to visualize and spatialize history, and to use the metaphor of a moving landscape to capture a shifting social formal history considered as a result of force and energy.

The production of the chart is a test of research, to see if such a general landscape of design positions exists at all in modern China. The research is carried out with simple rules. The chart has two dimensions: a horizontal axis of time from 1900 to 2010, and a vertical axis of basic design approaches. On this vertical axis, approaches that occurred later in China are placed further up (so that modernist approaches are placed above historicist approaches). Each and all design positions are identified based on research literature and existing knowledge; and each and all of them are plotted on the chart according to the time a particular design position occurred in history and the approach it belonged to. When these positions are located, connecting lines are put between them if there were relations in history. A continuous line signifies a direct link, a dashed line indicates a direct link that is historically interrupted, and a dotted line (with an arrow) refers to an indirect or hidden relationship which is by no means less important or powerful.

The research, in the development of this chart, is a process in which existing knowledge is visualized and spatialized according to the rules, which in turn results in a map or a landscape of new patterns that bring about new observations. In so far as current knowledge is limited, the chart describes empirical knowledge and involves hypothetical suggestions. In other words, it is an empirical history and a researched argument about what has happened in modern Chinese architecture.

In order to capture a real and messy history, the chart presented here contains a certain tolerance of inconsistency. Although only design positions in mainland China are covered, a significant moment in Taiwan in the 1970s is included on account of its close relation with one design position in mainland China of the 1930s (and therefore other positions through this), and also because of its significance in a larger comparison with Beijing and Nanjing. Similarly, although all 'positions' are about design practice, the scholarly work of the Society for Research in Chinese Architecture of the 1930s and 1940s is also included, owing to its great impact on design thinking and design practice from the 1930s to the 1950s and after.

A reading of the historical landscape

Let us now briefly go through this chart (Figure 10.1a) as an empirical representation and a theoretical argument that aim to capture a landscape of design positions in modern China across the twentieth century.

On the horizontal axis of time, crucial years in the political history of China are marked. They define the beginning (and sometimes the end) of political periods. They have clearly framed periods of design positions as well. Yet it is exactly against these framing dates that interrelations cutting through them reveal critical information. Here we can witness these political and architectural periods: (1) the 'Nanjing Decade' when central China was under the rule of the Kuomintang government with Nanjing as its capital (1927–37), (2) the Maoist era with Beijing as its capital since 1949, and (3) the post-Mao era since 1976. Before and in between are chaotic periods of wars, fragmentation and partial colonization. In a progression of ever longer periods of stability, those beginning in 1927 and 1949 have certainly witnessed the birth of new trends and building activities. In the post-Mao era after 1976, new trends and intensive building activities emerged somewhere in the mid-1980s, in the mid-1990s and then after 2000. These periods being defined, it is now the connections penetrating the politico-historical divisions that are most interesting. These occur mostly on horizontal and diagonal links between and within bands of design approaches defined by the vertical axis.

On the vertical axis, five design approaches or 'bands' are placed from bottom to top as they have appeared progressively in history:

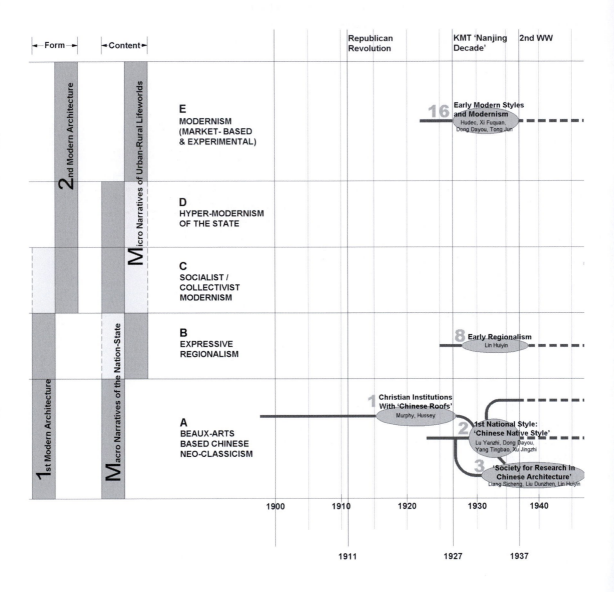

10.1a Twenty Plateaus: a historical landscape of modern architecture in mainland China.

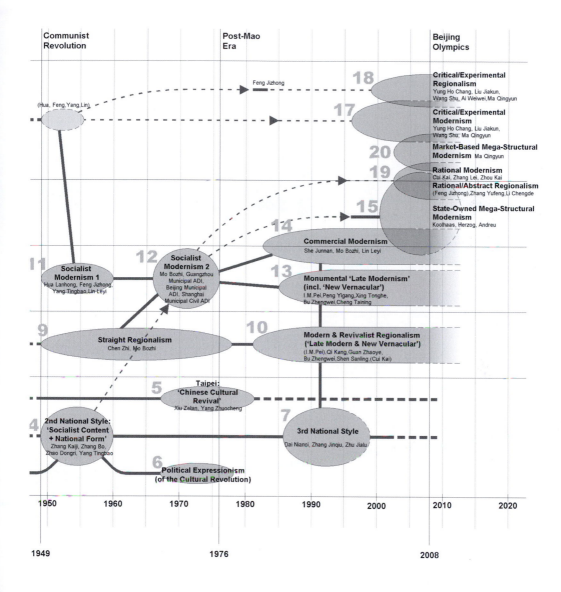

Communist
Revolution

Post-Mao
Era

Beijing
Olympics

18 Feng Jizhong

**Critical/Experimental
Regionalism**
Yung Ho Chang, Liu Jiakun,
Wang Shu, Ai Weiwei,Ma Qingyun

(Hua, Feng,Yang,Lin)

17

**Critical/Experimental
Modernism**
Yung Ho Chang, Liu Jiakun,
Wang Shu, Ma Qingyun

20

**Market-Based Mega-Structural
Modernism** Ma Qingyun

19

Rational Modernism
Cui Kai, Zhang Lei, Zhou Kai

Rational/Abstract Regionalism
(Feng Jizhong),Zhang Yufeng,Li Chengde

15

**State-Owned Mega-Structural
Modernism**
Koolhaas, Herzog, Andreu

14

11

**Socialist
Modernism 1**
Hua Lanhong, Feng Jizhong,
Yang Tingbao,Lin Leyi

12

**Socialist
Modernism 2**
Mo Bozhi, Guangzhou
Municipal ADI,
Beijing Municipal
ADI, Shanghai
Municipal Civil ADI

13

Commercial Modernism
She Junnan, Mo Bozhi, Lin Leyi

**Monumental 'Late Modernism'
(incl. 'New Vernacular')**
I.M.Pei,Peng Yigang,Xing Tonghe,
Bu Zhengwei,Cheng Taining

9

Straight Regionalism
Chen Zhi, Mo Bozhi

10

**Modern & Revivalist Regionalism
('Late Modern & New Vernacular')**
(I.M.Pei),Qi Kang,Guan Zhaoye,
Bu Zhengwei,Shen Sanling,(Cui Kai)

5

**Taipei:
'Chinese Cultural
Revival'**
Xiu Zelan, Yang Zhuocheng

4

**2nd National Style:
'Socialist Content
+ National Form'**
Zhang Kaiji, Zhang Bo,
Zhao Dongri, Yang Tingbao

7

3rd National Style
Dai Nianci, Zhang Jinqiu, Zhu Jialu

6

**Political Expressionism
(of the Cultural Revolution)**

1950   1960   1970   1980   1990   2000   2010   2020

1949   1976   2008

1 **2** **3** **4** **5** **6** **7** **8** **9** **10**

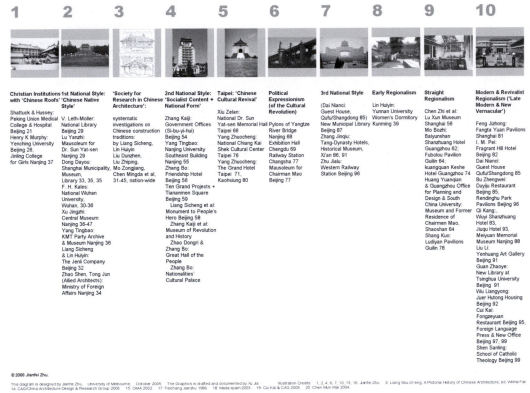

1
Christian Institutions
with 'Chinese Roofs'

Shattuck & Hussey:
Peking Union Medical
College & Hospital
Beijing 21
Henry K Murphy:
Yenching University
Beijing 26,
Jinling College
for Girls Nanjing 37

2
1st National Style:
'Chinese Native
Style'

V. Leth-Moller:
National Library
Beijing 29
Lu Yanzhi:
Mausoleum for
Dr. Sun Yat-sen
Nanjing 29
Dong Dayou:
Shanghai Municipality,
Museum,
Library 33, 35, 35
F. H. Kales:
National Wuhan
University,
Wuhan, 30-36
Xu Jingzhi:
Central Museum
Nanjing 36-47
Yang Tingbao:
KMT Party Archive
& Museum Nanjing 36
Liang Sicheng
& Lin Huiyin:
The Jenli Company
Beijing 32
Zhao Shen, Tong Jun
(Allied Architects):
Ministry of Foreign
Affairs Nanjing 34

3
'Society for
Research in Chinese
Architecture':

systematic
investigations on
Chinese construction
traditions:
by Liang Sicheng,
Lin Huiyin
Liu Dunzhen,
Liu Zhiping,
Mo Zongjiang,
Chen Mingda et al,
31-45, nation-wide

4
2nd National Style:
'Socialist Content +
National Form'

Zhang Kaiji:
Government Offices
(Si-bu-yi-hui)
Beijing 54
Yang Tingbao:
Nanjing University
Southeast Building
Nanjing 55
Zhang Bo:
Friendship Hotel
Beijing 56
Ten Grand Projects +
Tiananmen Square
Beijing 59
Liang Sicheng et al:
Monument to People's
Hero Beijing 58
Zhang Kaiji et al:
Museum of Revolution
and History
Zhao Dongri &
Zhang Bo:
Great Hall of the
People
Zhang Bo:
Nationalities'
Cultural Palace

5
Taipei: 'Chinese
Cultural Revival'

Xiu Zelan:
National Dr. Sun
Yat-sen Memorial Hall
Taipei 66
Yang Zhuocheng:
National Chiang Kai
Shek Cultural Center
Taipei 76
Yang Zhuocheng:
The Grand Hotel
Taipei 71,
Kaohsiung 80

6
Political
Expressionism
(of the Cultural
Revolution)

Pylons of Yangtze
River Bridge
Nanjing 68
Exhibition Hall
Chengdu 69
Railway Station
Changsha 77
Mausoleum for
Chairman Mao
Beijing 77

7
3rd National Style

(Dai Nianci:
Guest House,
Qufu/Shangdong 85)
New Municipal Library
Beijing 87
Zhang Jinqiu:
Tang-Dynasty Hotels,
Historical Museum,
Xi'an 86, 91
Zhu Jialu:
Western Railway
Station Beijing 96

8
Early Regionalism

Lin Huiyin:
Yunnan University
Women's Dormitory
Kunming 39

9
Straight
Regionalism

Chen Zhi et al:
Lu Xun Museum
Shanghai 56
Mo Bozhi:
Baiyunshan
Shanzhuang Hotel
Guangzhou 62;
Fubolou Pavilion
Guilin 64;
kuangquan Keshe
Hotel Guangzhou 74
Huang Yuanqian
& Guangzhou Office
for Planning and
Design & South
China University:
Museum and Former
Residence of
Chairmen Mao,
Shaoshan 64
Shang Kuo:
Ludiyan Pavilions
Guilin 78

10
Modern & Revivalist
Regionalism ('Late
Modern & New
Vernacular')

Feng Jizhong:
Fangta Yuan Pavilions
Shanghai 81
I. M. Pei:
Fragrant Hill Hotel
Beijing 82
Dai Nianci:
Guest House
Qufu/Shangdong 85
Bu Zhengwei:
Duyiju Restaurant
Beijing 85,
Rendinghu Park
Pavilions Beijing 96
Qi Kang:,
Wuyi Shanzhuang
Hotel 83,
Jiuqu Hotel 93,
Meiyuan Memorial
Museum Nanjing 88
Liu Li:
Yenhuang Art Gallery
Beijing 91
Guan Zhaoye:
New Library at
Tsinghua University
Beijing 91
Wu Liangyong:
Juer Hutong Housing
Beijing 92
Cui Kai:
Fongzeyuan
Restaurant Beijing 95,
Foreign Language
Press & New Office
Beijing 97, 99
Shen Sanling:
School of Catholic
Theology Beijing 99

10.1b Twenty Plateaus: a historical
landscape of modern architecture in
mainland China.

11	12	13	14	15	16	17	18	19	20

Socialist Modernism 1	Socialist Modernism 2	Monumental 'Late Modernism' (incl. 'New Vernacular')	Commercial Modernism	State-Owned Mega-Structural Modernism	Early Modern Styles and Modernism	Critical/Experimental Modernism	Critical/Experimental Regionalism	Rational Modernism	Market-Based Mega-Structural Modernism
Yang Tingbao: Peace Hotel Beijing 53 Hua Lanhong (Leon Hoa): Children's Hospital Beijing 54 Huang Yulin: Tongji University Wenyuan Building Shanghai 54 Feng Jizhong, Medical College Teaching Hospital Wuhan 55 Lin Leyi: Telephone & Telegraphy Building Beijing 57	Mo Bozhi: Baiyun Hotel Guangzhou 68, 75 Beijing Municipal ADI: International Club Beijing, Friendship Shop Beijing, Diplomats' Apartment Buildings Beijing 72, 72, 73 Guangzhou Municipal ADI: China International Trade Hall, Guangzhou 74, 74, 75 Shanghai Municipal Civil ADI: High-rise Apartments (Cao-xi-bei-lu) Shanghai 76	Chai Peiyi: China International Exhibition Centre Beijing 85 Qi Kang: Memorial Museum to the Nanking Massacre Victims Nanjing, 85 Peng Yigang: Tianjin University School of Architecture Tianjin 90 Bu Zhengwei: Chongqing 90 Wu Lusheng: Tongji University Yifu Building Shanghai 93 Xing Tonghe: Shanghai Museum 95 Wu Yue: Shixia/Futian Theatre Shenzhen 98 Cheng Taining: Hangzhou Railway Station 99	She Junnan & Mo Bozhi: White Swan Hotel Guangzhou 83 ECADI: Lianyi Mansion Shanghai 85 Lin Leyi: International Hotel Beijing 87	Jean-Marie Charpentier: Grand Theatre Shanghai 97 Paul Andreu: National Grand Theatre Beijing 05 Herzog & de Meuron + CAG: National Stadium Beijing 08 Rem Koolhaas/OMA + ECADI: CCTV Beijing 09	Ladislaus Hudec: Grand Theatre Shanghai 33, Woo Residence Shanghai 37 Xi Fuquan: Hongqiao Sanatorium Shanghai 34 Dong Dayou: Own Residence Shanghai 35 Zhuang Jun: Maternity Hospital Shanghai 35 Liang Sicheng, Lin Huiyin: Peking University Department of Geology & Students Dormitory, Beijing, 34, 35 Yang Tingbao: Dahua Theatre, International Club, Xin Sheng Club, Sun Ke Residence, Nanjing 35, 36, 47, 48 Tong Jun: Apartment Block A & B Nanjing 46	Yung Ho Chang: Book-Bike Store Beijing 96, Morningside Math Center Beijing 98, PKU Conference Center Qingdao 01, Pingod (Apple) Sales Center & Art Museum Beijing 03, Hebei Education Press Shijiazhuang 04 Liu Jiakun: Hedouling Studio Chengdu 97, Museum of Buddhist Art Chengdu 02 Wang Shu: Chenmo Studio 98, 'A Room with a View' (gallery) Shanghai 00, Wenzheng College Library Suzhou 00 Ma Qingyun: Edge Park Qingpu/Shanghai 04 Chen Yifeng/Deshaus: Xiayu Kindergarten Qingpu/Shanghai 04 Liu Yichun, Zhuang Shen, Chen Yifeng/Deshaus: DGIT Dongguan 04	(Feng Jizhong: Fangta Yuan Pavilions Shanghai 81) Yung Ho Chang: Villa Shanyujian 98, Split Hou 02, Villa Shizilin 04 Wang Shu: Wenzheng College Library Suzhou 00 China Academy of Art at Xiangshan Hangzhou 04 Ai Weiwei: China Art Archives & Warehouse Beijing 00 Liu Jiakun: Museum of Buddhist Art, Chengdu 02, Sichuan Academy of Fine Art Department of Sculpture Chongqing 04 Ma Qingyun: Father's House Xi'an, 03; Edge Park Qingpu/Shanghai 04 Liu Yichun, Zhuang Shen, Chen Yifeng/Deshaus: Three Houses Kunshan 03 Tong Ming: Dong's House Suzhou 04	Cui Kai: China Academy of Urban Planning and Research Beijing 03, Conference Centre of Foreign Language University Daxin/Beijing 04 Zhang Lei: Nanjing University Postgraduates' Dormitory Nanjing 01, DGIT Staff Housing Dongguan 04 Zhou Kai: Feng Jichai Institute of Art and Literature Tianjin 03 Tang Hua: Center for Scholarly Exchange Dongwan 03 Wang Hui/Urbanus: 'Grand Constellation' Sales Office Beijing 03 Zhang Bin & Zhou Wei: Tongji College of Architecture & Urban Planning Shanghai 04 Zhuang Shen, Chen Yifeng/Deshaus: DGIT Dongguan 04 (Zhang Yufeng: Historical Museum Hangzhou 01 Li Chengde: China Academy of Fine Arts Hangzhou 03)	Ma Qingyun: CCD Complex Ningbo 02 Riken Yamamoto: Jianwai SOHO Beijing 04 Peter Davidson/Lab: SOHO Shangdu Beijing 07 Rem Koolhaas/OMA: Beijing Books Building 08

rbank, Boston: MIT, 1984, pp. 46-9.   5. Fu Chao-qing, Zhongguo gudian shiyang xin jianzhu, Taipei: Niantian, 1993, p. 298.   8. Zhao Chen   9, 11, 12 Gong Deshun, Zou Denong, Douyide, Zhongguo xiandai jianzhu shigang, Tianjin: Science & Technology Press, 1989, p. 119, 32, 108.

(A) a Chinese neo-classical architecture based on the imported Beaux-Arts programme in design, teaching and research; (B) a regionalism that is largely expressive; (C) socialist modernism; (D) hyper-modernism of the state; (E) modernism for the market and modernism for critical experimentation. Although there are complex links and overlapping areas between them, all 'interesting' design positions in modern China on the mainland can be placed into one of these five groups or in between. Twenty design positions can be identified, and all can be grouped into the five bands or in some cases between them. Since these positions are part of the groups or bands, and since the emergence of each position reflects a critical moment of intense production of ideas and designs, these five bands can be referred to as 'mountain ranges' whereas these twenty positions can be likened to 'plateaus' in a naturalistic analogy.

The historical lining up of these five groups or ranges reveals crucial information in terms of form and content. In terms of form, if groups A and B belong to a historicist language for modern state and society (as appeared in nineteenth-century Europe if not earlier), groups C, D and E belong to modernism and its variations (which first appeared in the 1920s in Europe). And if the former and latter can be described as the first and second modern architecture, then the trend in the chart displays a significant domination of the first modern, and a gradual shift from the first to the second in Chinese architecture of the twentieth century. In terms of content, whereas major designs in groups A, C and D were cases of representation of the nation-state and its grand narratives (of various kinds), those 'interesting' designs in groups B and E have shifted towards a micro aesthetics of region, place, a specific theme, or the experience of the person, in an individualist exploration of these small life-worlds. There are in other words an expression of 'macro narratives of the nation-state' in the first (especially in the Beaux-Arts-based Chinese architecture of the state), and 'micro narratives of life-worlds' in an urban or rural setting in the second (especially in experimental modernism). In other words, if modern Chinese architecture involves a progression from A to E, then this development includes a shift from the first modern to the second modern in form (from A, B to C, D, E), and a general change of semantic interest from a grand narrative of the nation to a micro aesthetics of the local and the specific in content (from A to E, with a mixture in between).

We may now look more closely into these twenty plateaus, and the links that relate them together. Detailed description is beyond the scope of the present chapter, but a summary of them can be made. The strongest current, amongst all 'interesting' designs in modern China, is the development of a national style, the entire 'mountain range' of group A. Seven positions are found here (1–7). Whereas the first was the use of Chinese roofs and decorative details on modern structures made by foreign architects in the 1910s and 1920s, positions 2, 4 and 7 were the three major waves of the national style carried out by the Chinese architects in the 1930s, 1950s and 1980s–1990s respectively. Supporting these designs was a research programme carried out by the Society for Research in Chinese Architecture in the 1930s and 1940s led by Liang Sicheng and others. There have been interesting bifurcations since then: while the Kuomintang government of the 1930s moved to Taiwan and was behind a movement of 'Chinese cultural revival' in the 1970s there, the decorative expressionism of the 1930s and 1950s also led to a political expressionism of the 1970s for the Cultural Revolution on the mainland. Nanjing of the 1930s, Beijing of the 1950s and Taipei of the 1970s (positions 2, 4 and 5 respectively), in fact, form a triangle of three primary sites/moments in which the greatest efforts to represent a modern Chinese nation-state in architecture and urban design were made. The relationship among these three points deserves further research. The resurfacing of the use of Chinese roofs and other details in the 1980s and 1990s, on the other hand, was partly encouraged by the arrival of Post-Modernism from the West, and partly to do with a revival of interest in tradition and heritage in the retreat of the radical left and Maoism in China.

In group B, we find three moments of regionalist designs. The strongest were those of the 1950s to the 1970s and since the mid-1980s. The designs in the first were partially decorative (such as Lu Xun Museum, Shanghai, 1956), yet some also demonstrated a modernist inclination (Baiyunshan Hotel, Guangzhou, 1962, by Mo Bozhi). Those since the mid-1980s, however, remained decorative and often historicist. Still ongoing today, this moment's formal language has matured greatly in recent years, in which one finds a more austere use of expressive forms and textures (such as Shen Sanling's School of Theological Studies in Beijing, 1999).

Group C, a socialist modernism, occurred first in the 1950s (position 11), then resurfaced with great strength in the 1970s (position 12) with the new international outlook of the Beijing leadership under Mao and Zhou Enlai (Mao and Richard Nixon met in 1972 in Beijing, a meeting prepared by Zhou and Henry Kissinger for some time before). It is interesting to note that, whereas the modernism of the 1970s was related to that of the 1950s, that of the 1950s, often criticized for not following Stalinist ideas of 'socialist realism', had links with the capitalist era before 1949 (through architects surviving the political change). The modernism of the 1970s, furthermore, is also related to the regionalism of the 1960s and 1970s (position 9). Here Mo Bozhi and other architects in Guangzhou played a critical role: a 'naked' and authentic expression of local climatic conditions in a sub-tropical region and of modern construction methods had led to a simultaneous rise of regionalism and modernism in that period (positions 9 and 12). Moving further along the timeline, history has also witnessed a mutation of this earthy modernism into a 'wealthy' formalism in the mid-1980s in an increasing use of volumes and white surfaces, in a late modernism for cultural facilities such as museums (position 13) and commercial projects such as hotels and office towers (position 14).

Group D, hyper-modernism of the state, is a very new phenomenon emerging after the late 1990s and especially 2001 (when China joined the WTO and won the bid to host the 2008 Olympic Games). Futuristic, radical or super-modern forms were employed for cultural and sports facilities from Beijing to Shanghai to Guangzhou. The designs were selected through international competitions and European architects were the predominant winners. Yet this is part of the effort of the government to construct new spectacles of the nation and new spaces for the public. This is ideologically related to the modernism of the state in the 1970s (position 12) and, through this, to the national style of the 1950s (position 4). One connection is the representation of the nation found in all these moments. But a more intriguing link is between the present and the 1970s (positions 15 and 12): in both, modernism of a certain kind was adopted for a Chinese nation-state that was gradually opening up with a new international outlook.

Group E, modernism of the capitalist market and also experimental modernism, had a difficult time in China. As a modernism of the capitalist market and of 'bourgeois' critical experimentation, these designs only briefly emerged in the 1930s and 1940s (villas, apartments, cinemas, hospitals, in position 16). They then resurfaced briefly in the early 1950s, to be criticized (position 11) and 'reformed' into a socialist or collectivist modernism of efficiency and productivity, and also symbolic representation (position 12). Absent for decades, they have finally emerged in the mid-1990s, in the hands of a young generation of Chinese architects educated after 1977/8 in the post-Mao era. Here we can divide these designs into the experimental (17, 18) and the market-oriented, utilitarian and rational (19, 20). The experimental can be further divided into a regionalist trend (18) and a formalist or abstract trend (17), the two being closely related and designed by the same group of architects. Earlier precedents found in Xi Fuquan (1934), Tong Jun (1946), Hua Lanhong (1954), Lin Leyi (1957) and Feng Jizhong (1981) are important historically (to demonstrate that experimental modernism was possible in China in the earlier decades but was largely absent because of ideological and politico-economic limitations). Again, the socialist modernism of the state in the 1970s (position 12) shared important similarities with rational modernism of the present (position 19) so that the first had in fact prepared a basis for the second. Rational modernism of the present, furthermore, also shared certain features with the regionalism of the 1980s and 1990s (position 13), in a group of designs that can be described as 'late modern and new vernacular' (Li Chengde's China Academy of Art, Hangzhou, 2003).

General observations

Based on the readings above, we can now make some general observations regarding the whole landscape. Four aspects of the overall history appear most important: continuity, evolution, foreign influence, and the presence of the state.

1. *A continuous system*. What this map or chart demonstrates, first of all, is a continuous system running through the twentieth century. The continuity is found in the links and bifurcations, with some limited breakthroughs at the earliest historical moments. With these earliest incidents and with foreign influence coming in then or at later moments throughout the twentieth century, the rest of the chart, no matter how dramatic and full of 'new' beginnings, can all be contextualized into a web of relations in this history. We can find either early cases in a formal or ideological sense that had anticipated a later development, or larger formal and social categories in which a new breakthrough can be located. This is best represented at the beginning of new trends in the opening of a new political environment, when direct or indirect influences (marked as links on the chart) run into them from the past, a situation which challenges the divisions between the old and new periods. Throughout the century, we can identify new beginnings in 1927, 1949, 1978, the mid-1980s, the mid-1990s and 2001. In every case, we see lines moving from the old into the new eras (and also into later periods). In the post-Mao era after 1976/8, the mid-1980s, mid-1990s and 2001 are particularly interesting: they signalled the beginning of respectively a late modernism (10, 13, 14), an experimental modernism (17, 18) and a hyper-modernism (15 and, to an extent, 19, 20). Yet earlier developments in the 1930s, 1950s and 1970s (16, 11, 12) played a critical role in preparing in China a formal and ideological basis for the new breakthroughs of recent years to arrive. The modernism of the state of the 1970s (12) appears particularly important as it had summarized earlier trends and prepared for later developments in the presentation of the nation. The central position of the modernism of the 1970s requires further research. In the overall flow into the recent developments, none of the breakthroughs are entirely 'new'. This is the case not only in the sense of some early precedents preparing for them formally or politically, but also in the sense of an overall framework of the chart (with five bands from A to E) in which these breakthroughs are embedded. This is not to deny creativity in these spectacular developments in recent years in China (which should be fully appreciated). This is to suggest instead that, no matter how challenging or disorienting today's scene may appear, they can be clearly comprehended and precisely located.

2. *Formal evolutions*. We can also identify formal evolutions happening across this landscape. There is a shift from the first to the

second modern architecture as outlined above. This is a change from a Beaux-Arts-based decorative and historicist language to abstract and functionalist modernism and its recent and critical variations (from A, B to C, D, E). We can also identify a long gap or absence of modernism of the free market and individualist critical experimentation from the 1930s to the 1990s, for obvious political reasons. Furthermore, we also find a coupling of modernism and regionalism in their joint development. This happened in the 1960s and 1970s (9 and 12) and then after the mid-1990s (17 and 18). A common resistance against the decorative national style of the state (occurring across the entire range A) must have secured a common interest in the local, the authentic and sometimes the purist in these joint explorations in the 1970s and the 1990s. In the formal evolution of modern Chinese architecture, the latest situation can be found in the trends of B, C, D, E as they are reaching the date of 2008. Here we can say that the dominant language amongst the 'interesting' designs today is modernist (C, D, E), and the most powerful appears to be that of D and E, the modernism of the state, the market, and the experimental (positions 15, 17–20).

3. *Foreign influence*. Where are the foreign influences in this historical landscape? First of all, there have been influences from the outside and the West all the time, even in the Cold War or the Maoist period of 1949–78, as building technologies were introduced and 'bourgeois' thinking in design was also 'critically studied' in a favourite slogan of the time. A subtle and pervasive synchronization between China and the outside including the West has been going on quietly all the time. Yet not all of the influences had the same effect in all periods; it was the domestic politico-ideological climate of the time that had the immediate impact on how open China was to these influences. In this, we can identify five moments at which certain foreign influences were clearly absorbed *and* localized: (1) the historicist and Beaux-Arts use of Chinese roofs and other features on modern buildings by foreign architects in the 1910s and 1920s that was developed and localized by the Chinese in the 1930s (when the Beaux-Arts approach in teaching and historical research was also introduced); (2) the use of historicist features in the 1950s with the Soviet–Russian idea of socialist realism; (3) the introduction of Post-Modernism and of a formalistic late modernism in the 1980s, which encouraged not only a revival of the national style, but also a range of positions that can be described as 'late modern and new vernacular'; (4) the introduction of purist and tectonic modernism largely through the young Chinese architects themselves since the mid-1990s (which was perhaps partly to do with a rising new modernism at the time in the West); (5) a radical modernism introduced into China through foreign architects (European, American, Japanese) since the late 1990s and after 2001 for large-, medium- and small-scale buildings in which 'deconstructive'

and 'non-Cartesian' thinking for form and construction features prominently. Among all these historical moments (1910s–1930s, 1950s, 1980s, 1990s, 2001–8), the first and the last witnessed the largest number of foreign architects designing in and for China. Yet the two periods have a fundamental difference: whereas in the first a sovereign nation-state of China was weak, in the second it is strong and omnipresent, with decades of effort behind it in state building and national reconstruction after 1949.

4. *The presence of the state*. One of the earliest, and also strongest, design positions established in the history of modern Chinese architecture is the style of the nation, the historicist representation of the new republic using features of the imperial palace as a (constructed) classical tradition of the nation. The development of this position has occupied the entire 'mountain range' of group A. Having emerged in Nanjing in the 1930s, it resurfaced in Beijing of the 1950s and Taipei of the 1970s (a triangle of positions 2, 4, 5). A revival of that in the 1980s and 1990s with Post-Modern influence has witnessed exhaustion, as the language of the nation and of the public has already evolved in a new direction. In the matrix of relations of these positions, we can find a development from the national style of the 1950s to the modernism (of the state) of the 1970s, and further to a hyper-modernism of the state of the present in 2008 (from 4 to 12 to 15). Here the language has shifted to a modernism, and on to a more radicalized modernism of the present. It reveals a synchronization of China's design history with that of the world, yet the trajectory was implicit until after the late 1990s. In the architectural history of modern China, it reveals once again the critical centrality of the modernism of the 1970s as it carried a certain trust from the 1930s and 1950s into the 1990s and the present time.

Since the language of the state (about the government, the nation and the public) has survived, moved forward, and even absorbed the latest modern expressions as revealed now in 2008 (such as the CCTV building, the National Olympic Stadium, and all major civic and sports projects), one would ask the following question. Have we witnessed a shift from the grand narratives of the nation-state to the micro aesthetics of the local and the personal in modern Chinese architecture (from A to E)? If that is the case, then how to explain the ongoing presence of the state, with an ever more modernist language adopted for its presence and representation? If we look more closely at the design positions that dominate the architectural scene in China today, that is, positions 15 and 17–20, or modernism of the state, the market and the individual, what we are witnessing here in fact is an expansion of the spectrum of semantic interest which covers not just macro narratives for the nation in hyper-modernism (15) but also micro aesthetics of the local and personal in experimental modernism of the individual (17, 18). Therefore what is really happening today is an opening-up of a larger spectrum of semantic manifestations, that is, ideological positions, in which state, market and individuals all attain new expressions. This should be related to another important phenomenon: the post-Mao era is now three decades long, the longest period of stability and development in the entire history of modern China. All of this perhaps indicates the opening of a new era, one that has been and may continue to be liberal and sustained.

Notes

Chapter 1 Modern Chinese architecture: a social, historical and formal analysis

1 See Jianfei Zhu, 'Beyond revolution: notes on contemporary Chinese architecture', *AA Files*, 35 (1998), 3–14; and *2G: International Architectural Review*, 10 (1999) (special issue titled 'Instant China', which includes my article 'An archaeology of contemporary Chinese architecture', pp. 90–7); and Peter G. Rowe and Seng Kuan, *Architectural Encounters with Essence and Form in Modern China*, Cambridge, MA: MIT Press, 2002.

2 See Zhang Fuhe (ed.), *Zhongguo Jindai Jianzhu Yanjiu yu Baohu 1: 1998 Zhongguo Jindai Jianzhu Shi Guoji Yantaohui Lunwenji* (Anthology of 1998 international conference on history of modern Chinese architecture), Beijing: Qinghua Daxue Chubanshe, 1999; and the subsequent proceedings (volumes 2, 3 and 4) published in 2000, 2002 and 2004.

3 Jeffrey W. Cody, *Building in China: Henry K. Murphy's 'Adaptive Architecture', 1914–1935*, Seattle: The Chinese University Press and University of Washington Press, 2001.

4 Lai Delin, *Zhongguo Jindai Jianzhu Shi Yanjiu: Studies in Modern Chinese Architectural History*, Beijing: Qinghua Daxue Chubanshe, 2007.

5 Hou Youbin, 'Jindai zhongguo jianzhu' (Architecture in early modern China), in Pan Guxi (ed.), *Zhongguo Jianzhu Shi* (A history of Chinese architecture), Beijing: Zhongguo Jianzhu Gongye Chubanshe, 2001, pp. 299–391.

6 Yang Bingde, *Zhongguo Jindai zhongxi Jianzhu Wenhua Jiaoliu Shi* (A history of communication and integration of Chinese and Western architectural cultures in early modern China), Wuhan: Hubei Jiaoyu Chubanshe, 2002.

7 Fu Chao-ching, *Zhongguo Gudian Shiyang Xin Jianzhu* (Chinese neo-classical architecture: a historical research on a new imperial architecture in twentieth-century China), Taipei: Nantian Shuju, 1993.

8 Zou Denong, *Zhongguo Xiandai Jianzhushi* (A history of modern Chinese architecture), Tianjin: Tianjin Kexuejishu Chubanshe, 2001.

9 Rowe and Kuan, *Architectural Encounters*.

10 Caroline Klein and Eduard Kögel, *Made in China: neue Chinesische Architektur*, Munich: Deutsche Verlags-Anstalt, 2005.

11 Charlie Q. L. Xue, *Building a Revolution: Chinese Architecture since 1980*, Hong Kong: Hong Kong University Press, 2006.

12 Hao Shuguang, *Dangdai Zhongguo Jianzhu Sichao Yanjiu* (Research on architectural thoughts in contemporary China), Beijing: Zhongguo Jianzhu Gongye Chubanshe, 2006.

13 See Lai Delin, *Zhongguo Jindai*, and Li Shiqiao, 'Writing a modern Chinese architectural history: Liang Sicheng and Liang Qichao',

Journal of Architectural Education, 56 (2002), 35–45; and 'Reconstituting Chinese building tradition: the Yingzao fashi in the early twentieth century', *Journal of Society of Architectural Historians*, 62, no. 4 (2003), 470–89. For Wang's work, see Wang Chun-Hsiung, Chuan-Wen Sun and Horng-Chang Hsieh, 'Guomin zhengfu shiqi jianzhushi zhuanye zhidu xingcheng zhi yanjiu' (Formation of a professional institution of the architect in the Nationalist era), *Chengshi yu Sheji: Cities and Design*, 9/10 (September 1999), 81–116. For Lu's research, see Duanfang Lu, 'Third World modernism: modernity, utopia and the People's Commune in China', *Journal of Architectural Education*, 60, no. 3 (2007), 40–8; and her book, *Remaking Chinese Urban Form: Modernity, Scarcity and Space, 1949–2005*, London: Routledge, 2006.

14 Michael Dutton, *Streetlife China*, Cambridge: Cambridge University Press, 1998; Laurence J. C. Ma and Fulong Wu (eds), *Restructuring the Chinese City: Changing Society, Economy & Space*, London: Routledge, 2005; John Friedmann, *China's Urban Transition*, Minneapolis: University of Minnesota Press, 2005; and Joseph W. Esherick (ed.), *Remaking the Chinese City: Modernity and National Identity, 1900–1950,* Honolulu: Hawaii University Press, 2000.

Chapter 2 Perspective as symbolic form: Beijing, 1729–35

1 Descriptions of Matteo Ricci are based on He Zhaowu and He Gaoji, 'Zhong yi ben xuyan' (Preface for the Chinese edition), in Li Madou, *Li Madou Zhongguo Zaji* (China: the journals of Matteo Ricci), trans. He Gaoji, Wang Zunzhong and Li Shen, Guilin: Guangxi Shifandaxue Chubanshe, 2001, pp. 1–18. See also Jonathan D. Spence, *The Memory Palace of Matteo Ricci*, London: Faber and Faber, 1984, pp. xiii–xiv, 194–6; and Matteo Ricci, *China in the Sixteenth Century: The Journals of Matthew Ricci: 1583–1610*, trans. Louis J. Gallagher, S. J., New York: Random House, 1942.

2 He and He, 'Preface for the Chinese edition'.

3 On the rites controversy, see Kenneth Scott Latourette, *A History of Christian Missions in China*, New York: Russell & Russell, 1929, pp. 131–55.

4 This section on astronomy is based on Joseph Needham, *Science and Civilization in China*, vol. 3, *Mathematics and the Sciences of the Heavens and the Earth*, Cambridge: Cambridge University Press, 1959, pp. 171–461.

5 Needham, *Science*, pp. 437–8.

6 Needham, *Science*, pp. 438, 443–4, 447.

7 Needham, *Science*, pp. 444–5.

8 Needham, *Science*, p. 456.

9 This brief summary of mathematics in China in relation to the subject in India, Arabia and Europe is based on Needham, *Science*, pp. 53, 150–6.

10 Peter M. Engelfriet, *Euclid in China: The Genesis of the First Chinese Translation of Euclid's Elements Books I–VI (Jihe yuanben; Beijing, 1607) and its Receptions up to 1723*, Leiden: Brill, 1998, pp. 106–7.

11 Needham, *Science*, p. 52, 106.

12 Engelfriet, *Euclid*, pp. 106–7.

13 Engelfriet, *Euclid*, p. 451.

14 Engelfriet, *Euclid*, p. 139, 452.

15 Needham, *Science*, pp. 52–3.

16 Needham, *Science*, pp. 533–41.

17 Needham, *Science*, pp. 551–6.

18 Lu Liangzhi, *Zhongguo Dituxue Shi* (A history of cartography in China), Beijing: Cehui Chubanshe, 1984, pp. 176–7.

19 Needham, *Science*, pp. 583–5; Lu, *Zhongguo*, pp. 176–7.

20 Needham, *Science*, p. 585; Lu, *Zhongguo*, pp. 177–85.

21 This is Needham's comment in his *Science*, p. 585.

22 Wu Cong, 'Zai touying zhiwai' (Beyond projection), unpublished PhD thesis, Tianjin University, 1998, p. 103.

23 Yang Boda, *Qingdai Yuanhua* (Court paintings of the Qing dynasty), Beijing: Zijincheng Chubanshe, 1993, pp. 131–2.

24 Liu Yi, '*Shi Xue* pingxi' (Analysis and comments on *Shi Xue*), *Ziran Zazhi* (Nature), 10, no. 6 (1987), pp. 447–52. See also Michael Sullivan, *The Meeting of Eastern and Western Art*, Berkeley: University of California Press, 1989, pp. 54–5.

25 Nian Xiyao, *Shi Xue* (Principles of visual perspective), Beijing, 1735.

26 See Nian, *Shi Xue* and the following three studies: Liu Ruli, '*Shi Xue* – Zhongguo zuizao de toushixue zhuzou' (*Shi Xue*, the earliest book on perspective in China), *Nanyi Xuebao* (Journal of Nanjing Academy of Art), 1 (1979), 75–8; Shen Kangshen, 'Cong *Shi Xue* kan shibashiji dongxifang toushixue zhishi de jiaorong he yingxiang' (Confluence and influence between East and West in perspective studies in the case of the book *Shi Xue*), *Ziran Kexueshi Yanjiu: Studies in the History of Natural Sciences*, 4, no. 3 (1985), 258–66; and especially Liu Yi, '*Shi Xue* pingxi', pp. 447–52.

27 Both prefaces were published in the 1735 edition. See Nian, *Shi Xue*, pp. 1–5.

28 Although Ripa had made bronze engravings of Chinese landscape paintings and brought them to England and presented them in 1724 to Lord Berlington at Chiswick House, an encounter that had a 'major impact on the revolution of English garden design initiated by William Kent'. See Sullivan, *The Meeting of Eastern and Western Art*, pp. 76–7. See also Wu, 'Zai', pp. 100–1.

29 Yang, *Qingdai*, pp. 168, 174–7.

30 Yang, *Qingdai*, pp. 173–7.

31 Detailed descriptions of Castiglione's work here are based on Yang, *Qingdai*, pp. 131–77; and Wang Yong, *Zhongwai Meishu Jiaoliu Shi* (A history of communication between China and foreign countries in fine art), Hunan: Hunan Jiaoyu Chubanshe, 1998, pp. 176–84. See also Sullivan, *The Meeting of Eastern and Western Art*, pp. 67–77.

32 Yang, *Qingdai*, pp. 173–4.

33 Yang, *Qingdai*, pp. 175–7.

34 Yang, *Qingdai*, pp. 134–8, 174.

35 Yang, *Qingdai*, p. 174.

36 The sequence of events in the building of Xiyanglou and Changchunyuan is based on Yang Naiji, 'Yuanmingyuan dashi ji' (Chronology of the Yuanmingyuan Garden), *Yuanmingyuan*, 4 (October 1986), 29–38; and Shu Mu, 'Yuanmingyuan dashi nianbiao' (Annals of the Yuanmingyuan Garden), in Shu Mu, Shen Wei and He Naixian, *Yuanmingyuan Ziliaoji* (Archival materials concerning the Yuanmingyuan Garden), Beijing: Shumu Wenxian Chubanshe, 1984, pp. 361–89.

37 These Western-Style Pavilions and gardens, together with other

Chinese-style gardens of the whole Yuanmingyuan Garden, were burned down and looted by the Anglo-French Allied Forces in October 1860. The Xiyanglou remains in ruins today.

38 Tong Jun, 'Beijing Changchunyuan xiyang jianzhu' (Western-style buildings at the Changchunyuan Garden in Beijing), *Jianzhushi* (Architect), 2 (1980), 156–68. See also Wang Shiren and Zhang Fuhe, 'Beijing jindai jianzhu gaishuo' (An outline of early modern architecture in Beijing), in Wang Tan and Tengsen Zhaoxin (Terunobu Fujimori) (eds), *Zhongguo Jindai Jianzhu Zonglan – Beijing Pian: The Architectural Heritage of Modern China – Beijing*, Beijing: Zhongguo Jianzhu Gongye Chubanshe, 1992, pp. 5–6.

39 These elements are identified by Tong, 'Beijing Changchunyuan', pp. 165–6, and Wang and Zhang, 'Beijing jindai', pp. 5–6.

40 Tong, 'Beijing Changchunyuan', p. 165, and Wang and Zhang, 'Beijing jindai', pp. 5.

41 Tong, 'Beijing Changchunyuan', p. 165.

42 Tong, 'Beijing Changchunyuan', p. 165–6.

43 Wang and Zhang, 'Beijing jindai', pp. 1–4.

44 Wang and Zhang, 'Beijing jindai', pp. 5–6.

45 This style was referred to simply as 'Xiyanglou Style' or 'Yuanmingyuan Style'. See Wang and Zhang, 'Beijing jindai', pp. 5–6.

46 Liu, 'Shi Xue – Zhongguo', p. 77; Wu, 'Zai', p. 105.

47 This description of curriculum and university education in civil engineering and architecture is based on Lai Deling, 'Xueke de wailai yizhi – Zhongguo jindai jianzhu rencai de chuxian he jianzhu jiaoyu de fazhan' (Disciplines transplanted from abroad: the emergence of architects and architectural education in early modern China), in Lai Deling, *Zhongguo Jindai Jianzhu Shi Yanjiu: Studies in Modern Chinese Architectural History*, Beijing: Qinghua Daxue Chubanshe, 2007, pp. 115–80.

48 Zou Yuejin, *Xin Zhongguo Meishu Shi: A History of Chinese Fine Arts: 1949–2000*, Changsha: Hunan Meishu Chubanshe, 2002, pp. 1–15, 35–67. See also Sullivan, *The Meeting of Eastern and Western Art*, pp. 171–207.

49 Nie Chongzheng, *Zhongguo Jujiang Meishu Congshu: Lang Shining* (Books on great masters in Chinese art: Giuseppe Castiglione), Beijing: Wenwu Chubanshe, 1998, pp. 6–9.

50 Wang and Zhang, 'Beijing jindai', pp. 6–12.

51 Gaspard Monge's descriptive geometry of 1799 and Jacques-Nicolas-Louis Durand's history and design teaching texts of 1801–2, both developed at the Ecole Polytechnique in Paris, had a great impact on the teaching at the Ecole des Beaux Arts of the nineteenth century, from which in an Anglo-American version the Chinese students received a modern language of design and representation in the 1910s to 1930s mostly in the United States. Regarding the French development from Monge and Durand to the Beaux-Arts programme, see Alberto Pérez-Gómez, *Architecture and the Crisis of Modern Science*, Cambridge, MA: MIT, 1983, pp. 277–82, 288, 298–300, 304–14, 324; and Alberto Pérez-Gómez and Louie Pelletier, *Architectural Representation and the Perspective Hinge*, Cambridge, MA: MIT, 1997, pp. 71–87.

52 Erwin Panofsky, *Perspective as Symbolic Form*, trans. Christopher S. Wood, New York: Zone Books, 1997, pp. 63–6; and Martin Jay, 'Scopic regimes of modernity', in Hal Foster (ed.), *Vision and Visuality*, Seattle: Bay Press, 1988, pp. 3–23.

53 Robin Evans, *The Projective Cast: Architecture and its Three*

Geometries, Cambridge, MA: MIT, 1995, pp. xxv–xxxvii, 123–30, 351–70; Pérez-Gómez, *Architecture*, p. 174; and Pérez-Gómez and Pelletier, *Architectural*, pp. 19, 31, 55, 71, 82.

Chapter 3 The architect and a nationalist project: Nanjing, 1925–37

1 Hou Youbin, 'Jindai zhongguo jianzhu' (Architecture in early modern China), in Pan Guxi (ed.), *Zhongguo Jianzhu Shi* (A history of Chinese architecture), Beijing: Zhongguo Jianzhu Gongye Chubanshe, 2001, pp. 299–391. Some of the current analysis is based on empirical descriptions provided by Hou's comprehensive study. Yet there are different assumptions about political practice in Hou's work and mine. See the following sentences.

2 Hou, 'Jindai', p. 382.

3 This essay is a development from my earlier paper published in 2003 on the Nanjing decade. In that paper I focused on a few issues identified as critical: power relations between the state and architecture as a profession, the ideological position of the party-state, the political alliance of the architect, the contrast between leftist writers and nationalist architects, the use of architects' skills as a body of knowledge transferred from the West, and the making of a bourgeois public space in China. See Jianfei Zhu, 'Politics into culture: historical formation of the national style in the Nanjing decade (1927–1937)', in Zao Chen and Wu Jiang (eds), *Zhongguo Jindai Jianzhu Xueshu Sixian Yanjiu* (Research on ideologies and perspectives in early modern Chinese architecture), Beijing: Zhongguo Jianzhu Chubanshe, 2003, pp. 107–16. Lai Delin's essay in 2006 also adopted notions of 'knowledge' and 'public space', yet these social processes were not elucidated or analysed. It was nevertheless a comprehensive empirical account. See Lai Delin, 'Searching for a modern Chinese monument: the design of the Sun Yat-sen Musuem in Nanjing', *Journal of the Society of Architectural Historians*, 64, no. 1 (March 2005), 22–55.

4 More recently, I have encountered an essay by Chun-Hsiung Wang and colleagues that provides an interesting social analysis with valuable empirical details. It focuses on institutionalization of the profession and its relationship with state authority. However, it suffers from a few problems. The idea of 'institutionalization (of the profession)' is used literally, as applied to legal status of the profession, rather than the institutionalization of knowledge or knowledge production, including the building of university education and the work of the 'Society of Research in Chinese Architecture'. The state–profession relationship is dealt with internally within society (adopting established Anglo-American studies which are also 'internal'), rather than externally in a geo-political sphere involving colonialism. See Wang, Chuan-Wen Sun and Horng-Chang Hsieh, 'Guomin zhengfu shiqi jianzhushi zhuanye zhidu xingcheng zhi yanjiu' (Formation of a professional institution of the architect in the Nationalist era), *Chengshi yu Sheji: Cities and Design*, 9/10 (September 1999), 81–116. A social analysis of the 1930s, I believe, must move beyond these limitations (beyond the narrow use of 'institutionalization', and the internal study of the state–profession relationship). For a further critique, see the last few sections of the current chapter, especially 'A different kind of critical intellectual'.

5 Hou, 'Jindai', pp. 305–6.
6 Hou, 'Jindai', pp. 312–3.
7 Hou, 'Jindai', p. 355.
8 Hou, 'Jindai', p. 315.
9 See Marie-Claire Bergère, *The Golden Age of the Chinese Bourgeoisie 1911–1937*, trans. Janet Lloyd, Cambridge: Cambridge University Press, 1986; and Leo Ou-fan Lee, *Shanghai Modern: The Flowering of a New Urban Culture in China 1930–1945*, Cambridge, MA: Harvard University Press, 1999.
10 Hou, 'Jindai', pp. 355, 317–19. See also Wang Shiren and Zhang Fuhe, 'Beijing jindai jianzhu gaishuo' (An outline of early modern architecture in Beijing), in Wang Tan and Tengsen Zhaoxin (Terunobu Fujimori) (eds), *Zhongguo Jindai Jianzhu Zonglan – Beijing Pian: The Architectural Heritage of Modern China – Beijing*, Beijing: Zhongguo Jianzhu Gongye Chubanshe, 1992, pp. 1–26.
11 Hou, 'Jindai', p. 365.
12 Hou, 'Jindai', p. 357.
13 Hou, 'Jindai', p. 357.
14 Hou, 'Jindai', p. 365.
15 Hou, 'Jindai', p. 365.
16 Hou, 'Jindai', p. 366.
17 Hou, 'Jindai', p. 366. For the introduction of modern tertiary education in civil engineering and architecture in China, see Lai Delin, 'Xueke de wailai yizhi – Zhongguo jindai jianzhu rencai de chuxian he jianzhu jiaoyu de fazhan' (Disciplines transplanted from abroad: the emergence of architects and architectural education in early modern China), in Lai Delin, *Zhongguo Jindai Jianzhu Shi Yanjiu: Studies in Modern Chinese Architectural History*, Beijing: Qinghua Daxue Chubanshe, 2007, pp. 115–80.
18 Li Haiqing, *Zhongguo Jianzhu Xiandai Zhuanxing* (A structural transformation into modernity in Chinese architecture), Nanjing: Dongnan Daxue Chubanshe, 2004, pp. 132–3.
19 The account here is based on Hou, 'Jindai', pp. 361–2.
20 Hou, 'Jindai', p. 366.
21 Hou, 'Jindai', pp. 361–8.
22 Hou, 'Jindai', p. 367.
23 Regarding the May Fourth New Cultural Movement, see John K. Fairbank, 'The rise and decline of Nationalist China', in John K. Fairbank, Edwin O. Reischauer and Albert M. Craig (eds), *East Asia: Tradition and Transformation*, Boston: Houghton Mifflin, 1989, pp. 763–807; and Benjamin Schwartz, 'Themes in intellectual history: May Fourth and after', in John K. Fairbank (ed.), *The Cambridge History of China*, vol. 12: *Republican China 1912–1949, Part 1*, Cambridge: Cambridge University Press, 1983, pp. 406–50.
24 These two statements from *The Chinese Architect* and *The Builder* are quoted in Hou, 'Jindai', p. 368.
25 On the nationalist theme in the May Fourth Movement see Schwartz, 'Themes', pp. 406–50. On the background and the nationalist outlook of the Society of Research in Chinese Architecture, see Lin Zhu, *Koukai Luban de Damen: zhongguo yingzao xueshe silue* (Opening the doors to ancient Chinese building construction: a brief history of the Society of Research in Chinese Architecture), Beijing: Zhongguo Jianzhu Gongye Chubanshe, 1995, pp. 13–17, 19–22. For Liang Sicheng's nationalist outlook in relation to his father Liang Qichao (a major proponent for the study of national heritage in the May Fourth Movement), see Li Shiqiao, 'Writing a modern Chinese architectural history: Liang

Sicheng and Liang Qichao', *Journal of Architectural Education*, 56 (2002), 35–45.

26 About the exhibition see Wu Jiang, *Shanghai Bainian Jianzhu Shi 1840–1949* (A century of architecture in Shanghai, 1840–1949), Shanghai: Tongji Daxue Chubanshe, 1997, pp. 165–6. About Liang Sicheng's involvement in the design of the Central Museum, see Li Haiqing and Liu Jun, 'Zai jiannan tansuo zhong zuoxiang chengshu' (Towards maturity through difficult research: analysis of the origin of the National Central Museum and the related issues), *Huazhong Jianzhu* (Architecture in central China), 6 (2001), 85–6; 1 (2002), 15; and 2 (2002), 99–103; and Lai Delin, 'Sheji yizuo lixiangde zhongguo fengge de xiandai jianzhu' (Designing an ideal Chinese-style modern architecture), in Lai Delin, *Zhongguo*, pp. 331–62.

27 Liang Sicheng, 'Jianzhu sheji cankao tuji xu' (Preface to the Visual Dictionary for Architectural Design), in Liang Sicheng, *Liang Sicheng Quanji, di liu juan* (The complete works of Liang Sicheng, volume 6), Beijing: Zhongguo Jianzhu Gongye Chubanshe, 2001, pp. 233–6.

28 Lu Yanzhi (Y. C. Lu), 'Memorials to Dr. Sun Yat-sen in Nanking and Canton', *Far Eastern Review*, xxv, no. 3 (March 1929), 97–101.

29 Fairbank, 'The rise', pp. 763–807. See also the following two sources for Comintern's work in China: Kevin McDermott and Jeremy Agnew, *The Comintern: A History of International Communism from Lenin to Stalin*, London: Macmillan, 1996; and Guo Hengyu, *Gongchan Guoji yu Zhongguo Geming* (The Comintern and the Chinese revolution), Taipei: Dongda Tushu Gongsi, 1989.

30 This description of Chiang's rule during 1927–37 is based on: Lloyd E. Eastman, 'Nationalist China during the Nanking decade 1927–37', in John Fairbank and Albert Feuerwerker (eds), *The Cambridge History of China*, vol. 13, *Republic China 1912–49, Part 2*, Cambridge: Cambridge University Press, 1986, pp. 116–67; Lloyd E. Eastman, *The Abortive Revolution: China under Nationalist Rule 1927–1937,* Cambridge, MA: Harvard University Press, 1974, pp. 1–30, 31–84, 244–82; Fairbank, 'The rise', pp. 763–807; and *Zhongguo Jinxiandaishi Dashiji (1840–1980)* (A calendar of events: early modern Chinese history (1840–1980)), Shanghai: Zhishi Chubanshe, 1982, pp. 100–20.

31 Eastman, 'Nationalist', pp. 116–24, 136–41.

32 Eastman, 'Nationalist', pp. 145–7. See also William C. Kirby, *Germany and Republican China*, Palo Alto, CA: Stanford University Press, 1984, pp. 38–75, 102–44.

33 Eastman, 'Nationalist', pp. 142–4.

34 Eastman, 'Nationalist', pp. 146–7. See also Chiang Kai-shek, 'Xin shenghuo yundong zhi yaoyi' (The essence of the New Life Movement), in Chiang Kai-shek, *Jiang Zongtong Ji* (Collective works of President Chiang), Taipei: Guofang Yanjiu Yuan, 1961, pp. 733–7; and Arif Dirlik, 'The ideological foundations of the New Life Movement: a study in counterrevolution', *Journal of Asian Studies*, xxxiv, no. 4 (August 1975), 945–79.

35 V. I. Lenin, *Imperialism, the Highest Stage of Capitalism: A Popular Outline*, Moscow: Progress Publishers, 1970, pp. 117–23; Lenin, 'Communism and the east: theses on the national and colonial questions', in Robert C. Tucker (ed.), *The Lenin Anthology*, New York: Norton, 1975, pp. 619–25. See also Fairbank, 'The rise', pp. 772–3, 776–81.

36 Sun Yat-sen, 'Sanmin zhuyi' (Three principles of the people), in Sun
    Yat-sen, *Sun Zhongshan Xuanji* (Selected works of Sun Yat-sen),
    Hong Kong: Zhonghua Shuju, 1956, pp. 588–602, 588–838.
37 For Sun's revised ideas after 1923, see Sun Yat-sen, 'Zhongguo
    Guomindang diyici quanguo daibiao dahui xuanyan' (Manifesto
    at the first national congress of the Chinese Nationalist Party), and
    'Yizhu' (Will), in Sun, *Sun*, pp. 520–31, 921.
38 See especially Eastman, 'Nationalist', pp. 145–7, and Dirlik, 'The
    ideological', pp. 945–79.
39 For a comprehensive view of Chiang and his party's position, see
    the following delivered in 1943: Chiang Kai-shek, 'Zhongguo zhi
    mingyun' (China's destiny), in Chiang Kai-shek, *Jiang Zongtong
    Ji* (Collected works of President Chiang), Taipei: Guofang Yanjiu
    Yuan, 1961, pp. 119–70.
40 Li Mu, *Sanshi Niandai Wenyi Lun* (On the literature and arts of the
    1930s), Taipei: Liming Wenhua Shiye Gongsi, 1973, pp. 61–3; Leo
    Ou-Fan Lee, 'Literary trends: the road to revolution 1927–1949',
    in Fairbank and Feuerwerker (eds), *The Cambridge*, vol. 13, Part 2,
    pp. 421–91, especially 433. See also Hou, 'Jindai', p. 381.
41 This was first raised and explored in Jianfei Zhu, 'Politics into
    culture: historical formation of the national style in the Nanjing
    decade (1927–1937)', in Zao Chen and Wu Jiang (eds), *Zhongguo
    Jindai Jianzhu Xueshu Sixian Yanjiu* (Research on ideologies and
    perspectives in early modern Chinese architecture), Beijing:
    Zhongguo Jianzhu Chubanshe, 2003, pp. 107–16.
42 Wu, *Shanghai*, pp. 158–9.
43 Lin Zhu, Lou Qingxi, Wang Jun, 'Liang Sicheng nianpu' (Life of
    Liang Sicheng: a chronology), in Liang Sicheng, *Liang Sicheng
    Quanji, di jiu juan* (Complete works of Liang Sicheng, volume 9),
    Beijing: Zhongguo Jianzhu Gongye Chubanshe, 2001, pp. 101–
    11.
44 Li Haiqing, *Zhongguo*, pp. 293–4.
45 Jeffrey W. Cody, *Building in China: Henry K. Murphy's 'Adaptive
    Architecture' 1914–1935*, Seattle: Chinese University Press and
    University of Washington Press, 2001, pp. 182–97.
46 Hou, 'Jindai', pp. 355–6.
47 Hou, 'Jindai', pp. 355–6.
48 Wang, Sun and Hsieh, 'Guomin', pp. 81–116.
49 The description here is based on Nanjing Municipal Archive and
    Zhongshan Lingyuan Office (comp.), *Zhongshanling Dangan Shiliao
    Xuanbian* (Selected historical files and documents concerning
    Sun Yat-sen's mausoleum), Nanjing: Jiangsu Guji Chubanshe,
    1986, pp 12–16, 85–7, 384–9, 149–57; Liu Fan, 'Lu Yanzhi yu
    Nanjing Zhongshanling' (Lu Yanzhi and Sun Yat-sen's mausoleum
    in Nanjing), *Jianzhushi* (Architect) (Taipei), March 1994, 114–25;
    and Yao Qian and Gu Bing (eds), *Zhongshanling* (Sun Yat-sen's
    mausoleum), Beijing: Wenwu Chubanshe, 1981, pp. 1–14.
50 The competition was open to all nationals. The second and third
    prizes however also went to the Chinese (Fan Wenzhao, Yang
    Xizong), while the recommendation prize went to seven designs,
    six of which were by Western architects (Cyrill Nebuskad, Francis
    Kales, C. Y. Anney and W. Frey, W. Livin Goldenstaedt, Zdanwitch
    and Goldenstaedt, and Zdanwitch and Goldenstaedt). See Nanjing
    and Zhongshan, *Zhaongshangling*, pp. 15, 156–62, and Liu, 'Lu
    Yanzhi', pp. 116–7.
51 The content of the guidelines may be found in Nanjing and
    Zhongshan, *Zhongshanling*, pp. 149–52.

52 Nanjing and Zhongshan, *Zhongshanling*, pp. 149–53, 157. See also Lu, 'Memorials', pp. 97–8, which includes the statement that the design was 'in accordance with Chinese traditions in planning and in the form', being 'apparent in its Chinese origin, yet, [standing] out distinctively as a creative effort in monumental construction of modern times'.

53 Lu was self-conscious in the adoption of this Chinese ritual passage when he described the process as composed of a 'Tablet Pavilion', an entrance gate and a 'Pailo', and also the visual openness in the Western tradition when he described 'vistas' on the axis and the tomb visible and accessible to the public like 'Grant's Tomb in New York or Napoleon's Tomb in Paris'. See Lu, 'Memorials', pp. 97–8.

54 Lu was apparently also self-conscious about the combination of 'Chinese architecture' and the massive or heroic forms of European modern architecture when he said that 'it should be apparent in its Chinese origin, yet, must stand out distinctively as a creative effort in monumental construction of modern times'. See Lu 'Memorials', p. 98.

55 See Liu, 'Lu Yanzhi', p. 119; and Nanjing and Zhongshan, *Zhongshanling*, pp. 85–7, 384–9. See also Fan Fangzhen and Liao Jinhan (comp.), *Zhongshan Lingyuan Shihua* (Sun Yat-sen's mausoleum and the surrounding historical sites and relics), Nanjing: Zhongshan Lingyuan, 1995, pp. 69–71.

56 Hou, 'Jindai', pp. 321–3.

57 Cody, *Building*, pp. 182–3. Lin Yimin, Murphy and Goodrich in fact had all worked under Sun Ke in Guangzhou on its planning in 1926, a previous partnership that was surely inherited here for the Nanjing plan. See Wang, Sun and Hsieh, 'Guomin', p. 88 (note 6).

58 Cody, *Building*, p. 183.

59 Cody, *Building*, pp. 191–5.

60 *Shoudu Jihua* (Capital plan), Nanjing, 1929, p. 1.

61 *Shoudu*, pp. 25–8 and figures 12 and 14.

62 *Shoudu*, pp. 33–6.

63 *Shoudu*, pp. 25–8 and figure 16. It is interesting to note that as planned the capitol in Nanjing had a shorter central axis than that in Washington, yet the total area was larger than that in the American capital: 775.8 ha versus 650 ha.

64 Wu, *Shanghai*, pp. 168–9. See also Editorial Committee (comp.), *Shanghai Chengshi Guihua Zhi* (Annuals of urban planning for Shanghai), Shanghai: Shehui Kexue Yuan Chubanshe, 1999, pp. 66–70.

65 Wu, *Shanghai*, p. 168.

66 Wu, *Shanghai*, p. 169; Editorial Committee, *Shanghai*, pp. 67, 69–70.

67 Lee, *Shanghai*, pp. 312–15.

68 Hou, 'Jindai', p. 337.

69 See Wang, Sun and Hsieh, 'Guomin', pp. 96–8.

70 Liu, 'Lu Yanzhi', p. 114, and Cody, *Building*, p. 134.

71 See for example Jürgen Habermas, *The Structural Transformation of the Public Sphere: An Inquiry into a Category of Bourgeois Society*, trans. Thomas Burger, Cambridge, MA: MIT, 1989, pp. 25–6.

72 Michael Hays, 'Critical architecture: between culture and form', *Yale Architectural Journal: Perspecta*, 21 (1984), 15–29.

73 Peter Eisenman, 'Critical architecture in a geopolitical world', in

Cynthia C. Davidson and Ismail Serageldin (eds), *Architecture beyond Architecture: Creativity and Social Transformation in Islamic Cultures*, London: Academy Editions, 1995, pp. 78–81. It is interesting to note that Eisenman has acknowledged the national independence movements of the third world in a geo-political sphere, yet for him that doesn't seem to provide a basis upon which to reform or develop his basic formulation of the critical and the avant-garde in the European tradition. This article is nevertheless important precisely because it has entered a geo-political space but hasn't gone far enough.

74 Hou, 'Jindai', p. 386.
75 Wu, *Shanghai*, pp. 138–43.
76 Hou, 'Jindai', pp. 387–8. See also Li, *Zhongguo*, pp. 332–5.
77 Hou, 'Jindai', pp. 387–8.
78 Li, *Zhongguo*, pp. 336.
79 Li, *Zhongguo*, pp. 337–8.
80 Henry-Russell Hitchcock and Philip Johnson, *The International Style*, New York: W. W. Norton, 1966, pp. 259–60. Soviet Russia was soon to be governed by Stalin with his 'socialist realism' attack on modernism from the 1930s to the 1950s, which exerted an impact on China in the 1950s. The interesting inclusion of the Soviet Union in 1932 was perhaps more to do with the intimate exchange in avant-garde culture between Russia and Europe that had occurred before, but which was soon to be suppressed in the mid-1930s under Stalin.

Chapter 4 A spatial revolution: Beijing, 1949–59

1 Michel Foucault, *The Archaeology of Knowledge*, trans. A. M. Sheridan Smith, London: Routledge, 1972, pp. 25–30. See also Paul Hirst, 'Foucault and architecture', *AA Files*, 26 (Autumn 1993), 52–60. A study of discourse as external things, events and practices characterizes the approach proposed by Foucault. I find this useful here to transcend personal–moral readings of Liang in the current discussion in China. Ethical–political observations, nevertheless, must be brought back into the picture, as I will attempt to do at the end of the essay.

2 See online postings, available at <http://en.wikipedia.org/wiki/March_of_the_Volunteers>, <http://en.wikipedia.org/wiki/Flag_of_the_People's_Republic_of_China>, <http://news.xinhuanet.com/ziliao/2003–01/18/content_695296.htm> (accessed 25 September 2007).

3 The account here is based on Zhu Changzhong and Qin Youguo: Zhu Changzhong, 'Liang xiansheng yu guohui sheji' (Liang and the design for the national emblem), in Editorial Committee (ed.), *Liang Sicheng Xiansheng Danchen Bashiwu Zhounian Jinian Wenji* (A collection of essays in honour of Liang Sicheng's 85th birthday), Beijing: Qinghua Daxue Chubanshe, 1986, pp. 119–32; Qin Youguo, 'Liang Sicheng, Lin Huiyin yu guohui sheji' (Liang Sicheng, Lin Huiyin and the design for the national emblem), in Tsinghua University School of Architecture (ed.), *Liang Sicheng Xiansheng Baisui Danchen Wenji* (A collection of essays on the 100th birthday of Liang Sicheng), Beijing: Qinghua Daxue Chubanshe, 2001, pp. 111–19.

4 The account here is based on Liang Sicheng, 'Renmin yingxiong jinianbei sheji jingguo' (An account of how the Monument to the People's Heroes was designed), in Liang Sicheng, *Liang Sicheng*

Quanji, Di wu juan (Complete works of Liang Sicheng, vol. 5), Beijing: Zhongguo Jianzhu Gongye Chubanshe, 2001, pp. 462–4.

5   See also Wu Liangyong, 'Renmin yingxiong jinianbei de chuangzuo chengjiu' (Achievements in the design of the Monument to the People's Heroes), *Jianzhu Xuebao* (Architectural journal), 2 (1978), 4–7.

6   Wu Hong, 'Tiananmen Square: a political history of monuments', *Representations* 35, Summer 1991, 84–117.

7   Zou Yuejing, *Xin Zhongguo Meishushi 1949–2000* (A history of fine arts of New China 1949–2000), Changsha: Hunan Meishu Chubanshe, 2002, pp. 105–7.

8   Wang Jun, *Cheng Ji* (Beijing: a story of the city), Beijing: Sanlian Shudian, 2003, p. 38.

9   English spellings of the name of this advisor and of others from the Soviet Union mentioned in this article are provided by Professor Lu Fuxun of Tsinghua University of Beijing. I am very grateful for Prof. Lu's help.

10 Editorial Committee (comp.), *Jianguo Yilai de Beijing Chengshi Jianshe Ziliao, diyijuan, chengshi guhua* (Materials concerning Beijing's urban construction since 1949, volume 1, urban planning), Beijing: Beijing Jiansheshishu Bianji Weiyuanhui Bianjibu, 1987, pp. 5–14. See also Dong Guangqi, *Beijing Guihua Zhanlue Sikao* (Strategic thoughts on Beijing's planning), Beijing: Zhongguo Jianzhu Gongye Chubanshe, 1998, pp. 313–18.

11 Liang Sicheng, 'Guanyu zhongyang renmin zhengfu xingzheng zhongxinqu weizhi de jianyi' (On locating the administrative centre of the Central People's Government: a proposal), in Liang, *Liang* (vol. 5), pp. 60–81, especially 69–73.

12 Editorial (comp.), *Jianguo*, p. 14; Dong, *Beijing*, p. 318; Wang, *Cheng Ji*, p. 85, 101.

13 Editorial (comp.), *Jianguo*, p. 16; Dong, *Beijing*, p. 318.

14 Information on the 'Chang-guan-lou Plan' is based on Editorial (comp.), *Jianguo*, pp. 19–21, and Dong, *Beijing*, pp. 321–3.

15 Wang, *Cheng Ji*, p. 175.

16 Information on China's domestic and international affairs is based on Frederick C. Teiwes, 'Xin zhengquan de jianli he gonggu' (Chapter 2: Establishing and consolidating the new regime), and Nakajima Mineo, 'Waijiao guanxi: cong chaoxian zhanzheng dao wanlong luxian' (Chapter 6: Foreign relations: from the Korean War to the Bandung Principles), in Roderick MacFarquhar and John K. Fairbank (eds), *Jianqiao Zhonghua Renmin Gongheguo Shi: geming de Zhongguo de xingqi 1949–1965* (Cambridge History of China, vol. 14, The People's Republic: The emergence of revolutionary China, 1949–1965), trans. Xie Liangsheng, Beijing: Zhongguo Shehuikexue Chubanshe, 1990, pp. 55–149 and 273–306.

17 Wang Jianying (comp.), *Zhongguo Gongchangdang Zhuzhishi Zhiliao Huibian: lingdao jiguo yange he chengyuan minglu* (Collected materials on the Chinese Communist Party's organizational history: an evolution of institutions and a list of members' names), Beijing: Zhonggong Zhongyang Dangxiao Chubanshe, 1995, p. 963.

18 Zou Denong, *Zhongguo Xiandai Jianzhushi* (A history of modern Chinese architecture), Tianjin: Tianjin Kexuejishu Chubanshe, 2001, pp. 704–6.

19 I have received indispensable help from Professor Mario Gutjahr

from the University of Melbourne to determine the German names 'Walter Ulbricht' and 'Kurt Magritz'. The Russian names were confirmed by Prof. Lu Fuxun of Tsinghua University of Beijing. I am very grateful to Prof. Lu and Prof. Gutjahr on this. The name 'Jozsef Revai' was already printed in the journal.

20 Liang Sicheng, 'Jianzhu yishuzhong shehuizhuyi xianshizhuyi he minzu yichan de xuexi yu yuanyong de wenti' (On socialist realism in architectural art and on the study and use of national heritage), in Liang, *Liang* (vol. 5), pp. 185–96.

21 Liang Sicheng, 'Zhongguo jianzhu de tezheng' (Characteristics of Chinese architecture), *Jianzhu Xuebao*, 1 (1954), 36–9.

22 Liang Sicheng, 'Zuguo de jianzhu' (Architecture of the motherland), in Liang, *Liang* (vol. 5), pp. 197–234.

23 Liang, 'Zuguo de jianzhu', p. 233.

24 Liang, 'Zuguo de jianzhu', pp. 233–4.

25 This is evidenced in Liang's essays written after his visit to Moscow and other cities from February to May 1953. In these writings he referred to his conversations with Arkady Mordvinov, the president of the Academy of Architectural Science of the USSR. Liang also discussed the Moscow Plan in 1935, and the famous works in Moscow including the metro stations, the 'Tall Buildings', the Gorky Ulitsa, the Leningradskii Prospekt, and the axis from the Kremlin via the proposed Palace of Soviets to the Lenin Hills and Moscow State University. See Liang Sicheng, 'Wodui sulian jianzhu yishu de yidian renshi' (My reflections on architectural art in the Soviet Union), in Liang, *Liang* (vol. 5), pp. 175–8.

26 See for example Chen Dengao, 'Zai minzu xingshi gaoceng jianzhu sheji guocheng zhong de tihui' (Reflections upon my designs of high-rise buildings with national forms), *Jianzhu Xuebao*, 2 (1954), 104–7.

27 Mao Zedong, 'Zai Yanan wenyi zuotanhui shang de jianghua' (Speeches at the seminar on literature and art in Yanan), in Mao Zedong, *Mao Zedong Xuanji* (Selected works of Mao Zedong), vol. 3, Beijing: Renmin Chubanshe, 1966/70, pp. 804–35.

28 Liang Sicheng, 'Cong "shiyong, jingji, zai keneng tiaojian xia zhuyi meiguan" tandao chuantong yu gexin' (A talk on tradition and renovation based on the principle of 'function, economy, and moderate concerns of beauty'), *Jianzhu Xuebao*, 6 (1959), 1–4.

29 Liang Sicheng, 'Liang Sicheng de fayan' (Liang Sicheng's talk), *Jianzhu Xuebao*, 11 (1958), 6–7. The use of Fletcher's *History* as a model for documentation and representation for Liang and his assistants can be confirmed in Lin Zhu, *Koukai Luban de damen: zhongguo yingzao xueshe shilue* (Opening the door to the world of Lu Ban: a brief history of the Society for Research in Chinese Architecture), Beijing: Zhongguo Jianzhu Gongye Chubanshe, 1995, pp. 32–3.

30 Liang had in fact completed two such manuscripts by 1944. The other, written in English, was published in 1984 by the MIT Press. See Liang Ssu-cheng, *A Pictorial History of Chinese Architecture*, ed. by Wilma Fairbank, Cambridge, MA: MIT Press, 1984. The two manuscripts shared the same body of drawings, renderings and plates, which were annotated with Chinese characters and English letters.

31 See David Watkin, *The Rise of Architectural History*, London: The Architectural Press, 1980, pp. 23–4 and 85–6, for Durand, Fletcher, and the development on this path. For Durand's rationalism and universalism, see Alberto Pérez-Gómez, *Architecture and the Crisis*

of Modern Science, Cambridge, MA: MIT, 1983, pp. 298–314, and Hanno-Walter Kruft, *A History of Architectural Theory: From Vitruvius to the Present*, trans. Ronald Taylor, Elsie Callander and Antony Wood, London: Zwemmer, 1994, pp. 273–4.

32 For these drawings see Liang Sicheng, *Liang Sicheng Quanji* (Complete works of Liang Sicheng), Beijing: Zhongguo Jianzhu Gongye Chubanshe, 2001, vols 4 and 8; and Liang, *A Pictorial History*.

33 Erwin Panofsky, *Perspective as Symbolic Form*, trans. Christopher S. Wood, New York: Zone Books, 1997; Martin Jay, 'Scopic Regimes of Modernity', in Hal Foster (ed.), *Vision and Visuality*, Seattle: Bay Press, 1988, pp. 3–23.

34 For the idea of 'Cartesian perspectivalism', see Jay, 'Scopic Regimes', pp. 4–10.

35 The following discussion on China's international and domestic developments is based on Teiwes, 'Xin zhengquan', and Mineo, 'Waijiao guanxi', in MacFarquhar and Fairbank (eds), *Jianqiao*, pp. 55–149 and 273–306.

36 Editorial, 'Fandui jianzhu zhong de langfei xianxiang' (Against wasteful practice in building construction), *Renmin Ribao* (People's daily), 28 March 1955, p. 1, reprinted in *Jianzhu Xuebao*, 1 (1955), 32–4.

37 Bolan Jianzhushi Fanghua Daibiaotuan (Delegation of Architects from Poland), 'Dui Zhongguo chengshi guihua, jianzhu yishu he jianzhu jiaoyu de yixie yijian' (Observations on urban planning, architectural art and architectural education in China) and 'Dui Zhongguo jianzhushi tongzhimen suoti wenti de dafu' (Answers to the questions raised by the Chinese architect-comrades), *Jianzhu Xuebao*, 1 and 2 (1956), 102–11 and 87–98.

38 Yang Tingbao, 'Jiefanghou zai jianzhu sheji zhong cunzai de jige wenti' (A few issues in architectural design since the Liberation of 1949), *Jianzhu Xuebao*, 9 (1956), 51–3.

39 Wang, *Cheng Ji*, pp. 155–6.

40 Zhou Rongxing, 'Zhou Rongxing lishizhang de dahui zongjie' (Concluding speech at the conference by the President of the Society, Zhou Rongxing), *Jianzhu Xuebao*, 3 (1957), 14–15.

41 Information on China's domestic and international affairs in these years is based on Merle Goldman, 'Dang yu zhishi fenzi' (Chapter 5: The Party and the intellectuals), and Allen S. Whiting, 'Zhongsu fenlie' (Chapter 11: The Sino-Soviet split), in MacFarquhar and Fairbank (eds), *Jianqiao*, pp. 228–72 and 508–70.

42 Wang, *Cheng Ji*, p. 265.

43 Zhang, *Wode*, pp. 156–7; Wang, *Cheng Ji*, pp. 280–1.

44 Wang, *Cheng Ji*, p. 38–40.

45 Tiananmen Diqu Guanli Weiyuanhui, *Tiananmen* (DVD, a four-part TV documentary), Beijing: Zhongguo Luyin Luxiang Chubanshe, 1999.

46 Wang, *Cheng Ji*, p. 170.

47 Tiananmen, *Tiananmen*; Wang, *Cheng Ji*, p. 38.

48 Liu Xiufeng, 'Chuangzao zhongguo de shehui zhuyi de jianzhu xin fengge' (Creating new styles for China's socialist architecture), *Jianzhu Xuebao*, 9–10 (1959), 3–12.

49 Liu, 'Chuangzao', pp. 9–10.

50 Zhao Dongri, 'Jianzhu shiye shang jiti chuanzuo de fanli' (A model in collective design and creation in the architecture profession), *Jianzhu Xuebao*, 9–10 (1959), 17. See also Zou, *Zhongguo*, p. 232.

51 *Renmin Ribao* (People's daily), 2 October 1959, pp. 1, 3, 5, 8.
52 The four with Chinese roofs were the Cultural Palace for Nationalities, the Agricultural Exhibition Hall, Beijing Railway Station, and Diaoyutai State Guesthouse. The one with a 'Russian spire' was the Military Museum and the three 'modern' buildings were Beijing Workers' Stadium, Minzu Hotel and the Overseas Chinese Mansion. See *Jianzhu Xuebao*, 9–10 (1959), and Zou, *Zhongguo*, pp. 230–40.
53 Zhang, *Wode*, pp. 150–1, 156–7.
54 Information regarding the design and the final dimensions of the Great Hall is based on Renmin Dahuitang Shejizu (Design team for the Great Hall of the People), 'Renmin Dahui Tang' (The Great Hall of the People), *Jianzhu Xuebao*, 9–10 (1959), 23–30. Other information regarding Zhou Enlai's selection of Zhao's sachem and the expansion of the size of the building is based on Zhang, *Wode*, pp. 142–52. See also Wang, *Cheng Ji*, pp. 265–85.
55 Zhao Dongri, 'Tiananmen Guanchang' (The Tiananmen Square), *Jianzhu Xuebao*, 9–10 (1959), 18–22. See also Lu Bingjie, *Tiananmen*, Shanghai: Tongji Daxue Chubanshe, 1999, pp. 74–5.
56 Zhao, 'Tiananmen', pp. 18, 20, 21.
57 Zhang, *Wode*, pp. 154, 177.
58 Zhao, 'Tiananmen', p. 21.

Chapter 5 The 1980s and 1990s: Liberalization

1 Jianfei Zhu, 'Beyond revolution: notes on contemporary Chinese architecture', *AA Files*, 35 (1998), 3–14; Jianfei Zhu, 'An archaeology of contemporary Chinese architecture', *2G*, 10 (1999), 90–7; Jianfei Zhu, 'Vers un moderne Chinois: les grands courants architecturaux dans la Chine contemporaine depuis 1976' (Towards a Chinese modern: architectural positions in contemporary China since 1976), trans. Jean-François Allain, in Anne Lemonnier (ed.), *Alors, la Chine?*, Paris: Éditions du Centre Pompidou, 2003, pp. 193–9. Other studies on architecture of modern China can be found in Zou Denong, *Zhongguo Xiandai Jianzhushi* (A history of modern Chinese architecture), Tianjin: Tianjin Kexuejishu Chubanshe, 2001, and Peter G. Rowe and Seng Kuan, *Architectural Encounters with Essence and Form in Modern China*, Cambridge, MA: MIT Press, 2002. See also note 3 below for a different perspective.
2 Kenneth Frampton, *Modern Architecture: A Critical History*, London: Thames and Hudson, 1985, pp. 210–23.
3 Chuihua Judy Chung, Jeffrey Inaba, Rem Koolhaas and Sze Tsung Leong (eds), *Great Leap Forward*, Cologne: Taschen, 2001, p. 704.
4 Zhu, 'Beyond revolution', pp. 7–13; Zhu, 'An archaeology', pp. 93–4; especially Zhu, 'Vers un moderne Chinois', pp. 196–8.
5 Hans Ibelings, *Supermodernism: Architecture in the Age of Globalization*, Rotterdam: NAi Publishers, 2002.
6 Jianfei Zhu, 'Human space, China, 1990s: Cui Kai, a new generation, and a critique of a 20th-century master narrative', in Cui Kai (ed.), *Gongcheng Baogao: Projects Report*, Beijing: Zhongguo Jianzhu Gongye Chubanshe, 2002, pp. 172–85; Jianfei Zhu, 'Xiandaihua: zai lishi da guanxi zhong xunzhao zhang yonghe jiqi feichang jianzhu' (Modernization: locating Yung Ho Chang and his atelier FCJZ in a larger historical context), *Jianzhushi: Architect*, 108 (April 2004), 14–17.

7 They are also regarded as the fourth generation in the overall lineage of the twentieth century. Architects born around 1900, in the 1910s–1920s, and in the 1930s and the early 1940s, are respectively regarded as the first, second and third generations. In this division, for example, Lu Yanzhi and Liang Sicheng (b. 1894, 1901), Zhang Bo, Zhang Kaiji and Wu Liangyong (b. 1911, 1912, 1922), and Zhang Jinqiu and Bu Zhengwei (b. 1936, 1939) belong respectively to the first, second and third generations. There is a gap between the third and the fourth (such as Yung Ho Chang, Liu Jiakun and Cui Kai, b. 1956, 1956, 1957) when university education was suspended in the Cultural Revolution (1966–76).

8 Zhu, 'Human space', pp. 181–2; Zhu, 'Xiandaihua', p. 16.

9 The earliest and clearest expression of this to my knowledge is Yung Ho Chang, 'Pingchang jianzhu' (A basic architecture), *Jianzhushi: Architect*, 84 (October 1998), 27–37, especially 28–9. See also Yung Ho Chang, 'Xiang gongye jianzhu xuexi' (Learning from industrial architecture), in Yung Ho Chang (ed.), *Pingchang Jianzhu: For a Basic Architecture*, Beijing: Zhongguo Jianzhu Gongye Chubanshe, 2002, pp. 26–32.

10 Chang, 'Pingchang jianzhu', pp. 28–9; Chang, 'Xiang gongye jianzhu xuexi', pp. 29–31.

11 I am aware of a very different argument regarding autonomy in the West by scholars such as Manfredo Tafuri. Whereas to move out of bourgeois autonomy and the international discourse of architecture and to engage with society and political practice is much desired in the West (by Tafuri), in China the opposite, that is, to gain 'bourgeois' autonomy, was much desired. This arose from a very different situation in which the ideological state had been directing all aspects of discourse and practice, and it should be regarded as progressive with 'critical' potential in these historical conditions, in the late 1970s and 1980s, when China was moving out of Maoism and strict ideological indoctrination of society by the state.

12 The major–minor differentiation was first explored in Zhu, 'Human space, China, 1990s', pp. 172–85. See also Zhu, 'Xiandaihua', pp. 14–7.

13 My observations on Cui Kai can be found in Zhu, 'Human space, China, 1990s', pp. 172–85. I have also benefited considerably from a conversation with Li Xinggang and a visit to his studio in late September 2004.

14 I benefited a great deal from a conversation with Zhang Lei in Nanjing in late September 2004.

15 I used this phrase to describe Wang and to an extent Liu's work in a speech in a forum for the opening of the exhibition 'TUMU @ Home', Shanghai, 25 August 2002. This stimulated ongoing debate in China and on the web (abbs.com.cn).

16 This was clearly expressed by Wang in the 15th Architectural Congress on 'China Production' at the Architectural Center Vienna (Az W) on 24 November 2007, at which Wang, Cui Kai, Zhu Pei, Wang Mingxian and I each made a presentation on the contemporary scene in China.

17 Liu Jiakun, 'Xushihuayu yu dijicelue' (A narrative discourse and a low-tech strategy), *Jianzhushi: Architect*, 78 (October 1997), 46–50. See also Liu Jiakun, 'Guanyu wode gongzuo' (About my work) and 'Qianjin dao qiyuan' (March on to the beginning), in Liu Jiakun (ed.), *Cishi Cidi: Now and Here*, Beijing: Zhongguo Jianzhu Gongye Chubanshe, 2002, pp. 12–14 and 15–18.

18 Liu, 'Qianjin dao qiyuan', pp. 15–18.

19 Chang, 'Pingchang jianzhu', pp. 28–9; Chang, 'Xiang gongye jianzhu xuexi', pp. 29–31.

20 Chang says 'once the idea of signification is excluded, architecture is architecture in itself, a self-governed or autonomous existence, not an instrument of meaning or ideology, nor a secondary existence to express another entity'. See Chang, 'Xiang gonyye jianzhu xuexi', p. 27.

21 I benefited from communications with Yung Ho Chang, Liu Jiakun and Qingyun Ma between September and December 2004 regarding recent directions in China as discussed in this paragraph. Chang has specifically pointed out the rise of regionalism in recent years.

22 Yung Ho Chang, 'Disanzhong taidu' (The third approach), *Jianzhushi: Architect*, 108 (April 2004), 24–6.

23 Liu Jiakun, 'Guanyu wode gongzuo', pp. 12–14.

24 Ma Qingyun and Stephen Wright, 'A city without leftovers: a conversation with Ma Qingyun', *Parachute*, 114 (2004), 62–79, especially 71–2.

Chapter 6 Criticality between China and the West, 1996–2004

1 Chuihua Judy Chung, Jeffrey Inaba, Rem Koolhaas, Sze Tsung Leong (eds), *Great Leap Forward*, Cologne: Taschen, 2001, p. 704.

2 Peter Eisenman, 'Critical architecture in a geopolitical world', in Cynthia C. Davidson and Ismail Serageldin (eds), *Architecture beyond Architecture: Creativity and Social Transformations in Islamic Cultures*, London: Academy Editions, 1995, pp. 78–81.

3 Eisenman, 'Critical architecture', pp. 78–9.

4 Eisenman, 'Critical architecture', p. 79.

5 See for example Michael Hays, 'Critical architecture: between culture and form', *Perspecta*, 21 (1984), 15–29, especially 15, 17 and 27.

6 Rem Koolhaas and Bruce Mau, *S, M, L, XL*, Rotterdam: 010 Publishers, 1995, pp. 1008–86.

7 Rem Koolhaas, 'Pearl River Delta', in Rem Koolhaas, Stefano Boeri, Sanford Kwinter, Nadia Tzai and Hans Ulrich Obrist, *Mutations*, Barcelona: ACTAR, 2001, pp. 308–35.

8 Chung, *Great Leap Forward*, pp. 27–8, 704–9.

9 Rem Koolhaas, *Content*, Cologne: Taschen, 2004, pp. 450–1.

10 Koolhaas, 'Pearl River Delta', p. 309.

11 See John Rajchman, 'A new pragmatism', in Cynthia C. Davidson (ed.), *Anyhow*, New York: MIT, 1998, pp. 212–17; Michael Speaks, 'Tales from the Avant-Garde: how the new economy is transforming', *Architectural Record*, 12 (2000), 74–7; Joan Ockman, 'What's new about the "new" pragmatism and what does it have to do with architecture', *A+U*, 9, no. 372 (2001), 26–8. See also the debate on 'Architectural theory and education at the millennium', *A+U*, 6, 7, 9, 10 and 11 (2001), which includes essays by Michael Hays, Mary McLeod, Michael Speaks, Mark Wigley and William J. Mitchell. The argument evolves as described in the following notes 12 to 15.

12 George Baird, ' "Criticality" and its discontents', *Harvard Design Magazine*, 21 (Fall 2004/Winter 2005). Online. Available at <www.gsd.harvard.edu/hdm> (accessed 5 November 2004).

13 Robert Somol and Sarah Whiting, 'Notes around the Doppler

effect and other moods of modernism', *Perspecta 33: Mining Autonomy* (2002), 72–7.

14 Somol and Whiting, 'Notes', pp. 74–5. See also Gilles Deleuze and Felix Guattari, *A Thousand Plateaus: Capitalism and Schizophrenia*, trans. Brian Massumi, London: Athlone Press, 1987, p. 142.

15 Michael Speaks, 'Design intelligence and the new economy', *Architectural Record*, January 2002, 72–6; and 'Design intelligence: part 1, introduction', *A+U*, 12, no. 387 (2002), 10–18.

16 The following discussion on modern and contemporary China is based on these earlier studies. See Jianfei Zhu, 'Beyond revolution: notes on contemporary Chinese architecture', *AA Files*, 35 (1998), 3–14; Jianfei Zhu, 'An archaeology of contemporary Chinese architecture', *2G*, 10 (1999), 90–7; Jianfei Zhu, 'Vers un moderne Chinois: les grands courants architecturaux dans la Chine contemporaine depuis 1976' (Towards a Chinese modern: architectural positions in contemporary China since 1976), trans. Jean-François Allain, in Anne Lemonnier (ed.), *Alors, la Chine?*, Paris: Éditions du Centre Pompidou, 2003, pp. 193–9.

17 I am not saying that they are representative of Chinese architects. Instead, they represent a critical edge of the new generation opposing the mainstream practice in China.

18 I am grateful to Yung Ho Chang for the information provided about Rodney Place's involvement at the AA in the 1970s.

19 Yung Ho Chang, 'Pingchang jianzhu' (A basic architecture), *Jianzhushi: Architect*, 84 (October 1998), 27–37, especially 28–9. See also Yung Ho Chang, 'Xiang gongye jianzhu xuexi' (Learning from industrial architecture), in Yung Ho Chang (ed.), *Pingchang Jianzhu: For a Basic Architecture*, Beijing: Zhongguo Jianzhu Gongye Chubanshe, 2002, pp. 26–32.

20 Yung Ho Chang, 'Design philosophy of Atelier FCJZ', unpublished, January 2004.

21 Yung Ho Chang, 'Yong Ho Chang (about education)', in Michael Chadwick (ed.), *Back to School: Architectural Education: The Information and the Argument* (*Architectural Design*, 74, no. 5), London: Wiley-Academy, 2004, pp. 87–90.

22 Yung Ho Chang, 'Disanzhong taidu' (The third approach), *Jianzhushi: Architect*, 108 (April 2004), 24–6.

23 Liu Jiakun, 'Guanyu wode gongzuo' (About my work), in Liu Jiakun (ed.), *Cishi Cidi: Now and Here*, Beijing: Zhongguo Jianzhu Gongye Chubanshe, 2002, pp. 12–14.

24 Liu Jiakun, 'Qianjin dao qiyuan' (March on to the beginning), in Liu Jiakun (ed.), *Cishi Cidi: Now and Here*, pp. 15–18.

25 Ma Qingyun, 'Interview', 2004. Online posting. Available at <www.abbs.com/> (accessed 15 October 2004).

26 Ma, 'Interview'.

27 Ma Qingyun and Stephen Wright, 'A city without leftovers: a conversation with Ma Qingyun', *Parachute*, 114 (2004), 62–79, especially 71–2.

28 Arata Isozaki is another architect who has observed China in a sustained manner since the late 1990s. However, his position is more complex as his perspective is not 'Western', nor does he export pragmatism from China to the West. In fact, although he is an outsider, his position seems closer to the Chinese in that he imports 'quality' and 'criticality' into China. For example he has famously criticized the low standard of design in China. See for example Yuan Feng, 'Jiancheng yu weijiancheng: Jiqixin de

Zhongguo zhilu' (Built and unbuilt: Arata Isozaki in China), *Shidai Jianzhu: Time + Architecture*, 81 (2005), 38–45.

29 In September 2006, *Time + Architecture* (Tongji University, Shanghai) published a Chinese translation of my article together with the responses to it from Chinese and overseas architects and critics including George Baird, Peter Eisenman, Michael Speaks, Yung Ho Chang, Liu Jiakun, Zheng Shiling, Zhu Tao, Li Hua, Li Xiangning, Peng Nu and Zhou Shiyan. Around the same time, a debate occurred on the architectural website in China <www.abbs.com.cn> around my article and Zhu Tao's response, with 13,000 hits by the end of 2006. In late October, George Baird and I were invited to present our views to the staff and students at Tongji University in a five-hour seminar. Tao was also invited to present his research at Tongji later on. In late November, editors of *Domus China* brought me and Tao together in Beijing and organized a five-hour debate at Peking University. In early 2007, *Domus China* published the transcripts of the dialogue in the January and February issues, and *Time + Architecture* published Chinese translations of George Baird, Somol and Whiting, and Michael Speaks's essays in the second, third and fourth issues in 2007. These events revealed an earnest interest and a deep uncertainty about the current trajectories in design practice and a clear agenda one should adopt in contemporary China. It revealed more than anything else a call for a certain kind of criticality in a situation that is all too superficial and commercial.

30 Except in the case of Zhu Tao, to whom I have written a response (*Journal of Architecture*, 12, no. 2 (April 2007), 199–207), this is the first time I present my review of and response to the comments of all the critics and architects invited and published in the September 2006 issue of *Time + Architecture* at Tongji University of Shanghai.

31 Zheng Shiling, 'Dangdai jianzhu piping de zhuanxing: guanyu jianzhu pipingde dushu biji' (A transformation in contemporary architectural criticism), in Chinese and English, *Shidai Jianzhu: Time + Architecture*, 91, issue 5 (September 2006), 68–70. Zheng Shiling is a professor at the Institute of Architecture and Urban Space, Tongji University, Shanghai, and also an Academician of the Chinese Academy of Sciences.

32 Zhou Shiyan, 'Xiang kongqi zhong jiang kongqi' (Speaking air into the air), in Chinese and English, *Shidai Jianzhu: Time + Architecture*, 91, issue 5 (September 2006), 82–3. Zhou Shiyan is a postgraduate fellow of the Visual Art Research Center at Fudang University, Shanghai.

33 Li Hua, '"Piping" de yanshen' (Extending a critical space: questioning the categories of 'China' and the 'West'), in Chinese and English, *Shidai Jianzhu: Time + Architecture*, 91, issue 5 (September 2006), 78–80. Li Hua is a PhD candidate at the Architectural Association School of Architecture, London.

34 Peng Nu, 'Jianzhu sheji de pipingxing yu jianzhu piping' (Critical architecture and architectural criticism), in Chinese and English, *Shidai Jianzhu: Time + Architecture*, 91, issue 5 (September 2006), 81–2. Peng Nu, PhD, is an Associate Professor in the College of Architecture and Urban Planning, Tongji University, Shanghai.

35 Li Xiangning, 'Guanyu zhongguo jianzhu de duihua' (Dialogue with the other), in Chinese and English, *Shidai Jianzhu: Time + Architecture*, 91, issue 5 (September 2006), 80–1. Li Xiangning,

PhD, is a lecturer in the College of Architecture and Urban Planning, Tongji University, Shanghai.

36 Zhu Tao, 'Jinqi xifang "piping" zhi zheng yu dangdai zhongguo jianzhu zhuangtai' (The 'criticality' debate in the West and the architectural situation in China), in Chinese and English, *Shidai Jianzhu: Time + Architecture*, 91, issue 5 (September 2006), 71–8. An edited version of this comment was published together with my response to his criticism. See Tao Zhu, Jianfei Zhu, 'Critical dialogue: China and the West', *Journal of Architecture*, 12, no. 2 (April 2007), 199–207.

37 George Baird, 'Guanyu pipingxing de taolun: yixie zai sikao' (The criticality debate: some further thoughts), in Chinese and English, trans. from English into Chinese by Karey Huang, *Shidai Jianzhu: Time + Architecture*, 91, issue 5 (September 2006), 62–3.

38 Rem Koolhaas, 'Pearl River Delta (Harvard Project on the City)', in Rem Koolhaas, Stefano Boeri, Sanford Kwinter, Nadia Tazi and Hans Ulrich Obrist, *Mutations*, Barcelona: ACTAR, 2000, pp. 280–337, especially p. 310.

39 Koolhaas, 'Pearl River Delta', p. 309.

40 Yung Ho Chang, 'Jizhong pipingxing: huo xifang dui wo de yiyi' (Criticalities or what the West meant to me), in Chinese and English, trans. from English into Chinese by Ding Qing, *Shidai Jianzhu: Time + Architecture*, 91, issue 5 (September 2006), 66–7.

41 Peter Eisenman, 'Dui "qiguang" wenhua de zhiyi' (Contro lo spettacolo), in Chinese and English, trans. from English into Chinese by Wu Ming, *Shidai Jianzhu: Time + Architecture*, 91, issue 5 (September 2006), 61–2.

42 Liu Jiakun, 'Gei Zhu Jianfei de hui xin' (An open letter to Jianfei Zhu), in Chinese and English, trans. from Chinese into English by Chia Shi Chee, *Shidai Jianzhu: Time + Architecture*, 91, issue 5 (September 2006), 67–8.

43 Michael Speaks, 'Lixiang, yishi xingtai, shiyong zhiyui: zai zhongguo yu xifang' (Ideals, ideology and intelligence in China and the West), in Chinese and English, trans. from English into Chinese by Chia Shi Chee, *Shidai Jianzhu: Time + Architecture*, 91, issue 5 (September 2006), 63–5.

Chapter 7 A global site and a different criticality

1 This chapter is developed from the following previously published essays: Jianfei Zhu, 'Criticality in between China and the West', *Journal of Architecture*, 10, no. 5 (2005), 479–98; and 'China as a global site: in a critical geography of design', in Jane Rendell, Jonathan Hill, Murray Fraser and Mark Dorrian (eds), *Critical Architecture*, London: Routledge, 2007, pp. 301–8. The 'Criticality in between' paper covered the first half of a long draft that included in the second half an argument for a Chinese approach to criticality which has never been published before now. The argument is presented here at the end of this chapter. A draft of the whole chapter was first delivered at the 15th Architecture Congress on 'China Production' at the Architecture Center, Vienna, 24 November 2007.

2 Immanuel Wallerstein, 'The three instances of hegemony in the history of the capitalist world-economy', in Immanuel Wallerstein, *The Essential Wallerstein*, New York: The New Press, 2000, pp. 253–63; and 'The rise of East Asia, or the world-system in

the twenty-first century', in Immanuel Wallerstein, *The End of the World as We Know It: Social Science for the Twenty-First Century*, Minneapolis: University of Minnesota Press, 1999, pp. 34–48.

3 This contribution of the 1980s is still ongoing in the 1990s and today. Its heroic late modernism is still practised in the hands of younger architects such as Xu Weiguo and Wu Yue. The neo- or modern vernacular, on the other hand, has been gradually perfected in more recent designs in the 1990s such as Shen Sanling's Institute of Catholic Theology and Philosophy, Beijing, 1999, and Li Chengde's Main Teaching Buildings at China Academy of Art, Hangzhou, 2003. Despite this continuation into the younger generation, and into the 1990s and now with a perfection of formal skills in the above examples, this remains a contribution of the 1980s, not the 1990s, as a new historical breakthrough.

4 I am here using Pierre Bourdieu's concept modified by David Harvey as 'collective symbolic capital' and 'marks of distinction'. See pp. 404–6 of David Harvey, *Spaces of Capital: Towards a Critical Geography*, Edinburgh: Edinburgh University Press, 2001, pp. 394–411.

5 Rem Koolhaas, 'What ever happened to urbanism?', in O. M. A., Rem Koolhaas and Bruce Mau, *S, M, L, XL*, New York: The Monacelli Press, 1995, pp. 958–71.

6 Rem Koolhaas, 'Bigness, or the problem of large', in O. M. A., Koolhaas and Mau, *S, M, L, XL*, pp. 494–517.

7 Rem Koolhaas, 'Singapore songlines: thirty years of tabula rasa', in O. M. A, Koolhaas and Mau, *S, M, L, XL*, pp. 1008–89.

8 Rem Koolhaas, 'The generic city', in O. M. A, Koolhaas and Mau, *S, M, L, XL*, pp. 1238–64.

9 Rem Koolhaas, 'Pearl River Delta', in Rem Koolhaas, Stefano Boeri, Sanford Kwinter, Nadia Tazi and Hans Ulrich Obrist, *Mutations*, Barcelona: ACTAR, 2000, pp. 280–337, especially p. 309.

10 Koolhaas, 'Pearl River Delta', p. 309.

11 Rem Kollhaas, 'Introduction', in Chuihua Judy Chung, Jeffrey Inaba, Rem Koolhaas, Sze Tsung Leong (eds) *Great Leap Forward*, Cologne: Taschen, 2001, pp. 27–8.

12 Koolhaas, 'Introduction', p. 28.

13 See: Robert Somol and Sarah Whiting, 'Notes around the Doppler effect and other moods of modernism', *Perspecta 33: Mining Autonomy*, 2002, 72–7; Michael Speaks, 'Design intelligence and the new economy', *Architectural Record*, January 2002, 72–6; and 'Design intelligence: part 1, introduction', *A+U*, 12, no. 387 (2002), 10–8; and also George Baird, '"Criticality" and its discontents', *Harvard Design Magazine*, 21 (Fall 2004/Winter 2005). Online. Available at <www.gsd.harvard.edu/hdm> (accessed 5 November 2004).

14 I have raised this issue in my 'Criticality', 479 and 484.

15 The architects invited to design for the 'Commune by the Great Wall' (Beijing) as completed in 2002 were Gary Chang (China–Hong Kong), Shigeru Ban (Japan), Cui Kai (China), Chien Hsueh-yi (China–Taiwan), Antonio Ochoa (China), Kanika R'kul (Thailand), Yung Ho Chang (China), Nobuaki Furuya (Japan), Kay Ngee Tan (Singapore), Kengo Kuma (Japan), Rocco Yim (China–Hong Kong) and Seung H-Sang (South Korea). The architects invited by and currently designing and building for CIPEA (Nanjing) are Steven Holl (USA), Liu Jiakun (China), Arata Isozaki (Japan), Ettore Sottsass (Italy), Zhou Kai (China), Qingyun Ma (China), Kazuyo Sejima + Ryue Nishizawa (Japan), Zhang Lei (China), Mathias Klotz (Chile),

Hrvoje Njiric (Croatia), David Adjaye (UK), Luis M. Mansilla (Spain), Sean Godsell (Australia), Odile Decq (France), Liu Heng (China–Hong Kong), Kris Yao (China–Taiwan), Gabor Bachman (Hungary), Tang Hua (China), Wang Shu (China), Ai Weiwei (China), Yung Ho Chang (China), Cui Kai (China), Alberto Kalach (Mexico) and Matti Sanaksenaho (Finland).

16 Yung Ho Chang, 'Pingchang jianzhu' (A basic architecture), *Jianzhushi: Architect*, 84 (October 1998), 27–37, especially 28–9 and 34.

17 Yung Ho Chang, 'Xiang gongye jianzhu xuexi' (Learning from industrial architecture), in Yung Ho Chang (ed.), *Pingchang Jianzhu: For a Basic Architecture*, Beijing: Zhongguo Jianzhu Gongye Chubanshe, 2002, pp. 26–32.

18 Yung Ho Chang, 'Disanzhong taidu' (The third approach), *Jianzhushi: Architect*, 108 (April 2004), 24–6.

19 Yung Ho Chang and Zhou Rong, 'Duihua: xia yi shinian' (Dialogue: the next decade), *Jianzhushi: Architect*, 108 (April 2004), 56–8.

20 Zhu, 'Criticality', 479–98. This essay is reprinted here as Chapter 6.

21 Rem Koolhaas, 'Found in translation' and 'Zhuanhua zhongde ganwu' (trans. Wang Yamei), in *Volume 8: Ubiquitous China*, 2006, pp. 120–6 and 157–9. See also Yung Ho Chang, Shi Jian, Feng Keru, 'Interview: Yung Ho Chang', *Domus China*, 1 (July 2006), 116–19; and Ma Qingyun, Shi Jian and Feng Keru, 'Interview: Ma Qingyun', *Domus China*, 8 (February 2007), 116–17.

22 Wallerstein, 'The three instances', p. 254, and 'The rise of East Asia', pp. 35, 48. See also Enrique Dussel, 'Beyond eurocentrism: the world-system as the limits of modernity', in Fredric Jameson and Masao Miyoshi (eds), *The Cultures of Globalization*, Durham, NC: Duke University Press, 1998, pp. 3–31, especially 19–21.

23 David Harvey, *A Brief History of Neoliberalism*, Oxford: Oxford University Press, 2005, pp. 120–51, especially pp. 120, 141–2, 150–1, where observations on the Party's long-term commitment to egalitarianism, China's departure from neo-liberalism, and its government's policies to frustrate the capitalist class are made respectively. Harvey's study here, however, is comprehensive and has indeed pointed out other opposing tendencies as well, such as China's confluence with the United States in adopting neo-liberal and neo-conservative policies.

24 Peter Nolan, *China at the Crossroads*, Cambridge: Polity Press, 2004, pp. 174–7.

25 Satoshi Ikeda, 'U.S. hegemony and East Asia: an exploration of China's challenge in the 21st century', in Wilma A. Dunaway (ed.), *Emerging Issues in the 21st Century World-System, Volume II: New Theoretical Directions for the 21st Century World-System*, Westport, CT: Praeger Publishers, 2003, pp. 162–79.

26 Ikeda, 'U.S. hegemony and East Asia', pp. 177–8.

27 This idea was presented by Wang Shu at the 15th Architecture Congress on 'China Production', at the Architecture Center, Vienna, 24 November 2007.

28 See Yung Ho Chang, 'Yong Ho Chang (about education)', in Michael Chadwick (ed.), *Back to School: Architectural Education: The Information and the Argument (Architectural Design*, 74, no. 5, 2004), pp. 87–90, especially p. 88; and Qingyun Ma, 'Interview', 2004. Online. Available at <www.abbs.com> (accessed 15 October, 2004). See also Chang, 'Disanzhong taidu', pp. 24–6.

29 In François Jullien's comparison of Chinese and Greek/European philosophy, he demonstrated that, in the theory of war and strategy, the Chinese preferred an indirect and transformative approach whereas the European valued a direct confrontation, a final pitched battle, a decisive blow to the enemy as of the highest significance. Jullien's comparison leads us to other fields such as literature and painting but his final interest is in the philosophical tradition between the Chinese and the Greek. For this, which concerns a confrontational versus a relational dualism, in Aristotle and in the 'yin–yang' worldview, see François Jullien, *The Propensity of Things: Towards a History of Efficacy in China*, trans. Janet Lloyd, New York: Zone Books, 1995, pp. 249–58.

30 Jürgen Habermas, 'Further reflections on the public sphere', in Craig Calhoun (ed.), *Habermas and the Public Sphere*, Cambridge, MA: MIT Press, 1992, pp. 421–61.

31 Peter Eisenman, 'Critical architecture in a geopolitical world', in Cynthia C. Davidson and Ismail Serageldin (eds), *Architecture beyond Architecture: Creativity and Social Transformations in Islamic Cultures*, London: Academy Editions, 1995, pp. 78–81, especially 79.

32 Tu Wei-ming, 'Introduction' and 'Epilogue', in Tu Wei-ming (ed.). *Confucian Traditions in East Asian Modernity: Moral Education and Economic Culture in Japan and the Four Mini-Dragons*, Cambridge, MA: Harvard University Press, 1996, pp. 1–10, 343–9.

33 Jullien, *The Propensity*, pp. 249–58.

34 Regarding the difficulties of using a dualist conception of the 'public sphere' from the West in general and Habermas in particular, see Philip C. C. Huang, ' "Public Sphere"/ "Civil Society" in China? The third realm between state and society', *Modern China*, 19, no. 21 (April 1993), 216–40, and Timothy Brook and B. Michael Frolic (eds), *Civil Society in China*, New York: M. E. Sharpe, 1997, especially pp. 3–16.

Chapter 8 Beijing, 2008: a history

1 David Harvey, *A Brief History of Neoliberalism*, Oxford: Oxford University Press, 2005, p, 127. In Harvey's comparison, the entire Irish migration to North America from 1820 to 1930 involved 4.5 million people, whereas in China today 114 million have migrated to the cities to work, a figure that is expected to rise to 300 million in 2020 and eventually to 500 million.

2 Huang Ping and Zhan Shaohua, 'Internal migration in China: Linking it to development', *Regional Conference on Migration and Development in Asia*, Lanzhou: 2005, pp. 3–10; and *People's Daily Online*, 'China's urbanization, 10 per cent higher within 10 years'. Online. Available at <http://english.peopledaily.com.cn/200212/06/eng20021206_108064.shtml> (accessed on 13 February 2007).

3 Harvey, *A Brief History*, pp. 1–4.

4 Jianfei Zhu, *Chinese Spatial Strategies: Imperial Beijing 1420–1911*, London: RoutledgeCurzon, 2004, p. 29.

5 Dong Guangqi, *Beijing Guihua Zhanlue Sikao* (Thoughts on planning strategies for Beijing), Beijing: Zhongguo Jianzhu Gongye Chubanshe, 1998, pp. 404–5.

6 Dong, *Beijing*, pp. 386–8, 393–5.

7 Editorial Committee, *Jianguo Yilai de Beijing Chengshi Jianshe*

Ziliao, Di yi juan: Chengshi Guihua (Documenting materials of urban construction of Beijing since 1949, volume 1: Urban planning), Beijing: Beijing Jianshe Shishu Bianji Weiyuanhui Bianjibu, 1987, pp. 88–9.

8 The regulations in 1985, 1987 and 1990 are found in Dong, *Beijing*, p. 400.

9 Wang Hui, 'The historical origin of China's neo-liberalism', in Tian Yu Cao (ed.), *The Chinese Model of Modern Development*, London: Routledge, 2005, pp. 61–87.

10 Dong, *Beijing*, p. 417, and Ma Guoxin, 'Santan jiyu he tiaozhan' (Three comments on opportunities and challenges), *World Architecture*, 169 (July 2004), 19–21.

11 Fang Ke, *Dangdai Beijing Jiucheng Gengxin* (Contemporary renewal of the old city of Beijing), Beijing: Zhongguo Jianzhu Gongye Chubanshe, 2000, p. 52.

12 Dong, *Beijing*, p. 413.

13 Beijing Municipal City Planning Commission (ed.), *Beijing Lishi Wenhua Mingcheng Beijing Huangcheng Baohu Guihua* (Conservation Plan for the historical city of Beijing and the Imperial City of Beijing), Beijing: Zhongguo Jianzhu Gongye Chubanshe, 2004, p. 12; and Wang Jun, 'Zhenti baohu tichu zhihou' (What happens after the release of the comprehensive conservation plan), *Liaowang Zhoukan: Outlook Weekly*, 19 (8 May 2006), 20–1.

14 China News, 'Guowuyuan huiyi yuanze tongguo Beijing chengshi guihua 2004–2020' (The State Council has approved in principle the Beijing Plan 2004–2020), available at <http://news.sina.com.cn/o/2005–01–12/21284810260s.shtml> (accessed 7 February 2007).

15 Xinhua News, 'Interview with Long Yongtu on 18 September 2001'. Online. Available at <http://news.xinhuanet.com/fortune/2001-09/25/content_42797.htm> (accessed 13 February 2007).

16 Beijing Olympic Bid Committee, 'The Action Plan for the 2008 Olympics Games'. Online. Available at <www.china.com.cn/chinese/zhuanti/177019.htm> (accessed 13 February 2007).

17 Ma Guoxin, 'Santan jiyu he tiaozhan', pp. 19–21; and Li Bing, '1978 nian yilai wailai jianzhushi zai Beijing jianzhu de xiangguan yanjiu: projects designed by foreign architects in Beijing since 1978', *Shidai Jianzhu: Time + Architecture*, 81, issue 1 (January 2005), 14–18.

18 Mark Wigley, 'Deconstructivist architecture', in Philip Johnson and Mark Wigley, *Deconstructivist Architecture*, New York: The Museum of Modern Art, 1988, pp. 10–20, especially p. 19.

19 Rem Koolhaas, 'Bigness or the problem of large', in O. M. A., Rem Koolhaas and Bruce Mau, *S, M, L, XL*, New York: The Monacelli Press, 1995, pp. 494–516.

20 Jianfei Zhu, 'Criticality in between China and the West', *Journal of Architecture*, 10, no. 5 (November 2005), 479–98 (reprinted above as Chapter 6), especially 485.

21 Harvey, *A Brief History*, pp. 1–4.

22 Anthony D. King and Abidin Kusno, 'On Be(ij)ing in the world: "postmodernsim", "globalization," and the making of transnational space in China', in Arif Dirlik and Xudong Zhang (eds), *Postmodernism and China*, Durham, NC: Duke University Press, 2000, pp. 41–67, especially 61.

23 Jianfei Zhu, *Chinese Spatial Strategies*, pp. 222–34.

24 David Harvey, *Spaces of Capital: Towards a Critical Geography*, Edinburgh: Edinburgh University Press, 2001, pp. 394–411; and Charles Jencks, *The Iconic Building*, New York: Rizzoli, 2005, pp. 7–19, 101–12.

25 Foster and Partners, 'Project summary: Terminal 3 Beijing Capital Airport, Beijing, China'. Online. Available at <www.designbuild-network.com/projects/terminal-5-beijing/> (accessed 7 February 2007).

Chapter 9 Geometries of life and formlessness: a Chinese urban tradition

1 Henri Lefebvre, *The Production of Space*, trans. Donald Nicholson-Smith, Oxford: Blackwell, 1991, pp. 38–9.

2 Lefebvre, *The Production*, pp. 40, 41, 42 and 47.

3 Lefebvre, *The Production*, p. 42.

4 François Jullien, *The Propensity of Things: Towards a History of Efficacy in China*, trans. Janet Lloyd, New York: Zone Books, 1995, pp. 249–58.

5 Jullien, *The Propensity*, pp. 123–4.

6 Roland Barthes, *Empire of Signs*, New York: Hill & Wang, 1982, pp. 30–2 ('Center-city, empty center').

7 Barthes, *Empire*, p. 32.

8 Barthes, *Empire*, pp. 33–6 ('No address').

9 Barthes, *Empire*, p. 36.

10 The following observations on historical Beijing are empirically based on my earlier work, *Chinese Spatial Strategies: Imperial Beijing 1420–1911*, London: RoutledgeCurzon, 2004, especially chapters 3 and 9.

11 According to the cultural geographer and theorist Augustin Berque, 'at the scale of world history, the notion of landscape was first invented in Southern China towards the beginning of the fifth century'. See Augustin Berque, 'Beyond the modern landscape', *AA Files*, 25 (Summer 1993), 33–7, and also 'Landscape in Japan as a symbolic form', unpublished paper given to me in July 1997.

12 The debate on the concept of a 'mountain–water city' in the late 1990s in China is an indication of a renewed interest in the Chinese tradition of a landscape urbanity. See Bao Shixing and Gu Mengchao (eds), *Chengshi Xue yu Shanshui Chengshi* (Urban studies and a 'mountain–water' urbanism), Beijing: Zhongguo Jianzhu Gongye Chubanshe, 1996.

13 Wang Guxiang, *Dongxifangde Jianzhu Kongjian: wenhua kongjian tushi ji lishi jianzhu kongjian lun* (Architectural space in the East and West: a theory of space in cultural schema and historical construction), Beijing: Zhongguo Jianzhu Gongye Chubanshe, 1998, pp. 477–91; and Wang Qiheng, *Fengshui Lila Yanjiu* (Studies in the theory of feng shui), Tianjin: Tianjin Daxue Chubanshe, 1992, pp. 117–37.

14 Benoit B. Mandelbrot, *The Fractal Geometry of Nature*, San Francisco: W. H. Freeman, 1982.

15 See Mandelbrot, *The Fractal*, pp. 1–13.

16 See Peter M. Engelfriet, *Euclid in China: The Genesis of the First Chinese Translation of Euclid's Elements Books I–VI (Jihe yuanben; Beijing, 1607) and its Receptions up to 1723*, Leiden: Brill, 1998, pp. 106–7. I have touched on this issue, in Chapter 2 of the present book, in the context of Greek geometry being introduced

into China in 1607 and the gradual rise of formal geometry of the object in modern China.

17 Philip C. C. Huang, '"Public sphere"/ "civil society" in China: the third realm between state and society', *Modern China*, 19, no. 2 (April 1993), 216–40.

18 One of the earliest modern studies that has identified a relational and mediating relationship between state and society in the Chinese tradition is Fei Xiaotong's *Xiangtu Zhongguo* (Rural China), Shanghai: Guanchashe, 1948, pp. 22–30. For an English translation, see Fei Xiaotong, *From the Soil: The Foundations of Chinese Society*, trans. Gary G. Hamilton and Wang Zheng, Berkeley: University of California Press, 1992, pp. 69–70.

19 In Cecil Balmond's exposition of an 'informal' approach to the design of building structures, the local or local intensities are also considered a crucial generative moment for a non-Cartesian structure and, if I may add, a non-Euclidian or non-formal geometry. See Cecil Balmond, *Informal*, Munich: Prestel, 2002, pp. 217–28.

20 Mao Zedong, 'Xin minzhu zhuyi lun' (On new democracy), in Mao Zedong, *Mao Zedong Xuanji* (Selected works of Mao Zedong), vol. 2, Beijing: Renmin Chubanshe, 1970, pp. 623–70.

21 See Huang, '"Public sphere"', pp. 216–40, and Timothy Brook and B. Michael Frolic, 'The ambiguous challenge of civil society', in Timothy Brook and B. Michael Frolic (eds), *Civil Society in China*, New York: M. E. Sharpe, 1997, pp. 3–16. See also Fei, *From the Soil*, pp. 69–70.

22 The most eminent voice today to have criticized the Leninist tradition and supported European-style social democracy as an alternative to Soviet communism and American capitalism is Xie Tao in his 'Minzhu shehui zhuyi moshi yu zhongguo qiantu' (Social democracy and China's future), published in a Beijing-based monthly well circulated amongst Party members and high-ranking officials: *Yanhuang Chunqiu* (no. 2, 2007). For a report on this see Jiang Xun, 'Minzhu shehui zhuyi de tupo' (A breakthrough for social democracy), *Yazhou Zhoukan: the international Chinese newsweekly*, 25 March 2007, 30, and 'Zhonggong yuanlao zhichi huwen zhenggai' (Veterans of the Chinese Communist Party are supporting Hu and Wen's political reform), *Yazhou Zhoukan: the international Chinese newsweekly*, 10 June 2007, 32–4.

Chapter 10 Twenty plateaus, 1910s–2010s

1 The project was initially carried out in late 2005. The result was represented in two diagrams identical in content but one written in Chinese and the other in English. The diagrams were then exhibited in the First Shenzhen Biennale of Architecture and Urbanism during December 2005 and March 2006, Shenzhen, China. With a note of explanation, they were then published in Jianfei Zhu, 'Guanyu "ershipian gaodi"' (Twenty plateaus: a genealogy of styles and design positions of modern architecture in mainland China, 1910s–2010s), *Shidai Jianzhu: Time + Architecture*, 97, issue 5 (September 2007), 16–21. A shorter explanation was also published in Jianfei Zhu, 'Ershipian gaodi: zhongguo dalu xiandai jianzhu de lishi tujing' (Twenty plateaus: a historical landscape of modern architecture in mainland China), *Jinri Xianfeng: Avant-Garde Today*, 14 (2007), 103–14. What is published here is an edited version of the diagram in English, and

the most thorough explanation and reading of the diagram thus far.

2 The empirical historical materials are based primarily on the following sources: Pan Guxi (ed.), *Zhongguo Jianzhu Shi* (A history of Chinese architecture), Beijing: Zhongguo Jianzhu Gongye Chubanshe, 2001; Fu Chao-qing, *Zhongguo Gudian Shiyang Xinjianzhu* (A new architecture of classical styles in China), Taipei: Nantian, 1993; Gong Deshun, Zou Denong, Dou Yide, *Zhongguo Xiandai Jianzhu Shigang* (An outline of a history of modern Chinese architecture), Tianjin: Science & Technology Press, 1989; Zou Denong, *Zhongguo Xiandai Jianzhushi* (A history of modern Chinese architecture), Tianjin: Science & Technology Press, 2001; Dan Cruickshank (ed.), *Sir Banister Fletcher's A History of Architecture*, London: Architectural Press, 1996.

3 Gilles Deleuze and Felix Guattari, *A Thousand Plateaus: Capitalism & Schizophrenia*, trans. Brian Massumi, London: Athlone Press, 1987, pp. 3–25.

Glossary of Chinese
expressions

Baichi weixing, qianchi weishi	百尺为形，千尺为势
Baijun Tu	百骏图
Bei	碑
Beiwen	碑文
Bifa	笔法
Bili	笔力
Dazhuang	大壮
Dizheng si	地政司
Fa	法
Fangwu	房屋
Gengzhi Tu	耕织图
Gewu	格物
Gongwu ju	工务局
Gujin zhongwai	古今中外
Huangyu Quanlantu	皇舆全览图
Huaqi Toushuo	画器图说
Hutong	胡同
Jianshe ting	建设厅
Jianzao	建造
Jianzhu ke gongye jishi	建筑科工业技师
Jianzhu Sheji Cankuo Tuji	建筑设计参考图集
Jianzhu Xuebao	建筑学报
Jianzhu Yuekan	建筑月刊
Jihe	几何
Jihe Yuanben	几何原本
Jindai	近代
Jingdu Shizheng Gongsuo	京都市政公所
Jurui Tu	聚瑞图
Li	理
Liangfa	量法
Lilong	里弄
Miao	妙
Neizheng bu	内政部

Pingchang jianzhu	平常建筑
Qianlong Huangdi Chaofu Xiang	乾隆皇帝朝服像
Qin Tian Jian	钦天监
Qinding Xuetang Zhangcheng	钦定学堂章程
Qiu	求
Qiyun	气运
Shanghaishi Jianzhu Xiehui	上海市建筑协会
Sheji jianzhu shi	设计建筑师
Sheji zhe	设计者
Shenyi	神逸
Shi	势
Shi Xue	视学
Shidai Jianzhu	时代建筑
Shixing	适形
Shixue	实学
Shixue Jingyun	视学精蕴
Shoudu Jihua	首都计划
Shuli Jingyun	数理精蕴
Si zhang	司长
Toushi Xue	透视学
Wanshu Yuan Ciyan Tu	万树园赐宴图
Xiezhen	写真
Xin Jianshe	新建设
Xin Jianzhu	新建筑
Xing	形
Xingshi	形势
Xiyang Xinfa Lishu	西洋新法历书
Yiju	宜居
yin and yang	阴阳
Yingjian si	营建司
Yingzao Fashi	营造法式
Yiren weiben	以人为本
Yuanmingyuan Gongcheng Zuofa	圆明园工程作法
Zhen	真
Zhen er bu miao	真而不妙
Zhongguo Jianzhu	中国建筑
Zhongguo Jianzhu Shi	中国建筑史
Zhongguo Jianzhu Xuehui	中国建筑学会
Zhongguo Jianzhushi Xuehui	中国建筑师学会
Zhongguo Xiandai Jianzhu Shi	中国现代建筑史

Bibliography

2G: International Architectural Review, 10 (1999) (Special issue: 'Instant China').

AA Files, 35 (Spring 1998).

Baird, George, '"Criticality" and its discontents', *Harvard Design Magazine*, 21 (Fall 2004/Winter 2005). Online. Available at <www.gsd.harvard.edu/hdm> (accessed 5 November 2004).

Baird, George, 'Guanyu pipingxing de taolun: yixie zai sikao' (The criticality debate: some further thoughts), in Chinese and English, trans. from English into Chinese by Karey Huang, *Shidai Jianzhu: Time + Architecture*, 91, no. 5 (September 2006), 62–3.

Balmond, Cecil, *Informal*, Munich: Prestel, 2002.

Bao Shixing and Gu Mengchao (eds), *Chengshi Xue yu Shanshui Chengshi* (Urban studies and a 'mountain–water' urbanism), Beijing: Zhongguo Jianzhu Gongye Chubanshe, 1996.

Barthes, Roland, *Empire of Signs*, New York: Hill & Wang, 1982.

Beijing Municipal City Planning Commission (ed.), *Beijing Lishi Wenhua Mingcheng Beijing Huangcheng Baohu Guihua* (Conservation Plan for the historical city of Beijing and the Imperial City of Beijing), Beijing: Zhongguo Jianzhu Gongye Chubanshe, 2004.

Beijing Olympic Bid Committee, 'The Action Plan for the 2008 Olympic Games'. Online. Available at <www.china.com.cn/chinese/zhuanti/177019.htm> (accessed 13 February 2007).

Benevolo, Leonardo, *The History of the City*, trans. Geoffrey Culverwell, Cambridge, MA: MIT, 1980.

Bergère, Marie-Claire, *The Golden Age of the Chinese Bourgeoisie 1911–1937*, trans. Janet Lloyd, Cambridge: Cambridge University Press, 1986.

Berque, Augustin, 'Beyond the modern landscape', *AA Files*, 25 (1993), 33–7.

Berque, Augustin, 'Landscape in Japan as a symbolic form', unpublished paper presented in July 1997.

Bolan Jianzhushi Fanghua Daibiaotuan (Delegation of Architects from Poland), 'Dui Zhongguo chengshi guihua, jianzhu yishu he jianzhu jiaoyu de yixie yijian' (Observations on urban planning, architectural art, and architectural education in China), *Jianzhu Xuebao* (Architectural Journal), 1 (1956), 102–11.

Bolan Jianzhushi Fanghua Daibiaotuan (Delegation of Architects from Poland), 'Dui Zhongguo jianzhushi tongzhimen suoti wenti de dafu' (Answers to the questions raised by the Chinese architect-comrades), *Jianzhu Xuebao* (Architectural Journal), 2 (1956), 87–98.

Brook, Timothy and B. Michael Frolic, 'The ambiguous challenge of civil society', in Timothy Brook and B. Michael Frolic (eds), *Civil Society in China*, New York: M. E. Sharpe, 1997, pp. 3–16

Brook, Timothy and B. Michael Frolic (eds), *Civil Society in China*, New York: M. E. Sharpe, 1997.

Calhoun, Craig (ed.), *Habermas and the Public Sphere*, Cambridge, MA: MIT Press, 1992.

Chadwick, Michael (ed.), *Back to School: Architectural Education: The Information and the Argument* (*Architectural Design*, 74, no. 5 (2004).

Chang, Yung Ho, 'Design philosophy of Atelier FCJZ', unpublished, January 2004.

Chang, Yung Ho, 'Disanzhong taidu' (The third approach), *Jianzhushi: Architect*, 108 (April 2004), 24–6.

Chang, Yung Ho, 'Jizhong pipingxing: huo xifang dui wo de yiyi' (Criticalities or what the West meant for me), in Chinese and English, trans. from English into Chinese by Ding Qing, *Shidai Jianzhu: Time + Architecture*, 91, no. 5 (September 2006), 66–7.

Chang, Yung Ho, 'Pingchang jianzhu' (A basic architecture), *Jianzhushi: Architect*, 84 (October 1998), 27–37.

Chang, Yung Ho (ed.), *Pingchang Jianzhu: For a Basic Architecture*, Beijing: Zhongguo Jianzhu Gongye Chubanshe, 2002.

Chang, Yung Ho, 'Xiang gongye jianzhu xuexi' (Learning from industrial architecture), in Yung Ho Chang (ed.), *Pingchang Jianzhu: For a Basic Architecture*, Beijing: Zhongguo Jianzhu Gongye Chubanshe, 2002, pp. 26–32.

Chang, Yung Ho, 'Yong Ho Chang (about education)', in Michael Chadwick (ed.), *Back to School: Architectural Education: The Information and the Argument* (*Architectural Design*, 74, no. 5) (2004), pp. 87–90.

Chang, Yung Ho, Shi Jian and Feng Keru, 'Interview: Yung Ho Chang', *Domus China*, 1 (July 2006), 116–19.

Chang, Yung Ho and Zhou Rong, 'Duihua: xia yi shinian' (Dialogue: the next decade), *Jianzhushi: Architect*, 108 (April 2004), 56–8.

Chen Dengao, 'Zai minzu xingshi gaoceng jianzhu sheji guocheng zhong de tihui' (Reflections upon my designs of high-rise buildings with national forms', *Jianzhu Xuebao*, 2 (1954), 104–7.

Chiang Kai-shek, *Jiang Zongtong Ji* (A collection of works of President Chiang), Taipei: Guofang Yanjiu Yuan, 1961.

Chiang Kai-shek, 'Xin shenghuo yundong zhi yaoyi' (The essence of the New Life Movement), in Chiang Kai-shek, *Jiang Zongtong Ji* (A collection of works of President Chiang), Taipei: Guofang Yanjiu Yuan, 1961, pp. 733–7.

Chiang Kai-shek, 'Zhongguo zhi mingyun' (China's destiny), in Chiang Kai-shek, *Jiang Zongtong Ji* (A collection of works of President Chiang), Taipei: Guofang Yanjiu Yuan, 1961, pp. 119–70.

China News, 'Guowuyuan huiyi yuanze tongguo Beijing chengshi guihua 2004–2020' (The State Council has approved in principle the Beijing Plan 2004–2020). Online. Available at <http://news.sina.com.cn/o/2005-01-12/21284810260s.shtml> (accessed 7 February 2007).

Chung, Chuihua Judy, Jeffrey Inaba, Rem Koolhaas and Sze Tsung Leong (eds), *Great Leap Forward*, Cologne: Taschen, 2001.

Cody, Jeffrey W., 'American planning in Republican China', *Planning Perspective*, 11, no. 4 (1996), 339–77.

Cody, Jeffrey W., *Building in China: Henry K. Murphy's 'Adaptive Architecture' 1914–1935*, Seattle: Chinese University Press, 2001.

Colton, Timothy J., *Moscow: Governing the Socialist Metropolis*, Cambridge, MA: Belknap Press of Harvard University Press, 1995.

Cooke, Catherine and Alexander Kudriavtsev (eds), *Uses of Tradition in Russian & Soviet Architecture* (Architectural Design Profile, no. 68), London: Architectural Design, 1987.

Cruickshank, Dan (ed.), *Sir Banister Fletcher's A History of Architecture*, London: Architectural Press, 1996.

Cui Kai (ed.), *Gongcheng Baogao: Projects Report*, Beijing: Zhongguo Jianzhu Gongye Chubanshe, 2002.

Davidson, Cynthia C. (ed.), *Anyhow*, New York: MIT Press, 1998.

Davidson, Cynthia C. and Ismail Serageldin (eds), *Architecture beyond Architecture: Creativity and Social Transformation in Islamic Cultures*, London: Academy Editions, 1995.

Deleuze, Gilles and Felix Guattari, *A Thousand Plateaus: Capitalism and Schizophrenia*, trans. Brian Massumi, London: Athlone Press, 1987.

Dirlik, Arif, 'The ideological foundations of the New Life Movement: a study in counterrevolution', *Journal of Asian Studies*, 34, no. 4 (August 1975), 945–79.

Dirlik, Arif and Xudong Zhang (eds), *Postmodernism and China*, Durham, NC: Duke University Press, 2000.

Dong Guangqi, *Beijing Guihua Zhanlue Sikao* (Strategic thoughts on Beijing's planning), Beijing: Zhongguo Jianzhu Gongye Chubanshe, 1998.

Dunaway, Wilma A. (ed.), *Emerging Issues in the 21st Century World-System, vol. II: New Theoretical Directions for the 21st Century World-System*, Westport, CT: Praeger Publishers, 2003.

Dussel, Enrique, 'Beyond eurocentrism: the world-system as the limits of modernity', in Fredric Jameson and Masao Miyoshi (eds), *The Cultures of Globalization*, Durham, NC: Duke University Press, 1998, pp. 3–31.

Dutton, Michael, *Streetlife China*, Cambridge: Cambridge University Press, 1998.

Eastman, Lloyd E., *The Abortive Revolution: China under Nationalist Rule 1927–1937,* Cambridge, MA: Harvard University Press, 1974.

Eastman, Lloyd E., 'Nationalist China during the Nanking decade 1927–37', in John Fairbank and Albert Feuerwerker (eds), *The Cambridge History of China, vol. 13, Republic China 1912–49, Part 2*, Cambridge: Cambridge University Press, 1986, pp. 116–67.

Editorial Committee (ed.), *Dijiing Jiuying: As Dusk Fell upon the Imperial City*, Beijing: Palace Museum Press, 1994.

Editorial Committee (comp.), *Jianguo Yilai de Beijing Chengshi Jianshe Ziliao, Di yi juan: chengshi guihua* (Documents concerning urban construction of Beijing since 1949, vol. 1: urban planning), Beijing: Beijing Jianshe Shishu Bianji Weiyuanhui Bianjibu, 1987.

Editorial Committee (ed.), *Liang Sicheng Xiansheng Baisui Danchen Wenji* (A collection of essays at the 100th birthday of Liang Sicheng), ed. Tsinghua University School of Architecture, Beijing: Qinghua Daxue Chubanshe, 2001.

Editorial Committee (ed.), *Liang Sicheng Xiansheng Danchen Bashiwu*

Zhounian Jinian Wenji (A collection of essays in honour of Liang Sicheng's 85th birthday), Beijing: Qinghua Daxue Chubanshe, 1986.

Editorial Committee (comp.), *Shanghai Chengshi Guihua Zhi* (Annuals of urban planning for Shanghai), Shanghai: Shehui Kexue Yuan Chubanshe, 1999.

Editorial Committee (ed.), *Zhongguo Jinxiandaishi Dashiji* (1840–1980) (A calendar of events: early modern Chinese history, 1840–1980), Shanghai: Zhishi Chubanshe, 1982.

Editorial: 'Fandui jianzhu zhong de langfei xianxiang' (Against wasteful practice in building construction), *Renmin Ribao* (People's Daily), 28 March 1955, p. 1.

Eisenman, Peter, 'Critical architecture in a geopolitical world', in Cynthia C. Davidson and Ismail Serageldin (eds), *Architecture beyond Architecture: Creativity and Social Transformation in Islamic Cultures*, London: Academy Editions, 1995, pp. 78–81.

Eisenman, Peter, 'Dui "qiguang" wenhua de zhiyi' (Contro lo spettacolo), in Chinese and English, trans. from English into Chinese by Wu Ming, *Shidai Jianzhu: Time + Architecture*, 91, no. 5 (September 2006), 61–2.

Engelfriet, Peter M., *Euclid in China: The Genesis of the First Chinese Translation of Euclid's Elements Books I–VI (Jihe Yuanben; Beijing, 1607) and its Receptions up to 1723*, Leiden: Brill, 1998.

Esherick, Joseph W. (ed.), *Remaking the Chinese City: Modernity and National Identity, 1900–1950*, Honolulu: Hawaii University Press, 2000.

Evans, Robin, *The Projective Cast: Architecture and its Three Geometries*, Cambridge, MA: MIT, 1995.

Fairbank, John K. (ed.), *The Cambridge History of China, vol. 12: Republican China 1912–1949, Part 1*, Cambridge: Cambridge University Press, 1983.

Fairbank, John K., 'The rise and decline of Nationalist China', in John K. Fairbank, Edwin O. Reischauer and Albert M. Craig (eds), *East Asia: Tradition and Transformation*, Boston: Houghton Mifflin, 1989, pp. 763–807.

Fairbank, John K. and Albert Feuerwerker (eds), *The Cambridge History of China, vol. 13: Republic China 1912–49, Part 2*, Cambridge: Cambridge University Press, 1986.

Fairbank, John K., Edwin O. Reischauer and Albert M. Craig (eds), *East Asia: Tradition and Transformation*, Boston: Houghton Mifflin, 1989.

Fan Fangzhen and Liao Jinhan (comp.), *Zhongshan Lingyuan Shihua* (The Sun Yat-sen Mausoleum and the surrounding historical sites and relics), Nanjing: Zhongshan Lingyuan, 1995.

Fang Hao, *Zhongxi Jiaotong Shi* (A history of intercommunication between China and the West), Taipei: Huagang Chubanshe, 1977.

Fang Ke, *Dangdai Beijing Jiucheng Gengxin* (Contemporary renewal of the old city of Beijing), Beijing: Zhongguo Jianzhu Gongye Chubanshe, 2000.

Fei Xiaotong, *From the Soil: The Foundations of Chinese society*, trans. Gary G. Hamilton and Wang Zheng, Berkeley: University of California Press, 1992.

Fei Xiaotong, *Xiangtu Zhongguo* (Rural China), Shanghai: Guanchashe, 1948.

Foster, Hal (ed.), *Vision and Visuality*, Seattle: Bay Press, 1988.

Foster and Partners, 'Project summary: Terminal 3 Beijing Capital Airport, Beijing, China'. Online. Available at <www.designbuild-network.com/projects/terminal-5-beijing/> (accessed 7 February 2007).

Foucault, Michel, *The Archaeology of Knowledge*, trans. A. M. Sheridan Smith, London: Routledge, 1972.

Frampton, Kenneth, *Modern Architecture: A Critical History*, London: Thames and Hudson, 1985.

Friedmann, John, *China's Urban Transition*, Minneapolis: University of Minnesota Press, 2005.

Fu Chao-ching, *Zhongguo Gudian Shiyang Xinjianzhu* (A new architecture of classical styles in China), Taipei: Nantian Shuju, 1993.

Fujimori Terunobu and Wang Tan (eds), *A Comprehensive Study of East Asian Architecture and Urban Planning: 1840–1945*, Tokyo: Chikuma Shobo, 1996.

Goldman, Merle, 'Dang yu zhishi fenzi' (The Party and the intellectuals), in Roderick MacFarquhar and John K. Fairbank (eds), *Jianqiao Zhonghua Renmin Gongheguo Shi: geming de Zhongguo de xingqi 1949–1965* (Cambridge History of China, vol. 14, The People's Republic: The Emergence of Revolutionary China, 1949–1965), trans. Xie Liangsheng, Beijing: Zhongguo Shehuikexue Chubanshe, 1990, pp. 228–72.

Gong Deshun, Zou Denong and Dou Yide, *Zhongguo Xiandai Jianzhu Shigang* (An outline of a history of modern Chinese architecture), Tianjin: Tianjin Kexue Jishu Chubanshe, 1989.

Guo Hengyu, *Gongchan Guoji yu Zhongguo Geming* (The Comintern and the Chinese revolution), Taipei: Dongda Tushu Gongsi, 1989.

Habermas, Jürgen, 'Further reflections on the public sphere', in Craig Calhoun (ed.), *Habermas and the Public Sphere*, Cambridge, MA: MIT Press, 1992, pp. 421–61.

Habermas, Jürgen, *The Structural Transformation of the Public Sphere: An Inquiry into a Category of Bourgeois Society*, trans. Thomas Burger, Cambridge, MA: MIT Press, 1989.

Hao Shuguang, *Dangdai Zhongguo Jianzhu Sichao Yanjiu* (Research on architectural thoughts in contemporary China), Beijing: Zhongguo Jianzhu Gongye Chubanshe, 2006.

Harvey, David, *A Brief History of Neoliberalism*, Oxford: Oxford University Press, 2005.

Harvey, David, *Spaces of Capital: Towards a Critical Geography*, Edinburgh: Edinburgh University Press, 2001.

Hays, Michael, 'Critical architecture: between culture and form', *Yale Architectural Journal: Perspecta*, 21 (1984), 15–29.

He Chongyi and Zeng Zhaofen, *Yuanmingyuan Yuanlin Yishu* (The landscape design aesthetics of the Yuanmingyuan garden), Beijing: Kexue Chubanshe, 1995.

He Zhaowu and He Gaoji, 'Zhong yi ben xuyan' (Preface for the Chinese edition), in Li Madou (Matteo Ricci), *Li Madou Zhongguo Zaji* (China: the journals of Matteo Ricci), trans. He Gaoji, Wang

Zunzhong and Li Shen, Guilin: Guangxi Shifandaxue Chubanshe, 2001, pp. 1–18.

Hirst, Paul, 'Foucault and architecture', *AA Files*, 26 (Autumn 1993), 52–60.

Hitchcock, Henry-Russell and Philip Johnson, *The International Style*, New York: W. W. Norton & Company, 1966.

Hou Youbin, 'Jindai zhongguo jianzhu' (Architecture in early modern China), in Pan Guxi (ed.), *Zhongguo Jianzhu Shi* (A history of Chinese architecture), Beijing: Zhongguo Jianzhu Gongye Chubanshe, 2001, pp. 299–391.

Huang, Philip C. C., ' "Public sphere"/"civil society" in China?: the third realm between state and society', *Modern China*, 19, no. 21 (April 1993), 216–40.

Huang Ping and Zhan Shaohua, 'Internal migration in China: linking it to development', *Regional Conference on Migration and Development in Asia*, Lanzhou: China Academy of Social Sciences Press, 2005, pp. 3–10.

Ibelings, Hans, *Supermodernism: Architecture in the Age of Globalization*, Rotterdam: NAi Publishers, 2002.

Ikeda, Satoshi, 'U.S. hegemony and East Asia: an exploration of China's challenge in the 21st century', in Wilma A. Dunaway (ed.), *Emerging Issues in the 21st Century World-System, Volume 2: New Theoretical Directions for the 21st Century World-System*, Westport, CT: Praeger Publishers, 2003, pp. 162–79.

Jameson, Fredric and Masao Miyoshi (eds), *The Cultures of Globalization*, Durham, NC: Duke University Press, 1998.

Jay, Martin, 'Scopic regimes of modernity', in Hal Foster (ed.), *Vision and Visuality*, Seattle: Bay Press, 1988, pp. 3–23.

Jencks, Charles, *The Iconic Building*, New York: Rizzoli, 2005.

Jiang Xun, 'Minzhu shehui zhuyi de tupo' (A breakthrough for social democracy), *Yazhou Zhoukan: The International Chinese Newsweekly*, 25 March 2007, 30.

Jiang Xun, 'Zhonggong yuanlao zhichi huwen zhenggai' (Veterans of the Chinese Communist Party are supporting Hu and Wen's political reform), *Yazhou Zhoukan: The International Chinese Newsweekly*, 10 June 2007, 32–4.

Jianzhu Xuebao (Architectural Journal), 1954–1962 and 1978.

Johnson, Philip and Mark Wigley, *Deconstructivist Architecture*, New York: Museum of Modern Art, 1988.

Jullien, François, *The Propensity of Things: Towards a History of Efficacy in China*, trans. Janet Lloyd, New York: Zone Books, 1995.

King, Anthony D. and Abidin Kusno, 'On Be(ij)ing in the world: "postmodernism," "globalization," and the making of transnational space in China', in Arif Dirlik and Xudong Zhang (eds), *Postmodernism and China*, Durham, NC: Duke University Press, 2000, pp. 41–67.

Kirby, William C., *Germany and Republican China*, Palo Alto, CA: Stanford University Press, 1984.

Klein, Caroline and Eduard Kögel, *Made in China: neue Chinesische Architektur*, Munich: Deutsche Verlags-Anstalt, 2005.

Koolhaas, Rem, 'Bigness, or the problem of large', in Rem Koolhaas and Bruce Mau, *S, M, L, XL*, New York: Monacelli Press, 1995, pp. 494–517.

Koolhaas, Rem, 'Found in translation' and 'Zhuanhua zhongde ganwu' (trans. Wang Yamei), in *Volume 8: Ubiquitous China*, 2006, pp. 120–6 and 157–9.

Koolhaas, Rem, 'The generic city', in Rem Koolhaas and Bruce Mau, *S, M, L, XL*, New York: Monacelli Press, 1995, pp. 1238–64.

Kollhaas, Rem, 'Introduction', in Chuihua Judy Chung, Jeffrey Inaba, Rem Koolhaas, Sze Tsung Leong (eds), *Great Leap Forward*, Cologne: Taschen, 2001, pp. 27–8.

Koolhaas, Rem, 'Pearl River Delta (Harvard Project on the City)' in Rem Koolhaas, Stefano Boeri, Sanford Kwinter, Nadia Tazi and Hans Ulrich Obrist, *Mutations*, Barcelona: ACTAR, 2000, pp. 280–337.

Koolhaas, Rem, 'Singapore songlines: thirty years of tabula rasa', in Rem Koolhaas and Bruce Mau, *S, M, L, XL*, New York: Monacelli Press, 1995, pp. 1008–89.

Koolhaas, Rem, 'What ever happened to urbanism?', in Rem Koolhaas and Bruce Mau, *S, M, L, XL*, New York: Monacelli Press, 1995, pp. 958–71.

Koolhaas, Rem, Stefano Boeri, Sanford Kwinter, Nadia Tazi and Hans Ulrich Obrist, *Mutations*, Barcelona: ACTAR, 2000.

Koolhaas, Rem and Bruce Mau, *S, M, L, XL*, New York: Monacelli Press, 1995.

Kruft, Hanno-Walter, *A History of Architectural Theory: From Vitruvius to the Present*, trans. Ronald Taylor, Elsie Callander and Antony Wood, London: Zwemmer, 1994.

Lai Delin, 'Searching for a modern Chinese monument: the design of the Sun Yat-sen Musuem in Nanjing', *Journal of the Society of Architectural Historians*, 64, no. 1 (March 2006), 22–55.

Lai Delin, 'Sheji yizuo lixiangde zhongguo fengge de xiandai jianzhu' (Designing an ideal Chinese-style modern architecture), in Lai Delin, *Zhongguo Jindai Jianzhu Shi Yanjiu: Studies in Modern Chinese Architectural History*, Beijing: Qinghua Daxue Chubanshe, 2007, pp. 331–62.

Lai Delin, 'Xueke de wailai yizhi – Zhongguo jindai jianzhu rencai de chuxian he jianzhu jiaoyu de fazhan' (Disciplines transplanted from abroad: the emergence of architects and architectural education in early modern China), in Lai Delin, *Zhongguo Jindai Jianzhu Shi Yanjiu: Studies in Modern Chinese Architectural History*, Beijing: Qinghua Daxue Chubanshe, 2007, pp. 115–80.

Lai Delin, *Zhongguo Jindai Jianzhu Shi Yanjiu: Studies in Modern Chinese Architectural History*, Beijing: Qinghua Daxue Chubanshe, 2007.

Latour, Alessandra, *Birth of a Metropolis: Moscow 1930–1955*, Moskva: Iskusstvo – XXI vek, 2002.

Latourette, Kenneth Scott, *A History of Christian Missions in China*, New York: Russell & Russell, 1967.

Lee, Leo Ou-fan, 'Literary trends: the road to revolution 1927–1949', in John Fairbank and Albert Feuerwerker (eds), *The Cambridge History of China, vol. 13: Republic China 1912–49, Part 2*, Cambridge: Cambridge University Press, 1986, pp. 421–91.

Lee, Leo Ou-fan, *Shanghai Modern: The Flowering of a New Urban Culture in China 1930–1945*, Cambridge, MA: Harvard University Press, 1999.

Lefebvre, Henri, *The Production of Space*, trans. Donald Nicholson-Smith, Oxford: Blackwell, 1991.

Lemonnier, Anne (ed.), *Alors, la Chine?*, Paris: Éditions du Centre Pompidou, 2003.

Lenin, V. I., 'Communism and the east: theses on the national and colonial questions', in Robert C. Tucker (ed.), *The Lenin Anthology*, New York: Norton, 1975, pp. 619–25.

Lenin, V. I., *Imperialism, the Highest Stage of Capitalism: A Popular Outline*, Moscow: Progress Publishers, 1970.

Li Bing, '1978 nian yilai wailai jianzhushi zai Beijing jianzhu de xiangguan yanjiu: projects designed by foreign architects in Beijing since 1978', *Shidai Jianzhu: Time + Architecture*, 81, no. 1 (January 2005), 14–18.

Li Haiqing, *Zhongguo Jianzhu Xiandai Zhuanxing* (A structural transformation into modernity in Chinese architecture), Nanjing: Dongnan Daxue Chubanshe, 2004.

Li Haiqing and Liu Jun, 'Zai jiannan tansuo zhong zuoxiang chengshu' (Towards maturity through difficult research: analysis of the origin of the National Central Museum and the related issues), *Huazhong Jianzhu* (Architecture in central China), 6 (2001), 85–6; 1 (2002), 15; and 2 (2002), 99–103.

Li Hua, '"Piping" de yanshen' (Extending a critical space: questioning the categories of 'China' and the 'West'), in Chinese and English, *Shidai Jianzhu: Time + Architecture*, 91, no. 5 (September 2006), 78–80.

Li Madou (Matteo Ricci), *Li Madou Zhongguo Zaji* (China: the journals of Matteo Ricci), trans. He Gaoji, Wang Zunzhong and Li Shen, Guilin: Guangxi Shifandaxue Chubanshe, 2001.

Li Mu, *Sanshi Niandai Wenyi Lun* (On the literature and arts of the 1930s), Taipei: Liming Wenhua Shiye Gongsi, 1973.

Li Shiqiao, 'Reconstituting Chinese building tradition: the Yingzao fashi in the early twentieth century', *Journal of the Society of Architectural Historians*, 62, no. 4 (2003), 470–89.

Li Shiqiao, 'Writing a modern Chinese architectural history: Liang Sicheng and Liang Qichao', *Journal of Architectural Education*, 56 (2002), 35–45.

Li Xiangning, 'Guanyu zhongguo jianzhu de duihua' (Dialogue with the other), in Chinese and English, *Shidai Jianzhu: Time + Architecture*, 91, no. 5 (September 2006), 80–1.

Li Yuese (Joseph Needham), *Zhongguo Kexue Jishushi* (Science and civilisation in China), *vol. 3, Shu Xue* (Mathematics), trans. Translation Team, Hong Kong: Zhonghua Shuju, 1980.

Li Yuese (Joseph Needham), *Zhongguo Kexue Jishushi* (Science and civilisation in China), *vol. 4, Tian Xue* (Science of the Heavens), trans. Translation Team, Hong Kong: Zhonghua Shuju, 1978

Li Yuese (Joseph Needham), *Zhongguo Kexue Jishushi* (Science and civilisation in China), *vol. 5, Di Xue* (Science of the Earth), trans. Translation Team, Hong Kong: Zhonghua Shuju, 1978.

Liang Sicheng, 'Cong "shiyong, jingji, zai keneng tiaojian xia zhuyi meiguan" tandao chuantong yu gexin' (A talk on tradition and renovation based on the principle of 'function, economy, and moderate concerns of beauty'), *Jianzhu Xuebao* (Architectural Journal), 6 (1959), 1–4.

Liang Sicheng, 'Guanyu zhongyang renmin zhengfu xingzheng zhongxinqu weizhi de jianyi' (On locating the administrative centre of the Central People's Government: a proposal), in Liang Sicheng, *Liang Sicheng Quanji, di wu juan* (Complete works of Liang Sicheng, vol. 5), Beijing: Zhongguo Jianzhu Gongye Chubanshe, 2001, pp. 60–81.

Liang Sicheng, 'Jianzhu sheji cankao tuji xu' (Preface to the Visual Dictionary for Architectural Design), in Liang Sicheng, *Liang Sicheng Quanji, di liu juan* (The complete works of Liang Sicheng, vol. 6), Beijing: Zhongguo Jianzhu Gongye Chubanshe, 2001, pp. 233–6.

Liang Sicheng, 'Jianzhu yishuzhong shehuizhuyi xianshizhuyi he minzu yichan de xuexi yu yuanyong de wenti' (On socialist realism in architectural art and the study and use of national heritage), in Liang Sicheng, *Liang Sicheng Quanji, di wu juan* (Complete works of Liang Sicheng, vol. 5), Beijing: Zhongguo Jianzhu Gongye Chubanshe, 2001, pp. 185–96.

Liang Sicheng, 'Liang Sicheng de fayan' (Liang Sicheng's talk), *Jianzhu Xuebao* (Architectural Journal), 11 (1958), 6–7.

Liang Sicheng, *Liang Sicheng Quanji, di si juan* (Complete works of Liang Sicheng, vol. 4), Beijing: Zhongguo Jianzhu Gongye Chubanshe, 2001.

Liang Sicheng, *Liang Sicheng Quanji, di wu juan* (Complete works of Liang Sicheng, vol. 5), Beijing: Zhongguo Jianzhu Gongye Chubanshe, 2001.

Liang Sicheng, *Liang Sicheng Quanji, di liu juan* (Complete works of Liang Sicheng, vol. 6), Beijing: Zhongguo Jianzhu Gongye Chubanshe, 2001.

Liang Sicheng, *Liang Sicheng Quanji, di ba juan* (Complete works of Liang Sicheng, vol. 8), Beijing: Zhongguo Jianzhu Gongye Chubanshe, 2001.

Liang Sicheng, *Liang Sicheng Quanji, di jiu juan* (Complete works of Liang Sicheng, vol. 9), Beijing: Zhongguo Jianzhu Gongye Chubanshe, 2001.

Liang Sicheng, 'Renmin yingxiong jinianbei sheji jingguo' (An account of how the Monument to the People's Heroes was designed), in Liang Sicheng, *Liang Sicheng Quanji, di wu juan* (Complete works of Liang Sicheng, vol. 5), Beijing: Zhongguo Jianzhu Gongye Chubanshe, 2001, pp. 462–4.

Liang Sicheng, 'Wodui sulian jianzhu yishu de yidian renshi' (My reflections on architectural art in the Soviet Union), in Liang Sicheng, *Liang Sicheng Quanji, di wu juan* (Complete works of Liang Sicheng, vol. 5), Beijing: Zhongguo Jianzhu Gongye Chubanshe, 2001, pp. 175–8.

Liang Sicheng, 'Zhongguo jianzhu de tezheng' (Characteristics of Chinese architecture), *Jianzhu Xuebao* (Architectural Journal), 1 (1954), 36–9.

Liang Sicheng, 'Zuguo de jianzhu' (Architecture of the motherland), in Liang Sicheng, *Liang Sicheng Quanji, di wu juan* (Complete works of Liang Sicheng, vol. 5), Beijing: Zhongguo Jianzhu Gongye Chubanshe, 2001, pp. 197–234.

Liang Ssu-cheng, *A Pictorial History of Chinese Architecture*, ed. Wilma Fairbank, Cambridge, MA: MIT Press, 1984.

Lin Zhu, *Koukai Luban de Damen: zhongguo yingzao xueshe shilue* (Opening the door to the world of Lu Ban: a brief history of the Society for Research in Chinese Architecture), Beijing: Zhongguo Jianzhu Gongye Chubanshe, 1995.

Lin Zhu, Lou Qingxi and Wang Jun, 'Liang Sicheng nianpu' (Life of Liang Sicheng: a chronology), in Liang Sicheng, *Liang Sicheng Quanji, di jiu juan* (Complete works of Liang Sicheng, vol. 9), Beijing: Zhongguo Jianzhu Gongye Chubanshe, 2001, pp. 101–11.

Liu Dunzhen, *Zhongguo Gudai Jianzhushi*, Beijing: Zhongguo Jianzhu Gongye Chubanshe, 1980.

Liu Fan, 'Lu Yanzhi yu Nanjing Zhongshanling' (Lu Yanzhi and Sun Yat-sen's mausoleum in Nanjing), *Jianzhushi* (Architect), March 1994, 114–125.

Liu Jiakun (ed.), *Cishi Cidi: Now and Here*, Beijing: Zhongguo Jianzhu Gongye Chubanshe, 2002.

Liu Jiakun, 'Gei Zhu Jianfei de hui xin' (An open letter to Jianfei Zhu), in Chinese and English, trans. from Chinese into English by Chia Shi Chee, *Shidai Jianzhu: Time + Architecture*, 91, no. 5 (September 2006), 67–8.

Liu Jiakun, 'Guanyu wode gongzuo' (About my work), in Liu Jiakun (ed.), *Cishi Cidi: Now and Here*, Beijing: Zhongguo Jianzhu Gongye Chubanshe, 2002, pp. 12–14.

Liu Jiakun, 'Qianjin dao qiyuan' (March onto the beginning), in Liu Jiakun (ed.), *Cishi Cidi: Now and Here*, Beijing: Zhongguo Jianzhu Gongye Chubanshe, 2002, pp. 15–18.

Liu Jiakun, 'Xushihuayu yu dijicelue' (A narrative discourse and a low-tech strategy), *Jianzhushi: Architect*, 78 (October 1997), 46–50.

Liu Ruli, '*Shi Xue* – Zhongguo zuizao de toushixue zhuzou' (*Shi Xue*, the earliest book on perspective in China), *Nanyi Xuebao* (Journal of the Nanjing Academy of Art), 1 (1979), 75–8.

Liu Xiufeng, 'Chuangzao Zhongguo de shehui zhuyi de jianzhu xin fengge' (Creating new styles for China's socialist architecture), *Jianzhu Xuebao* (Architectural Journal), 9–10 (1959), 3–12.

Liu Yi, '*Shi Xue* pingxi' (Analysis and comments on *Shi Xue*), *Ziran Zazhi* (Nature), 10, no. 6 (1987), 447–52.

Lu Bingjie, *Tiananmen*, Shanghai: Tongji Daxue Chubanshe, 1999.

Lu, Duanfang, *Remaking Chinese Urban Form: Modernity, Scarcity and Space, 1949–2005*, London: Routledge, 2006.

Lu, Duanfang, 'Third World modernism: modernity, utopia and the People's Commune in China', *Journal of Architectural Education*, 60, no. 3 (2007), 40–8.

Lu Liangzhi, *Zhongguo Dituxue Shi* (A history of cartography in China), Beijing: Cehui Chubanshe, 1984.

Lu Yanzhi (Y. C. Lu), 'Memorials to Dr. Sun Yat-sen in Nanking and Canton', *Far Eastern Review*, 25, no. 3 (March 1929), 97–101.

Ma Guoxin, 'Santan jiyu he tiaozhan' (Three comments on opportunities and challenges), *World Architecture*, 169 (July 2004), 19–21.

Ma, Laurence J. C. and Fulong Wu (eds) *Restructuring the Chinese City: Changing Society, Economy & Space*, London: Routledge, 2005.

Ma Qingyun, 'Interview', 2004. Online. Available at <www.abbs.com/> (accessed 15 October 2004).

Ma Qingyun, *MADA s.p.a.m. on SITE*, Berlin: Aedes, 2004.

Ma Qingyun, Shi Jian and Feng Keru, 'Interview: Ma Qingyun', *Domus China*, 8 (February 2007), 116–17.

Ma Qingyun and Stephen Wright, 'A city without leftovers: a conversation with Ma Qingyun', *Parachute*, 114 (2004), 62–79.

McDermott, Kevin and Jeremy Agnew, *The Comintern: A History of International Communism from Lenin to Stalin*, London: Macmillan, 1996.

MacFarquhar, Roderick and John K. Fairbank (eds), *Jianqiao Zhonghua Renmin Gongheguo Shi: geming de Zhongguo de xingqi 1949–1965* (Cambridge History of China, vol. 14, The People's Republic: The Emergence of Revolutionary China, 1949–1965), trans. Xie Liangsheng, Beijing: Zhongguo Shehuikexue Chubanshe, 1990.

Mandelbrot, Benoit B., *The Fractal Geometry of Nature*, San Francisco: W. H. Freeman & Company, 1982.

Mao Zedong, *Mao Zedong Xuanji* (Selected works of Mao Zedong), vol. 2, Beijing: Renmin Chubanshe, 1970.

Mao Zedong, *Mao Zedong Xuanji* (Selected works of Mao Zedong), vol. 3, Beijing: Renmin Chubanshe, 1970.

Mao Zedong, 'Xin minzhu zhuyi lun' (On new democracy), in Mao Zedong, *Mao Zedong Xuanji* (Selected works of Mao Zedong), vol. 2, Beijing: Renmin Chubanshe, 1970, pp. 623–70.

Mao Zedong, 'Zai Yanan wenyi zuotanhui shang de jianghua' (Speeches at the seminar on literature and art in Yanan), in Mao Zedong, *Mao Zedong Xuanji* (Selected works of Mao Zedong), vol. 3, Beijing: Renmin Chubanshe, 1970, pp. 804–35.

Mineo, Nakajima, 'Waijiao guanxi: cong chaoxian zhanzheng dao wanlong luxian' (Chapter 6: Foreign relations: from the Korean War to the Bandung Principles), in Roderick MacFarquhar and John K. Fairbank (eds), *Jianqiao Zhonghua Renmin Gongheguo Shi: geming de Zhongguo de xingqi 1949–1965* (Cambridge History of China, vol. 14, The People's Republic: The Emergence of Revolutionary China, 1949–1965), trans. Xie Liangsheng, Beijing: Zhongguo Shehuikexue Chubanshe, 1990, pp. 273–306.

Musgrove, Charles D., 'Building a dream: constructing a national capital in Nanjing, 1927–37', in Joseph W. Esherick (ed.), *Remaking the Chinese City: Modernity and National Identity, 1900–1950*, Hawaii: University of Hawaii Press, 2000, pp. 139–57.

Nanjing Municipal Archive and Zhongshan Lingyuan Office (comp.), *Zhongshanling Dangan Shiliao Xuanbian* (Selected historical files and documents concerning Sun Yat-sen's mausoleum), Nanjing: Jiangsu Guji Chubanshe, 1986.

Nanjing Municipal Archive and Zhongshan Lingyuan Office (comp.), *Zhongshanling Shiji Tuji* (Historical photos of Sun Yat-sen's mausoleum), Nanjing: Jiangsu Guji Chubanshe, 1996.

Needham, Joseph, *Science and Civilization in China, vol. 3, Mathematics and the Sciences of the Heavens and the Earth*, Cambridge: Cambridge University Press, 1959.

Nian Xiyao, *Shi Xue* (Principles of visual perspective), Beijing, 1735.

Nie Chongzheng, *Zhongguo Jujiang Meishu Congshu: Lang Shining* (Books on great masters in Chinese art: Giuseppe Castiglione), Beijing: Wenwu Chubanshe, 1998.

Nolan, Peter, *China at the Crossroads*, Cambridge: Polity Press, 2004.

Ockman, Joan, 'What's new about the "new" pragmatism and what does it have to do with architecture', *A+U*, 9, no. 372 (2001), 26–8.

Palace Museum (comp.), *Qingdai Gongting Huihua* (Paintings from the Qing palace), Beijing: Wenwu Chubanshe, 1992.

Pan Guxi (ed.), *Zhongguo Jianzhu Shi* (A history of Chinese architecture), Beijing: Zhongguo Jianzhu Gongye Chubanshe, 2001.

Panofsky, Erwin, *Perspective as Symbolic Form*, trans. Christopher S. Wood, New York: Zone Books, 1997.

Peng Nu, 'Jianzhu sheji de pipingxing yu jianzhu piping' (Critical architecture and architectural criticism), in Chinese and English, *Shidai Jianzhu: Time + Architecture*, 91, issue 5 (September 2006), 81–2.

People's Daily Online, 'China's urbanization, 10 per cent higher within 10 years'. Online. Available at <http://english.peopledaily.com.cn/200212/06/eng20021206_108064.shtml> (accessed 13 February 2007).

Pérez-Gómez, Alberto, *Architecture and the Crisis of Modern Science*, Cambridge, MA: MIT Press, 1983.

Pérez-Gómez, Alberto, 'The revelation of order: perspective and architectural representation', in Kester Rattenbury (ed.), *This Is Not Architecture: Media Constructions*, London: Routledge, 2002, pp. 3–25.

Pérez-Gómez, Alberto and Louie Pelletier, *Architectural Representation and the Perspective Hinge*, Cambridge, MA: MIT, 1997.

Qi Kang (comp.), *Yang Tingbao Jianzhu Sheji Zuopin Xuan: Selected Architectural Works of Yang Tingbao*, Beijing: Zhongguo Jianzhu Gongye Chubanshe, 2001.

Qin Feng (ed.), *Minguo Nanjing 1927–1949* (Republican Nanjing 1927–1949), Shanghai: Wenhui Chubanshe, 2005.

Qin Youguo, 'Liang Sicheng, Lin Huiyin yu guohui sheji' (Liang Sicheng, Lin Huiyin and the design for the national emblem), in Editorial Committee (ed.), *Liang Sicheng Xiansheng Baisui Danchen Wenji* (A collection of essays on the 100th birthday of Liang Sicheng), ed. Tsinghua University School of Architecture, Beijing: Qinghua Daxue Chubanshe, 2001, pp. 111–19.

Rabinow, Paul, *French Modern: Norms and Forms of the Social Environment*, Cambridge, MA: MIT Press, 1989.

Rajchman, John, 'A new pragmatism', in Cynthia C. Davidson (ed.), *Anyhow*, New York: MIT Press, 1998, pp. 212–17.

Rattenbury, Kester (ed.), *This Is Not Architecture: Media Constructions*, London: Routledge, 2002.

Rawski, Evelyn S. and Jessica Rawson (eds), *China: The Three Emperors 1662–1795*, London: Royal Academy of Arts, 2006.

Rendell, Jane, Jonathan Hill, Murray Fraser and Mark Dorrian (eds), *Critical Architecture*, London: Routledge, 2007.

Renmin Dahuitang Shejizu (Design team for the Great Hall of the People), 'Renmin Dahui Tang' (The Great Hall of the People), *Jianzhu Xuebao* (Architectural Journal), 9–10 (1959), 23–30.

Renmin Ribao (People's Daily), 28 March 1955 and 2 October 1959.

Ricci, Matteo, *China in the Sixteenth Century: The Journals of Matthew Ricci: 1583–1610*, trans. Louis J. Gallagher, S. J., New York: Random House, 1953.

Rowe, Peter G. and Seng Kuan, *Architectural Encounters with Essence and Form in Modern China*, Cambridge, MA: MIT Press, 2002.

Ryabushin, Alexander and Nadia Smolina, *Landmarks of Soviet Architecture 1917–1991*, New York: Rizzoli, 1992.

Schwartz, Benjamin, 'Themes in intellectual history: May Fourth and after', in John K. Fairbank (ed.), *The Cambridge History of China, vol. 12: Republican China 1912–1949, Part 1*, Cambridge: Cambridge University Press, 1983, pp. 406–50.

Shen Kangshen, 'Cong *Shi Xue* kan shibashiji dongxifang toushixue zhishi de jiaorong he yingxiang' (Confluence and influence between East and West in perspective studies in the case of the book *Shi Xue*), *Ziran Kexueshi Yanjiu: Studies in the History of Natural Sciences*, 4, no. 3 (1985), 258–66.

Shoudu Jihua (Capital plan), Nanjing, 1929.

Shu Mu, 'Yuanmingyuan dashi nianbiao' (Annals of the Yuanmingyuan Garden), in Shu Mu, Shen Wei and He Naixian, *Yuanmingyuan Ziliaoji* (Archive materials concerning the Yuanmingyuan Garden), Beijing: Shumu Wenxian Chubanshe, 1984, pp. 361–89.

Shu Mu, Shen Wei and He Naixian, *Yuanmingyuan Ziliaoji* (Archive materials concerning the Yuanmingyuan Garden), Beijing: Shumu Wenxian Chubanshe, 1984.

Somol, Robert and Sarah Whiting, 'Notes around the Doppler effect and other moods of modernism', *Perspecta 33: Mining Autonomy*, 2002, 72–7.

Speaks, Michael, 'Design intelligence and the new economy', *Architectural Record*, January 2002, 72–6.

Speaks, Michael, 'Design intelligence: part 1, introduction', *A+U*, 12, no. 387 (2002), 10–18.

Speaks, Michael, 'Lixiang, yishi xingtai, shiyong zhiyui: zai zhongguo yu xifang' (Ideals, ideology and intelligence in China and the West), in Chinese and English, trans. from English into Chinese by Chia Shi Chee, *Shidai Jianzhu: Time + Architecture*, 91, no. 5 (September 2006), 63–5.

Speaks, Michael, 'Tales from the Avant-Garde: how the new economy is transforming', *Architectural Record*, 12 (2000), 74–7.

Spence, Jonathan D., *The Memory Palace of Matteo Ricci*, London: Faber and Faber, 1984.

Sullivan, Michael, *The Meeting of Eastern and Western Art*, Berkeley: University of California Press, 1989.

Sun Yat-sen, 'Sanmin zhuyi' (Three principles of the people), in Sun Yat-sen, *Sun Zhongshan Xuanji* (Selected works of Sun Yat-sen), Hong Kong: Zhonghua Shuju, 1956, pp. 588–838.

Sun Yat-sen, *Sun Zhongshan Xuanji* (Selected works of Sun Yat-sen), Hong Kong: Zhonghua Shuju, 1956.

Sun Yat-sen, 'Yizhu' (Will), in Sun Yat-sen, *Sun Zhongshan Xuanji* (Selected works of Sun Yat-sen), Hong Kong: Zhonghua Shuju, 1956, p. 921.

Sun Yat-sen, 'Zhongguo Guomindang diyici quanguo daibiao dahui xuanyan' (Manifesto at the First National Congress of the Chinese Nationalist Party), in Sun Yat-sen, *Sun Zhongshan Xuanji* (Selected works of Sun Yat-sen), Hong Kong: Zhonghua Shuju, 1956, pp. 520–31.

Tafuri, Manfredo, *Architecture and Utopia: Design and Capitalist Development*, trans. Barbara Luigia La Penta, Cambridge, MA: MIT Press, 1976.

Teiwes, Frederick C., 'Xin zhengquan de jianli he gonggu' (Chapter 2: Establishing and consolidating the new regime), in Roderick MacFarquhar and John K. Fairbank (eds), *Jianqiao Zhonghua Renmin Gongheguo Shi: geming de Zhongguo de xingqi 1949–1965* (Cambridge History of China, vol. 14, The People's Republic: The Emergence of Revolutionary China, 1949–1965), trans. Xie Liangsheng, Beijing: Zhongguo Shehuikexue Chubanshe, 1990, pp. 55–149.

Tian Yu Cao (ed.), *The Chinese Model of Modern Development*, London: Routledge, 2005.

Tiananmen Diqu Guanli Weiyuanhui, *Tiananmen* (DVD, a 4-part TV documentary), Beijing: Zhongguo Luyin Luxiang Chubanshe, 1999.

Tong Jun, 'Beijing Changchunyuan xiyang jianzhu' (Western-style buildings at the Changchunyuan Garden in Beijing), *Jianzhushi* (Architect), 2 (1980), 156–68.

Tu Wei-ming (ed.), *Confucian Traditions in East Asian Modernity: Moral Education and Economic Culture in Japan and the Four Mini-Dragons*, Cambridge, MA: Harvard University Press, 1996.

Tu Wei-ming, 'Introduction' and 'Epilogue', in Tu Wei-ming (ed.), *Confucian Traditions in East Asian Modernity: Moral Education and Economic Culture in Japan and the Four Mini-Dragons*, Cambridge, MA: Harvard University Press, 1996, pp. 1–10, 343–9.

Tucker, Robert C. (ed.), *The Lenin Anthology*, New York: Norton, 1975.

Wallerstein, Immanuel, *The End of the World as We Know It: Social Science for the Twenty-First Century*, Minneapolis: University of Minnesota Press, 1999.

Wallerstein, Immanuel, *The Essential Wallerstein,* New York: New Press, 2000.

Wallerstein, Immanuel, 'The rise of East Asia, or the world-system in the twenty-first century', in Immanuel Wallerstein, *The End of the World as We Know It: Social Science for the Twenty-First Century*, Minneapolis: University of Minnesota Press, 1999, pp. 34–48.

Wallerstein, Immanuel, 'The three instances of hegemony in the history of the capitalist world-economy', in Immanuel Wallerstein, *The Essential Wallerstein,* New York: New Press, 2000, pp. 253–63.

Wang, Chun-Hsiung, Chuan-Wen Sun and Horng-Chang Hsieh, 'Guomin zhengfu shiqi jianzhushi zhuanye zhidu xingcheng zhi yanjiu' (Formation of a professional institution of the architect in the Nationalist era), *Chengshi yu Sheji: Cities and Design*, 9/10 (September 1999), 81–116.

Wang Guxiang, *Dongxifangde Jianzhu Kongjian: wenhua kongjian tushi ji lishi jianzhu kongjian lun* (Architectural space in the East and West: a theory of space in cultural schema and historical construction), Beijing: Zhongguo Jianzhu Gongye Chubanshe, 1998.

Wang Hui, 'The historical origin of China's neo-liberalism', in Tian Yu Cao (ed.), *The Chinese Model of Modern Development*, London: Routledge, 2005, pp. 61–87.

Wang Jianying (comp.), *Zhongguo Gongchangdang Zhuzhishi Zhiliao Huibian: lingdao jiguo yange he chengyuan minglu* (Collected materials on the Chinese Communist Party's organizational history: an evolution of institutions and a list of members' names), Beijing: Zhonggong Zhongyang Dangxiao Chubanshe, 1995.

Wang Jun, *Cheng Ji* (Beijing: a story of the city), Beijing: Sanlian Shudian, 2003.

Wang Jun, 'Zhenti baohu tichu zhihou' (What happens after the release of the comprehensive conservation plan), *Liaowang Zhoukan: Outlook Weekly*, 19 (8 May 2006), 20–1.

Wang Nengwei (ed.), *Nanjing Jiuying* (Old photos of Nanjing), Beijing: Renmin Meishu Chubanshe, 1998.

Wang Qiheng, *Fengshui Lilun Yanjiu* (Studies in the theory of feng shui), Tianjin: Tianjin Daxue Chubanshe, 1992.

Wang Shiren and Zhang Fuhe, 'Beijing jindai jianzhu gaishuo' (An outline of early modern architecture in Beijing), in Wang Tan and Terunobu Fujimori (eds), *Zhongguo Jindai Jianzhu Zonglan – Beijing Pian: The Architectural Heritage of Modern China – Beijing*, Beijing: Zhongguo Jianzhu Gongye Chubanshe, 1992, pp. 1–26.

Wang Tan and Terunobu Fujimori (eds), *Zhongguo Jindai Jianzhu Zonglan – Beijing Pian: The Architectural Heritage of Modern China – Beijing*, Beijing: Zhongguo Jianzhu Gongye Chubanshe, 1992.

Wang Yong, *Zhongwai Meishu Jiaoliu Shi* (A history of communication between China and foreign countries in fine art), Hunan: Hunan Jiaoyu Chubanshe, 1998.

Watkin, David, *The Rise of Architectural History*, London: Architectural Press, 1980.

Weng Lianxi (comp.), *Qingdai Gongting Banhua* (Engravings from the Qing palace), Beijing: Wenwu Chubanshe, 2001.

Whiting, Allen S., 'Zhongsu fenlie' (Chapter 11: The Sino-Soviet split), in Roderick MacFarquhar and John K. Fairbank (eds), *Jianqiao Zhonghua Renmin Gongheguo Shi: geming de Zhongguo de xingqi 1949–1965* (Cambridge History of China, vol. 14, The People's Republic: The Emergence of Revolutionary China, 1949–1965), trans. Xie Liangsheng, Beijing: Zhongguo Shehuikexue Chubanshe, 1990, pp. 508–70.

Wigley, Mark, 'Deconstructivist architecture', in Philip Johnson and Mark Wigley, *Deconstructivist Architecture,* New York: Museum of Modern Art, 1988, pp. 10–20.

Wu Cong, 'Zai touying zhiwai' (Beyond projection), unpublished PhD thesis, Tianjin University, 1998.

Wu Hong, 'Tiananmen Square: a political history of monuments', *Representations*, 35 (Summer 1991), 84–117.

Wu Jiang, *Shanghai Bainian Jianzhu Shi 1840–1949* (A century of architecture in Shanghai, 1840–1949), Shanghai: Tongji Daxue Chubanshe, 1997.

Wu Liangyong, 'Renmin yingxiong jinianbei de chuangzuo chengjiu' (Achievements in the design of the Monument to the People's Heroes), *Jianzhu Xuebao* (Architectural Journal), 2 (1978), 4–7.

Xie Fenggang (ed.), *Lang Shining Huaji* (Collection of Giuseppe Castiglione's paintings), Tianjin: Tianjin Renmin Meishu Chubanshe, 1998.

Xinhua News, 'Interview with Long Yongtu on 18 September 2001'. Online. Available at <http://news.xinhuanet.com/fortune/2001-09/25/content_42797.htm> (accessed 13 February 2007).

Xue, Charlie Q. L., *Building a Revolution: Chinese Architecture since 1980*, Hong Kong: Hong Kong University Press, 2006.

Yang Bingde, *Zhongguo Jindai Zhongxi Jianzhu Wenhua Jiaoliu Shi* (A history of communication and integration of Chinese and Western architectural cultures in early modern China), Wuhan: Hubei Jiaoyu Chubanshe, 2002.

Yang Boda, *Qingdai Yuanhua* (Court paintings of the Qing dynasty), Beijing: Zijincheng Chubanshe, 1993.

Yang Naiji, 'Yuanmingyuan dashi ji' (Chronology of the Yuanmingyuan Garden), *Yuanmingyuan*, 4 (October 1986), 29–38.

Yang Tingbao, 'Jiefanghou zai jianzhu sheji zhong cunzai de jige wenti' (A few issues in architectural design since the Liberation of 1949), *Jianzhu Xuebao* (Architectural Journal) 9 (1956), 51–3.

Yao Qian and Gu Bing (eds), *Zhongshanling* (Sun Yat-sen's mausoleum), Beijing: Wenwu Chubanshe, 1981.

Yuan Feng, 'Jiancheng yu weijiancheng: Jiqixin de Zhongguo zhilu (Built and unbuilt: Arata Isozaki in China), *Shidai Jianzhu: Time + Architecture*, 81, no. 1 (2005), 38–45.

Zao Chen and Wu Jiang (eds), *Zhongguo Jindai Jianzhu Xueshu Sixian Yanjiu* (Research on ideologies and perspectives in early modern Chinese architecture), Beijing: Zhongguo Jianzhu Chubanshe, 2003.

Zhang Fuhe (ed.), *Zhongguo Jindai Jianzhu Yanjiu yu Baohu 1: 1998 Zhongguo jindai jianzhu shi guoji yantaohui lunwenji* (Anthology of 1998 international conference on history of modern Chinese architecture), Beijing: Qinghua Daxue Chubanshe, 1999.

Zhao Dongri, 'Jianzhu shiye shang jiti chuanzuo de fanli' (A model in collective design and creation in the architecture profession), *Jianzhu Xuebao* (Architectural journal), 9–10 (1959), 17.

Zhao Dongri, 'Tiananmen Guanchang' (Tiananmen Square), *Jianzhu Xuebao* (Architectural Journal), 9–10 (1959), 18–22.

Zheng Shiling, 'Dangdai jianzhu piping de zhuanxing: guanyu jianzhu pipingde dushu biji' (A transformation in contemporary architectural criticism), in Chinese and English, *Shidai Jianzhu: Time + Architecture*, 91, no. 5 (September 2006), 68–70.

Zhou Jiyan (ed.), *Zheng Banqio Shufa Ji* (A collection of calligraphic works of Zheng Banqiao), Nanjing: Jiangsu Meishu Chubanshe, 1985.

Zhou Rongxing, 'Zhou Rongxing lishizhang de dahui zongjie' (Concluding speech at the conference by the President of the Society Zhou Rongxing), *Jianzhu Xuebao* (Architectural journal), 3 (1957), 14–5.

Zhou Shiyan, 'Xiang kongqi zhong jiang kongqi' (Speaking air into the air), in Chinese and English, *Shidai Jianzhu: Time + Architecture*, 91, no. 5 (September 2006), 82–3.

Zhu Changzhong, 'Liang xiansheng yu guohui sheji' (Liang and the design for the national emblem), in Editorial Committee (ed.), *Liang Sicheng Xiansheng Danchen Bashiwu Zhounian Jinian Wenji*

(A collection of essays in honour of Liang Sicheng's 85th birthday), Beijing: Qinghua Daxue Chubanshe, 1986, pp. 119–32.

Zhu Tao, 'Jinqi xifang "piping" zhi zheng yu dangdai zhongguo jianzhu zhuangtai' (The 'criticality' debate in the West and the architectural situation in China), in Chinese and English, *Shidai Jianzhu: Time + Architecture*, 91, no. 5 (September 2006), 71–8.

Zhu, Jianfei, 'An archaeology of contemporary Chinese architecture', *2G: International Architectural Review*, 10 (1999), 90–7.

Zhu, Jianfei, 'Beyond revolution: notes on contemporary Chinese architecture', *AA Files*, 35 (1998), 3–14.

Zhu, Jianfei, 'China as a global site: in a critical geography of design', in Jane Rendell, Jonathan Hill, Murray Fraser and Mark Dorrian (eds), *Critical Architecture*, London: Routledge, 2007, pp. 301–8.

Zhu, Jianfei, *Chinese Spatial Strategies: Imperial Beijing 1420–1911*, London: RoutledgeCurzon, 2004.

Zhu, Jianfei, 'Criticality in between China and the West', *Journal of Architecture*, 10, no. 5 (November 2005), 479–98.

Zhu, Jianfei, 'Ershipian gaodi: zhongguo dalu xiandai jianzhu de lishi tujing' (Twenty plateaus: a historical landscape of modern architecture in mainland China), *Jinri Xianfeng: Avant-Garde Today*, 14 (2007), 103–14.

Zhu, Jianfei, 'Guanyu "ershipian gaodi" ' (Twenty plateaus: a genealogy of styles and design positions of modern architecture in mainland China, 1910s–2010s), *Shidai Jianzhu: Time + Architecture*, 97, no. 5 (September 2007), 16–21.

Zhu, Jianfei, 'Human space, China, 1990s: Cui Kai, a new generation, and a critique of a 20th-century master narrative', in Cui Kai (ed.), *Gongcheng Baogao: Projects Report*, Beijing: Zhongguo Jianzhu Gongye Chubanshe, 2002, pp. 172–85.

Zhu, Jianfei, 'Politics into culture: historical formation of the national style in the Nanjing decade (1927–1937)', in Zao Chen and Wu Jiang (eds), *Zhongguo Jindai Jianzhu Xueshu Sixian Yanjiu* (Research on ideologies and perspectives in early modern Chinese architecture), Beijing: Zhongguo Jianzhu Chubanshe, 2003, pp. 107–16.

Zhu, Jianfei, 'Vers un moderne Chinois: les grands courants architecturaux dans la Chine contemporaine depuis 1976' (Towards a Chinese modern: architectural positions in contemporary China since 1976), trans. Jean-François Allain, in Anne Lemonnier (ed.), *Alors, la Chine?*, Paris: Éditions du Centre Pompidou, 2003, pp. 193–9.

Zhu, Jianfei, 'Xiandaihua: zai lishi da guanxi zhong xunzhao zhang yonghe jiqi feichang jianzhu' (Modernization: locating Yung Ho Chang and his atelier FCJZ in a larger historical context), *Jianzhushi: Architect*, 108 (April 2004), 14–17.

Zhu, Tao and Jianfei Zhu, 'Critical dialogue: China and the West', *Journal of Architecture*, 12, no. 2 (April 2007), 199–207.

Zou Denong, *Zhongguo Xiandai Jianzhu Shi* (A history of modern Chinese architecture), Tianjin: Tianjin Kexuejishu Chubanshe, 2001.

Zou Yuejing, *Xin Zhongguo Meishushi 1949–2000* (A history of fine arts in New China 1949–2000), Changsha: Hunan Meishu Chubanshe, 2002.

Index

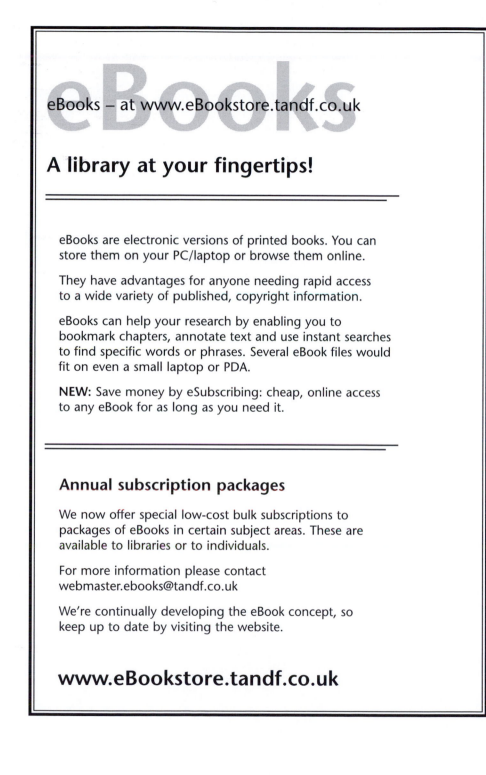